JACK THE RIPPER
THE AMERICAN CONNECTION

JACK THE RIPPER

THE AMERICAN CONNECTION

INCLUDES THE DIARIES OF JAMES MAYBRICK

SHIRLEY HARRISON

POSTSCRIPT BY DAVID CANTER

BLAKE

Published by Blake Publishing Ltd,
3, Bramber Court, 2 Bramber Road,
London W14 9PB, England

First published in hardback in 2003

ISBN 1 85782 590 X

British Library Cataloguing-in-Publication Data:

A catalogue record for this book is available from the British Library.

Design by ENVY

Printed in Great Britain by CPD

1 3 5 7 9 10 8 6 4 2

Papers used by Blake Publishing are natural, recyclable products made from wood grown in sustainable forests. The manufacturing processes conform to the environmental regulations of the country of origin.

This book is dedicated to those often-forgotten women of Whitechapel who were savagely butchered in 1888 and whose deaths have been eclipsed since by the mystery of their killer.

If this Diary is a modern forgery – which I am sure it is not – and if I were the faker, then I would consider it to have been the summit of my literary achievement.

Bruce Robinson, Oscar nominee
and scriptwriter of *The Killing Fields*
and *Withnail and I*

Contents

Acknowledgements

The opportunity to work on such an extraordinary project happens once in a lifetime. Since the day in 1992 when the Diary was first shown to me I have sought the help and guidance of literally hundreds of people. There have been experts, amateur enthusiasts in an astonishing range of subjects from pub signs to body snatching and descendants of anyone connected to the cases of James Maybrick and Jack the Ripper. This time we owe a great deal to friends in America, especially to the indefatigable Otto Gross and his patient wife Patty who have voluntarily spent innumerable hours beavering away on our behalf in libraries and research centres. As the material has continued to pour in it has been collated, researched and checked by my colleague Sally Evemy and forms the backbone of this new, fully updated anniversary edition. There are far too many individuals to mention but in particular we are grateful to:

Doreen Montgomery, our agent, whose iron glove conceals a velvet hand and without whose vision the project would not have been born.

Robert Smith, our original publisher. His enthusiasm and consumption of midnight oil went well beyond the call of duty.

Keith Skinner, Paul Begg and Martin Fido who so generously guided our first faltering footsteps into the world of Jack the Ripper.

Richard Nicholas of Roberts, Moore, Nicholas and Jones of Liverpool, who advised and supported Albert Johnson in all matters relating to the watch.

Roger Wilkes, whose generous support and research material launched our investigation.

Paul Feldman, whose enthusiasm kept us on our toes and yielded some useful leads.

Caroline Morris for her time line.

Naomi Evett of Liverpool Library whose limitless patience was invaluable.

Professor David Canter; Dr Nicholas Eastaugh; Dr David Forshaw; Sue Iremonger; Anna Koren; Melvyn Fairclough; art collector the late Sidney Sabin; Nicholas Campion; John Astrop; Jeremy Beadle; Camille Wolfe and Loretta Lay; scriptwriter Bruce Robinson; Lindsay Siviter; forensic handwriting examiner Lawrence Warner; Dr Glyn Volans of Guy's Hospital; Judge Richard Hamilton, Liverpool; Bill Waddell former Curator, Scotland Yard Black Museum; the late Tony Miall, music historian; Richard and Molly Whittington Egan; Paul Dodd; the late Brian Maybrick; David Maybrick; Gerard Brierley; Berkeley Chappelle Gill; Derek Warman and John Matthews in the Isle of Wight; Sister Ursula Maybrick; Dr. W. Taylor, the Fazakerley Hospital; Seddons Funeral Service, Southport; Phil Maddox of Wordplay Public Relations; Kevin Whaye of Outhwaite and Litherland, auctioneers, Liverpool; David Fletcher Rogers; Walkleys Clogs; the staff of Stanstead Hall; Gordon Wright of the Inn Sign Society; The Special Hospitals Service; Andrew Brown of the Metropolitan Police Archives, New Scotland Yard; Colin Inman of the Financial Times; Nick Pinto of the Public Record Office; R.H. Leighton and Co., Southport; Colin Wilson; Donald Rumbelow; the Liverpool Cotton Association; The British Medical Association Library; Mrs Gill Wokes of Hampshire and Mrs Delphine Cummings in Canada (descendants of Arthur Siminson Wokes); Des McKenna for help with the Museum of Anatomy; The

Royal Netherlands Embassy; Peter O'Toole BEM and Lee Charles Allen of the Museum of the S.A.S Regiment and the Artists' Rifles;Clive Emson, antiquarian bookseller; Brian Pugh of the Conan Doyle Establishment; Stephen Shotnes of Simons, Muirhead and Burton; the staff of libraries and local history departments throughout the country. In the United States: Dorothy MacRitchie of South Kent School and Peggy Haile McPhillips of Norfolk Public Library; Carole Cain of the Mobile Register; the American Heritage Centre, University of Wyoming for permission to use excerpts from the Trevor Christie Collection and to HarperCollins for permission to use an excerpt from *Hunting the Devil*; Chris George; Skip Hollandsworth; John Chapman; the staff in the public libraries of New Orleans, Austin, Dallas, Richmond and Norfolk; the Austin History Centre; the American Baptist Foreign Missionary Society. In Australia: Victoria Vickery; Amanda Pruden; Derek Strahan and Steve Powell.

PRINCIPAL SOURCES

The College of Heralds; Freemasons' Hall; Public Record Office, Kew; Public Record Office, Chancery Lane; the IGI Index; The Scottish Record Office; the Governor of Walton Prison, Liverpool; General Register Office, St Catherine's House; Principal Registry of the Family Division, Somerset House; Patent Office; Companies House; British Library; National Newspaper Library, Colindale; American State Archives, Washington DC; Bibliothèque Nationale, Paris; Victoria State Library, Australia; HM Land Registry; New Scotland Yard, Black Museum; Merseyside Police; Lancashire Constabulary; Ministry of Defence; Liverpool University; University of Wyoming, Christie Collection; Royal Liverpool University Hospital; Fazakerley Hospital, Histopathology Department; Historic Manuscripts Commission; Post Office Archives; Postal Museum; Post Mark Society; Shoe Museum; Liverpool Maritime Museum; Whitworth Museum, Manchester; Cotton Association, Liverpool; Liverpool Chamber of Commerce; Coldestone Park Cemetery; Lewisham Cemetery; Southwark Cemetery; Seddons Funeral Service; Parker

Pens; John Lewis Partnerships Archives Dept; Boddingtons; Scottish College of Textiles; The Poetry Library; Peter Bower, paper historian; Dr Earl Morris, Dow Chemicals; Stephen Ryder editor of the *Internet Ripper Casebook*.

Local History departments of Liverpool, Lambeth, Lewisham, Tower Hamlets, Southwark, Edinburgh, Manchester, Selkirk and Galashiels.

Libraries: Guildhall, Tunbridge Wells, Morden, Carlshalton, Sutton, Sunderland, Camden, Westminster, Liverpool, Chester, Manchester, Rochdale, Royal College of Surgeons, Royal College of Psychiatrists, Royal Society of Medicine, British Toxicological Society, Wellcome Research Institute, Science Library, Patent Office.

Record Offices: West Sussex, Lancashire, Chester, Newport, Isle of Wight.

Register Offices: Liverpool, Caernarfon.

NEWSPAPERS AND PERIODICALS

New Penny; Touchstone; Punch; Review of Reviews; Liverpool Review; Pall Mall Gazette; Family Tree; Brooklyn Eagle; Pall Mall Budget; Stuart Cumberland's Illustrated Mirror; the Police Review 1931; the Daily Express; New York Herald; New York Times; New Milford Times; Bridgeport Sunday Post; Police Gazette; Daily Telegraph; Liverpool Daily Post; Liverpool Echo; Liverpool Mercury; Liverpool Courier; Liverpool Citizen; Porcupine; The Times; Star; Graphic; Manchester Guardian; Yorkshire Post; Independent; Evening News; Pictorial News; Southport Guardian; Whitehaven News; Liverpool Medico Chirulogical Journal; New Scientist; Nature; Criminologist; True Detective; Murder Casebook; Ripperana; Ripperologist; Crime and Detection; Norfolk Virginian; St Louis Evening Chronicle and Texas Monthly.

BIBLIOGRAPHY

Steps to the Temple: Delights of the Muses, Richard Crashaw, reprinted Cassell 1881

The Sphere History of English Literature Volume 2, ed. Christopher Ricks, revised 1986

The Faber Book of English History in Verse, ed. Kenneth Baker, Faber and Faber
Just a Song at Twilight, Anthony Miall, Michael Joseph 1974
The Parlour Song Book, Anthony Miall, Michael Joseph 1972
Gore's Directories of Liverpool
Kelly's Directories
Who was Who, A & C Black
The Trial of Mrs Maybrick, H.B. Irving (ed. William Hodge), 1912
Treatise on the Maybrick Case, A.W MacDougall, Bailliere, Tindall and Cox 1891
The Necessity for Criminal Appeal, J.H.Levy, P.S. King and Son 1899
A Dictionary of Sea Terms, A. Anstead, Brown Son and Ferguson 1985
My Fifteen Lost Years, Florence Elizabeth Maybrick, Funk and Wagnalls 1909
A Toxicological Study of the Maybrick Case, C.N. Tidy and R. Macnamara, Bailliere, Tindall and Cox 1891
The Maybrick Case, Helen Densmore, Swan Sorrenschein 1892
Etched in Arsenic, Trevor L. Christie, George C. Harrap 1960
This Friendless Lady, Nigel Morland, Frederick Muller 1957
The Poisoned Life of Mrs Maybrick, Bernard Ryan and Sir Michael Havers, Kimber 1977
Victorian Murderesses, Mary S. Hartman, Robson 1977
Victorian England, W.J. Reader, Batsford 1974
Liverpool's Legion of Honour, written and published B.G. Orchard 1899
Materia Medica of Homeopathic Remedies, James Tyler Kent, republished Homeopathic Book Service 1989
Oxford English Dictionary
Webster's Dictionary
Dictionary of Jargon, Jonathon Green, Routledge Keegan Paul 1987
Encyclopedia of Australia, A.T.A. Learmouth, Warne 1968
Law's Grocer's Manual c1900
Enquire Within Upon Everything, Herbert Jenkins, 1923
American Illustrated Medical Dictionary (22nd edition)
The Trials of Israel Lipski, Martin L. Friedland, Macmillan 1984

Encylopedia of Chemical Technology (3rd edition, vol 3)
Merck Index (Ninth ed)
Casebook on Jack the Ripper, Richard Whittington Egan, 1976
The Complete Jack the Ripper, Donald Rumbelow, Penguin 1988
The Jack the Ripper A–Z, Paul Begg, Martin Fido and Keith Skinner, Headline 1996
The Ripper Legacy, Martin Howells and Keith Skinner, Warner Books 1987
Jack the Ripper: Summing Up and Verdict, Colin Wilson and Robin Odell, Corgi 1987
Jack the Ripper, The Uncensored Facts, Paul Begg, Robson Books Ltd, 1987
The Ripper and the Royals (*2nd edition*) Melvyn Fairclough, Gerald Duckworth and Co. Ltd., 1992
The Ripper File, Melvin Harris, W.H. Allen, 1989
The True Face of Jack the Ripper, Melvin Harris, Michael O'Mara 1994
The Encylopedia of Serial Killers, Brian Lane and Wilfred Gregg, Headline 1992
Hunting the Devil, Richard Lourie, Grafton 1993
The Lighter Side of My Official Life, Sir Robert Anderson, Blackwoods Edinburgh Magazine 1910
The Police Encyclopedia, Hargrave Lee Adam, Waverley Book Co 1920
Days of My Years, Sir Melville Macnaghten, Edward Arnold 1914
From Constable to Commissioner, Sir Henry Smith, Chatto and Windus 1910
The Mystery of Jack the Ripper, Leonard Matters, W.H. Allen 1929
I Caught Crippen, Walter Dew, Blackie and Son Ltd. 1938
The Identity of Jack the Ripper, Donald McCormick, Jarrold Books, 1959
The Crimes and Times of Jack the Ripper, Tom Cullen, Bodley Head 1965
Jack the Ripper, The First American Serial Killer, Stewart Evans and Paul Gainey, 1996
Jack the Ripper, The Final Chapter, Paul H. Feldman, Virgin 1997
The Lodger, Marie Belloc Lowndes, OUP 1913
The Complete History of Jack the Ripper, Philip Sugden, Robinson 1994
The Guinness Book of Names, Leslie Dunkling, Guinness 1993

Dan Leno and the Limehouse Golen, Peter Ackroyd, Sinclair Stevenson 1994

Jack the Ripper Revealed, John Wilding, Constable Volcano 1993

Who was Jack the Ripper?, ed. Camille Wolfe, Grey House Books 1995

Murder, Mayhem and Mystery in Liverpool, Richard Whittington Egan, Gallery Press 1985

Death, Dissection and the Destitute, Ruth Richardson, Routledge 1988

The Suicide Club, Robert Louis Stevenson, Blackie 1961

Dr Jekyll and Mr Hyde, Robert Louis Stevenson, McDonald 1960

Jack the Ripper, The Final Solution, Stephen Knight, Grafton 1977

The Simple Truth, Bruce Paley, Headline 1995

Pen, Ink and Evidence, Dr Joe Nickell, 1995

Criminal Shadows, David Canter, HarperCollins 1994

The Chemistry of Dyestuffs, Font and Lloyd, Cambridge University Press 1919

Printing Ink Technology, Apps, Leonard Hill 1959

Cyclopaedia of the Practice of Medicine, Dr H. Von Ziemenssen, William Wood and Co. New York 1878

The Uncollected Sherlock Holmes, Richard Lancelyn Green, Penguin 1983

Dr Joe Bell, Model for Sherlock Holmes, Ely Liebow, Bowling Green University Popular Press, 1982

Letters from Hell, Keith Skinner and Stewart Evans, Sutton 2001

The Secret to the Maybrick Poisoning Case, Eleanor Mason, D'Vauz Press, Rangoon, 1890 board from a cracker box, thereon painted in large letters:

N.Y. Times Oct 7, 1888

AL GEDDY,

A GOOD FELLOW,

BUT OUT OF LUCK.

The bones of poor Al were never buried. They were gathered in by the buffalo bone hunters, thrown in with the buffalo bones, and shipped East. They were perhaps utilized in refining sugar or found their way to some fertilizing establishment.

THE LONDON AND AUSTIN MURDERS.

AUSTIN, Texas, Oct. 4.—In 1885 there was a series of murders and assassinations of women, which extended at intervals throughout the year. Eight women in all were killed, including two white married women. The others were colored women and girls. Among the colored were Mary Rancy and Gracie Vance. The white women were Mrs. Hancock and Mrs. Eula Phillips. These murders have never been explained. The assassin left no trace whatever to identify him. There was a fearful similarity among all these murders—nearly all were killed about midnight and usually within a few days of full-moon nights. All of the victims were struck with some sharp instrument about the head and on the same side of the head. All were slain in profound silence, even persons in an adjoining room hearing nothing. The bodies were all found in the same position. All were dragged out into the back yard. On reading of the London Whitechapel murders citizens of Austin recognize a likeness to the servant-girl murders, as they are called, so startling as to lead to the conclusion that the London assassin s the Austin murder fiend of 1885.

FLOUR PRICES ADVANCED.

Introduction

On October 7th 1888, when Jack the Ripper was rampaging in Whitechapel, London, the *New York Times* carried an article from its correspondent in Austin, Texas. It was headed:

> THE LONDON AND AUSTIN MURDERS.
>
> In 1885 there was a series of murders and assassinations of women, which extended at intervals throughout the year. Eight women in all were killed, including two white married women. The others were colored women and girls. Among the coloured were Mary Rancy and Gracie Vance. The white women were Mrs Hancock and Mrs Eula Phillips. These murders have never been explained. The assassin left no trace whatever to identify him. There was a fearful similarity among all these murders – nearly all were killed about midnight and usually within a few days of full-moon nights. All of the victims were struck with some sharp instrument about the head and on the same side of the head. All were slain in profound silence, even persons

> in an adjoining room hearing nothing. The bodies were all found in the same position. All were dragged out into the back yard. On reading of the London, Whitechapel murders, citizens of Austin recognise a likeness to the servant-girl murders, as they are called, so startling as to lead to the conclusion that the London assassin is the Austin murder fiend of 1885.

* * *

In the Spring of 1992, I was introduced to an innocuous looking journal. It had clearly been a photograph album and the writing raged erratically over 63 pages, revealing a horrific account of murder, cannibalism and drug abuse, interlaced with a tragic longing for love and forgiveness. The book was a confession, signed, starkly, 'Jack the Ripper'.

The true author was unnamed, but clues within its text enabled us to identify him as James Maybrick, an arsenic-addicted Liverpool cotton merchant, with offices in Norfolk, Virginia, who died in suspicious circumstances in 1889, at the age of 50.

That year, 9 months after the last of the Whitechapel killings, Maybrick's pretty 26-year-old American wife, Florence, was convicted of poisoning him in what is today acknowledged by the legal profession to have been a shocking miscarriage of justice. She was condemned to death and although the sentence was commuted, she was, nevertheless, imprisoned for 15 terrible years. Her case became a '*cause célèbre*' with the American president and hundreds of thousands of people petitioning for clemency. The name of Maybrick was headline news around the world.

The arrival of the journal posed three hugely controversial questions. Who did kill James Maybrick? Who was Jack the Ripper? Is the diary a forgery?

* * *

The diary provenance was disastrous. It had been brought to London from Liverpool by former scrap-metal merchant, Michael Barrett. He claimed that it had originally been given to him by an invalid pal, who told him to 'do something with it', but who refused to reveal its origins and died soon after.

However, a few basic enquiries at the British Museum and also with some scientific experts encouraged me that, at the very least, the document should be taken seriously. I agreed to write a book which, I hoped, would enable me to underpin the cost of research. It seemed so simple at the time. What a lot I had to learn!

The first hardback edition of that book was published in 1993. As a result I found myself at the centre of a storm which has not abated to this day.

I became convinced that the diary was, indeed, genuine, but although much of the circumstantial evidence I collated supported my belief, it did not prove that I was right.

The *Sunday Times* screamed FAKE in banner headlines.

I discovered that I was entering a passionate, sometimes fanatical world, the existence of which I had been completely unaware. The world of Jack the Ripper.

There is a small elite of experts, whose depth of historical knowledge about the Whitechapel killer is awe-inspiring. There is also an international band of enthusiasts, themselves steeped in the hundreds of books, plays, and films created around the story of Jack the Ripper. Collectively they are known as Ripperologists.

Between them, they have named almost 100 suspects, including Lewis Carroll, the British artist Walter Sickert and, of course, best known of all, the royal connection with the Duke of Clarence. There are quality publications such as *Ripperologist* and *Ripperana* in Britain, in America *Ripper Notes* and in Australia *Ripperoo*. There is also a Cloak and Dagger club which meets regularly in London's East End.

To most of these people Maybrick was an irritating irrelevance. Yet after ten years of exhausting, scientific, genealogical and historical research, the mystery remains very much alive. For every time evidence appears which points to the end of the trail, a new clue emerges which tells a different story.

* * *

Ripper historians regularly ask themselves the question: Why did the Whitechapel killings stop in 1888? What happened next? Where did the Ripper go? The fact that Maybrick died in 1889 dealt neatly with that problem.

It was only when the *New York Times* article was brought to my notice in 2002 that I realised it could be time to change tack. Time to look backwards, not forwards and to focus more on the American life and connections of the man I believe could have killed the Whitechapel women.

The *New York Times* had stirred my imagination. It offered a new seam of untapped material that might throw light on the Maybricks and even the mystery of Jack the Ripper – not only in England but also in America. I then discovered that there were bands of enthusiasts in Texas who, much like our Ripperologists, were eagerly trying to unravel the identity of their Austin killer.

Consequently, this anniversary edition has taken me from Norfolk, Virginia, by rail down the cotton line, to America's deep South. Its tentacles have reached as far as New Orleans, to Canberra and Sydney in Australia, to Paris and to the textile mills of Scotland and the Border country of the river Tweed.

The diary itself emerged from the shadowy back streets of Victorian history to cast a flickering light on the sombre life and times of the Maybricks and their friends. Eventually, I believe, the truth about its origins will be revealed from their story and not from science and I believe that the Diary will have the last word.

We still do not know for certain that James Maybrick was the Ripper; neither can we say that he was not. Readers must follow their own instinct. Remember, always, the words of Sherlock Holmes himself: 'When you have eliminated the impossible then whatever remains, however improbable, must be the truth.'

I intend to follow his example. In 1894 Conan Doyle suggested to an American journalist that, faced with the enigma of Jack the Ripper, Holmes would have thrown the case open to the public and 'enlisted millions of people as detectives in the case.' So now, read on …

1

Perhaps in my Tormented Mind I Wish for Someone to Read this and Understand

Late one May afternoon in 1889, three doctors gathered in Aigburth, a suburb of Liverpool, to conduct a most irregular post-mortem. The body of a middle-aged businessman lay on the bed, where he had died, in his plush and mahogany bedroom, while his young American widow, distraught and confused, was in a mysterious swoon in the adjoining dressing room. Under the watchful eye of a police superintendent, two of the doctors dissected and inspected the internal organs while the third took notes.

The brain, heart and lungs seemed normal and were returned to his body. There was slight inflammation of the alimentary canal, a small ulcer on the larynx and the upper edge of the epiglottis was eroded. The stomach, tied at each end, the intestines, the spleen and parts of the liver were put into jars and handed to the police officer.

About two weeks later the same three doctors drove to Anfield cemetery, where the body had by that time been buried. They arrived at 11 p.m. and, in the yellow light of naphtha lamps, stood by the fresh grave while four men dug up the coffin. Without lifting the body from its container, they removed the heart, brain, lungs, kidneys and tongue for further investigation. An eye witness reported: 'there was scarcely anyone present who did not experience an involuntary shudder as the pale, worn features of the dead appeared in the flickering rays of a lamp held over the grave by one of the medical men.

'What everyone remarked was that, although interred a fortnight, the corpse was wonderfully preserved. As the dissecting knife of Dr Barron pursued its rapid and skilful work there was, however, whenever the wind blew, a slight odour of corruption.'

Eventually the authorities concluded that 50-year-old James Maybrick, a well-known Liverpool cotton merchant with business connections in London and America, had been poisoned. His death certificate issued on June 8th shockingly pre-empted the course of justice: it stated – before Florie had even been tried let alone judged – that Maybrick died from 'irritant poison administered to him by Florence Elizabeth Maybrick. Wilful murder.'

That August, after a sensationally disorganised trial that gripped Britain and America alike, Maybrick's 26-year-old widow, Florie, was convicted of his murder and condemned to death. She was the first American woman to be tried in a British court.

* * *

Six months before Maybrick's death, Thomas Bowyer walked through Whitechapel, a squalid neighbourhood in London's East End. He was on his way to collect the overdue rent of 13 Miller's Court, let by John McCarthy to Mary Jane Kelly. It was about 10.45 a.m. on November 9th, and cheerful crowds were making their way to watch the passing of the gold coach amid the traditional celebrations that, even today, mark the annual inauguration of the City of London's Lord Mayor.

There was no response to Bowyer's knock. Reaching through the broken widow, he pulled back the grubby, makeshift curtain and peered into the hovel that was Mary Kelly's pathetic home. On the blood-drenched bed lay all that remained of a girl's body.

It was naked, apart from a skimpy shift. There had been a determined attempt to sever the head. The stomach was ripped wide open. The nose, breasts and ears were sliced off, and skin torn from the face and thighs was lying beside the raw body. The kidneys, liver and other organs were placed around the corpse, whose eyes were wide open, staring terrified from a mangled, featureless face.

Mary Jane Kelly was the latest victim of a fiend who had been butchering prostitutes since the end of August. The killings all took place around weekends and within the same sordid square mile of overcrowded streets that was, and is, one of London's most deprived areas. The women were strangled, slashed and mutilated, in progressively more brutal attacks.

Mary Ann ('Polly') Nichols, the first victim, was a locksmith's daughter in her early forties who moved from workhouse to workhouse. Then came Annie Chapman, 47, Elizabeth Stride, 44, and Catharine Eddowes, 46. Now there was Mary Kelly, at about 25 the youngest of them all.

Hideous as these crimes were, they might have been forgotten or dismissed as an occupational hazard of the 'unfortunates', as prostitutes were called, had the police not been taunted by notes and clues. These came apparently from the murderer who, in one infamous, mocking letter had given himself a nickname that sent shudders through London and far beyond: Jack the Ripper.

No one in 1889 had reason to link the exhumation of James Maybrick in a windy Liverpool graveyard with that earlier blood bath in a squalid London slum, 220 miles away. Neither the police nor the medical men in Liverpool could possibly have connected the doctors' macabre midnight dissection of a respectable middle-aged businessman and the gruesome disembowelling of a young Whitechapel prostitute. That link was finally made 103 years later, in 1992, when a newly found Diary exposed the possibility that James Maybrick was Jack the Ripper.

* * *

On March 9th of that year, my literary agent Doreen Montgomery, managing director of Rupert Crew Limited, one of the capital's longest-established and best-respected agencies, took a call from Liverpool. It was from a 'Mr Williams'. He said that he had found the Diary of Jack the Ripper and would like to bring it to her for publication.

She was naturally cautious. Doreen had been my agent for many years so she suggested I should be present at the meeting; she would welcome a second opinion. In fact 'Mr Williams' turned out to be Michael Barrett, the former scrap metal dealer with a taste for drama. He arrived in the Rupert Crew office, wearing a smart new suit and clutching a briefcase. Inside, in brown paper wrapping, was the book which was about to have such a cataclysmic effect on so many of those whose lives it touched and cause uproar in the hitherto peaceful world of Ripper historians. It appeared to be a dark blue, cross grain leather, quarterbound guard book. The binding and paper were of medium to high quality and well preserved. To judge by the evidence of the glue stains and the oblong impressions left on the flyleaf, the book had served the common Victorian practice of holding postcards, photographs, reminiscences, autographs and other mementoes. The first 64 pages had been removed. The last 17 were blank. The writer's reference to his fear of being caught as early as page three – '*I am beginning to think it is unwise to continue writing*' clearly indicates that what we are reading is the end of the story – not the beginning. For whatever reason the earlier text has been destroyed. Then followed 63 pages of the most sensational words we had ever read. Their tone veered from maudlin to frenetic; many lines were furiously crossed out, with blots and smudges everywhere. We were sickened by the story that unfolded in an erratic hand, reflecting the violence of the subject.

> *I will take all next time and* eat it. *Will leave* nothing *not even the head. I will boil it and eat it with freshly picked carrots. The taste of blood was sweet, the pleasure was overwhelming.*

Towards the end the mood softened:

Tonight I write of love.
tis love that spurned me so,
tis love that does destroy.

Finally, we read the words:

Soon, I trust I shall be laid beside my dear mother and father. I shall seek their forgiveness when we are reunited. God I pray will allow me at least that privilege, although I know only too well I do not deserve it. My thoughts will remain in tact, for a reminder to all how love does destroy... I pray whoever should read this will find it in their heart to forgive me. Remind all, whoever you may be, that I was once a gentle man. May the good lord have mercy on my soul, and forgive me for all I have done.

I give my name that all know of me, so history
do tell, what love can do to a gentle man born.
Yours truly
Jack the Ripper
Dated this third day of May 1889

I was not a Ripper historian, but even after some 50 years as a professional writer I sensed, in this rather drab looking journal, the thrill of the chase! Was it true? Was it a forgery? I listened, still suspicious, anxiously waiting for clues as Michael Barrett talked.

Those who have read the original, hardback edition of my book and the subsequent paperback editions will be aware that some details of Michael's recollections have changed. We have been accused of altering the story to meet objections and so compounding a lie with a lie. Quite the reverse. Research is organic, it is not static. Over the five years since my first meeting with Michael I have learned a great deal. New information emerges every week and I have revised some of my interpretation of events accordingly, not to pervert the course of history, but to come nearer to the truth.

MICHAEL BARRETT'S STORY

Michael told us how he had spent all his life in Liverpool, apart from time as a merchant seaman and working on the oil rigs. He was also a barman and then a scrap metal dealer. In 1976 he met Anne Graham in the city's Irish Centre and fell in love.

They were married within weeks. Michael described how some years ago he was injured in an accident and had been on invalidity benefit, unable to work ever since. So Anne went out to work as a secretary and he stayed at home to care for the couple's little girl Caroline, born in 1981.

'I did everything for that girl. I bonded with her. Housework, cooking, I did it all and I also looked after the tiny garden in our back yard. That was my pride and joy. From 1989 Caroline went to school in Kirkdale and on the way to collect her I would drop off in the Saddle pub where Tony Devereux and I became good friends. He was about 67 at the time and I was 38. Tony fractured his hip around Christmas 1990 and I did a bit of shopping for him, smuggling in a spot of sherry which he hid under the sink.

'In March 1991 Tony went into hospital for a hip replacement but during that summer his health deteriorated. One day I dropped in and Tony was sitting there with a brown paper parcel on the table. He wouldn't tell me what it was. All he said was "Take it. I want you to have it. Do something with it."

'I went home and opened the parcel with Caroline. Inside was this book. I tried to read it but the handwriting was difficult and then when I turned to that last entry I just laughed.

'It was like a knife going into me,' Michael recalled. 'I just didn't believe it. Who's going to believe that in a million years? I telephoned Tony straight away and said, "Who are you trying to kid?"'

The next day, Caroline remembers, her dad went down to Tony's house and pestered him about the origins of the Diary. How long had he had it? All Tony would say was 'You are getting on my fucking nerves. I have given it to you because I know it is real and I know you will do something with it.'

Eventually, Michael said, Tony lost his temper when asked, 'Who else knows about it?' The reply: 'Absolutely no fucking bugger alive today.'

Caroline remembers clearly how her dad continued to pester Tony for information on the telephone. 'I trusted him,' Michael said. 'He didn't want any money for it. He would not have let me down. Anne and I sat together that evening and tried to make it out. There were some names of people and places which meant nothing to me. Battlecrease, Bunny, Gladys and Michael. Who were Lowry and Mrs Hammersmith? We didn't know anything about Jack the Ripper either.'

On that day the Barretts' world was turned upside down. The Diary, which should have secured their happiness, was to destroy their marriage and prove the final straw for Michael's already fragile health. Anne told us much later that, like many people in Liverpool, she was aware of the Maybrick case, but not its details. Michael became obsessed and threw himself into fact finding about the Ripper. He had always had dreams of being a writer and had actually published some short interviews with visiting celebrities and made up simple word puzzles for *Look-in,* a D.C. Thomson children's magazine. He liked to call himself a journalist. 'In fact,' Anne admits now, 'I usually tidied them up for him.'

In April 1986, Michael had bought himself an Amstrad word processor with money lent by Anne's father, Billy Graham, and now, at last, it came into its own. He told us that he made copious notes in the Liverpool library, which Anne latterly transcribed onto the Amstrad. But at this stage Michael had not connected the Diary with James Maybrick. One day, he told me, when he was in a Liverpool bookshop, he found a copy of *Murder, Mayhem and Mystery in Liverpool* by Richard Whittington Egan, a much-respected crime historian whose family hailed from the city and had even driven with the Maybricks to the races. In the book there was a piece entitled 'Motif in Fly Papers' which began: 'When first I beheld it in the fast fading light of a late May evening, Battlecrease House looked very much like any other of the solid respectable relics of the mid-Victorian period...'

This was the connection Michael needed. The name 'Battlecrease' also appeared on page two of the Diary. In fact, Battlecrease House, in the agreeable suburb of Aigburth, is a name still known to many Liverpudlians acquainted with the tragedy of the ill-fated couple. James and Florence Maybrick had moved there early in 1888, their last turbulent year together. Could it be that the Diary in Michael's possession linked the stories of the outwardly respectable, loving father, a middle-aged merchant broken by a lifetime of secret drug-taking, with the best-known murder mystery of all time?

'I suddenly realised that I could become the man who had finally caught Jack the Ripper,' he said.

In August 1991 Tony Devereux died in Walton Hospital and with him, we assumed, had died the key to the mystery of the Whitechapel killings. By February 1992 Michael knew he was out of his depth. He had no idea how to verify the Diary, much less how to get it published. So he rang Pan Books because he had some of their paperbacks at home and asked if they would like to publish his story. London publishers are not so easily enthused and advised Michael to get himself a literary agent, recommending Doreen Montgomery. Anne apparently panicked and tried to destroy the Diary. She was extremely shy at that stage and not one to seek publicity; but since she could not, for personal reasons, tell Mike that it was, in fact, she who had secretly given the Diary to Tony, she decided to let him get on with it, believing that London publishers would throw him out. They didn't.

* * *

We listened to Michael with suppressed disbelief. On the face of it the Diary's pedigree was extremely doubtful. A former scrap-metal worker from Liverpool? A friend in a pub who was now dead? I suggested, on the spur of the moment, that we should take the Diary immediately to the British Museum round the corner from the Rupert Crew offices and see if we could elicit an opinion from their experts. An instant appointment was made with Robert Smith, then a curator of 19th century manuscripts. It all seemed so easy at the beginning!

The front entrance to the British Museum is monumental. Inside, the scale is no less massive; the silence of 3 million learned tomes carpeting the walls, envelops the visitor. Michael clutched my arm nervously as we walked, carrying the Diary, through the maze of corridors that form the administrative arteries of the building. Elderly manuscript historians peered at the pages through magnifying glasses, poring over the dramatic words again and again.

'Fascinating,' said Robert Smith. 'Quite extraordinary. It looks authentic. But of course you will have to take it to a document examiner. We just don't have the facilities here.' I was astonished by this admission.

On a whim, I popped into Jarndyce, the antiquarian bookshop opposite the museum, where Brian Lake looked up from his first edition Dickens and was also reassuringly enthusiastic. Brian, the shop's owner, is a specialist in 19th century literature and recognised the potential value of the Diary. But he agreed with Robert Smith that we should have to find a forensic scientist to establish the book's precise date.

On April 30th 1992 a collaboration agreement was drawn up to be signed by Michael Barrett, his wife Anne and myself. It bound us to share the responsibilities, expenses and royalties from any future book. In the meantime we had all also signed confidentiality agreements, binding anyone with access to the Diary to secrecy. Because of its potentially sensational nature, we were all afraid the story would leak before we were ready and so lessen its impact.

Michael Barrett went home to Liverpool. He returned with Caroline, his daughter, on June 3rd to be present at the two-day auction which Doreen Montgomery had decided to hold for the publishing rights to a book about the Diary, which I would write. My colleague, researcher Sally Evemy, took Caroline off for a day's sightseeing and then Caroline and her father spent the night at my home. Anne was still working and unable to join us. Among the contenders the next day, June 4th, was another Robert Smith, managing director of Smith Gryphon publishers. He had some years earlier published *The Ripper Legacy* by Martin Howells and Keith Skinner and had invited Keith to accompany him to Doreen's office.

Robert pored over the Diary for what seemed like hours, saying very little, while Michael told him that all he hoped for was enough money to buy a greenhouse. The bid which Robert eventually made for the Diary was not large – and understandably reflected caution. From a publisher's point of view it was a dangerous prospect – no one had forgotten the fiasco of the Hitler diaries, which had been published by the *Sunday Times* in 1982 and then proved to be a forgery within weeks. But Robert Smith, a shrewd businessman and a keen historian himself, had a hunch that the Diary could be genuine, and he decided to back that hunch. By July 29, 1992, Michael Barrett and I had signed a contract with Robert Smith. We were in business.

It is not usually customary for an author to discuss the terms of a publishing contract, but since these are exceptional circumstances and such unbelievably exaggerated figures have been bandied about I shall, where necessary, bend the rules now. I was eventually offered an advance against royalties of £15,000 – to be divided equally between Michael and me and to be returned should the Diary prove to be a forgery. From this I knew I would be expected to pay for any scientific testing and additional researchers' fees that would be needed to enable me to meet the terrifyingly short deadline. As it turned out, the concept of sharing expenses was unworkable, and for the last few years I have borne that cost myself. I needed a team of helpers, including academics. Initially I turned to Keith Skinner, Paul Begg and Martin Fido (who is a former university don), the co-authors of the *Jack the Ripper A-Z*, widely respected for their integrity and profound knowledge of the subject.

At the time, they were working on a documentary for producer Paul Feldman. Eventually he too was introduced to Diary and by November had signed a contract for the video and film rights of my book. He became a man obsessed. Cigar in one hand and a large Scotch in the other, he worried at theat Diary for five years, spending a fortune and all but breaking himself financially, emotionally and physically.

Philip Sugden, the academic historian and author of the mammoth, much-praised *Complete History of Jack the Ripper* (published 1996), has since expressed the view that it would have been better had the Diary been directed along the academic path. He has said that its entry into the commercial world of publishing has meant that research has been directed by commercial motivation and that serious academic historians should have investigated the Diary. I question this view. Academics are not always right. After all, the late Lord Dacre of Glanton (Hugh Trevor Roper), who confirmed the Hitler diaries as 'genuine' was a greatly respected academic. Besides, in time the Diary attracted its share of academics, too. The fact is that this project was handed to me and I doubt that any professional writer in my position would have acted differently. The only way I knew to meet the cost of researching this Diary was to find a publisher prepared to offer an advance which would be enough to facilitate some basic investigation. Few people realise that it is always the writer's responsibility to finance research and at that stage I had little idea of the likely expense involved, still less of the likely financial outcome.

Of course I hoped the Diary was genuine – indeed, I was sure that it was – but had there been, at any stage, proof positive that it was a forgery I would have stopped work. So would any one of the team that was involved. Ten years on Keith Skinner and Paul Begg are still baffled and always available for help and advice. They have devoted an inordinate amount of time and interest to the enigma of the Diary for very little return. Judging by the history of hoaxes, such as the Hitler and Mussolini Diaries, I was somewhat naively confident that if the Diary were a modern forgery we should all know very quickly.

On the other hand, like most of those who have decided the Diary is a forgery, Martin Fido is convinced it was written within the two or three years prior to Michael Barrett's arrival in London.

For ten years our team has been immersed in the story of the Barretts, the Maybricks and the Whitechapel murders. We have met and worked with the friends and families of all those in Liverpool who have any connections with the central players in the drama. We have stayed with them, attended family gatherings, funerals and festivities. We have listened to their troubles, borne the brunt of their anger. A few have been amused, many have been helpful and eager to unravel the truth. Most have been distraught by the Diary's unwelcome intrusion into their private lives and the publicity it has brought.

*   *   *

Michael Barrett and Caroline returned to Liverpool that evening. Michael was elated with the excitement of the new life he thought he had begun, peopled with agents, publishers and academics. On the train he got talking to the then owner of a free newspaper in Liverpool, Phil Maddox.

Phil recalls: 'I saw this chap clutching a brown paper parcel – he was sitting on the opposite side of the carriage, slipping up and down to the bar to get these small bottles of whisky. Then he came over – just started talking. "Bet you don't know what this is – Jack the Ripper's Diary." I thought he was a nutter. He was fluttering his hands all over it to prevent me looking. I tried to see it – I collect old books, mostly of the printed variety. Then I got interested but he wouldn't show me the bloody thing. Kept messing about. He mentioned the auction but "I am sworn to secrecy". Then he mentioned scrap metal; and about his child being in a band or winning some British Legion award, so I thought "That's how I'll trace him when I need to." I didn't need to push him or anything.'

*   *   *

I had begun preliminary efforts to investigate the Diary's origins scientifically before a publisher was involved. I was naively optimistic, having no idea at this stage of the bitter controversies that would be involved in such a task or of the fallibility of experts!

Not only was a leading expert in the history and composition of ink to be consulted but I also enlisted the help of a document examiner, a graphologist, a psychiatrist and medical consultants. The first step was, I felt, to establish as nearly as possible that the Diary was indeed Victorian and that the ink had been put on the paper over 100 years ago.

First I took it to Dr David Baxendale of Document Evidence Limited, a former Home Office forensic examiner whose team in Birmingham had an excellent reputation. Dr Baxendale was asked, in particular, to tell us the age of the ink and, if possible, when it was applied to the paper. His first brief report on July 1st 1992, in summary, said that he viewed the Diary with suspicion. We asked for a fuller account of his reasoning. This, on July 9th, had it been factually correct, would have been a bombshell. The paragraph dealing with the ink said:

> The ink of the Diary was readily soluble in the extractant and only a small amount of insoluble black residue was left on the paper. The chromatogram showed only a partial separation: much of the ink remained on the baseline but there was a strip of partially resolved coloured components, and a few colourless fluorescent spots. This pattern is characteristic of inks based on a synthetic dye called nigrosine, which is a complex mixture of substances but one which has been used in many inks at least since the 1940s. There was nothing to suggest the presence of iron.

Then I learned from another well respected scientific analyst, Dr Nicholas Eastaugh, that in tests on the ink which he had taken from several parts of the Diary he had, indeed, found iron and that the observation that the ink was 'freely soluble' was unsupported. With the help of the Science Library in London it took very little time to establish that nigrosine was patented in 1867 by Coupier and was in general use in writing inks by the 1870s! Indeed, there is a statement in one of the standard reference works *Pen, Ink and Paper*, published in 1990, by Dr Joe Nickell (who was later asked to testify against us). It confirms my continuing concern over the fallibility of experts.

> ...Subsequent writing fluids which were not of the corrosive iron-gall variety included ...certain other coloured inks (made possible by the discovery of aniline dyes in 1856) as well as nigrosine ink (first produced commercially in 1867).

One of the key reasons Dr Baxendale dismissed the Diary was, quite simply, inaccurate. We lost confidence in the value of his report and agreed, in writing, with his request that it would not be used in my book or 'for any purpose whatsoever'. That restriction has now been removed by mutual agreement.

Dr Eastaugh, who then became our chief scientific adviser on the ink, paper and binding of the Diary, is primarily a specialist in identifying and dating materials used on Old Masters and manuscripts. He has worked for the Museum of London, the National Gallery, the Tate Gallery and Christie's. He said straight away that documents as potentially important as the Diary I had brought him were rare.

Dr Eastaugh examined the Diary at his studio in Teddington, south-west London. It lay in distinguished company. On his desk was a 16th century painting by Bruegel the Elder, the provenance of which he was hoping to establish. He would begin by studying the ink to establish the Diary's age and, if possible, when it was applied to the paper. Later he would attempt to date the paper itself. Dr Eastaugh also proposed an investigation of what was left of the missing pages, and to examine some black powder that had been found deeply embedded in the 'gutter' between the pages of the Diary.

The most crucial tests were carried out with a proton microprobe. Dr Eastaugh told me this employs 'a non-destructive method of exciting atoms in a small target area on a page with an accelerated beam of protons, in order to detect, to the parts per million, what chemicals are present in inks, papers, parchments and pigments tested.' Minute samples of ink, painstakingly lifted from the Diary were prepared and mounted on slides before being taken into the Star Wars world of the laboratory. Such a device was used by the Crocker National Laboratory in California to determine how the *Gutenburg* Bible was printed and to investigate the Vinland Map, which appears to be mediaeval in origin but is still controversial.

These were the first of a number of laboratory tests conducted over the next four years, not only by us but by a group determined to prove the Diary a forgery. The conflicting results were bewildering. But at that early stage in our quest Dr Eastaugh seemed encouraging. 'The results of various analyses of ink and paper in the Diary performed so far have not given rise to any conflict with the date of 1888/9.'

As my confidence grew, my attention turned to the kind of man who might have written the Diary. There seemed to be three likely possibilities. It could be an old forgery by someone who knew Maybrick was the Ripper and wanted to destroy him; it could be the work of a modern forger; or it could be genuine. In an attempt to throw some light on the personality of the man behind the Diary I first went to see Dr David Forshaw, who was then a specialist consultant in addiction at the Maudsley Psychiatric Hospital in London. (At the time of Jack the Ripper the hospital was better known as the notorious Bedlam lunatic asylum.)

Dr Forshaw was born in Liverpool and had completed three years' research into forensic psychiatry in London; he holds a diploma in the History of Medicine from the Society of Apothecaries and has published extensively on psychiatry and addiction. He is now a consultant at Broadmoor Hospital, where Peter Sutcliffe, the Yorkshire Ripper, is serving a life sentence.

I did not ask him to prove that the author of the Diary was Jack the

Ripper but to assess whether, in his view, the writer had genuinely committed the crimes described or whether he could indeed be merely a sick or cynical forger. Dr Forshaw spent several months examining the Diary, eventually producing a 15,000 word report, excerpts of which will be presented later. But his conclusions focused my mind more and more on the significance of the personality of the Diary writer and the psychopathology of the Diary itself. Here Dr Forshaw said:

> A thorough examination of the Diary and its provenance are essential components of deciding if it is authentic. If such an examination proves indecisive and all falls back on the content, then I would argue in that case, on the balance of probabilities from a psychiatric perspective, it is authentic.

From the beginning, it was my instinctive response to the psychopathology of the Diary that convinced me it was genuine. I could not believe that the violent mood swings, the anguish and the nauseating pleasure of cannibalism was the writing of, as some claimed, a money-conscious con man, a Maybrick/Ripper expert or even of a member of the Maybrick family with a lust for revenge. I did not believe that any one man or woman could master the scientific knowledge needed to make and fade the ink, the understanding of arsenic addiction revealed in the Diary and, at the same time, accumulate all the historical data to make the progression of events fit the known facts of the case.

In 1997, five years older and wiser, I also went to see Professor David Canter of Liverpool University, and Director of its Institute of Investigative Psychology, whose book *Criminal Shadows* won the Golden Dagger Award and whose book *Mapping Murder* is published in 2003. Probably the country's best-known expert on the profiling of serial killers, he was immensely reassuring and confirmed that my earliest 'gut' response to the Diary's emotional ebb and flow was not simply a case of wishful thinking. In fact, he has found it valuable source material for his students. He agreed to write a new postscript for this edition.

In all the years since that autumn of terror, the evidence surrounding the Whitechapel murders has remained as confused as ever. Very little hard documentary material has emerged for us to state with total confidence exactly what happened. Evidence was contradictory, few people wore watches to be sure of precise times, roads were dimly lit and press statements were understandably unreliable. Jack the Ripper struck at a time when newspapers were thirsting for sensation. The new banner headlines whipped up a hysterical panic never known before. Better education and improved technology led to a newspaper circulation war. The Ripper's gruesome crimes and taunts to the authorities – and their apparent inability to stop him – were headline news.

Where did he come from? What drove him on to kill and kill again? Why did he mutilate his victims? What compulsion made him leave clues? All this was the stuff of Victorian gothic horror, at a time when Robert Louis Stevenson's *Dr Jekyll and Mr Hyde* had been scaring audiences at London's Lyceum Theatre.

Despite the greatest manhunt Britain had ever seen, the killer was never captured. The Ripper remained an obsession, spawning penny dreadfuls, scholarly investigations, novels and music hall verse. An entire literary and theatrical industry is based on his awful exploits. In the years that followed, memoranda emerged and books were written; documents vanished and came mysteriously to light again. With each new 'discovery' came a flood of theories. In 1959, the late Daniel Farson, was shown a document by Lady Aberconway, daughter of Sir Melville Macnaghten, who became Assistant Chief Constable CID at Scotland Yard in 1889. This document was a transcribed copy of her father's original notes, written in 1894. Two versions of the document exist and a third has been described. In the version that Farson saw, the Assistant Chief Constable named for the first time the three men who, he said, were suspected by Scotland Yard in 1888. They were Montague John Druitt, Kosminski and Michael Ostrog.

MONTAGUE JOHN DRUITT

Druitt, described erroneously as a doctor, was a barrister, but had also become a schoolteacher at Mr Valentine's school in Blackheath by the time of the murders. He was mysteriously dismissed and was found drowned in the Thames at Chiswick in December 1888, his pockets full of stones. The body had been in the water for about a month. Macnaghten named Druitt as a suspect largely because his body was discovered soon after the Kelly murder, the assumption being that Druitt's mental state had collapsed just before his suicide. Macnaghten also claimed that he had access to 'private information' that Druitt's own family believed him to be the killer and that Druitt was 'sexually insane'. He added that 'the truth will never be known.'

By contrast, in 1903, Inspector Abberline of the Metropolitan Police, who had been in charge of detectives investigating the Whitechapel murders, said: 'I know all about that story but what does it amount to? Simply this. Soon after the last murder in Whitechapel the body of a young doctor was found in the Thames but there is absolutely nothing beyond the fact that he was found at that time to incriminate him.' Nevertheless Montague John Druitt remains among the front-running suspects.

KOSMINSKI

Sir Robert Anderson (Assistant Commissioner of the Metropolitan Police CID at the time) does not name Kosminski, but in speaking of the Ripper says: 'In saying that he was a Polish Jew I am merely stating a definitely ascertained fact'. Kosminski was a misogynist with homicidal tendencies who had become insane from years of indulgence in 'solitary vices'. He was sent to Stepney Workhouse and then, in 1891, to Colney Hatch Lunatic Asylum when, it was said, 'he goes about the streets and picks up bits of bread out of the gutter.' However, in the police evidence against him, dates, times and places are wrongly listed.

In 1987 there came to light some pencil notes by Chief Inspector Donald Swanson, who had also played a leading role in the

Whitechapel investigation. These were comments, written in about 1910 in the margins and on the endpapers of his own personal copy of the memoirs of Sir Robert Anderson. Published in the *Daily Telegraph*, Swanson's marginalia identified Anderson's own, unnamed suspect: Kosminski. Nevertheless the marginalia contained inaccuracies which only served to fuel rather than end the debate.

MICHAEL OSTROG

The remaining police suspect was the Russian sneak thief and confidence trickster, Michael Ostrog. Little is known about him beyond his appalling criminal record and his being habitually cruel to women. It is probable that suspicion fell on him largely because he carried surgical knives and instruments when he roamed the streets of Whitechapel. He was 'wanted' in October 1888 (not for the Whitechapel crimes) but his whereabouts at the time of the murders was never established.

Macnaghten also stated with apparent authority that the Whitechapel murderer had claimed five victims and five victims only, contradicting the belief of the public and many fellow policemen alike that there had been at least two more.

* * *

Of course, there have been a number of other suspects.

THE DUKE OF CLARENCE

In the 1970s when the great surge of Ripper books really began, several writers produced a sensational new candidate. The public loves a royal scandal, which is probably why Prince Albert Victor, the Duke of Clarence, and grandson of Queen Victoria, has become the best-remembered suspect.

This story arose in November 1970, from an article in *The Criminologist* by Dr Thomas Stowell. He based his arguments on the alleged private papers of Sir William Gull, physician to the Queen, who treated the Prince for syphilis and said that he died of softening of the brain. (He, too, is on the suspect list along with Dr Barnardo and Lewis Carroll!). These papers were never expertly examined and are now missing. However, it is known from diaries and court circulars of the time that the Prince was in Yorkshire, Scotland and the royal retreat of Sandringham in Norfolk, at the time of the murders.

DR FRANCIS TUMBELTY

In 1993, while I was hard at work exploring the background to the Maybrick Diary, former policeman Stewart Evans and author of several Ripper books and press officer Paul Gainey discovered the Littlechild letter naming an 'American quack', Francis Tumbelty, as a hitherto unknown police suspect. Their book, *Jack the Ripper, the First American Serial Killer* appeared in 1995. Chief Inspector John Littlechild, head of Special Branch, was a greatly respected detective in 1888 and this letter, written 24 years later, suggests that the infamous 'Dear Boss' letter which gave the name of Jack the Ripper to the world was not written by Jack at all, and names the alleged authors.

Curiously, research into the Littlechild letter was to present some interesting similarities with the information I was receiving about James Maybrick. Both focused heavily on Liverpool and America – as did police enquiries at the time. But, at the end of the day, in a book of 274 pages only 40 relate to the alleged connections between Tumbelty and Whitechapel. He is a fascinating man with a murky history but the hard evidence against him is thin.

* * *

In 1997, the finger of suspicion was pointed at Jimmy Kelly, the Broadmoor escapee and lover of Mary Jane Kelly (no relation) in a book by Jim Tully; horse-breeder Terry Saxby was compiling evidence at his home in Australia to support his belief that Henry Tabram, estranged husband of Martha, was the man, while Andy and Sue Parlour launched their own publication, written by Kevin O'Donnell, *Jack the Ripper: The Whitechapel Murders*.

In 2002 best-selling American crime author, Patricia Cornwell arrived in Britain on a publicity tour for her book *Portrait of a Killer*. She was protected by square-shouldered, square-jawed, unsmiling minders and received a rather cool welcome for her graphic television demonstration of the Ripper's methods of dissection and her pummelling of a hunk of red raw meat. Her man was the British artist Walter Sickert, backed, she claimed, by samples of DNA from his letters and those in the Scotland Yard archives...

But the experts were unimpressed with her arguments.

The entire worldwide Ripper industry has been built on such speculation. In 1996 the first Ripper Conference was held in Ipswich. By 2001 support for the Conference had ballooned and Bournemouth became the hugely well-attended venue for the now International Ripper Conference. In 2003 Liverpool was chosen to host the event and delegates flew in from all over the world. Speakers included Professor David Canter and Bill Rubinstein, Professor of Modern History at Aberystwyth University.

The regular lunches hosted by the renowned true crime specialist Camille Wolfe also became an informal forum for civilised discussion. Daily groups of amateur sleuths trail behind professional guides around the backstreets of Whitechapel and The London Dungeon attracts some two and a half thousand visitors per day to its Jack the Ripper Experience and, not surprisingly, there is a strong lobby by various women's movements who protest at the commercial exploitation of the 'unfortunates'.

The Internet is buzzing with theories and the results of a surfers' poll conducted in January 1997 placed James Maybrick at the top of the list of 29 Ripper suspects. In 2002, Discovery Channel viewers watched a trial of Jack the Ripper in which Kosminski, Tumbelty, Gull and Maybrick were defended by such celebrity advocates as Angela Rippon and Jeremy Beadle. The jury was a record-breaking countrywide audience, and it condemned Maybrick.

As Philip Sugden, the academic and author of one of the classic Ripper bibles, *The Complete History of Jack the Ripper*, himself proposes: 'eye witness testimony is at best treacherous'. In fact, after 500 pages based on impeccable original source material, Mr Sugden admits:

> Sadly, by the end of my study two things had become painfully apparent... First, there was no single police view on the matter. Different officers espoused different theories... The second conclusion is... none of their theories seems to be based on tangible evidence linking a suspect to the crimes... History can take us no further. Perhaps psychology can...

So my attention was now focused. I knew that I had a unique opportunity. So far everyone had tried to solve the Whitechapel murders by examining unreliable evidence. I had a document, which tallied in some ways with what was known and differed in others. This no longer troubled me. Suppose the Diary was right. Suppose the police, the witnesses and the Ripperologists had all been wrong!

2

I am Jack. A Watch is Discovered

A few weeks before the first edition of this book was due at the printers, our publisher at the time, Robert Smith, took a phone call. The voice at the other end of the line, in an unmistakable Liverpool accent, said, 'I think I have got James Maybrick's watch.'

On June 4th 1993, Robert Smith received a rough drawing of the inside of the watch, from its owner Albert Johnson of Wallasey in Cheshire. This drawing convinced Robert that he should meet Albert and his younger brother Robbie, and on June 14th they brought their prize to London. At this stage Robert Smith was playing his cards very close to his chest – even Sally Evemy and I were not yet aware of the existence of the watch, although Robert had spoken of it with Keith.

When I was brought into the picture, I was far from elated; instead I felt a sense of near panic. Here, more than likely, was the first of the bandwagon riders we had imagined might try to capitalise on the Diary. Yet we dared not ignore the possibility that the call could be genuine and so Sally and I drove up to Liverpool to meet the owner, Albert Johnson, at his younger brother Robbie's modern bungalow in the Wirral.

At first sight they were an oddly assorted pair. Albert was clearly a straightforward family man, semi-retired from his college security job. Robbie was wiry, frenetically eager and anxious, and worked on the fringes of the pop music industry.

The watch lay on the glass-topped table in front of us. It was a small, elaborately engraved pocket-watch. Gently, Albert opened the back of the case and I could just see some very faint scratches on the inside cover. Try as we could, neither Sally nor I could make out the words. So the brothers produced a small microscope and we took the watch to better light in the kitchen. There, I could just make out a signature – it read 'J. Maybrick', and I felt that the *K* and the *M* seemed very like those on Maybrick's wedding certificate. Across the centre, even less distinct, appeared to be the words 'I am Jack'. Around the edge were five sets of initials: they were those of the murdered women in Whitechapel.

I could see there were other initials, which meant nothing to me. On the back the monogram 'J.O' had at some time been professionally engraved. I was speechless, but overwhelmingly suspicious.

Like everything else connected with the Diary, the discovery of the watch provoked furious controversy. Albert told us that he had first seen the watch in Stewart's jewellery shop window in Wallasey and had passed it several times. 'I'd always had a liking for antique bits and pieces, so I thought I'd buy it as an investment for my little granddaughter, Daisy. The shop receipt dates the purchase as July 14th 1992. I paid £225. I took it home and put it in a drawer and thought no more about it.'

Later, Sally, Keith Skinner and I went to visit Albert's pal, John White, who had worked with him at Liverpool Polytechnic for 12 years. John was also a sensible, family man. He recalled the first time the watch was mentioned. 'It all stemmed from the *Antiques Road Show*... we were talking about gold and Albert said he had this watch; he said it was 18 carat gold and one of our group said they didn't have 18 carat gold in Victorian times. So Albert brought the watch in to show us – Albert collects anything, his house is full of stuff. We could see the scratches but we couldn't make them out. The light was bad so we said we'd take it over to the Science and Technology block. When Albert came back he said, "It's just initials and there's a name – Maybrick – in it and there's also something about Jack." I said to him, "I tell you whose watch that is – it's Jack the Ripper's". And he said, "What do you mean?" I said "Well, that Maybrick could be Jack the Ripper. I was reading his diary in the *Echo*. He is supposed to have murdered his wife and buried her body under the floorboards and gone off to America." Albert phoned the *Echo* and they knew nothing about it. I was wrong, it was the *Liverpool Daily Post* and they said it wasn't Maybrick that murdered his wife anyway but she was supposed to have murdered him. So we went to the college library and we couldn't find anything about Maybrick but then we looked in this one on Jack the Ripper. The initials in the watch belonged to the murder victims. That was where it all started.'

The *Liverpool Post*, sensing scandal, ran an article. As was to happen so often in the future, the Maybrick/Ripper possibility was condemned before it was investigated.

Albert realised by this time that his watch might be important. He told his brother Robbie about it and during the first week in June they decided to telephone Robert Smith. Towards the end of the month they also sought the support of Wallasey solicitor, Richard Nicholas. 'I would never have dreamed of representing Albert if I was not convinced of his honesty,' Mr Nicholas reassured me when we went to his office.

By this time, Paul Feldman had also telephoned Albert and Robbie and the brothers offered to meet him at his home on July 5th, with Richard Nicholas. They were all very excited. Paul was immediately 'sold' on the watch but that visit sowed in his mind the seeds of an imaginative story within a story.

He also became convinced that Albert Johnson is a Maybrick!

It is an intriguing and confusing story based on the Feldman team's discovery of a hitherto unknown nest of Maybricks and of a birthday book belonging to an Olga Maybrick Ellison who died in 1989. The book notes the name of a Mrs Johnston (as opposed to Johnson), 160 Goodwin Avenue, Bidston.

Was this name wrongly spelt and was there truly a connection?

Olga's niece, Norma Meagher, is an Ellison by birth and so Paul

Feldman's researcher Carol Emmas went to see her in Birkenhead in July 1995. Norma recalled that in the mid-1980s Olga had told her 'there's a watch that James Maybrick had and someone in Goodwin Avenue has got it.'

The focus was now on Goodwin Avenue. Robbie Johnson confirmed that he and Albert had indeed lived there in the 1960s. Albert Johnson takes all this with a wry smile and a pinch of salt. But he maintains that he bought the watch exactly how he said he did. So if he *is* a Maybrick, he says that his stumbling across this particular watch 'is a miracle' and being a deeply religious man, this is exactly what he means.

I spoke to Norma Meagher myself many years later and asked her to respond in writing to the contents of the 1998 edition of my book. She was forthright in her reply. 'I only know, from my Aunt Olga, the sister of my father, Norman Ellison, that a man in Goodwin Avenue had the watch which he got from Liscard, Wallasey. The watch had James Maybrick's name on it but I do not believe for one moment that he engraved the other initials on it. I never heard of John Over ...'

Sally and I meantime had been pursuing our own line of research. We went to see Ron and Suzanne Murphy whose little shop in Sea View Road, Wallasey, was about to achieve national fame. A second meeting in February 1997 confirmed their original story and their astonishment at what had happened. 'We'd never have sold the watch if we'd realised it could be valuable', they laugh. 'Some time after Mr Johnson got the watch he kept coming back and asking questions about where it came from. We honestly got a bit fed up and thought there must be something wrong. We even offered to buy it back but he said "no". Now we know why!'

In around 1980, Suzanne's father had given them the watch when he retired, along with all the other gold stock from his shop in Lancaster, Firth Antiques. The watch was not then in working order and eventually in 1992 they sent it, with some other watches, to Tim Dundas, of The Clock Workshop, West Kirby, Wirral. He was asked to repair the movement. Later, before it was finally placed in their own shop window, Ron himself cleaned the watch and it was then that he noticed the scratches in the back. 'I tried to buff them out with jeweller's rouge', he recalls ruefully.

After Albert's discovery of what the scratches really were, the Murphys tried to find out from Suzanne's father who had brought the watch to him all those years before. But he was already ill with the onset of Alzheimer's disease, and all he could recall was buying it from a chap with a Liverpool accent.

Before returning to London after that first visit, Sally and I took the watch to the Prescot Watch Museum for a professional technical description. We saw the curator, John Griffiths.

'It is,' he wrote, 'a gold pocket watch hallmarked for 1846/7 at London, the casemaker's mark being RS in an oval, the inner back marked 20789 and the initials J.O engraved in a cartouche on the outside of the back: the full plate, fusee, English lever movement inscribed on the back, Verity, Lancaster and numbered 1286.'

It was from David Thompson, superintendent of the Aladdin's cave of a watch and clock department deep within the British Museum in London that we learned exactly what this meant. Henry Verity ran a family watch retailing business that had been founded in Lancaster around 1830. R. S. were the initials of Ralph Samuel, who by 1845 was a partner with Jacob Lewis Samuel and Co., watch and dial makers of 54 Wood Street, Liverpool, and of Clerkenwell, London. Mr Thompson was puzzled about the numbers which he thought could have been produced by the implement that made the other scratches... Certainly, he said, the 20789 on the inside rim was a repair mark. 'Although I have not examined the watch scientifically,' he said, 'I would not have any immediate reason to doubt the age of the scratches'.

It was Richard Nicholas who suggested that the brothers should take the watch to be forensically tested in the hope that they could prove the age of the scratches. Albert agreed. He knew he had nothing to fear. Richard Nicholas arranged for the brothers to see Dr Stephen Turgoose of the Corrosion Protection Centre at the University of Manchester Institute of Science and Technology (UMIST). On 28th July 1993

Albert and Robbie took the watch to Manchester, in a state of considerable excitement, and left it there.

The result of that examination by scanning electron microscope was ready by August 10th 1993 and sent to Albert. It read:

> On the basis of the evidence... especially the order in which the markings were made, it is clear that the engravings pre-date the vast majority of superficial surface scratch marks (all of those examined). The wear apparent on many of the engravings, evidenced by the rounded edges of the markings and 'polishing out' in places, would indicate a substantial age for the engravings. The actual age would depend on the cleaning or polishing regime employed, and any definition of number of years has a great degree of uncertainty and, to some extent, must remain speculation. Given these qualifications, I would be of the opinion that the engravings are likely to date back more than tens of years and possibly much longer.
>
> However, whilst there is no evidence which would indicate a recent (last few years) origin of the engravings, it must be emphasised that there are no features observed which conclusively prove the age of the engravings. They could have been produced recently and deliberately artificially aged by polishing, but this would have been a complex multi-stage process using a variety of different tools, with intermediate polishing of artifical wearing stages. Also, many of the features are only resolved by the scanning electron microscope, not being readily apparent in optical microscopy, and so, if they were of recent origin, the engraver would have to be aware of the potential evidence available from this technique, indicating a considerable skill and scientific awareness.

This report had cost Albert Johnson several hundred pounds of his own money, which was proof enough to me that there was no skulduggery afoot. Had Albert forged the scratches himself, or was collaborating with anyone who had, he could not have dared to throw himself on the mercy of an independent scientist such as Dr Turgoose.

In January 1994, Albert agreed to submit the watch to a second test. It was taken to the Interface Analysis Centre at Bristol University. There, the eminent metallurgist Dr Robert Wild tested it under his electron microscope using a technique of scanning auger microscopy. His findings were better than we dared to hope. Like Dr Turgoose, Dr Wild photographed slivers of brass embedded within the scratch marks. They were blackened with age. The penultimate paragraph of his detailed report (which also stresses the need for much more lengthy work to pinpoint the precise age of the scratches) reads:

> Provided the watch has remained in a normal environment, it would seem likely that the engravings were at least of several tens of years age. This would agree with the findings of Dr Turgoose (1993) and in my opinion it is unlikely that anyone would have sufficient expertise to implant aged, brass particles into the base of the engravings.

Dr Wild told Robert Smith privately that he personally felt the scratches could be as old as 1888/9.

So both Dr Turgoose and Dr Wild agreed that the likelihood of anyone acquiring the considerable technical and scientific expertise necessary to create scratches that would pass their test was very remote. Both agreed, too, that the scratches were at least several decades old, thus ruling out any possibility that the watch is a modern forgery. But even these reports did not convert the disbelievers. As late as July 7th 1997 Martin Fido (who, like all the other critics, had never met Albert Johnson) wrote to Keith Skinner: 'while recognising the impressive two concurring lab reports on the watch I do not think they have proved the watch to be genuine; in fact without having any easy explanation for the scientific reports I think it most probably a modern forgery and most probably inspired by the diary.'

Vociferous as they were being about the Diary itself, for the most part the press response to the arrival of the watch was a disappointing, thunderous silence. Because they could not explain it, they chose to ignore it. The story of the watch was made all the more curious when Bob Davis and Stanley Dangar were beamed up, as it were, from outer space. They have since both died – Stanley Dangar in 2002 and Bob Davis in 2003.

Bob Davis was the boss of Davis Bros, a major publishing company in Dallas, Texas. Stanley Dangar lived near Gerona in north east Spain. Mr Davis offered $40,000 on spec for the watch, which Albert turned down. He was not interested in money. Mr Dangar, a watch expert and founder member of the British Horological Society, was a man with a mission.

Fortunately Stanley Dangar and Bob Davis never met, for each was, in his way, coiled tight like the springs of the watch that, for a time, overtook their lives – and mine. Each spent a fortune on pursuing his particular hunch – Stanley Dangar that the watch was forged, Bob Davis that it was genuine.

Stanley Dangar telephoned Robert Smith and arrived in London in February 1995. We had lunch and he brought me flowers.

His favourite description of anyone (or anything) of whom he did not approve was 'mickey mouse', and over the time that he was in touch with us all, I think only Albert and I escaped that label. He met the two brothers with Robert Smith and me in a pub near the Smith Gryphon office and was instantly suspicious of the golden glint in Robbie's eye.

Robbie was always more commercially-minded and hyperactive than Albert and had led a somewhat more colourful life. We did not learn the complex story of their filial financial arrangements until much later. Albert had privately arranged a partnership with his brother and had agreed to give him a 25% share should the watch be sold.

At that stage Robbie was up-front and eager for action and seemed as keen as Albert to have the watch scientifically tested again.

By the time Stanley had returned to Spain he had, himself, already employed a watch expert from the British Horological Society and was then to muster a graphologist and a scientific laboratory in Germany, to attempt simulation tests. Of course they did not have the watch itself and eventually, he admitted, 'we have had a little difficulty'.

Mr Dangar then informed me that he was collaborating with Melvin Harris, Alan Gray a private detective and with Peter Birchwood, a professional genealogist. In 1996 he employed Alan to take statements from Tim Dundas and the Murphys. That from Tim Dundas, which then appeared on the Internet, insisted that when he had cleaned the watch there were no scratches. 'The marks on the watch relating to Jack the Ripper have been made on the watch since I repaired it in 1992, the whole suggestion that this watch belonged to Jack the Ripper is completely false.'

But he also told Paul Feldman that the watch he examined had a white face and the name 'Verity' on the front in black letters. Albert's watch does not. Neither did Mr Dundas recall the engraved initials on the back. Most likely he was simply confusing two watches.

The Murphys were indignant. 'He was asked only to repair the movement, not clean the watch – he would not have needed to look inside the back at all. He would hardly have noticed the scratches anyway. After all, we tried to clean them and because they were so faint we didn't realise what they were.'

Melvin and Stanley eventually fell out. Alan Gray, Peter and his wife, and I had been, separately, invited to Gerona at the Dangars' expense. I arrived in May 1995 with my husband, who payed his own fare. Stanley was, by then, a man obsessed and needed some willing ears. We were welcomed warmly by his wife Janet and treated to Stanley's homemade paella – the best in the world. Two days later, after some fairly inexplicable, explosive exchanges, my husband suddenly found himself a bewildered member of Stanley's mickey-mouse club and we left, in unseemly haste. The Grays and the Birchwoods suffered much the same fate.

Robbie Johnson was tragically killed by a hit and run motorbike in southern Spain that Autumn. Stanley was convinced of foul play and that Robbie, in financial trouble, was involved in a conspiracy. He rang me on September 26th to say that he had been visited by the *Guardia Civil* who had taken away all papers relating to the Diary. By then he had decided that Paul Feldman and Robbie had together forged the watch but, not surprisingly, was never able to support this belief!

By the Autumn of 1996, Stanley Dangar had decided conclusively that the watch was a lady's watch and the diary had been written by a woman.

In May 1999, he phoned 'Shirley darling' to say that Peter Birchwood had discovered a letter from a lady in Liverpool which came from Battlecrease House and confirmed the Diary's authenticity. He offered to send me a copy. He then claimed that reports on the watch from Barcelona University confirmed that it was not a modern forgery. 'I want you to put this in your next edition with my blessing.' The letter never arrived and I began to suspect that Stanley's eagerness was probably by now supported by a large degree of fantasising. Peter Birchwood denies it ever existed.

Sadly, Stanley was beginning to lose his sight and so Janet Dangar, herself an academic author, took over the painstaking labour of typing his many, many reports on the watch. These she generously gave to Seth Linder and Keith Skinner for their book *The Ripper Diary: The Inside Story* after Stanley died.

Meanwhile, back at the ranch, Bob Davis had been establishing long distance pen-friendship with Albert but in November 1995 wrote to me saying that he had 'gotten nowhere'.

Eventually he planned a marathon trip to England and Europe (for which I set out the itinerary) with his wife and a friend. They arrived in September 1999 presenting both Albert and me, to our astonishment and delight, with the badges and insignia of the Texas Rangers. It was all very warm and friendly at that stage. Bob was even more enthusiastic to confirm his offer once he had seen the watch and returned to America to make arrangements.

But things began to turn sour.

Eventually Albert had agreed to a sale for $190,000. Bob Davis returned to Liverpool having already transferred money to an English bank. A meeting was arranged in Albert's solicitor's office. What Bob did not know was that shares in the watch had been divided between Albert (75%) and his late brother (25%). Worse, Robbie, unbeknown to Albert, had sold some of his shares to two other parties. They were now claiming their percentage of the £1 million Robbie had assured them the watch was worth and were waiting, menacingly, in the office for Bob Davis to arrive. There was a heated discussion which ended with threats of legal action by Bob Davis who told me later that he had spent at least $15,000 on travel alone.

He returned to Texas without the watch.

Albert has continued, often with a patient shrug of the shoulders, to bring the watch to London whenever he is asked by the press or television. There is absolutely no sense of secrecy. He is proud of his watch and curious too. He was even among the guests at the 2000 Jack the Ripper Conference in Bournemouth – an event attended by some of the highest-ranking officers from Scotland Yard.

There is another twist in this ever increasingly bizarre story. On the back of the watch are the engraved initials 'J.O.' Does this place the watch in the possession of John Over, who married the Maybrick nanny? Or did it pass to Florie's dressmaker – Sarah Jones-Osborne?

In that first year, before publication, I realised that all the theories in the world would not be enough. I needed to back my own growing belief that the Diary and the watch were material evidence of an historic drama, fired by uncontrollable passions and resulting in the complete mental disintegration of one man – James Maybrick.

I was never convinced, even in those days, that science alone would give us the answers to the origins of the diary and, in the light of everything that has happened since, that original hunch has proved correct.

The watch is still ticking loudly, like a time bomb amidst the silence of its critics. The message inside it cannot be a fake. Together

Albert Johnson's watch and Michael Barrett's Diary present powerful support for my belief that James Maybrick, a man obsessed by time was indeed, Jack the Ripper.

3

They Will Suffer Just as I. I Will See to That

In the months before the launch of the book in October 1993, an epidemic swept England. We called it Rippermania. I was quite unprepared for its devastating and long-lasting repercussions.

Perhaps we should have been more alert to the dangers. Despite our best endeavours the story leaked. On September 5th 1992, the *Liverpool Echo* had written an article 'Murder on her Mind', describing Sally (who was calling herself Sally MacDonald) as Miss Marple. Then, in a two-page spread on March 26th 1993 the *Daily Express* picked up the baton with WILL THEY EVER REALLY UNMASK JACK THE RIPPER? and the other nationals followed hard on their heels.

By this time we were consulting experts in various fields and talking to people in Liverpool familiar with the Maybrick case. Judge Richard Hamilton, whose play based on the trial of Florence had been produced in St George's Hall, told us, 'If Maybrick is not Jack the Ripper I'm a monkey's uncle.' The rest of the world was joining in; two surviving Maybricks had been found – Brian Maybrick, a descendant of James Maybrick's cousin, and Sister Ursula, a

Dominican nun. Sister Ursula was initially uneasy about speaking of her connections, whereas Brian Maybrick was genially enthusiastic.

The *Liverpool Post* finally told the sensational story as relayed to them by Phil Maddox, now a public relations director, about 'the man on the train who may or may not own the Diary of Jack the Ripper.'

In April 1993, Robert Smith met one of the Sunday Times' most senior executives to discuss possible serialisation of the book. Well aware that the Sunday Times, of all newspapers, would need to examine and test the Diary carefully before going ahead, Robert offered them an option agreement. For £5,000 against a final purchase price of £75,000, the newspaper was given access to the Diary, my preliminary commentary and any consultants on the project. Robert Smith insisted that any experts employed by them would have to sign a confidentiality agreement. This procedure is intended to protect all parties from the common practice whereby one paper runs a 'spoiler', printing revelations that pre-empt exclusive serialisation by another.

In America on July 30th, The Washington Post expressed doubts about the Diary and, as a result, the US publisher, Warner Books, commissioned their own investigation and issued a press statement that, if any report were critical, they would withdraw, despite having made over 200,000 advance sales to booksellers.

The tensions were mounting as increasingly I worked in a maelstrom. Sensing trouble ahead, Doreen Montgomery was concerned about the Sunday Times' involvement at this stage, Paul Feldman was making dust storms with his documentary, an angry author, Melvin Harris, himself writing a book on his own Ripper suspect, took on the role of defender of the moral high-ground, denouncing the diary as 'C.R.A.P.' – a position he maintains today, and Anna Koren a graphologist flew in from Israel. Then, out of the blue, a watch appeared, engraved with Maybrick's name.

On August 20th Robert Smith flew to America, in a spirit of friendly co-operation, taking the Diary and a number of key documents. The investigation was being co-ordinated by Kenneth

Rendell a well-known Antiquarian bookseller who had been involved with the exposure of the Hitler Diaries. He had hurriedly assembled a team of experts including Maureen Owens, former President of the American Questioned Document Examiners and Joe Nickell, best known for his work on the Turin shroud, research ink chemist Robert Kurantz and scientist Rod McNeil, who had devised an ion migration test which, he claimed, could date when ink had been placed on paper.

By this time I had been working on background historical research for more than 12 months. Yet after only two weeks the American team decided that "on the evidence provided in the book" the Diary was a forgery. In other words they were sitting in judgement on my book and not on the Diary itself.

This was despite the fact that Robert Kurantz's test on ink and paper agreed with Dr Eastaugh that there was no element in either inconsistent with the date of 1889. Rod McNeil's ion migration test judged that the diary had been written in 1921 give or take 12 years. No one commented that this placed the diary to within 20 years of the date we believed it to have been written but up to 80 years before the 'modern forgery' theorists were claiming.

On the basis of this report Warner panicked and withdrew and delighted press headlines were flashed around the world.

Almost no one reported that, the same week, Hyperion, the publishing company owned by Disney, made an offer to publish – and to include the Rendell report, with a rebuttal by Robert Smith.

It is worth repeating Kenneth Rendell's own summary of his report:

> The basis of the book and the text of the purported Jack the Ripper Diary is that James T [sic] Maybrick was Jack the Ripper and wrote the Diary. Handwriting comparisons by a number of leading experts, including the one selected by the English publisher, definitely show that Maybrick did not write this Diary.

A major factor cited in this book linking the Diary to Jack the Ripper is the fact that highly unusual phrases and expressions that first appeared in 1888 in a letter signed 'Jack the Ripper', sent to a London newspaper, widely publicised since, are used throughout the Diary. The Diary is thus inexorably linked to that letter. All comparisons of the two handwritings conclude they are written by different people.

The style of handwriting is not Victorian. The type of handwriting is indicative of the early to mid-twentieth century at the earliest – not late 19th century. The layout, pen pressure and ink distribution all indicate that many entries were written at one time, they are completely inconsistent with the Diary but consistent with a forgery of a Diary.

The ion migration test conducted by its developer, Rod McNeil, to determine how long the ink has been on the paper concluded a median date of 1921 plus or minus 12 years...

The Diary is not written in a Victorian Diary book but in a scrap book – highly unusual. The first twenty pages are torn out, which is illogical, unless one assumes a forger bought a Victorian or Edwardian era scrap book, tore out the used pages and then filled in the Diary.

There is no credible evidence whatsoever that this Diary is genuine. Every area of analysis proves, or indicates the Jack the Ripper Diary is a hoax.

Robert Smith's reply, in part, said:

Kenneth Rendell's report on the Diary of Jack the Ripper is fundamentally flawed, inaccurate and unreliable. The tests and report on the Diary were rushed through in two weeks and largely ignore 16 months of research and testing

> by our writer, researchers and experts ... Furthermore, his opinions are more subjective than scientific; he makes many false assumptions and conclusions; and, crucially, all of his points of disagreement are dealt with fully in the book.

I spoke with Bill Waddell, the former curator of Scotland Yard's Black Museum, some time afterwards. He is now an international lecturer and a man with a lifetime's experience of crime and particularly of fraud and forgery. 'You could have driven a coach and horses through that American evidence,' he told me.

The *Sunday Times* had already decided in July that the Diary had been forged after three of their own experts had been called in to examine it before the clinching of any serialisation deal. They were: Dr Audrey Giles, a forensic document examiner who looked at the Diary for only a few minutes in Robert Smith's office on June 22nd and performed no tests on it; Dr Kate Flint, a lecturer at Oxford University specialising in Victorian literature rather than language; Ripperologist Tom Cullen whose vague report started unpromisingly by mistaking the year of the Whitechapel murders!

However, the standard confidentiality agreement which had been signed prevented them from publishing these results. Meanwhile, to their frustration, the competition was already also on the trail of the Diary. 'Is this man Jack the Ripper?' asked the *Independent on Sunday* on August 29th.

So it was that the *Sunday Times* took the publishers, Smith Gryphon, to court, to overturn the confidentiality agreement and persuade a High Court judge that it was 'in the public interest' for the newspaper to print their article before the agreed date. The upshot of two court appearances and astronomical legal costs was that the *Sunday Times* was finally given permission to go to press just one week before the confidentiality agreement allowed anyway!

On September 19th 1993, a banner headline was splashed over a double page spread: 'FAKE!' The article, under the by-line of the associate news editor, Maurice Chittenden, fell well short of the biting indictment that the headline promised.

No forger was named. No evidence was presented to suggest when or how the Diary had been forged. Much of the evidence produced to support the accusations was entirely subjective. We were even accused of suppressing damaging expert evidence when Maurice Chittenden discovered that we had adhered to Dr Baxendale's request, at the time, that his report should not be used in any way.

Yet in the 'small print' tucked away towards the bottom of the page Mr Chittenden made, in the circumstances, an astonishing suggestion which did not support the headline. He said:

'The Diary of Jack the Ripper has to be one of four things:

1. A genuine document
2. A modern hoax
3. A fantasy written by James Maybrick
4. A Victorian forgery, perhaps invented to secure the release of Florence Maybrick but never used.

Options 3 and 4 can be quickly discounted... the Diary must therefore be genuine or a modern hoax...'

Their conclusion was that the Diary was a modern fake and so began a determined effort to find the forgers. But no forgers have ever been found...

My book was published on October 3rd. Anne Barrett, who had kept a very low profile throughout, was extremely unwilling to attend the launch in London. Not for another year would we learn the true reason why. But eventually she was persuaded by Doreen Montgomery, and so Michael and she travelled down with their daughter, Caroline, to stay at Doreen's home.

The event was attended by large numbers of press and one disruptive but uninvited guest who stood up, waving his arms and shouting accusations at us all. This was Melvin Harris, recent founder of the Committee for Integrity which has taken a great deal of interest in our work on the Diary. He believed that my book was being published as part of a cynical commercial plot based entirely on greed and that all of us involved knew we were promoting a fraud.

The facts were less exciting. Besides, any potential golden goose's egg was swiftly being gobbled up by legal fees and research expenses. On October 21st 1993 there was yet another blow. We learned from the *Daily Express* that there was to be a 'Ripper Diary Probe by Yard' into what they suggested could be the 'biggest publishing hoax since the Hitler diaries'. Knowing the London team involved with the Diary as I did, such dark insinuations were amusing and hard to take seriously. They bore no relation to the honest people with whom I was working but of course they looked alarming in print.

We had known that the *Sunday Times* had deposited all its papers with New Scotland Yard's International and Organised Crimes Branch. If such a move is taken, the Yard is obliged to act. Their brief, we understood, was to discover if Robert Smith, or anyone else, had knowingly passed off a fake document as genuine. Their intention was not to prove whether the Diary was genuine or a forgery, but in order to unravel the facts they would, incidentally, have to examine its provenance.

In charge of the case was Detective Sergeant Thomas, known to his colleagues as 'Bonesy' – famous in the force for his superb home-made pickled onions. I heard on the grapevine that Detective Sergeant Thomas had travelled to Liverpool and was interviewing everyone involved in the story. Among them were Tony Devereux's daughters, the landlord of the Saddle Public House, a witness of Tony's will, the local press and of course the Barretts.

Anne has since described that day as the worst in her life. She prepared refreshments and hardly said a word while Detective Sergeant Thomas grilled Michael who kept asking for beer. In the middle of it all Anne's father, Billy Graham, turned up and Michael asked Detective Sergeant Thomas to pretend he was the insurance man rather than admit his true identity. Among other things Michael denied that he had a word processor. He was terrified that Scotland Yard would know of a confrontation with the police over 20 years before and that he would be condemned before they arrived. He was right. When asked to sign a statement Michael refused unless a solicitor was present.

We all knew that, in many ways understandably, Michael Barrett was suspected of being the forger. The rumour and innuendo was getting out of hand and the pressure on the Barrett family was intolerable.

* * *

In November 1993, I was invited to the USA to take part in an exciting red-carpet, coast-to-coast promotional tour for the book and to appear with Kenneth Rendell himself, first on the Larry King show and later to participate in a radio phone-in from Pasadena. Ken Rendell told me on air that there had been a 'sinister development' and that he had heard that a word processor had been found with the Diary on disc.

The facts are these. Michael Barrett invited the police into his house. There was no word processor in sight. No notes. Detective Sergeant Thomas left empty handed. The explanation about Michael Barrett's original research and his use of a word processor was, in any case, in the first edition of my book for all to see. Interestingly, by the time I met Kenneth Rendell he had shifted his stance. He still had absolutely no doubt the Diary was a modern forgery. But he now felt it was a modern forgery of within the last few years. Rod McNeil had re-examined his own report and issued a statement admitting that the storage conditions of a document could affect the tests he conducted and that a controlled study to test the Diary scientifically could take 20 years. I was astonished during our discussion to find that so much reliance could be placed by Mr Rendell on matters of personal opinion. For instance, he condemned the Diary because, he said, it is written in a scrap book with pages torn out, whereas Maybrick, an affluent man, he claimed, would have bought a purpose-made Diary. But we are not talking of the actions of a rational man; these are very extraordinary circumstances.

I have myself seen a Victorian album which is almost identical to the Maybrick Diary – it was used as a scrap book for photographs, visiting cards and letters by the prosperous Doubleday family in Essex. Its contents have been glued in casually and show that even Victorians varied in their artistic competence and design skills!

By the time I went to the USA, I had also received a letter, dated November 11th, from the curator of 19th century manuscripts at the British Museum. It said, 'By the late 19th century the term "Victorian handwriting" becomes difficult to define. From that time onwards a wide variety of hands, some quite modern in appearance can be found. Examples of the many different handwriting styles of the period can be seen in the large collections of late Victorian letters held by the British Library.'

I have corresponded amicably with Kenneth Rendell since those tumultuous times. Rod McNeil, working as part of the Rendell team, originally placed the Diary somewhere in the 1920s – give or take 12 years. Rendell himself had said to me and written several times that he now believed it to be a modern forgery with the clear implication that it was the work of Michael Barrett. On March 14th 1996, I wrote and asked him to explain, since the rest of his team had roundly condemned the Diary as a forgery, exactly when they thought it had been forged.

I had a reply by return. 'I did not state a definite opinion as to when I thought the forgery was done because my job was only to determine whether it was forged or not … It did however appear to be quite recent… I think everybody had the opinion that it was done fairly recently but nobody really thought very much about it because that was not a question we needed to deal with. It would be a mistake, therefore, to conclude that was our opinion – it was only an impression ...'

An 'impression' that did a great deal of damage. This was the report that seemed to me to destroy 16 months' work! It was not, of course, the end of the story. The police investigations rumbled expensively on, although no one ever came to interview me. We waited anxiously for their findings but such findings never came our way.

On November 26th, the *Daily Express* followed up its original story with 'Ripper Diaries are Fake'. The report said, 'a Scotland Yard investigation into the alleged diaries of Jack the Ripper concludes they are fake... detectives... are convinced the 65 page document was penned within the last decade.' Here was yet another date!

I rang the *Daily Express* to know the source for this statement and they claimed the information came from New Scotland Yard itself. I rang the Yard and was put through to Detective Sergeant Thomas' office who denied having made any statement to the *Daily Express*. They transferred me to the press office who, they alleged, would have issued any statement. The Press Office refused to speak to me because they said I was not a journalist. As a former member of the NUJ for some 30 years and then with the British Institute of Journalists, this seemed unreasonable.

I asked when we would receive a statement. 'There is no statement,' I was told.

Finally, on January 15th 1994, we learned the truth from Harold Brough of the *Liverpool Post*: 'Yard Clears Diary Publisher of Fraud'. This was the subject of the investigation – not, as already mentioned, the authenticity of the Diary, which was an internal matter and not one on which they were entitled to comment in the press.

The Yard had sent their findings to the Crown Prosecution Service (CPS) who had made a statement when deciding to go no further with the matter. The CPS told Harold: 'We have decided against a prosecution because there is not enough evidence to have a realistic prospect of getting a conviction.' It was a totally unsatisfactory conclusion. We, who had suffered such headline damage as 'The Great Ripper Rip-Off', were to be given no official written response to the harm that had been done.

4

My Hands are Cold, my Heart I do Believe is Colder Still

Behind the scenes, while these dramas were being enacted, my own team had begun, patiently, to reconstruct the bones of the story. I went first in search of its soul. I wanted to understand Maybrick's world of the late 1880s.

On June 28th 1992, Sally and I joined one of the Ripper walks around Whitechapel with crime writer and academic Martin Fido as our guide. We then drove on for the first of many visits to Liverpool, a city in which neatly painted Victorian terraces march in orderly rows over the hill, which drops down through acres of council houses to Albert Dock and the River Mersey. Windows were boarded up, shops and offices were derelict and beer cans sprouted on wasteland. Yet the pubs were noisy and full behind their ornately patterned glass and shiny, tiled façades. Liverpool, once a prosperous city, was struggling to survive, its heart torn out by poverty and unemployment. The ships that once served the busiest port in Britain had long since gone. Amidst this dereliction had been raised some of the great names in British entertainment such as The Beatles and Cilla Black. Over the last few years there has been a dramatic regeneration and new confidence has been born, which, in 2003, enabled the city to win the coveted title of 'European Capital of Culture'.

The city is surrounded by a protective cloak of beautiful parks and fine suburbs. There, the ornate mansions of wealthy Victorian merchants stand, proud mausoleums, recalling an energetic past but occupied today by students and their landladies and the elderly residents of eventide homes. One such suburb, Aigburth, lies to the south of the city centre, on the banks of the Mersey.

Battlecrease House is, as it was when the Maybricks lived there, half of an impressive mansion, built in a time when horse-drawn carriages bumped along the unpaved lane. Now known simply as 7 Riversdale Road, Battlecrease House is a 20-roomed, mushroom-coloured house set well back from the road. It stands opposite the Cricket Club of which James Maybrick was an enthusiastic member. Riversdale Road runs from the Aigburth Road down to the river and views across the Mersey to the distant Welsh mountains are uninterrupted still.

Maybrick was probably aware of the rumours that a murder had taken place at the house many years before. Nevertheless he moved in, with his young American wife and their two children. In 1889, not much more than a year later, sightseers gathered by the entrance – as they still do – pointing curiously at the upstairs windows of the room where Maybrick died. Some broke twigs from the shrubs surrounding the garden, as mementoes, unaware that the house could have another, even more shocking claim to notoriety.

James Maybrick has never before been associated with the case of Jack the Ripper and, like Michael Barrett, I found myself drawn to retrace the steps of the man who I believed had confessed to terrorising London and shocking the world. I walked along the narrow alley at the side of the former grounds of Battlecrease House which leads to tiny Aigburth station where Maybrick had boarded the train into town.

The gravel crunched as I walked up the driveway. I knocked at the door once used by the Maybricks and found myself talking to Paul Dodd, a primary school teacher who grew up in Battlecrease House. As I walked with him around the still splendid rooms, it was easy to imagine the whispered gossip of servants below stairs, to conjure up the immaculate figure of Maybrick himself, with his sandy hair and moustache, striding down the drive, and the coquettish Florie, the sun lighting her golden hair, reading romances in the conservatory.

The house has suffered structurally over the years. It was the only building in the road to escape the bombs of World War II, but was damaged by a landmine, and then by an earth tremor in 1984. A falling tree destroyed the conservatory. Even so, little imagination is needed to re-awaken the past.

Through the reception hall and the dining-room, with its stained-glass windows picturing water birds, is the ballroom that opens on to the garden. Intact are the beautiful, ornate ceiling mouldings and the Italian marble fireplace with its exquisite carved grapes and large mirror above. Up the splendid oak staircase are rooms for guests, family and staff, a nursery for the children. Overlooking the cricket pitch is the rather sombre bedroom where Maybrick died. Today it is Paul Dodd's sitting room.

Later that day I also paced the 'Flags', the vast open forum in the centre of Liverpool that was once the hub of Britain's cotton industry, and visited the grave where Maybrick is buried. The large cross that once capped the headstone was, mysteriously, missing and on a return visit in February 1997 I saw that the stone had been desecrated further by graffiti and a serious attempt to smash it in two.

* * *

At the time of Maybrick's birth there had been Maybricks in Liverpool for 70 years. They hailed from the West Country and one branch settled in the Stepney and Whitechapel area of London's East End. Later, when unemployment became bad, some moved on to the busy port of Liverpool. From there they emigrated – to Australia and to America. There had been a scattering of Maybricks in America for many years. In fact, one of James's Whitechapel antecedents, Charles (alias John Jones), was a convict, shipped off from London to Maryland in July 1775 to fight in the Civil War. Ephraim Maybrick was a private in the Confederate 43 Georgia Infantry. Maybrick is a comparatively unusual surname, numbered in genealogical sources in dozens rather than in hundreds. The American census records list a handful in the late 19th and 20th centuries in Connecticut, Detroit, Alabama and Illinois. The name seems to have finally died out with Leonora Maybrick from Kansas City whose death was recorded in the Social Security Index in 1988.

The parish church of St Peter, in the centre of Liverpool (where Woolworths stands today), had long been a focus for James's well-respected family. There had been Maybricks at the organ, Maybricks on the parish council and, when James was born on October 24th 1838, his grandfather was parish clerk.

St Peter's was consecrated in 1704 as the cathedral church and, according to the *Liverpool Courier*, was the first building in Church Street, 'originally surrounded by a picturesque belt of stately elms whose foliage harmonising with the summer livery of hedgerows and the floral beauty of the meadows, completed the charm of rural peace.' A somewhat different view of the church which dominated so much of Maybrick's childhood was that it was 'plain almost to ugliness.' Inside, the building was lofty, dark and oppressively sombre.

James' christening, on November 12th, must have been a particularly happy affair for his parents, William, an engraver, and Susannah, who had lost a four-month-old son the year before. They decided to follow the Victorian custom and name the new baby James, after his dead brother. James' older brother, William, was then aged three.

By the time James was six, his grandfather was dead and his father had succeeded him as parish clerk. Yet, despite their childhood involvement with St Peter's and respect for Victorian convention, none of the Maybrick brothers remained churchgoers as they grew up. Interestingly, though William and James were married in church, the three younger boys defied convention and preferred the registry office.

The family was living at 8 Church Alley, a narrow lane in the shadow of St Peter's that ran into busy Church Street. It was only a few seconds' walk from the road whose name was later to play so large a part in the story – Whitechapel. This Whitechapel, in contrast to its London namesake, was a fashionable shopping street. Just around the corner was the Blue Coat Hospital, a school for poor boys and girls. In Church Street itself James could linger at the Civet Cat, a nick-nack shop that sold exciting foreign toys. Or he could dream of faraway places while peering in the window of Mr Marcus the tobacconist, who ran flag-bedecked train excursions from Liverpool to London.

With the arrival of three younger brothers, Michael, born 1841, Thomas, born 1846, and Edwin, born 1851 (another brother, Alfred, had died at the age of four in 1848), the family moved to a more spacious house around the corner: 77 Mount Pleasant. They led a simple life, with no staff until after James left home, when the 1861 Census credits them with a house-servant named Mary Smith. Nothing is known about the parents' influence and personality and little about the boys' childhood or schooling. James probably attended Liverpool College, like Michael, but records were lost during World War II. We do know the boys threw themselves into sport, especially cricket.

However, there were other, more sinister entertainments on tap in the area of the Maybrick family home. Just round the corner, in Paradise Street, was the notorious Museum of Anatomy, reputed to contain the greatest number of preserved anatomical specimens in Britain. In 1850, the year that James was twelve, a four-wheeled landau had driven up Lime Street carrying one 'Dr' Joseph Thornton Woodhead, who had just arrived from America with 750 waxen models of anatomical parts and genitalia. The heavily loaded cab overturned, spilling its grisly contents into the street and Dr Woodhead decided, on the spot, to rent nearby premises for their display. In James Maybrick's young days, the Museum of Anatomy became one of Liverpool's most popular and shocking 'sights'. We looked at the catalogue for 1877. They surround the exhibition with typical Victorian religious and moral justification. 'Man know thyself' was the legend over the door. Ladies were admitted for only three hours on Tuesday and Friday afternoons. Gentlemen were admitted at all other times. They were warned: 'If any man defile the Temple of God, him will God destroy.'

These exhibits, intended to 'advance science and learning', included freaks of nature and a section on masturbation labelled as 'self pollution – the most destructive evil practised by fallen man.' There were full-sized models of operations on the brain and stomach and of a hysterectomy, 'a young lady in the act of parturition' and a man 'discovered in the family way.' It would not have been difficult for any visitor to pick up rudimentary anatomical knowledge. I remembered that Nick Warren, editor of *Ripperana* magazine and himself a surgeon, believes that the Ripper must have had anatomical experience, though whether he was actually a doctor is disputed.

The museum was not closed until 1937 when it was removed to Blackpool and finally, most strangely, to the seaside resort of Morecambe Bay on the Lancashire coast. There, it was re-opened by former Madame Tussaud's employee, George Nicholson, alongside a waxworks display which included the usual range of historic figures, including, of course, Jack the Ripper. It was here, during the late 1960s, that another notorious killer – Peter Sutcliffe, 'The Yorkshire Ripper' – spent hours, peering through the peepholes of the Torso Room at the sordid, offensive and by then seedily dilapidated models. There were to be many occasions over the next few years that I sensed the spirits of Peter Sutcliffe and James Maybrick walking side by side.

* * *

From an early age, according to a later profile in *The New Penny* magazine, Michael was the shining star of the family with the musical gift of 'harmonious invention'. At the age of 14, one of his compositions was even played at Covent Garden Opera in London and he was awarded a book of sacred music for his performance in the choir of St George's Church. The dedication reads: 'Presented to Master Michael Maybrick as a token of regard for his musical perception.'

He was organist at St Peter's Church between 1855 and 1865. William and Susannah encouraged Michael to study and in 1866 he went to Leipzig where it was discovered that he had a fine baritone voice. From there he moved on to the Milan Conservatoire. He made his London debut as a singer in 1869 and appeared with the National Opera Company at the St James's Theatre in October 1871. He went on to sing during the inaugural season of the Carl Rosa Operatic Company and there is reason to believe that he, and possibly James, had friendly links with the Rosa family. Michael was present at the funeral of Parepa Rosa in 1874. James Maybrick's physician in New York was a Dr Seguin, whose family pioneered opera in America and were related to the Rosas. Michael once referred to his profession as 'the shouting game'. He gave himself the stage name Stephen Adams (Adam being the first man, he explained) and formed a partnership with the equally successful librettist, Frederick Weatherly.

For his siblings, Michael was a hard act to follow. William became a carver and gilder's apprentice. Thomas and Edwin went into commerce. By 1858 James Maybrick had gone to work in a shipbroking office in the capital. That period of his life has been a blank to us – until now.

* * *

In 1891, two years after Florence's trial, Alexander William MacDougall, a tall, distinguished, if loquacious, Scottish lawyer, published a 606 page *Treatise on the Maybrick Case* in which he asserted, among many other things, that, 'There is a woman who calls herself Mrs Maybrick and who claims to have been James Maybrick's real wife. She was staying on a visit at a somewhat out of the way place, 8 Dundas Street, Monkwearmouth, Sunderland, during the trial; her usual and present address is 265 Queen's Road, New Cross, London SE.' No. 265 is still there, now a shadow of its Victorian elegance. It was a substantial property with a garden much larger than its neighbours. MacDougall also claimed that Maybrick was known to have had five children prior to his marriage to Florie.

Who was the mysterious 'Mrs Maybrick'? Census records, street directories and certificates of birth, death and marriage can resurrect the skeleton of any life long after it is over. But it is a long, slow process, fraught with problems, since form-filling was not always accurate and very often dates and details are incorrectly given. Census records for 1891 were not released until January 2nd 1992, according to British custom. Only then could the truth of MacDougall's assertion be established. Only then was it possible to fill in some of the details of Maybrick's secret life in London.

We found those details and for the first time established the names of the inhabitants of 265 Queen's Road. They were Christiana Conconi, a 69-year-old widow of independent means from Durham, her surprisingly young daughter, Gertrude, aged 18, and a 13-year-old visitor. There were two other persons in the household: a lodger named Arthur Bryant and Christiana's niece, Sarah Robertson, single, listed as aged 44 from Sunderland, County Durham. We realised that these ages did not tally with certificates we unearthed later. Christiana was more probably 74 and Sarah 54.

Gradually the story of Sarah Ann Robertson/Maybrick unfolded. She was first found in 1851, at the age of 13, living with Aunt Christiana at 1, Postern Way, Tower Hill, which runs into Whitechapel. Christiana's father was Alexander Hay Robertson, a general agent, who died in 1847. That same year Christiana married Charles James Case, a tobacconist, their residence being 40, Mark Lane which lies near Tower Hill between the City of London and Whitechapel.

James Maybrick went to London in 1858 and it seems probable that since shipbroking tends to centre on the City itself, this was where he met Sarah Ann. Charles Case died in 1863 and three years later Christiana re-married. Her new bridegroom was a paymaster in the Royal Navy named Thomas David Conconi. Their address was said to be 43, Bancroft Road. One of the witnesses at their wedding signed her name 'Sarah Ann Maybrick'.

In 1868, Thomas Conconi added a codicil to his will: 'in case my said wife shall die during my life then I give and bequeath all my household goods furniture plate linen and china to my dear friend Sarah Ann Maybrick, the wife of James Maybrick of Old Hall Street, Liverpool, now residing at No 55 Bromley Street, Commercial Road, London.'

This was the house then occupied by the Conconis. Whether the codicil means that Maybrick was also living with the family is unclear. But according to the 1871 census, Sarah Ann, listed as a 'merchant's clerk wife' [sic] was there. James was not. The street still exists, its modest two-storey houses restored in 1990 are now framed by shiny black railings. Number 55 was demolished for redevelopment after World War I. Turn right at the end of the street on to Commercial Road and it is but a brisk ten-minute walk to Whitechapel, the scene of Jack the Ripper's murders.

At Wyoming University, amongst the file of hand-written notes by Trevor Christie, author of '*Etched in Arsenic*', was one headed 'Russell's Brief'. Russell was Sir Charles Russell who later became Florie Maybrick's leading counsel. It said of James:

> At the age of 20 (1858) he went to a shipbroker's office in London and met Sarah Robertson, 18, an assistant in a jeweller's shop, she lived with him on and off for 20 years. Her relatives thought they were married and she passed as Mrs M with them. They had five children, all now dead.

Author Nigel Morland, who wrote *This Friendless Lady* (1957), claims that two of these offspring were born after James' marriage to Florie. However no source is given for this information and neither have we ever unearthed a marriage certificate for James and Sarah, or relevant birth certificates for the little Maybrick/Robertsons.

When Thomas Conconi died in 1876, at Kent House Road, Sydenham, South London, 'S. A. Maybrick niece' of the same address was the informant. When Christiana herself died in 1895 at Queen's Road, Sarah once again signs herself Sarah Ann Maybrick. But she is listed in the 1891 census as Robertson. However at the time of her own death on January 17th 1927, the records refer to 'Sarah Ann Maybrick, otherwise Robertson, spinster of independent means of 24 Cottesbrook Street, New Cross.' She was then living with William and Alice Bills. She was buried, un-named in a common grave in Streatham, London.

In 1995 Keith Skinner, hot on the trail for Paul Feldman, went to meet Alice's daughter, Barbara. She remembers that Sarah was known in the family as 'Old Aunty' and that she was a lonely, sweet old lady who was very good with children. Barbara showed Keith a large Bible which had been given by Sarah Ann to Alice. Inside was written, 'To my darling Piggy. From her affectionate husband J.M. On her birthday August 2nd 1865.' Was Maybrick a bigamist?

* * *

Where was James Maybrick in 1871? He was back in Liverpool after the death of his father in June 1870. According to the 1871 census he was with his 54-year-old mother, Susannah, at 77 Mount Pleasant. He was unmarried. His occupation is described simply as 'commercial clerk', whereas brother Thomas was a 'cotton merchant' and Edwin a 'cotton merchant/dealer'. He was in business with G. A. Witt, Commissioning Agent, in Knowsley Buildings, Tithebarn Street, off Old Hall Street. Two years later, he was still working with Witt from the same, overcrowded premises, where some 30 cotton merchants and brokers were crammed into one building. Maybrick established Maybrick and Company, Cotton Merchants, around this time and Edwin eventually joined him as a junior partner. The building was finally demolished in the late 1960s to make way for an imposing modern development, Silk House Court. Witt's main offices in London, which Maybrick visited from time to time, were in Cullum Street, on the boundaries of the City and Whitechapel.

It was a rough world, vigorously characterised in 1870 in the April 30th edition of the local magazine, *Porcupine*. An article headed 'Cotton Gambling' described the ever-more unscrupulous world that had attracted Maybrick. A once prestigious trade changed almost overnight after the cotton famine that followed the American Civil War; it became a business open to 'anyone, with no capital whatever, anyone with a shadow of credit', reported the magazine.

In 1868 a system of 'bear' sales had been introduced which was similar to that of the London Stock Exchange. This involved 'selling cotton you have not got in the hope you may cover the sale by buying at a lower price at a later period.' It brought to the market an element of pure gambling. 'It is to be regretted' noted *Porcupine* that 'the Cotton Brokers' Association should have given their sanction to this system of trade and thus lower the tone and character of the market.'

Maybrick was an opportunist who thrived in a world of ruthless competition. In 1874, when he was only 35, he went off to start a branch office in the newly booming cotton port of Norfolk, Virginia, in the United States. Traders there were engaged in all manner of tricks and illegal practices to hold their own in a cut-throat world. Rocks were used and bales were soaked in water, to make them weigh more. James seems to have established a reliable reputation and when he became a member and, eventually in November 1881, a director of the Norfolk Cotton Exchange, he would have been in the responsible position of overseer, trying to ensure that there was no such illegal dealing afoot.

Norfolk had been ruined by the Civil War, but its recovery had been energetic. One third of the town's 37 square miles was water-logged, especially round the mosquito-infested Dismal Creek Swamp. To encourage foreign investment, a piped supply of fresh water was needed. So the water system was modernised and the improved conditions coincided with the opening of the railway connecting Norfolk with the cotton growing states of the Deep South. The town was transformed into a successful international port, nearly half of whose ships plied between Liverpool and America. We now believe that Maybrick also had an office in Galveston, Texas, at the far end of the Norfolk and Western railway to New Orleans, via Atlanta. This was known as the Cotton Line. The journey to the Southern cities of Austin, St Louis, New Orleans or Mobile would have presented no problem – the Victorians were ardent travellers. Maybrick's close friend and business associate, John Aunspaugh, was head of the firm of Inman, Swan and Co of Dallas, Texas and Atlanta, Georgia. The family of

Alfred Brierley, who was later to achieve notoriety as Florence Maybrick's lover, had offices in New Orleans and in Savannah. Another friend was Brigadier John Gardiner Hazard who fought with great distinction for the North in the Civil War and whose obituaries, in 1897, described him as 'one of the country's foremost citizen soldiers'. After the war, General Hazard, with his fine drooping moustache and dashing good looks, had embarked on a mercantile career in cotton. A member of the Boston Cotton Exchange and this is, presumably, how he first met Maybrick.

In 1876, during one of James's return visits to Liverpool, all three Maybrick brothers – James, Thomas and Edwin – had been made Freemen of the City of Liverpool. This was not quite the prestigious event that it appears, the award being a purchasable commodity, costing £100. Nevertheless, it brought with it certain social and commercial perks – Freemen enjoyed immunity from tolls and other taxes.

In the year that Maybrick arrived in Norfolk, the town's Cotton Exchange was set up, giving rise to a tidal wave of commerce back and forth across the Atlantic. Three years later, while Maybrick was living in York Street with Nicholas Bateson and a negro servant, Thomas Stansell, he caught malaria. When the first prescription of quinine did no good, a second, for arsenic and strychnine, was dispensed by Santo's, the chemist on Main Street.

'He was very nervous about his health,' recalled Bateson, when he later testified for the defence at Florie's trial. 'He rubbed the backs of his hands and complained of numbness in his limbs. He was afraid of paralysis. The last year I lived with him he became worse. He became more addicted to taking medicines.'

When it was his turn to give evidence, the servant Stansell remembered running errands for Maybrick during their time in Norfolk. 'When I brought him the arsenic, he told me to go and make him some beef tea... he asked me to give him a spoon... he opened the package and took a small bit out. This he put in the tea and stirred it up.'

Stansell was surprised at the quantity of pills and potions in

Maybrick's office. 'I am,' the cotton merchant once told him 'the victim of free living.'

Maybrick's constant companion in Norfolk at the time was Mollie Hogwood (also known as Mary Howard). Her status, according to the 1881 Norfolk Census, was 'keeps house'. By then she was about 59 and her 'house' was a well-known brothel, in Church Street.

The chemical element, arsenic, is found widely in nature, usually associated with metal ores. It has claimed innumerable victims, including, it is believed, Napoleon Bonaparte, who was possibly fatally poisoned by arsenic in the colouring of his prison sitting-room wallpaper in St Helena. But it has also had a wide variety of medicinal and other uses. For example, in the 16th century, Queen Elizabeth I used arsenic as a cosmetic, applying it to her face to make it more white, just as Florie Maybrick used an arsenical preparation for her complexion. In 1786 Dr T. Fowler reported on the medical benefits of arsenic in cases of fever and sporadic headaches. Fowler's Solution was a popular tonic in Maybrick's time. The Greek word for arsenic – arsenikon – means 'potent'. Maybrick, like many men of his day, believed that it increased his virility. Because he was addictive by nature, he became hooked.

* * *

The year 1880 was crucial for Maybrick, for at the age of 41 he fell in love. He was booked, as usual, to return to Liverpool aboard the *SS Baltic*. The *Baltic* was one of the White Star Line's powerful screw-driven trans-Atlantic steamers, designed to 'afford the very best accommodation to all classes of passengers.' The six-day voyage cost 27 guineas. Advertisements proclaimed that the ships carried 'neither cattle, sheep, nor pigs.

On March 12th the *Baltic*, in the command of Captain Henry Parsell, steamed from New York. Among the 220 first-class passengers was General Hazard. Also on board was the impulsive, cosmopolitan Belle of the South, Florence Chandler, known as Florie. She was 17, in the care of her mother, the formidable Baroness Von Roques, and they were on their way to Paris. James and Florie may have become acquainted socially before that fateful voyage through General Hazard, who had homes in New York and Lancashire and was a mutual friend.

Their romance blossomed in unseemly haste among the opulent bars and ballrooms of the *Baltic* and was then nurtured at the Hazards' home at Childwall outside Liverpool, where Florie was invited to be a guest before going on to join her mother in Paris.

Maybrick was dazzled, not only by Florie's charms but also by her society connections and the prospect of wealth from her expected inheritance in America. A Victorian husband was still automatically heir to his wife's property and possessions.

Maybrick learned that this lively 5' 3" strawberry blonde hailed from America's high society. She had been born on September 3rd 1862, during the American Civil War, in the sophisticated city of Mobile, Alabama. Her mother, Carrie Holbrook, 'a brilliant society woman', was a descendant of President John Quincy Adams and Chief Justice Salmon P. Chase.

Among other achievements, Carrie's swashbuckling Yankee father, Darius, had founded the town of Cairo, Illinois, which Charles Dickens was to condemn after a visit in 1842 as a 'place without one single quality, in earth or air or water to commend it.' Darius Holbrook himself was caricatured as Zephaniah Scadder in *Martin Chuzzlewit*. Her uncle, the Reverend Joseph Ingraham, had enjoyed an adventurous career as a soldier of fortune and had written blood and thunder novels.

Her first husband, William Chandler, was head of the banking house of St John Powers & Co of 54 Francis Street and one of Mobile's most eligible bachelors, and Florie was born in the magnificent family home on Government Street (demolished in 1955 to make way for the Admiral Semmes Motor Hotel). But Florie never knew her father for he died on July 4th 1862, two months before she was born, leaving her and her older brother, Holbrook St John, fatherless. His headstone reads: 'William G. Chandler. Gifted and good, the Joy, the Pride, the Hope and the Light of our life.'

He was only 33. The entire family was convinced that his wife had poisoned him and, although there was not a shred of evidence, Carrie was ostracised by Mobile society and moved the children away to Macon, Georgia. Six months later, she married the distinguished soldier Captain Franklin du Barry, but, soon after their marriage, he too died unexpectedly, aboard ship bound for Scotland.

From then on for several years little Florie and her brother seem to have been feathers on the wind, blowing this way and that between Paris, England, New York and Cologne. In about 1869 the family lived for two years in a house called The Vineyards, at Kempsey near Worcester. A German governess educated the children, and local residents remembered Madame du Barry as a fine, handsome woman and good company. The house was always full of visitors.

When she returned to America she entered, with gusto, the ribald social life of New York. It was a frenetic, violent often scandalous time after the Civil War, known as 'The Flash Age' and Madame du Barry lived it to the full. She mixed in New York society where families such as the Vanderbilts were her friends. During 1870-71, back in Europe, she was caught up in the Siege of Paris, as a result of which she fell in love again. This time it was the dashing Prussian Cavalry Officer, the Baron Adolph von Roques, who fell prey to her attentions.

But the marriage was a disaster. The couple led 'an adventurous life' from Cologne to Wiesbaden and on to St Petersburg, squandering money, incurring massive debts and leaving devastation everywhere they went. Even so, Florie recalled, through rose-coloured spectacles, what must have been the appallingly lonely confusion of that time. She was virtually fatherless and being lodged, as it suited her mother, with relatives and friends. Yet in her autobiography, *My Fifteen Lost Years,* she wrote:

> My life was much the same as that of any girl who enjoys the pleasures of youth with a happy heart... My special pastime however was riding and this I could indulge to my heart's content when residing with my stepfather, Baron

> Adolph Von Roques, now retired, who was at that time a cavalry officer in the Eighth Cuirassier regiment of the German army and stationed at Cologne.

Her writing reveals ingenuousness and a preference for glossing over the true facts which coloured the rest of her life. She could never face unpleasant reality and surrounded herself with cheap fiction, dreams, and, towards the end, with cats. There is no mention in her story that the Baron beat her mother and finally left her in 1879 when Florie was 17 years old. It is true that the entrepreneurial, well-connected but often improvident Holbrooks had won and lost fortunes through various enterprises in the South. The flamboyant Baroness herself had originally inherited some 2,500,000 acres in Virginia, West Virginia and Kentucky. She willed one third of this to Florie. In 1879 she had signed an agreement with Kentucky promoter David Armstrong to sell this land on a 50/50 basis. But there were no buyers. Judging by later correspondence, the Baroness painted a more colourful and tempting picture of the value of that land, rather than a true one. However, James wasted no time in taking an interest in the Baroness's 'estates'. In March 1881, even before his marriage, he was in correspondence with David Armstrong about the sale of some of the lands.

In November 1881, four months after her wedding, by which time the couple had returned to live in America, Florie wrote to Mr Armstrong.

> ... the Baroness trusts to your honour and discretion with regard to any private matters she may have confided to you, and as my husband is quite ignorant of her personal affairs I must beg of you only to give information in reference to the Virginia claim and on no others!

The complex legal twists and turns of the Baroness's inheritance do not belong to the story of the Diary. But the increasingly heated correspondence rumbled on until 1906, when the Baroness finally took

David Armstrong to the Chancery Court of Virginia for tricking her into signing agreements she claimed she did not understand.

* * *

On board that day in 1880 James Maybrick must have appeared to Florie to be the perfect mix: at once the mature father figure she had never known and a worldly self-assured man with a taste for dangerous living. And she, he must have imagined, was to be his entrance into a class and a way of life that were not his by birth but to which he, nevertheless, aspired. She would bring him cachet among the socially-conscious worthies of Liverpool and, perhaps, a fortune. With breathtaking speed Maybrick swept young Florie off her feet and by the end of the voyage he had proposed. When they disembarked in Liverpool, plans were already being made for a stylish wedding the next year.

There followed a truly action-packed year. But what, I wonder, was really afoot in the Maybrick family at this time? In March 1880 James returned to tell his widowed mother of the hasty engagement. She was by now living in a boarding house run by an old friend, Mrs Margaret Machell at 111, Mount Pleasant. It seems inconceivable that she knew nothing of Sarah Ann or of the children she was alleged to have borne. Did Susannah express disapproval of his behaviour? If so, Maybrick was unmoved and by April was strolling the chestnut-lined streets of Paris with his bride-to-be.

On May 1st his mother died. He was present at her death but living at Ashley Broad Green. Her death certificate states the cause of death, curiously, as 'Bronchitis Hepatic'.

Ruth Richardson, author of *Death, Dissection and the Destitute* and an expert on Victorian death certificates says: 'This is odd. It doesn't really make sense. I have not seen one quite like it.' Bronchitis concerns the bronchial tract. Hepatic means 'of the liver'. But there is nothing which accurately explains what was really wrong with Susannah's liver. We can only wonder. Did she have a drink problem? Or had she become addicted to drugs like her son? Or could there possibly have been another, more sinister, explanation?

James's mother was dead. She was no longer able to cast a shadow over the proceedings by revealing 'any lawful impediment' why her son should not marry Florence Elizabeth Chandler. By September, Maybrick was back in Norfolk, actively speaking at the Corn Exchange. He was still there in January 1881, far from his fiancée.

With typical delusions of grandeur, he had arranged for the wedding to be at the suitably named St James's Church, not in Liverpool but in Piccadilly, one of the most fashionable settings in London. At the ceremony on July 27 1881, conducted by the Reverend J. Dyer Tovey, the bride wore a gown of pleated satin and ivory lace and her bouquet was of white columbines with lilies of the valley. The bridegroom, 24 years her senior, wore a white satin waistcoat embroidered with roses and lilies of the valley and a cutaway coat lined with elaborately quilted satin.

Florie's brother, Holbrook St John, came from Paris to give her away. Although Maybrick's brothers Edwin, Thomas and Michael were there, he must have been disappointed that there was no great enthusiasm for the match. Michael, who dominated the trio, was sceptical. Guests reported, with some justification, that he did not believe the Baroness' tales of estates to be inherited but saw in her scheming a crafty plot to secure for herself a settled British home in her old age. (After Florie's trial, however, she wrote somewhat fancifully to the Home Secretary that Florie had no pecuniary temptation to murder as she had assisted the family for years.)

At the time of the wedding, Maybrick had taken out an insurance policy, with Florie as beneficiary, for £2,000, which he later increased to £2,500. He also set up a trust fund of £10,000, a sum equal today to 40 times this amount, but he never paid in a penny. Florie herself had a small income of £125 a year from her grandmother's house in New York, and there was occasional income from her late father's lands near Mobile. There was hardly enough money to finance the kind of façade that the newly married Maybricks wished to present.

From the outset, the match was founded on deception: even the marriage certificate reveals Maybrick in his true colours. His profession he gives as 'esquire', his father's as 'gentleman, deceased' and his residence as St. James's.

Hardly more than a child, why should Florie suspect that his life was based on hypocrisy and deceit? Besides she had known little else herself. Nevertheless she would soon discover the awful truth that there was, already, a 'Mrs Maybrick'.

On March 1st 1882, when Florie was at least seven months pregnant, 'Mr and Mrs James Mayboick' [sic] were registered on board the *SS Baltic* once again ... returning to Liverpool for the birth of their first child. For a fragile Florie, the buffeting of the Atlantic must have been a terrible ordeal and doubtless raised a few eyebrows among fellow passengers.

On arrival in Liverpool, she was confronted by three of her husband's closest friends – the Janion sisters. Mrs Matilda Briggs, Mrs Martha Louise Hughes and Miss Gertrude Janion, were the daughters of Mrs Domatila Janion. They were shocked by Florie's lack of propriety. Bernard Ryan wrote, 'They took it upon themselves to tell Florence that ladies in her condition simply were not seen on the street. Wasn't it time now for her to remain in seclusion at home?'

Florie was irritated but she did not have long to wait. About two weeks after her return to Liverpool and eight months after the wedding, James Chandler, affectionately known as 'Bobo', was born to the Maybricks on March 24th 1882. He was a sickly, premature baby and Florie had a difficult birth.

That spring, Maybrick returned with the family to America. For the next two years they spent half their time in Liverpool, half in Norfolk, Virginia, living in a rented house in Freemason Street. Freemason Street was an area of 'wealth and refinement' according to Thomas J. Wertenbaker's book *Norfolk, Historic Southern Port*. The tree-lined streets were cobbled and the broad sidewalks fringed with flower-filled gardens. Maybrick's passion for horseracing was well catered for by the Norfolk Turf Association. Together James and Florie took business and pleasure trips by train down the cotton line. At 8 a.m. every morning Maybrick left home and walked to work. Rather than go directly to his office in Main Street near Boston Quay, he would stop at C.F. Greenwood's, a chemist in Freemason Street, to buy his daily supply of arsenic.

It was during this time that John Fleming, a merchant sailor from Halifax, Nova Scotia, spotted him adding a greyish powder to hominy grits (an American form of porridge). Later he recalled Maybrick telling him: 'You would be horrified, I daresay, if you knew what this is. It is arsenic. We all take some poison, more or less. For instance I am now taking arsenic enough to kill you. I take this arsenic once in a while because I find it strengthens me.'

From the chemist Maybrick would go on to the Cotton Exchange, where exporters, brokers and buyers mingled. Lunch was at one p.m. and the rest of the day was spent on letters and paperwork before calling at one of Norfolk's many clubs. The minutes of the Cotton Exchange record his regular attendance as a committee member.

Florie later wrote in a letter that it was about this time that her husband started rubbing the backs of his hands. What she did not know was that dry, itchy skin is one of the long term symptoms of arsenic abuse.

Maybrick was hardly alone in his indulgence. Use of arsenic, along with strychnine, which had similar effects, was a rapidly growing fashion among professional men in both Britain and America. Indeed, the *Liverpool Citizen* commented at the time of Florie's trial:

> We are all perfectly aware that men-about-town are much in the habit of taking these dangerous drugs, strychnine, arsenic and what-not, as they are of drinking champagne and smoking tobacco. Why, we are told there is enough taken on the Exchange Flags alone to poison all Castle Street.
>
> When once they contract the habit of arsenic eating they remain slaves for life... Once they enter on the downward path, there is no looking back, as it is asserted by

> toxicologists that if they are ever prevented obtaining their daily dose they may say, with truth 'the pains of Hell got hold of me' and they experience all the dreadful horrors of slow arsenic poisoning.

The classic specialist book, *The Materia Medica of Homeopathic Remedies* by Dr James Tyler Kent (1849-1916) was first published in 1912. It is a medical practitioners' book not readily found on public library shelves. It gives an analysis of arsenic addiction:

> *Arsenic affects every part of man; it seems to exaggerate or depress almost all his faculties... The anxiety that is found in arsenic is mingled with fear, with impulses, with suicidal inclinations, with sudden freaks and with mania... there is a burning in the brain the stomach the bladder and the throat. The skin itches with burning. The mental symptoms show... a disturbance of intellect and will. He thinks he must die.*

Dr Kent talks of 'screaming with pains', delirium in bed, and says the arsenic patient is always freezing (despite the burning sensations) and longing for warmth. Apart from the fact that Florie noticed James rubbing his hands, no other symptoms of arsenic addiction were mentioned at her trial nor in the literature that appeared subsequently. Yet they unconsciously colour the narrative of the diary from beginning to end.

> *My hands are cold... Summer is near... the warm weather will do me good... the pain burned into my mind... June is such a pleasant month... I am afraid to go to sleep for fear of my nightmares reocurring... I feel a numbness in my body... I do not have the courage to take my life. I pray each night I will find the strength to do so but the courage alludes me...*

Whoever wrote this diary had either discovered the symptoms of arsenic addiction such as described in the *Materia Medica* or he had experienced the real thing.

* * *

Coal began to replace cotton as Norfolk's prime export, so in March 1884 James decided to take his wife and young Bobo home to Liverpool for good. There, on August 22nd 1884, James posted his letter of resignation from the Norfolk Cotton Exchange. The minutes of the meeting on September 10th 1884 record that James Maybrick's resignation as 'an active member' had been accepted. Brother Edwin was to take over the running of the business in Norfolk and Galveston. The Exchange also recorded Maybrick's later request – their first ever – for 'information as to the action of Committee in regard to Foreign or non-resident members.' He clearly did not intend to sever all contact with America.

During Florie's trial in 1889, remarks made by Dr Hopper, Maybrick's Liverpool physician since 1882, confirmed that his patient had, indeed, spent more time in America after 1884 than we had realised. He admitted that only a few months prior to the trial, he had himself destroyed 'a bundle' of prescriptions written by Dr Seguin of New York, which had been given to him by Maybrick. Dr Hopper said that between 1882 and 1889 Maybrick had visited him 'a number of times' but between June and September 1888 he claimed the number of appointments rose sharply to '15 to 20'. This suggests that either there had been a dramatic escalation of Maybrick's hypochondria or, more likely, since hypochondria is a chronic condition, not acute, that prior to 1888 Maybrick was often away from Liverpool. Newspapers in America say that he was a frequent visitor until at least 1886.

Michael Maybrick, a well-known figure in the American concert halls, was touring the United States and Canada in 1884 and acknowledged at Florie's trial that his brother had visited the United States several times since his marriage. By now they were renting a brand-new detached house in Liverpool, called Beechville, in the exclusive suburb of Grassendale. The house belonged to Matilda Briggs.

The *United Press* reported darkly: 'It turns out that Mrs Maybrick was not the only woman in love with Maybrick. Mrs Briggs was a power in the Maybrick household and she had an unmarried sister, Gertrude ... who she wanted to see engaged to Maybrick.'

The article claims that when James married Florence, Gertrude spitefully turned her affections to the kindly Alfred Brierley ... but he did not appear to reciprocate the affection.

The Janions were a formidable family and when Gertrude was spurned, first by James and then by Brierley, the gullible Florie was no match for their scheming fury. They interfered in every aspect of her life. The voluble Scottish lawyer, Alexander McDougall, who was later to devote much of his time to exposing what many people saw as a conspiracy against Florence, likened them to Macbeth's witches:

> Double, double toil and trouble,
> Fire burn, and cauldron bubble ...

5

The American Connection

On December 30th 1884, the mutilated body of a black cook, Mollie Smith, was discovered in Austin, Texas, lying in the snow at the back of her employer's home, a gaping hole in her head. This was the first murder by America's earliest recorded serial killer who, all through 1885, terrorised Austin to become known as 'The Midnight Assassin'.

He was never found.

The Assassin's early victims were black servant girls. But a year later, on Christmas Day 1885, the *Austin Statesman* screamed:

> Blood! Blood! Blood!
> A woman has been chopped.

In fact there were two women murdered that night. They were white, they were pretty and they were the last to die.

There is no obvious similarity between the methods of the Austin killer and those of Jack the Ripper. The Ripper strangled and disembowelled his victims, with no apparent sexual motive; the Austin women were battered, a railway coupling pin driven into their brains. There were, in some cases, signs of rape. But in both places the killer struck in the dead of night and slipped silently into the dark. There were no witnesses.

In the ten years that I have been investigating the origins of the Maybrick Diary I have learned to question every shred of evidence that has arisen. Even official documents can be misleading and wrong – and where there are gaps in our knowledge of events, I know now, from experience, how easy it is to fill them with wishful thinking.

My initial response to the *New York Times* was one of curiosity but detachment. I saw no immediate link with my own research. But as I probed more deeply into the complex web of James Maybrick's American connections, there were aspects of his life which tempted me to check out his movements in 1884-5.

Robert Smith of Smith Gryphon had by this time changed tack and become a literary agent. My new publisher, John Blake, a former national newspaper editor, had an encouraging nose for a good story. Needless to say, he became very excited by the possibility that we had stumbled across a genuine, historic, discovery. Once again the pressure was on for me to share his excitement and not to sit on the fence. 'Jack the Ripper was the Midnight Assassin' made a tempting headline.

I refused. There was not yet enough supporting material for such a dramatic statement.

But I did agree that, so far, I had found no record that Maybrick was *not* in America at the time of the various murders. I have no diary dates for him in Liverpool that clash with the killings. On the contrary, over this period friends were reporting how increasingly unwell he looked and how lonely Florie was becoming. It seems very likely that he was, indeed, often away from home

At least I had a blank sheet on which to work.

So let us imagine that on Christmas Eve, 1885, the night of the Austin 'double event' when two women were butchered by the light of the full moon, their killer was not an American at all...

Three years later, the double event in London horrified the world and made headline news. Yet the possibility (as suggested by the American press) that these US/UK killings might have been the work of one man has never been thoroughly explored.

We should not forget that James Maybrick, with business connections, family and friends in Whitechapel, was already a secret, womanising, arsenic-driven, cotton merchant when he lived in Virginia. Well known and respected throughout the southern states, with a young wife from Mobile society, he was leading a double life.

Where was he on the night of December 24th 1885? Where was he on December 30th 1884?

What follows is a reconstruction of what might have happened. It is for you, the reader, to decide if it is a mere hypothesis, or if we have stumbled on a new chain of linked events that would make the Ripper's reign of evil even more terrible than we thought.

* * *

On December 23rd 1884, the *Times* in London reported, at length, the opening of the world's largest ever International Cotton Exposition in New Orleans. The event celebrated the centenary of the departure, in 1784, of the first ship bearing six bags of cotton from the United States to Liverpool.

The exhibition was opened by President Arthur 1,300 miles away in Washington: he turned a key which, sensationally for the time, sent an electrical charge to start the Exposition machinery in New Orleans. The band played 'The Star Spangled Banner' and 'God Save the Queen'!

Extending over 249 acres, along the banks of the Mississippi, exhibitors came also from Russia, France and Belgium. The British stand was said, the week previously, to be 'in a condition of unreadiness ...but much ahead of other foreign sections.'

In the harbour, nearly all the ships were British, awaiting cargoes of cotton and dressed overall with flags. 'It was a fine sight,' said the *Times*.

The Exposition was generally regarded as 'the most important event in the history of the south since the Civil War'. It boasted the largest conservatory in the world and one of the wonders was an electrically illuminated fountain around which 20,000 pieces of fruit, tropical plants, flowers and shrubs were displayed. 'High appreciation is shown by press and public,' said the *Times* 'of the English interest shown in the undertaking.'

It seems unlikely that Maybrick would have missed such an important business opportunity to return from England and contact his many friends in the region. Galveston, Dallas, St Louis and Mobile were all linked by the railway line, whose hub was Austin. W.T. Walke was advertising tickets for the two-day journey from Norfolk to New Orleans at $37.

Maybrick would, at the very least, have read those blood-curdling, unremittingly sensational press accounts of events in Austin in 1885.

But could there have been more to it than that?

During the 20 years before the Exposition, Austin had been transformed from a shanty town where pigs and cattle ran wild through mud streets to a thriving home for 23,000 residents. It had telephones, an opera house and an ice-cream parlour, hotels, colleges and electric light. Austin had emerged from the Civil War as an enlightened city with an unusually relaxed and progressive approach to its black residents. There were even black shopkeepers in the largely white Pecan Street, and many former slaves had been given land by their owners.

The Midnight Assassin was to threaten all that because, at first, he directed his savagery at black women. Their vile mutilations were reported in unrelenting detail and, as panic spread throughout the South, when the killer finally turned his fury on white women the newspapers spared their readers nothing. They were far more explicit in their bloodthirsty, vampire-like detail than anything produced during the London terror of 1888.

Sue Hancock was 53 and had been described as 'one of the most refined women in Austin'. Christmas concerts and celebrations were in full swing on December 24th 1885 and the Reverend R.K. Smoot had delivered his regular sermon, when Moses Hancock discovered the body of his wife in their back yard where the Four Seasons Hotel stands today. Her head was split open and a thin, sharp metal object was lodged in her brain.

An hour later, 17-year-old Eula Phillips was found in an unlit alley, to which she had been dragged, her face 'turned upward in the dim moonlight, with an expression of agony that death itself could not erase'. She too had been attacked with a coupling pin. Her unconscious husband was found in bed, beside their sleeping son.

Eula Phillips was the daughter of a hotelier. She was one of the city's great beauties with her billowing white dresses, her soft contemplative eyes and curling hair. In 1883, she had married the rakish musician and violent drunk, Jimmy Phillips. By 1885, when she was only 17, she had turned, for comfort, to one of the city's smartest and most exclusive brothels. She had been there on the night she was murdered and, just as in the case of Jack the Ripper, there were rumours about the illustrious identity of some of her clients and of a conspiracy in high places.

The murder of the 'achingly pretty' but unhappy young Eula Phillips and the respectable Sue Hancock offered the newspapers everything they needed. The *Austin Statesman* reported that:

> ...the skull was fractured in two places and blood was oozing from both ears. Her groans of agony were piercing with what appeared to be her expiring breath, cupfuls of blood were emitted from her mouth... The body was entirely nude and a piece of timber was laid across the bosom and arms and evidently used for the most hellish and damnable of purposes ...

The 'Texas Tidings' column in the *Statesman* commented that ladies were afraid to walk the streets in New Orleans. 'They need a few hangings in New Orleans ... ropes rather than exposition is the cure.'

The confusion and disorganisation of competitive police forces that marked the Austin investigations is reminiscent of what happened later in London in 1888. Journalist and author, Skip Hollandsworth, whose book *The Midnight Assassin* was commissioned in 2003, has described how the hunt was hampered by 'incompetence and a clash of egos' in a force too often to be found in the town's bordellos and saloons and headed by a 'lackadaisical' young police chief, Grooms Leigh.

Bloodhounds, led by a fearsome monster called Old George, raced up and down the streets of Austin, baying for blood and terrorising residents. No wonder they ran out of guns.

There is today a group of amateur detectives in Texas, of whom Skip is probably the best known. Like the Ripperologists, they have been mesmerised by the mystery and devote much of their spare time to analysing and dissecting this 'spellbinding narrative'. A few, I discovered, believe that Jack and the Midnight Assassin could have been one and the same.

Skip Hollandsworth regrets that 'this tale of murder and insanity, replete with shocking twists and turns, is almost entirely absent from the annals of American history'. Yet the killer brought Austin to the brink of chaos.

On Christmas Day, 1885, 500 community leaders and professional men met, determined to co-ordinate a new approach. There were proposals to fully light the darker areas of the city, to activate fire alarms whenever there was an attack. It was even suggested that residents should be put under a curfew and the city ring-fenced by guards at night.

But they were already too late. The killings stopped and, just like the Ripper's, they ended with a diabolical flourish. Eula Phillips and Mary Jane Kelly were the youngest and prettiest of the victims.

There followed the inevitable run of red herrings and list of unlikely suspects. In January 1886 Jimmy Phillips was arrested for the murder of Eula and soon after, Moses Hancock was charged with the death of his wife, Sue. Two separate trials for a single killer? It seemed unpromising and in the end both men were acquitted.

Another Texan author, Allan McCormack, has for many years, been researching the life of Yorkshire-born Ben Thompson. Thompson emigrated with his parents from Britain to Austin in 1851. He grew up to become a gambler, a gunslinger and eventually Austin's respected Marshal. He was there during the time of the killings and was a member of the 'dream team' employed to defend Jimmy Phillips.

Allan McCormack believes that Ben Thompson knew the Austin killer, although he probably did not suspect his true identity. He also claims that the British police in 1888 had investigated the possibility that London's Jack the Ripper was indeed their Midnight Assassin.

The *Austin Statesman* of September 5th 1888, commented that, 'There is a striking similarity which must be mere coincidence between these murderers across the water and the servant girl murderers in 1885, which latter remains a mystery as profound and unravelled as that of Whitechapel. All were perpetrated in the same mysterious and impenetrable silence and what makes the coincidence more singular is that the Austin murder fiend, who was seen on one occasion was, like "Leather Apron" [an early name given to the Whitechapel Killer] a short, heavy-set personage.'

The Littlechild letter, unearthed by Stewart Evans and Paul Gainey in 1993, names the bizarre, be-whiskered American quack, Dr Francis Tumbelty, a self-declared homosexual, as a police suspect.

Tumblety was certainly in Whitechapel at the time of the killings and had been arrested on November 7th for gross indecency with a number of men. Evans and Gainey say that he was released on unrecorded police bail. He was then re-arrested on suspicion of murder on November 12th and again released on bail. According to Stewart Evans, he broke bail and escaped aboard the steamer *La Bretagne* on November 24th for New York.

On December 1st 1888 in Missouri, the *St Louis Evening Chronicle* reported the arrival of a quiet British detective named Jordan. He was wearing an eye-glass and carrying a cane. This story is most likely to be linked to the known British police interest in the American Connection at the time.

In 1888, Scotland Yard had despatched a team of detectives to scour the United States – a serious step. The American press was hot on their heels, avidly reporting every move and conducting interviews in bars from New York to St Louis. Oddly, the British papers hardly mentioned the turn the Ripper trail had taken.

But on December 22nd 1888, Detective Inspector Walter Andrews, one of that original team, admitted in New York that, despite 23 detectives, two clerks and one inspector being employed on the case, they were 'without a jot of evidence' on which to convict anyone. But the seeds of suspicion had been sown.

Tumbelty gave them the slip and disappeared. Unsubstantiated claims were later made for his reappearance in Jamaica and Central and South America, where from time to time Ripper-like murders occurred. In his later years he lived quietly with his elderly sister in Rochester, New York, before dying in a nursing home run by the Sisters of Mercy in 1903.

So with Tumbelty out of the frame – what of James Maybrick?

6

A Dark Shadow Lays Over the House, it is Evil

Back in Liverpool, in late 1884, the Maybricks seemed to be enjoying life, at least superficially. Maybrick had taken over an office at 32 Knowsley Buildings, in Tithebarn Street. His staff there included the young clerk Thomas Lowry and bookkeeper George Smith. The couple took drives in the carriage, played whist and, above all, shared a passion for horse racing. They were regular visitors to Aintree, home of the world-famous Grand National.

They were accepted at Liverpool's social centre, the Wellington Rooms, in Mount Pleasant, where carpet was laid over the pavement for the five annual balls. Ladies emerged from carriages 'dressed with such gorgeousness as befits the wives and daughters of the wealthiest men in Britain's greatest seaport.'

Maybrick also belonged to the fashionable Palatine Club. The Diary refers to dining at the Club with 'George' – his closest friend was businessman George Davidson. But socially, the couple did not quite qualify for what was known as the 'currant jelly set'.

However, marriage and Liverpool life did nothing to curb a habit that was, for Maybrick, becoming more and more pernicious. He had ready access to drugs through his cousin, William, who worked for a wholesale chemist – John Thompson at 58, Hanover Street. When William was dismissed in 1886 Maybrick even asked Thompson to reinstate him but the move failed. (Cousin William died in Liverpool Workhouse in October 1888.)

No matter, for Maybrick already had another source for his 'medicine': a dispensing chemist named Edwin Garnett Heaton in Exchange Street East. Heaton served him for about ten years in total, over which time the dose he prescribed had increased from four to seven drops. (Arsenic was commonly dispensed in liquid as well as in powder form.) Maybrick went regularly to the shop, sometimes five times a day, for what the chemist described as his 'pick-me-up' to 'excite passion.' Seven drops five times a day would be nearly equivalent to one third of a grain of arsenic, and one grain is enough to kill. When Maybrick went away on business trips Heaton would make up several bottles containing eight or sixteen doses.

The drug was clearly having an impact on Maybrick. Florie's brother Holbrook St John Chandler, who was by now a doctor in Paris, became concerned about his brother-in-law's behaviour and wrote in 1884: 'I don't pretend to know his tricks, but he has forbidden Florie telling us a word of his affairs and has completely thrown dust in her eyes. We, unfortunately, cannot write to her or hear from her except through him, and he dictates her letters. I greatly regret this most unexpected attitude of Maybrick's, turning out to be such a bully and a brute, but such being the fact we have to protect ourselves as far as practicable.' About the same time, the Baroness wrote that James had forced Florie to suggest: "that I best allow my house to be sold. I ought to take an *attic room* and do my *own work*; it was absurd to keep a servant or a little dog (my only companion)." He also continued to see various mistresses, one of whom was whispered on the Exchange flags to be Christina Samuelson, the giddy wife of his friend Charles.

The cracks were beginning to show by 1884.

About this time Maybrick contacted a Pauline Cranstoun in London, who had advertised that she cast horoscopes and so was able to diagnose obscure diseases. Her story is mentioned by J.H. Levy in his book on the Maybrick case, *The Necessity for Criminal Appeal* (1899). 'He wrote me', she said, 'a strange account of his various ailments and told me he was in the habit of taking large quantities of arsenic, and put it in his food as he found that the best and safest way of taking it. He said it aided his digestion and calmed his nerves.'

In an interview with the *New York Herald* after Florie's trial, Pauline Cranstoun said: 'I wrote to him that he should stop using arsenic or it would certainly result in his fatal illness some time. I received no reply from him to that.'

Sadly, Levy tells us, all that correspondence was destroyed. Richard Lancelyn Green in his book *The Uncollected Sherlock Holmes* (Penguin 1983) refers to a letter received by Sir Arthur Conan Doyle in 1903 from a lady living with 'the Hon Pauline Cranstoun, daughter of the 10th Baron Cranstoun'.

During 1884 there was a brief economic downturn in Britain. Friends said that Maybrick became as worried about his money as he was about his health. Florie herself had never been taught to budget. She was extravagant in her passion for pretty clothes, which she bought in quantity from Woollright's. The fashionable department store in Bold Street was a snare for any clothes-conscious woman, with its glossy image and immense stock of furs, jewellery and exotic fabrics. In 1999, I received a letter from Annapolis in Maryland, USA, from British-born Mandy Johnson, a genealogist, telling me that her great-grandmother had made dresses for Florie. Her name was Sarah Ann Jones-Osborne – a multi-talented lady who inherited her mother's various businesses in Liverpool. She bought property and leased it to immigrant tailors as well as owning a laundry and a boarding house.

In December of that year, Florie's brother fell ill with consumption and died four months later. Maybrick went to his funeral, which took place in Paris at the American Episcopal Church on April 17th 1885.

*　　*　　*

On May 23rd 1885, during the closing celebrations at the New Orleans Exposition, Eliza Shelley was murdered in Austin. Maybrick could easily have made the journey to America from Paris or via England in time.

Florie had few close friends. To the ladies of Liverpool she was an outsider. Only the sisters, Matilda Briggs and Louisa Hughes, called regularly, and they were far from friendly. After her brother's death, Florie asked Mrs Briggs for a loan of £100 to quieten creditors, which she repaid in instalments.

On July 20th the following year, 1886, a daughter, Gladys Evelyn, was born. In attendance was the dapper, sharp-featured Dr Hopper, from Rodney Street, who had cared for the Maybricks since their marriage. Gladys's birth did nothing to restore marital bliss. In 1887 a distraught Florie discovered what others already knew: there was another woman in her husband's life.

Who was this woman – referred to several times in the Diary? Could she have been Sarah Ann Robertson who disappeared from the records between 1876 and 1891? There is no evidence of her whereabouts at this time. Is it possible that she followed James to Liverpool?

After James's death in 1889, several bills from a dressmaker arrived at Battlecrease House. They were for gowns destined not for Florie, but for his mistress, who was also discovered to have items of jewellery bought by Maybrick.

So far, we do not know. Florie's friend, John Baillie Knight, said in an affidavit in 1889 that Florie had told him in 1888 that she knew that Maybrick had a woman in Liverpool. The local papers at the time of Florie's trial also reported that a woman was living in Liverpool who had been his mistress for 20 years. When visited by Michael and Edwin she was found also to possess jewellery and clothes belonging to Florie, which she said had been given her by James in part payment for money lent. Moreover, William Stead, the editor of the Victorian weekly magazine *Review of Reviews*, and Bernard Ryan, in his 1977 book *The Poisoned Life of Mrs Maybrick*, both maintain that 1887 was when, at Florie's insistence, the couple moved into separate beds.

In Richard Whittington Egan's *Murder, Mayhem and Mystery in Liverpool* he speaks of Maybrick's increasing absences and the 'long lonely nights' that Florie endured.

In the Spring of 1887 when a scarlatina epidemic swept Britain and five year old Bobo became ill, Florie remained to look after him while, somewhat unconventionally, James and the children's nurse Emma Parker took Gladys away to Wales for six weeks. They stayed at the Hand Hotel in Llangollen. The hotel seems to have been a family favourite; James had stayed there previously with Florie and Gertrude Janion, and in 1889 the register records him on holiday there with four male companions.

When he returned, Maybrick cut Florie's allowance for food, servants' wages and other household expenses. In October that year she wrote to 'my darling Mammy' that Maybrick had made only £125 profit in the previous five years and that his assets were reduced to £1,500. She claimed that they had been using capital to furnish their home and complained:

> I am utterly worn out and in such a state of overstrained nervousness I am hardly fit for anything. Whenever the doorbell rings I feel ready to faint for fear it is someone coming to have an account paid and when Jim comes home at night it is with fear and trembling that I look into his face to see whether anyone has been to the office about my bills... my life is a continual state of fear of something or somebody. There is no way of stemming the current. Is life worth living? I would gladly give up the house and move elsewhere but Jim says it would ruin him outright. For one must keep up appearances until he has more capital to fall back on to meet his liabilities, since the least suspicion aroused, all claims would pour in at once and how could Jim settle with what he has now?

Maybrick was far from consistent and not always honest in his handling of their finances. When he died he left over £5,000, the equivalent of about £200,000 today. He was not as impoverished as Florie believed. In addition to all the financial worries, Florie was also concerned about the well-being of little Gladys. In the same letter she adds:

> Nurse is quite changed since baby's birth. Poor little mite, it gets neither petting nor coaxing when I am not with it and yet it is such a loving little thing and ready with a smile for every cross word that nurse says to her. I cannot understand why she does not take to the child. I am afraid she is getting too old for a young baby and has not the... patience to look after Gladys which she had for Bobo. With him it was a labour of love, with poor little Gladys it is a labour of duty only.

So it was that a new nurse – Alice Yapp – described by the *Liverpool Echo* as a 'somewhat prepossessing young woman' joined the family in September 1887. Alice Yapp had grown up with a brother and four sisters in the Nag's Head, Ludlow, Shropshire, where her parents were innkeepers. The girls were always extremely well dressed.

She lived with her then employers, Mr and Mrs David Gibson, in Birkdale, Southport. Maybrick again flouted convention by going alone to engage her. This was considered the task of the lady of any household. There were hints in the newspapers that relations between James and Alice Yapp were not all that they should have been.

The strain on Florie became even more intense. She knew – what no one else realised – that her life was out of control. She was in debt and worried about her husband's drug habit, his health and his infidelity. In addition to suspecting adultery, Florie was by now also worried that her husband was overdosing himself on his 'medicines'. Friends who saw Maybrick occasionally when they came on business trips from America remarked at his broken and rapidly ageing condition, despite the fact that he was still only 48. Such was Florie's state of mind when she first met the personable 36-year-old Alfred Brierley.

* * *

In the winter of 1887/8 the Maybricks gave a dinner party. Alfred Brierley, a Liverpool cotton broker, was among the guests. His company, Brierley Wood and Co., was in Old Hall Street, just around the corner from Maybrick's office.

Like James he had offices in America and had lived in Savannah as a member of the exporting house of Brierley, Maitland and Dougal.

Brierley was born in Rochdale, in 1851, and grew up with nine brothers and sisters. The Brierleys were pillars of the community, having risen within the security of the Church of England and the Tory party to a position of considerable affluence and influence, thanks to the cotton trade. Streets were named after them. Brierley was unmarried, attractive and susceptible. Later he always insisted, unconvincingly, that he met Florie only in company throughout the next year and that they were no more than 'distant acquaintances'. The press in America claimed constantly that their friendship had already been established by 1886.

Troubled as she was by her husband's affairs, Florie was herself a flirt, an animated woman who loved the attention of men. Moreover, as she explained to her mother, 'He was kind to me.'

At the same time the increasingly bewildered and naturally flirtatious Florie became the subject of a whispering campaign on the Exchange. It was said that she was receiving the attentions not only of Maybrick's impressionable young brother Edwin, who was in love with her, but also of a solicitor in London by the name of Williams.

In Liverpool, in those censorious times, it would have taken very little for a high-spirited girl from America's Deep South to step out of line. And this was someone who, according to an American friend, had grown up in a 'swift place, where the women were much swifter.' There, an unchaperoned girl might join a group of male and female friends on a Saturday evening to take a chartered river boat and dance and drink all night before returning home to sleep all day. Such behaviour would not have been tolerated in Victorian England.

Whatever the truth about Florie's feelings for Brierley, or whether she had even begun to indulge them as early as 1887, the Diary implies that James Maybrick nursed a growing paranoia about her suspected infidelities.

* * *

Probably in March 1888, the Maybricks moved from Grassendale to Aigburth, less than a mile away, into the far more imposing and better situated Battlecrease House, on which they took a five year lease. They were accompanied by nurse Yapp, gardener James Grant, who had just married the former housemaid Alice, and the waitress Mary Cadwallader. Cook Elizabeth Humphreys and housemaid Bessie Brierley (no relation) joined them later in the year.

The quality of the Maybricks' female staff was remarkable. A reporter described the girls at the time of Florie's arrest: 'One thing struck me with interest and wonder, not unmingled with admiration, was the smart appearance of the female servants and nurses... they were all dressed "*à la mode*", and the cook, especially, looked very fascinating, not to say coquettish.'

On August 18th 1889, the *New York Herald* front page was filled with the Maybrick story and, in particular, with descriptions of the servants. Subtitled 'Looking up Miss Alice Yapp' they said: 'She is a native of Ludlow, Shropshire and her parents were well-to-do. After the death of her father … she went into service as a nurse … She managed to ingratiate herself so with the Maybricks and to obtain such an all-powerful voice in the management of affairs in the servants' hall …'

She had, it was alleged, a most prying nature.

Mary Cadwallader, known as 'gentle Mary', grew up on a 160 acre farm, also in Shropshire, and was privately educated. Why Mary, eldest of 14 children, went into service is a mystery. She was tiny, with deep auburn hair, and was generally described as a 'lady'. She shared the Maybricks' passion for horses, rode well and every week asked a man friend to put sixpence on a horse for her since women were not allowed to bet. Years afterwards she kept a white rabbit and took it for walks on a lead.

Neither of these girls was of the servant class.

The couple's neighbours in Riversdale Road were professional people and businessmen, although cows wandered up and down the lane and made the going heavy for carriages. Florie wasted no time in furnishing the house in style. Every room had velvet carpets, and curtains in dark red plush lined with pale blue satin. The gold-painted furniture was upholstered in dark red with blue. Maybrick's den, which was always locked, had deep, comfortable leather chairs. It was here that he kept wine, cigars, tobacco, cards and the poker chips he used while entertaining men friends. Upstairs, his dressing room, which was reached through the main bedroom, was forbidden territory to everyone.

That summer there was a guest at Battlecrease from whom, in later life, would come some recollections of the strange domestic scene.

'Little Miss' was Maybrick's pet name for young Florence Aunspaugh, a boisterous eight-year-old American, who stayed with the family while her father, John, head of Inman Swann and Co. was in Europe.

When she was an old lady in America, Florence told her story to author Trevor Christie. Most of the notes made by Christie did not appear in his book *Etched in Arsenic*. Along with these notes, the unused material has only recently come to light. Stored in the archives at the University of Wyoming, Laramie, it figures prominently among the many archives and memorabilia that have proved invaluable to me in the present reconstruction of the couple's life and times. Florence told Christie:

> Battlecrease was a palatial home. The grounds must have consisted of five or six acres and were given most excellent care. There were large trees, luxuriant shrubbery and flowerbeds. Dotted around the grounds were little rock nooks or summer houses, with seats, covered with old

> English ivy and other running vines. A conservatory was near the house and a pair of peacocks roamed the grounds... running through the grounds was a small, natural stream of water, part of which had been broadened and deepened to form a small lake... this pool was stocked with fish and swans and ducks were swimming on the surface. I think I remember the pool better than anything else as I fell in it twice and was pulled out by the yard man.
>
> Mr Maybrick was very fond of hunting and had quite a few dogs... I saw six horses, a pair of handsome looking blacks which were always hitched to the carriage, a pair of greys which were hitched to what they called the trap, and two bay saddle horses: one Mr Maybrick used, the other Mrs Maybrick.

To young Florence, Florie was a beguiling figure:

> The crowning glory of her person was her hair. It was blonde, but not the dead faded-out type of yellow, had just enough of a tinge of red in it to make a glossy, rich golden.
>
> Mrs Maybrick's eyes were the most beautiful blue I have ever seen. They were a large, round eye of such a very deep blue that at times they were violet; but the expression was most peculiar... you would focus your eyes on hers with a steady gaze and they would appear entirely without life or expression as though you were gazing into the eyes of a corpse. Utterly void of animation and expression. As you continued your gaze her eyes seemed to change and have the look of a frightened animal.
>
> At no time was there any expression of intellectuality, either in eyes or face, yet there was a magnetic charm about her countenance that... seemed irresistible.
>
> She was extremely conscious of her beauty and attractiveness and courted admiration, especially from the

> male sex. She seemed to be very fond of being very close to them... I have seen her pat a man on the top of his head, put her arm on another's arm and rest her hand on another's knee. She acted that way before Mr Maybrick. Since I have reached the years of maturity I have wondered that he tolerated it, but he did.

The James Maybrick of young Florence's memory was stern and formidable, but with flashes of tenderness for his children.

> After breakfast Mr Maybrick would take his little boy and myself on each knee and talk to us. He would tease me to see what kind of pert answer I would give...
>
> One day Mr Maybrick instructed Nurse Yapp to have the little boy and myself dressed unusually well, as he wished to have us in the parlour a while before dinner was announced... I don't think I ever looked better in my life... we were taken down the beautiful stairway in the front hall by the upstairs housemaid. Mr Maybrick met us at the door of the hall leading to the front parlour. Taking me by the hand and walking me to the arch between the parlours he said: 'Ladies and gentlemen, I want to introduce you to this charming little miss from the USA.'
>
> While you would not term him a handsome man... he had a fine forehead, very pleasant intellectual face and an open, honest countenance. He had light, sandy coloured hair, grey eyes and a florid complexion. He had none of that blunt, abrupt manner, so characteristic of the English but was exceedingly cultured, polished and refined in his manners and was a superb host.
>
> But there were two unfortunate features in his make-up. That was his morose, gloomy disposition and extremely high temper. He also imagined he was afflicted with every ailment to which 'the flesh was heir.'

> Yes, Mr Maybrick was an arsenic addict. He craved it like a narcotic fiend. He used it right in our home.

Florence Aunspaugh was eight in 1888. This suggests that Maybrick had been a visitor to the family in Atlanta, certainly after his official departure from Norfolk in 1884. The little girl would have been far too young to recall events any earlier than that.

> He was always after the doctor to prescribe it and the druggist to make him up a tonic with arsenic in it. He said once to my mother, 'They only give me enough to aggravate and worry me and make me always craving for more.'
>
> He was always taking strychnine tablets and was great on beef broth and arsenic. My father once said, 'Maybrick has got a dozen drug stores in his stomach.'
>
> I have seen him angered on several occasions, and twice he was furious. I was the cause of his second outburst... His baby [Gladys] had a little bed with high railings all round... One morning the baby cried and I ran to the bed to try and get her out. I was tugging to get her over the railings but I became so exhausted I could not hang on to her any longer and let her go... If I had gotten her outside and she had fallen on the floor it might have broken her back...
>
> The nurse came in and was mad. She seized me by the back of the neck, jerked me round and said: 'If you do it again I will slap your jaws black and blue.'
>
> As this scene was being enacted Mr Maybrick passed by the door... Mr Maybrick was furious... he said: 'I saw you grab that child by the back of the neck – you might have broken her neck. This child is far from her father and mother, in my house under my protection and if I ever hear you talking to her in that way again I will kick you down the stairs and break every God damn bone in you.'

Though only a girl, Florence sensed something was amiss at Battlecrease House. 'A current of mystery seemed to circulate all round which gave you an uncanny feeling, a feeling that something was going on that you could not understand. In the yard you would see the servants conversing in low suppressed tones. If anyone came up they would stop abruptly and disperse.'

The cast of characters at Battlecrease House included Mrs Briggs, who Florence recalled 'was a woman near Mr Maybrick's age, and my father was told she had been madly in love with him and had made a desperate effort to marry him. It is very evident he did not reciprocate.' Florence also described Nurse Yapp as 'a very efficient capable woman' but also 'a most deceitful and treacherous one':

> Both Mrs Briggs and Nurse Yapp despised and hated Mrs Maybrick and the most pathetic part about it was that Mrs Maybrick did not have the brain to realise their attitude towards her...
>
> Mrs Briggs took all kind of authority around the place and with the servants. She would address Mr Maybrick as 'James'. At the table I have heard her say things like this: 'James, don't you think a roof on the porch by the side of your den would be much better... James, I suggest you wear your heavy coat... James, a pork roast would be nice for dinner today.' Not one time did she ever address Mrs Maybrick.
>
> When Mr and Mrs Maybrick were gone she would go into every room in the house. Mr Maybrick's bedroom and Mrs Maybrick's bedroom. Only one room escaped her – that was Mr Maybrick's den. He had a Yale lock on the door and it was never opened, only when he was there. It was never cleaned up. Only when he was there.

* * *

Among the regular callers and overnight visitors to Battlecrease House were Maybrick's brothers Thomas and Edwin and, much less frequently, Michael. William, the eldest brother, although resident in Liverpool, apparently never came.

Michael was thought to be the brains of the family. According to Florence Aunspaugh, 'He had a very pretentious estate which surpassed James's in every way.' He was unmarried in 1888 and was looked after by a housekeeper.

For a man who had already achieved something of star status, both as a singer and a composer, Michael is an enigma. Michael Maybrick's role in the Maybrick tragedy has excited the curiosity and suspicion of many people. Australian composer Derek Strahan, whose partner is Edwin Maybrick's great-granddaughter, Amanda Pruden, has written extensively about him and is a collector of his music. He says Michael was 'one of Britain's greatest composers of light music.'

For a short time he collaborated with American composer and novelist Hamilton Aidé on 'The Maid of the Mill' (1884) and 'My Life for Thee'. But it was the partnership with Frederick Weatherly which brought international renown. Together they wrote hundreds of songs such as 'Nancy Lee' and 'A Warrior Bold'. 'The Holy City', which appeared in 1892 after his brother's death, was to sell about 60,000 copies within a year of publication and remains a firm favourite today. Ironically, he also later wrote a lively ditty 'They all Love Jack'.

At the time of the Ripper murders Stephen Adams was a household name. He had more music being published than Arthur Sullivan of Gilbert and Sullivan fame and, according to Derek Strahan, should rank with Cole Porter, Jerome Kern and George Gershwin. He had performed with the Hallé Orchestra, the Glasgow Choral Union and the Birmingham Festival Choral Society although it was possibly the inauguration of 'Ballad Concerts' by his publishers Boosey and Hawkes, that brought him most popular acclaim.

Yet very little is known about the personal life and character of Michael Maybrick. Until the emergence of the Diary, even biographical dictionaries gave only the bare bones of his life. There are no books, no recordings, no diaries, no warm memories from friends or fellow composers. He remains a strangely dark shadow in the background.

Apart from his appearances at the London Ballad Concerts and on the concert stage, he was a member of the Constitutional Club and could be seen sporting the uniform of the Artists Rifles Volunteers, where his training would have included bayonet practice. He had enrolled in 1886 at the age of 45. According to the muster roll, the rest of the recruits that year were in their twenties. Was this why 45 year old Michael gave his age as 40 when he signed on?

He had also by this time achieved considerable status as a Freemason, where he was a member of the Athenaeum and St Andrew's Lodges and founder and first Principal of the Orpheus Lodge for Musicians. He rose to the coveted level of 30 degrees rite. By 1889 he had reached the even greater position of organist to the Grand Lodge.

Manchester teacher James Beswick Whitehead has been prompted by the Diary to speculate on the links between Stephen Adams, Weatherly, the Freemasons and James Joyce's stream-of-consciousness book *Ulysses*.

He writes on the Internet: 'It turns out that the 1922 modernist masterpiece has things to say about Florence Maybrick, Jack the Ripper and the Holy City as well as the Craft. It is not surprising that the ballad should feature in the book for Joyce was well acquainted with the contents of the Victorian Music stool ... However, there is something very suggestive in the way these particular references are arranged which indicate that Joyce knew of some gossip to link the Maybrick case with the Ripper many years before the Diary emerged.'

The late Tony Miall, musical historian, wrote of Michael Maybrick: 'He is one of the less attractive musical figures of the period. His endless pursuit of respectability and money is at variance with the image of an artist concerned with his art. One seeks in vain for any sympathetic bone in his body. His relations with his family and friends were more formal than warm. One suspects deeply that his relationship later with his wife was similar – all in all, a cold fish.'

Over the years since the Diary emerged, a number of people have pointed a finger at Michael Maybrick – including Bruce Robinson, scriptwriter of *The Killing Fields* and *Withnail and I*, who became immersed in the Maybrick saga after reading the first edition of my book and is now working on a film script.

There are those who feel that with his masonic connections and high society, even Royal, contacts, it was he and not James who stalked the streets of Whitechapel; that it could have been he who framed his brother and sister-in-law. There can be no doubt that brother Michael's role in the whole miserable Maybrick saga is murky and there is much still to learn.

The Diary refers repeatedly to Maybrick's jealousy of Michael, whom he called 'the sensible brother'.

The youngest brother, Edwin, was, according to the impressionable Florence, 'one of the handsomest men I have ever seen.' He was of medium height, fair, with a well-proportioned and finely formed figure. He had a beautiful singing voice, 'even better than Michael's', but no opportunity to make the most of it. At 37 he too was unmarried.

Edwin's daughter Amy acknowledged many years later that her father 'would not do up his shoes without consulting Michael.' But James was close to Edwin, with whom he worked and missed him greatly when he was away. It would not have been surprising if Florie had sought solace from her brother-in-law. Rumours about Florie's feelings had been circulating for some time at the Cotton Exchange. There was even suspicion of an affair. After Maybrick's death many love letters were found from Edwin to Florie. John Aunspaugh told his daughter Florence that Michael had destroyed those letters. However, she also recalled an incident told by her father that justified that suspicion.

> The first indication my father had of anything amiss was the night of the formal dining. There were twenty couples, which, of course, made a long table. The conversation was in groups. Mr Edwin was near Mrs James Maybrick and they were laughing and talking. My father glanced at Mr James and as he did he heard Mrs

Maybrick say to Edwin, with a laugh, 'if I had met you first things might have been different.'

It could have been a harmless joke. But Mr Maybrick took it at face value. He dropped his knife, clenched his fist and his face flushed the colour of fire. In a second he had recovered, picked up his knife and everything went off smoothly.

As Florence Aunspaugh and Bobo played by the pool and raced around the flowerbeds, a storm was about to break which would overwhelm them all.

7

There are Times when I Feel an Overwhelming Compulsion to Place my Thoughts to Paper

The Poste House in Cumberland Street near Liverpool Docks has hardly changed since 1888 when its lunchtime hot-pot was celebrated far and wide. Customers still crowd into the tiny, dimly lit bar, with its green ceiling and deep red walls closed in by a heavy drape of curtains. Prince Louis Napoleon drank here. So too, we understood at first from the Diary, did James Maybrick:

> *I took refreshment at the Poste House it was there I finally decided London it shall be. And why not, is it not an ideal location? Indeed do I not frequently visit the Capital and indeed do I not have legitimate reason for doing so. All who sell their dirty wares shall pay, of that I have no doubt. But shall I pay? I think not. I am too clever for that... The bitch and her whoring master will rue the day I saw them together.*

Not far from the Poste House is the once-fashionable shopping centre of Whitechapel. In those days it was a far cry from its namesake in London. It was in this street in 1888 that the Diary records Maybrick sighting Florie with the man he believed to be her lover. Florie's lover is never mentioned by name in the Diary – he becomes 'the whoremaster', and Florie is no longer 'my darling Bunny' but 'the bitch' or 'the whore'.

It was not until some time after my first visit to the Poste House in June 1992 that I became fully aware of the conflicts and contradictions with which this Diary would present me. For here, in one short paragraph, were two statements – one, referring to the Poste House, was eventually to cast doubt on the authenticity of the Diary and the second, referring to Maybrick's London connections, to support it dramatically!

During our visit to Liverpool we met Roger Wilkes, a BBC scriptwriter at the time, who had presented a programme on Michael Maybrick and generously gave us his research material. It was Roger who first threw a spanner in the works. 'The Poste House was not called the Poste House in 1888,' he said!

It is certainly correct that in 1888 the building now called the Poste House was affectionately known then as 'The Muck Midden'. In 1882 it had been called 'The Wrexham House' but in brewery records of 1888/9 no name is mentioned; the names of A. H. Castrell and Walter Corlett are given as licensees. The present owners of The Poste House – Pyramid – acquired it from Paramount in Chester who told us that they had bought the pub from Boddingtons, who had in turn bought it from Higsons. Higsons had acquired it from the Gartside and Gibson families. Tantalisingly in the 1848 Deed of Annuity between Richard and Betty Gibson and Abraham Gartside reference is made to 'premises in Cumberland Street, formerly a ware-room and now a public house under the sign of........' Again the name is missing!

It was not until the 1960s that the decision was made to smarten up what had become a seedy establishment and to re-name it The Poste House.

In the first few weeks it seemed we may have hit a problem. We went on to explore the history of the Post Office, pubs and post houses to see if there was another solution. Was the Poste House somewhere else? We turned for help to a number of local historians, such as Gordon Wright of the Inn Sign Society and Dick Daglish who has specialised in the history of Liverpool pubs. I learned that post houses were simply places where mail was collected or delivered and were seldom signposted as such. The term could be applied to any number of pubs or coffee houses such as the George, the Red Lion or the White Hart. They were not, necessarily, main coaching inns.

We learned too that the main Liverpool Post Office, probably opened first in Water Street in 1753, seemed to have frequently changed its location. In 1839, the year after Maybrick's birth, 'The Old Post Office' was situated off Church Street round the corner from the family home.

"It is now quite an exhilarating game of hide and seek... to find its whereabouts', wrote J. James Hewson in an article on the Liverpool post in 1899 – the year that the fifth main Post Office was opened finally. By 1904 the building known as the Muck Midden had become 'The New Post Office Restaurant'.

There is a pub at the Church Alley/School Lane crossing which is today called the Old Post Office. Licensee George Duxbury told my publisher Robert Smith that the pub was part of the old Post Office buildings and goes back to at least 1840 when it was a busy coaching inn. The stables, of which some cobbles remain, open on to Hanover Street, the main thoroughfare down to the main Post Office. Behind the pub was a second Post Office – from which it took its name. The Old Post Office Inn is close to Central Station where Maybrick would have caught the train for Aigburth; it is also near Church Street and Whitechapel and could be a strong contender to be the Diary's Poste House.

However, another idea was growing in my mind. Perhaps the Poste House was not in Liverpool at all – the Diary does not place it there. Amongst the papers which Roger had handed over to us was a list of the Maybrick files at the Public Record Office in Kew. These had recently been opened for general research after 100 years. A little time later Sally Evemy and I made our first visit to this vast building which houses many of the nation's historical records – war records, shipping records, army careers, government papers, maps, time tables. We had ordered the 'Maybrick boxes', unsure what to expect, and these were eventually delivered on the 'paternoster' – a kind of escalator carrying documents from the vaults. Gingerly we looked inside at bundle after bundle of crisp, fragile papers and letters all tied in red tape and numbered. Very few people indeed had looked at this material before us. Who knew what we would find?

We were to return many, many times, always coming across new snippets of helpful information. On one of these occasions much later on, we spotted lurking among those papers a letter which had not seemed important in our original searches. It was sent by Gustavus A. Witt who was Maybrick's colleague. This long letter, addressed to the Home Secretary, Sir Henry Matthews, in 1889 and which was never published makes an interesting statement:

> 4, Cullum Street
> London E.C., August 29th 1889
>
> Sir, Though you are no doubt more than tired of the unfortunate Maybrick affair permit me as one of the late Mr James Maybrick's most intimate friends (he was my partner in Liverpool up to 1875 and continued to do my London firm's business up to the time of his death)...

Another enigma! Did Witt mean that Maybrick did his business in Liverpool – or in London? Maybrick was still working for Witt at the time of the Whitechapel murders. Presumably such a partnership would have necessitated inter-office travel? So our attentions turned to London. But despite hours of trawling through Post Office archives and street directories, looking for refreshment places and coffee houses that could have borne the name, we found nothing.

There is a spelling later in the Diary which intrigues me; the expression 'post haste' is mis-spelt 'poste haste'. 'Haste post, haste' was a well known instruction to the Victorian post boy and was written on any envelopes when urgency was required. The word 'post' did not have an *e*. Could that spelling 'Poste House' simply reflect Maybrick's ignorance?

The Post(e) House file in my cabinet remains open – another unresolved puzzle at the heart of a now rapidly growing paper mountain of evidence. I have returned to my original idea that the Diary could possibly be right since there is no record of the Muck Midden's official name.

Wherever the Poste House was located, the Diary is clear on what happened next. Undermined by his own failing health, his drug addiction and banishment from Florie's bed, Maybrick was insanely jealous. It was without doubt the developing friendship with Brierley that sowed the seed for murder. Maybrick had the motive. He now needed the location.

> *I said Whitechapel it will be and Whitechapel it shall. Whitechapel Liverpool Whitechapel London,* Ha Ha. *No one could possibly place it together. And indeed for there is no reason for anyone to do so.*

There is a reference in the Diary, probably entered in March 1888, to a communication from brother Thomas requesting Maybrick to meet him in Manchester, where Thomas lived in the suburb of Moss Side. He was then manager of the Manchester Packing Company. Maybrick apparently agreed, although his mind was already preoccupied with matters other than business.

> *Tomorrow I travel to Manchester. Will take some of my medicine and think hard on the matter... I will force myself not to think of the children...*
>
> *Time is passing much too slowly. I still have to work up the courage to begin my campaign. I have thought long and hard over the matter and still I cannot come to a decision when I should*

> *begin. Opportunity is there, of that fact I am certain... My medicine is doing me good, in fact I am sure I can take more than any other person alive.*

Just as Maybrick used Michael and Witt as his 'cover' for his journeys to London, so Thomas provided a reason for a business trip to Manchester. The train to Manchester ran direct from Aigburth Station and the journey took just over an hour. It was there, in Manchester, that the Diary suggests Maybrick tried his first murder.

> *My dear God my mind is in a fog. The whore is now with her maker and he is welcome to her. There was no pleasure as I squeezed. I felt nothing. Do not know if I have the courage to go back to my original idea. Manchester was cold and damp very much like this hell hole. Next time I will throw acid over them.*

According to Dr David Forshaw such behavioural 'try-outs' are common. Studies of a number of psychopathic patients have shown them to be preoccupied with sadistic sexual fantasies. 'Over time' he explains, 'these became more extreme and they started to act out parts of the fantasy... For example, following potential victims.'

If Dr Forshaw is correct and the Manchester murder was a 'try-out' which gave Maybrick no pleasure, this would account for the fact that in the Diary he refers only to the aspect of killing which really thrilled him – the cutting and ripping.

Researcher Caroline Morris has made the interesting comment that the throwing of acid over victims – vitriolage – was a fashionable crime of the 1880s.

Police records are incomplete, coroners' records have been destroyed and, so far, we have found no murder in Manchester in February or March 1888. Henry Mayhew, in his classic *London Labour and London Poor* (first published in 1851 and reprinted many times) estimated there were probably 80,000 prostitutes working in London alone and a strangulation in Manchester would not have merited more than a simple routine investigation. Even the vicious murder of Emma Smith, who was mutilated in London in April 1888, was not widely reported.

Paul Feldman unearthed a copy of the *Manchester Evening Mail* of February 6th 1888 in which the 'Singular Disappearance of a Woman' was reported. The woman – Mary Ann Crawshaw – was a grieving widow who had abandoned her two children and the new home she was trying to furnish in James Street, Blackley, and who had not been seen for two weeks.

The timing was right for the Diary murder and so I felt justified in looking deeper. Sadly the street directories found her two years later, safe and apparently well, still in James Street. Unless she had been attacked and lived to tell the tale, she was not our murder victim.

In the Manchester attack the Diarist is acting entirely as could be expected of a potential serial killer. But if the Diary has been forged, its author is laying banana skins in his path by daring to weave fact and fiction together into the story.

From the beginning Maybrick is compelled to record his thoughts and deeds on paper. David Forshaw says his language is that of a man playing games, perversely giving himself confidence by pretending to be less clever than he is. There is a morbid delight in distorting grammar, in solecisms and in word play.

> It is not uncommon for intelligent, but insecure people to adopt a less educated personality on paper. There are many errors of spelling, grammar and punctuation which appear to play no part in the Diary's verbal games. While these may well be part of the less educated persona Maybrick adopted, they could result from genuinely modest schooling, for Maybrick was a self-made man with no pretensions to learning.

The entire undertaking was dangerous, of course, which is probably why it was easier for Maybrick to write in the security of his office, away from the prying eyes of his family and servants. After several entries he speaks of 'returning', presumably to Battlecrease House, and there is nothing to contradict the idea that the whole Diary was written in Knowsley Buildings. Even here he would have needed to exercise extreme caution to protect his secret from his book-keeper, George Smith, or his young clerk, Thomas Lowry.

> *If Smith should find this then I am done before my campaign begins... I am beginning to believe it is unwise to continue writing. If I am to down a whore then nothing shall lead the persuers [sic] back to me and yet there are times when I feel an overwhelming compulsion to place my thoughts to paper.... However, the pleasure of writing off all that lays ahead of me... thrills me so. And oh what deeds I shall comit. For how could one suspect that I could be capable of such things, for am I not, as all believe, a mild man, who, it has been said would never hurt a fly.*

Thomas Lowry, the 19-year-old clerk, son of a Liverpool clog maker had, in 1888, been with Maybrick and Co for five years. He played no part in his employer's personal life, at least on the face of it.

His appearance as a witness for the prosecution at Florie's trial was short and contained no clues as to his relationship with Maybrick. So, once again, the Diary enters into the dangerous realm of fiction, describing apparently historic events which any good researcher might later debunk with facts. Mrs Hammersmith is another example. The mystery of Mrs Ham(m)ersmith is one of the oddest but, I suspect, most important pointers to the Diary's authenticity.

The Diary says: 'I encountered Mrs Hamersmith in The Drive ... Mrs Hammersmith [sic] is a bitch ...'

The Drive is a pleasant sweeping thoroughfare near Battlecrease House, where people and dogs still take exercise. I found Mrs Ham(m)ersmith first in the 1881 Census. There she is listed as M.A Hamersmith, 17-year-old wife of Benjamin Hamersmith, a labourer. They are living with her parents, John (coal miner) Mousdell [sic] and

Catherine, all of 21 Peter Street, Prescot. Prescot is about 11 miles from Liverpool. We then checked the marriage registers and sure enough, there she was in 1880.

But we had a problem! Margaret Ann Mousedale [sic] was married on November 28th 1880 in Sutton Parish Church, Prescot to Benjamin Hamilton, a painter, and not to a Ham(m)ersmith at all. Even by the inaccurate standards of Victorian form-filling it is bizarre that a clerk should mistake the name of Hamilton for Hammersmith.

More importantly, why did the Diary writer select that most unusual name for his cast of characters? There were, as far as I can tell *no* other Ham(m)ersmiths living in England in 1881.

In 1882 Robert Louis Stevenson wrote a series of short stories *The New Arabian Nights*. Among these was the strange tale of 'The Suicide Club'. This concerned a mysterious superman nicknamed Prince Florizel. He does not suffer from normal pain or problems. and was modelled on the Prince of Wales who was accustomed to wandering the East End in disguise. His friend is Major Hammersmith. The Club, described as 'Death's private door', is a place where would-be suicide cases meet to discuss their lives and death.

I turned again to more practical research and looked for the birth of baby Hamiltons in the years up to 1889. There were several Hamilton births in Prescot, the last being in 1887.

Did the family move then from Prescot to Liverpool and, if so, could they have lived in the Aigburth area?

If this document is not the work of Maybrick, then its author is again writing with the imagination of a novelist. There is a dramatic episode with Lowry which similarly cannot be sourced in any newspaper or book. It is powerful and leaves us longing to know more. Its very simplicity is convincing. A forger would have been tempted to embellish.

> *If I could have killed the bastard Lowry with my bare hands there and then I would have done so. How dare he question me on any matter, it is I that should question him. Damn him damn him*

damn him. Should I replace the missing items? No that would be too much of a risk. Should I destroy this? My God I will kill him. Give him no reason and order him poste haste [sic] to drop the matter, that I believe is the only course of action I can take. I will force myself to think of something more pleasant.

Whatever the interfering young Lowry had said or done had placed him in more danger than he realised. He seems to have known far more than was good for him. But exactly what did he know? Whatever the 'missing items' were and whatever the 'matter' was, Lowry's appearance is completely convincing. For a second the office door to Maybrick and Co is ajar and we catch a fleeting glimpse of a dark corner of Maybrick's personality; one which the scandal-hungry press never reported. It is the same James Maybrick that Florence Aunspaugh saw threatening Nurse Yapp but did not reveal until she was an old lady.

* * *

There was a regular train service from Liverpool to London Euston and Willesden Junction, and the journey took about five hours. When there James sometimes went to fashionable Regent's Park where he stayed with his brother. Michael's neighbours in Wellington Mansions included an editor, an artist, a fine-art publisher, three comedians and Arthur Wing Pinero, the dramatist.

Maybrick was not relaxed in the company of his arrogant, self-satisfied younger brother, but the Regent's Park chambers were comfortable and convenient and provided a base for visiting Michael's friend, Dr Charles Fuller, in the endless quest for medicaments.

I will visit Michael this coming June. June is such a pleasant month, the flowers are in full bud, the air is sweeter and life is almost certainly much rosier. I look forward to its coming with pleasure. A great deal of pleasure.

June, to which he looked forward so much, started disappointingly unsettled and wet that year, but by the end of the month a heatwave brought water rationing to Liverpool. Commerce was fair – 'steady but idle' was how the newspapers put it.

According to the Diary, James went to see Michael with the idea of starting his 'campaign' but something went wrong. He was not ready; he had not laid his plans carefully enough although the urge to strike was becoming almost too much for him to control. Indeed he was forced to resort to using Michael as his jailer.

> *How I succeeded in controlling myself I do not know. I have not allowed for the red stuff, gallons of it in my estimation. Some of it is bound to spill onto me. I cannot allow my clothes to be be blood drenched, this I could not explain to anyone, least of all Michael. Why did I not think of this before? I curse myself. The struggle to stop myself was overwhelming and if I had not asked Michael to lock me in my bedroom for fear of sleepwalking, to which I had said I had been prone to do recently, was that not clever? I would have done my dirty deeds that very night.*

On a second visit to Michael the echoes of *Jekyll and Hyde* are unmistakable: 'I cursed my own stupidity, had I not informed Michael that I no longer sleep-walked I was forced to stop myself from indulging my pleasure by taking the largest dose I have ever done. The pain burnt into my mind. I vaguely recall putting my handkerchief into my mouth to stop my cries. I believe I vomited several times. The pain was intolerable, as I think, I shudder. No more.'

Is this the writing of a man who had read his medical journals or a man speaking through experience?

How Michael was able to testify later that he never saw James take drugs or knew of his habit is breathtaking. For reasons best known to himself he must have been hiding what he knew to be the truth.

We know from the medical evidence at Florie's trial that her husband was in an increasing state of panic about his health that June and this is clear too from the Diary. His usual hypochondria fuelled a craving for medical attention and a downward spiral of drug abuse. Between June and September he paid about 20 visits to Dr Arthur Hopper of Rodney Street, the family physician. He complained of violent headaches that had begun in June, around the time of the Royal Ascot race meeting, along with the numbness in his feet and legs.

Had the advantages of modern science been available to Dr Hopper, he would have realised that his patient's health was in a dangerous condition. But the doctor was sceptical and unsympathetic about Maybrick's hypochondria, as well as irritated that his patient was dosing himself between visits with remedies recommended by friends. One of these, Fellows' Syrup, was a brew containing arsenic, strychnine, quinine, iron and hypophosphites. Maybrick also doubled the dose of Dr Hopper's prescriptions when he felt they were having no effect. The doctor warned him that he would 'do himself a great injury'.

Strychnine pills were formerly sold widely for a variety of medical purposes, especially as a tonic or an aphrodisiac. Their long term effects have never been studied, according to doctors at the Poisons Unit at Guy's Hospital, London. Pills containing strychnine are no longer marketed and are considered ineffective and dangerous. However, the substance is sometimes used to 'cut', or increase the volume of, street drugs such as amphetamines. Its presence in the body can result in excessive neuron activity although, under strict medical supervision, it has a participatory role in the treatment of impotence, among other complaints.

James Maybrick used strychnine pills recklessly, like sweets. Once Maybrick gave Dr Hopper some prescriptions written for him by Dr Seguin in New York, a city he had often passed through on business. They were for strychnine and *nux vomica*, a strychnine-based medicine popular with Victorians that was also used as an aphrodisiac.

Dr Hopper destroyed them. 'I thought he was seriously hipped', he said at Florie's trial, explaining that this meant Maybrick 'attached too much importance to trifling symptoms.'

At Easter there was a family holiday at the Hand Hotel, in Wales and in July, at the doctor's suggestion, Maybrick went off to take the waters at Harrogate Spa, Yorkshire. He booked into the Queen Hotel, a modest establishment, and his name was duly recorded in the Visitors' Register, a regular feature in the *Harrogate Advertiser*. He stayed there, alone, for four days.

Goodwood Races at the beginning of August were a social must for the Maybricks. They journeyed together down to the gloriously situated racecourse in Sussex, where they met John Baillie Knight, Florie's childhood friend, and his Aunts Margaret and Harriet Baillie, who were friends of the Baroness. Afterwards they all dined together at the Italian Exhibition in Kensington, London.

The Misses Baillie, who owned property and industrial premises in London, had first become acquainted with the Baroness and her daughter at a small hotel in Switzerland. Florie had stayed with them several times as a girl and they visited Liverpool after her marriage. They later told their nephew that they had noticed all was not well between the Maybricks. John and Florie did not meet again until 1889, but she wrote to him several times and confided her unhappiness at her husband's infidelities.

Such domestic details are hardly described in the Diary which focuses on the relentless progress of his campaign of terror. Thoughts of murder and little else obsessed him and drove him to use it as a confessional.

* * *

On August 6th – Bank Holiday Monday – at the same time as Maybrick was in the South with Florie, a prostitute, Martha Tabram, was murdered in Whitechapel, London. She had been out drinking and looking for men in the evening. At 4.50 the next morning she was found in a pool of blood on the first floor landing of George Yard Building. She had suffered 39 stab wounds, mainly to her breasts, stomach and genitals.

Many Ripperologists believe that Martha was killed by an unidentified soldier – the Guards private who was her last client. But the press and police decided that she and Emma Smith, who had been murdered on Easter Monday, were victims of the same man. When the terror began in earnest that autumn, they linked Martha Tabram and Emma Smith with the Whitechapel killings of Jack the Ripper. At the time, the public believed they were all committed by the same maniac.

Some time during August, several weeks after his last stay with Michael, Maybrick went down to London again. But this time the Diary says that he rented a room in Whitechapel.

8

Tomorrow I will Purchase the Finest Knife Money Can Buy, Nothing Shall be Too Good for My Whores

I have taken a small room in Middlesex Street, that in itself is a joke. I have paid well and I believe no questions will be asked. It is indeed an ideal location. I have walked the streets and have become more than familiar with them ...I have no doubts, my confidence is most high. I am thrilled writing this, life is sweet, and my disappointment has vanished. Next time for sure.

Middlesex Street is today better known as Petticoat Lane, site of the London street market. Cullum Street, where the offices of Gustavus Witt were based, is just a short walk from the Whitechapel end of Middlesex Street. The Diary's suggestion that Middlesex Street was the location could explain the Ripper's ability to move freely around the neighbourhood, an easy place in which a stranger could have gone to ground.

Nearby, according to the street directory of 1888, lived Mrs Polly Nathan, who ran the fish and chip shop; Solran Berlinski, a rag merchant; George Bolam, cowkeeper; Isaac Woolf, a dealer in playing cards, and Samuel Barnett who ran the coffee rooms.

Why Middlesex Street was a joke we can only guess. Perhaps Maybrick liked its titillating name. Or perhaps it was because Middlesex Street was the commercial centre for London's Jewish community and therefore the focus of anti-Semitic unrest. Maybrick had already made it clear in the Diary that he was no friend of the Jews.

> *Why not let the Jews suffer? I have never taken to them, far too many of them on the Exchange for my liking.*

Towards the end of his life, however, he seems to have felt remorse over this prejudice. After meeting a former colleague on the Exchange floor, he wrote:

> *I felt regret for was he not Jewish. I had forgotten how many Jewish friends I have. My revenge is on whores not Jews.*

There are a number of genuine reasons why Middlesex Street was a good choice as a hideout. It was reasonably close to the office of Gustavus Witt but, more importantly, the boundary between the rival Metropolitan Police and the City Police lay down the centre of Middlesex Street. It would not have been too difficult to profit from a conflict of interests and tease the police by border-hopping from side to side.

Before the 19th century, Whitechapel was an area of respectable merchants and quiet prosperity. But by 1888 the area had declined. The dingy back yards and stinking, rubbish-littered alleys surrounding Middlesex Street were over-populated and violent. There were hundreds of lodging houses where, for threepence a night, a bed could be bought in a fetid, unheated room. Those with no money slept in gutters or in stairwells. Families squeezed, seven to a tiny room, with one bed and broken, rag-plugged windows. There was a choking stench of urine, mildew and rotting fruit, vegetables and fish. There were innumerable 'unfortunates' working the area. Like so many Victorian working class women, they were mostly old before their time, worn out by inhuman conditions, poverty, beatings and drink.

On August 18th, less than two weeks before the first attack in Whitechapel, Maybrick's brother Edwin left for America, aboard the *SS Adriatic*. Dr Forshaw believes this is significant. Emotionally, the absence of the devoted younger brother would have left James free from restraint. Effectively, there was no one looking over his shoulder when he said that he was off to London on business. And so the scene was set.

At 12.30 a.m. on Friday August 31st, Mary Ann Nichols, known as Polly, left the Frying Pan public house in Brick Lane, Whitechapel, and walked into history. Polly Nichols had been refused lodgings at 18 Thrawl Street but, undeterred, was overheard saying: 'I'll soon get my doss [rent] money.' She went off, wearing a 'jolly new bonnet', to earn her bed for the night. She looked young for a woman in her early forties and Dr Rees Ralph Llewellyn, who eventually examined her body, commented on the 'surprising cleanliness of her thighs'. But she was an alcoholic, and drink and lodgings had to be paid for.

Polly Nichols was seen by at least three people, wandering the murky streets, looking for a customer in need of a 'fourpenny knee trembler'. The clock on the parish church of St Mary Matfellon struck 2.30 a.m. as she staggered off along Whitechapel Road. There she must have met her killer. By 3.40 that morning she was dead.

They would have walked away from the main road into Buck's Row, a cobbled street which was, according to the *Evening News* 'not overburdened with gas lamps.' A terrace of new workers' cottages ran along one side. On the other were tall warehouses.

The Diary is consistent with medical reports of what happened next.

> *I have shown all that I mean business, the pleasure was far better than I imagined. The whore was only too willing to do her business. I recall all and it thrills me. There was no scream when I cut. I was more than vexed when the head would not come off. I*

> *believe I will need more strength next time. I struck deep into her. I regret I never had the cane, it would have been a delight to have rammed it hard into her. The bitch opened like a ripe peach. I have decided next time I will rip all out. My medicine will give me strength and the thought of the whore and her whoring master will spur me on no end.*

Maybrick's fantasy and obsession with decapitation is a recurring theme in his accounts of the murders, and inquest records show that there were indeed deep cuts around the neck of each victim.

Afterwards he walked silently away. None of the residents or night watchmen had heard a thing.

Charles Cross, a carter, was on his way to work down Buck's Row when he saw what he thought was a useful tarpaulin bundled against the gates to some stables. It was Polly Nichols. Because she was dead before her throat was cut, there had been no mess – only a wine glassful of blood in the gutter. The body was still warm, with Polly's prized black velvet-lined bonnet lying nearby.

Dr Llewellyn was summoned from his surgery in the Whitechapel Road to make an examination and pronounced her dead. A few hours later, two mortuary attendants were told to clean the body and only then was it discovered she had been mutilated. Dr Llewellyn was called again to make a further examination. He reported a jagged wound running for two or three inches on the left side of the abdomen. It was very deep and tissues had been cut through. There were several other incisions across the abdomen and three or four cuts running down the right side, all of which had been caused by a knife.

From this report arose the original belief that the killer stood in front of his victim, steadied her jaw with his right hand and cut her throat from left to right holding the knife in his left hand. By contrast, the authors of The *Jack the Ripper A-Z* suggest that he:

> Stood in front of his victim in a normal position for standing intercourse; that he seized them round the throat with both

> hands, thus instantly silencing them and rapidly inducing unconsciousness; that he pushed them to the ground with their heads to his left, and cut their throats dragging the knife towards him. The initial arterial blood flow would thus be away from him and he would avoid heavy bloodstaining. Also, this suggests he was right-handed.

The inquest, which began on September 1st and was re-convened on the 3rd, 17th and 23rd took place in the packed Whitechapel Working Lads Institute, next to the present Whitechapel Underground station. It was conducted by the stylish coroner Wynne Edwin Baxter, who turned up fresh from a Scandinavian tour, in black and white check trousers, white waistcoat and a crimson scarf.

The hunt was on.

On Saturday, September 1st the *Liverpool Echo* reported under the heading 'Who is Jim?':

> There is another point of some importance on which the police rely. It is the statement of John Morgan, a coffee stall keeper, who says that a woman whose description answers that given him of the victim, called at his stall, three minutes walk from Buck's Row early yesterday morning. She was accompanied by a man whom she addressed as 'Jim'.

The description of the man given by Mr Morgan does not fit Maybrick. All we can safely note is that a man named Jim *was* at the murder site within minutes of the murder.

* * *

The Diary suggests that at home in Liverpool Maybrick was eagerly scanning the newspapers for reports of the killing. He was not disappointed.

> *The wait to read about my triumph seemed long, although it was not... They have all written well. The next time they will have a great deal more to write, of that fact I have no doubt... I will remain calm and show no interest in my deed, if anyone should mention it so, but I will laugh inside, oh how I will laugh.*

A reporter for the *Star* in London, probably either Lincoln Springfield or Harry Dam, combed the local pubs and doss houses seeking descriptions of the killer. He claimed to have interviewed about 50 women in three hours, each of whom had given identical details of a man the locals called 'Leather Apron'. This claim may well have been true if, as is likely, the reporter plied the women with beer first and then asked them to rubber stamp his own suspicions.

So 'Leather Apron' made his first appearance – in the *Star*.

He was described as about 40 years old, short and Semitic looking, with an exceptionally thick neck and a black moustache. His movements were 'silent and sinister', his eyes gleamed and he had a 'repulsive smile.'

In fact, the Polish Jew they called Leather Apron – a boot finisher, whose real name was John Pizer – was innocent, although he had been charged with a couple of minor assaults in the past. On the night of Polly Nichols' murder, he was in Seven Sisters Road, Holloway, watching a glow in the sky from two huge fires at the docks and he was seen not only by a lodging-housekeeper but also by a policeman. So despite the eagerness of Sergeant William Thick to arrest him, he could not be linked with the murder and even received some small compensation for libel from the press. Even so, the certainty was that the murderer must be foreign and probably Jewish since no Englishman would sink to such depths. Sensationalism was a Victorian novelty, and the case provided ideal material for an unwholesome craving for the macabre, for vampires, monsters and real-life fat ladies and freaks such as Joseph Merrick, Whitechapel's very own Elephant Man. Readers were confronted with words never before printed in their newspapers and full frontal anatomical illustrations of shockingly mutilated bodies. The prurient Victorians lapped up every appalling detail.

Even the American press revelled in the case, likening it to Edgar Allen Poe's story *The Murders in the Rue Morgue*. American newspapers wrote of a small man with wicked black eyes moving silently with a 'queer run'. One imaginative reporter for the *New York Times* described how Polly Nichols had run from the scene of her attack and was found several streets away, with her head almost severed.

This kind of coverage did nothing to help the police, who also came under fire. They were castigated for their failures and not until police files were opened in 1976 was it really possible to appreciate just how much energy and initiative had been channelled into the the biggest manhunt Britain had ever known. But the police had no experience upon which to draw, their methods were unsophisticated, even crude, and their policy of secrecy at the time only served to provoke the press into creative reporting. The task set by the Ripper was beyond them.

All the Whitechapel murders except one came within the jurisdiction of the Metropolitan Police Force. Founded in 1829 the department was responsible for all of London except the square mile of the City. The 'Met's' area was then organised in divisions, Whitechapel being H Division. The press compared the 'Met' unfavourably with the City police.

The 'Met' officials were answerable to the Home Office, whose civil servants had considerable power and it was they who made many of the decisions for which the public blamed the police. For example, the bureaucrats forbade the offer of a government reward for anyone providing information that led to an arrest. The Home Secretary Henry Matthews was a witty man with a fine legal mind who, nevertheless, became unpopular over the Whitechapel affair. He managed to provoke the resignation of two Metropolitan Police Commissioners during his tenure. Less than a year later Matthews was to find himself facing challenging decisions over the alleged murder of James Maybrick.

One of the Police Commissioners was Sir Charles Warren. An

Evangelical Christian and former soldier, he ruled with military precision and was still being pilloried by the press for his heavy-handed treatment of a mass demonstration against unemployment the year before. The London newspaper, the *Star*, wrote on September 10th:

> To add to the list of clumsy follies, Sir Charles Warren whose name stinks in the nostrils of the people of London, has lately transferred the whole of the East End detectives to the West and transferred the West End team to the East.

This was an action which was to guarantee that the men on the ground had little or no knowledge of their new patches!

The capital was also in the thick of the first London County Council elections, in which the radicals sought control of the East End. The banner headlines referring to the Ripper's crimes threw light on the unemployment and disgraceful living conditions of London's underclass. The Ripper murders became a political hot potato: his terrible deeds were, in part, responsible for later social reforms as well as improvements in police procedure. So it was that the women murdered in Whitechapel became martyrs to a cause.

Inspector Frederick George Abberline (1843-1929) was the best-known name on the case, probably because he had a well-developed sense of his own importance. But because he knew the area and its villains so well, he was in charge of day-to-day investigations. It was Abberline whom Maybrick selected as the butt of his sarcasm:

> *Oh, Mr Abberline he is a clever little man*

Inspector Abberline remembered the seemingly endless sleepless nights after he had come off duty, trawling the streets of Whitechapel only to be called, exhausted, from his bed in the early hours of the morning to examine yet more evidence. Every statement had to be read, every witness – and there were hundreds – to be interviewed. He and his team alone made out 1,600 sets of papers about their investigations.

It was a coincidence, of course, that Robert Louis Stevenson's *Dr Jekyll and Mr Hyde* was thrilling London audiences at the time. Although the play was not about sexual repression, it was nearer the truth than anyone then imagined. It tells of the elderly, respectable Dr Jekyll, who discovered a potion which freed the hidden side of his personality – 'comparative youth, the light step, the leaping pulse, and secret pleasures' – but which also awakened in him the 'spirit of Hell' and sent him forth to kill in the streets of London.

The American press went wild. 'London is thrown into a ferment of terror,' screamed the *Virginian*. 'The word "Whitechapel" has passed as a verb into the vocabulary of the criminal classes ... No less than a dozen women of the street have complained of an assailant in the police courts this week that threatened to "Whitechapel" them ... the word has assumed a horrible significance.'

The *New York World* of September 11th also ran an article headed 'A Study for Morbologists' once again reminding readers of the similarities with the Austin crimes in 1884-5. 'A real Hyde seems to be glutting his thirst for horrors,' it wrote.

'The Austin crimes,' continues the report, 'were mostly done in the same way by some hideous night-fiend ... The same demonaic cunning in covering up his tracks was developed here as in London ... The awful realism of the Hyde of Stevenson's marvellous story is not too real or too unnatural to fit such cases.'

Such a divided spirit was James Maybrick. Within a week of Polly Nichols' death, the Diary finds him plotting his next murder.

9

I Look Forward to Tomorrow Night's Work, it Will do me Good, a Great Deal of Good

Maybrick was now apparently enjoying his notoriety. The Diary records him discussing the murder of Polly Nichols with his friend George (probably Davidson). The two apparently praised the excellent Liverpool police and agreed that events such as the Whitechapel killing would not happen there, in Liverpool, where women could safely walk the streets.

> *Indeed they can, for I will not play my funny little games on my own doorstep.* ha ha

Exhilarated, he immediately planned to repeat the thrill.

> *I will not allow too much time to pass before my next. Indeed I need to repeat my pleasure as soon as possible. The whoring Master can have her with pleasure and I shall have my pleasure with my thoughts and deeds. I will be clever. I will not call on Michael on my next visit. My brothers would be horrified if they knew, particularly Edwin after all did he not say I was*

> *one of the most gentlest of men he had ever encountered. I hope he is enjoying the fruits of America. Unlike I, for do I not have a sour fruit.*
>
> *The gentle man with gentle thoughts will strike again soon. I have never felt better, in fact, I am taking more than ever and I can feel the strength building up within me. The head will come off next time, also the whore's hands. Shall I leave them in various places about Whitechapel? Hunt the head and hands instead of hunt the thimble* ha ha. *Maybe I will take some part away with me to see if it does taste like fresh fried bacon.*

The next weekend he was off to London again. None of the passengers on the train that Friday September 7th 1888 would have suspected that they were travelling in the company of the most wanted man in Britain. Maybrick would have made the journey in the comfort of an upholstered maroon and gold carriage of the London and North Western Railway. In such luxury, the Diary tells us, he jotted down his first clumsy attempts at verse.

> *One dirty whore was looking for some gain*
> *Another dirty whore was looking for the same.*

After all the subsequent murders there are such doggerel verses packed with puzzling references of obvious significance to Maybrick himself. The rhymes become an obsession, with much scratching out and re-writing. They seem to be a rather pathetic attempt to establish some kind of superiority over Michael, the younger brother. Deep-rooted jealousy underlies the Diary.

> *... if Michael can succeed in rhyming verse then I can do better, a great deal better he shall not outdo me. Think you fool, think. I curse Michael for being so clever. I shall outdo him, I will see to that. A funny little rhyme <u>shall</u> come forth.*

James Maybrick's sense of inferiority and the desperate compulsion to write about his deeds are all part of an attempt to prove intellectual and physical prowess. The word 'clever' appears no fewer than 25 times in the Diary. 'Sir Jim' seems to be his favourite nickname. In fact Florence Aunspaugh remembered Nurse Yapp referring somewhat impudently to her master as 'Sir Jim'.

* * *

The Ripper's second Whitechapel victim was Annie Chapman. The daughter of a lifeguardsman, she had abandoned her husband and her two children to live by selling flowers and, occasionally, herself.

At the time of her death she was already terminally ill with a disease of the lungs and brain, but was forced to continue earning a bed for the night. She was short and stout but well proportioned and friends described her as a steady woman who drank only on Saturday nights.

At about 5.30 a.m. on September 8th, Albert Cadosh, a carpenter, heard someone talking in the yard behind 29 Hanbury Street. He thought he heard a voice say 'no' and then a thud against the fence. But he took no notice and walked off down Hanbury Street. There was not a soul about. This was just a few hundred yards from Dorset Street, where Annie was then living in Crossingham's Lodging House. Mrs Amelia Richardson, a packing case maker; Mrs Hardyman, a cats' meat woman; Mr Walker and his simple-minded son, car man Thompson and Mr and Mrs Copsey, who were cigar makers; and the elderly John Davis, his wife and their three sons – all slept undisturbed a few feet away.

When John Davis woke up at 5.45 a.m. he went down into the yard and was horrified to see the mangled, bloody corpse of Annie Chapman. 'What was lying beside her I can't describe,' he said, 'it was part of her body.'

It did not take long for an excited crowd to gather. What they all later remembered was the grotesque spectacle of Annie's striped woollen stockings protruding from beneath her dishevelled skirt. It was a tale to terrify friends and relations.

The murdered woman was covered with a sack and removed to the mortuary, leaving behind all her worldly goods arranged in a strangely formal manner. It seems generally agreed by most Ripper authors that there was a piece of coarse muslin, a small tooth comb and a pocket comb. There was also a scrap of envelope enclosing two pills.

But were there any farthings? These items have become the focus of much attention and have also played their part in the debate about the authenticity of the Diary which offers its own but quite logical version of events.

THE ENVELOPE

At about 1.45 a.m. on September 8th, Timothy Donovan, manager of Crossingham's Lodging House, had let Annie Chapman into the kitchen. William Stevens, a printer, told the police a week later that Annie had been to the hospital that day and he saw her in Crossingham's on the day of her death. She had taken a box containing two pills from her pocket and when the box broke she wrapped them in a torn envelope which, he alleged, she had found on the floor.

According to the authors of *The A-Z of Jack the Ripper*, the envelope bore the crest of The Sussex Regiment, the post office stamp 'London, August 28th 1888' and a letter *M* in a man's handwriting. Philip Sugden, in *The Complete History of Jack the Ripper,* says that the initials on the envelope were, indeed, an *M* but there was also *Sp*. This has been assumed to be part of the address of Spitalfields.

It was only when Paul Feldman obtained the private collection of papers belonging to the late Stephen Knight, author of *Jack the Ripper, The Final Solution*, that he found a document, transcribed by Knight from the original and written by Inspector Chandler. It followed his visit to the depot of the 1st Battalion of The Sussex Regiment at North Camp, Farnborough, on September 14th to check on the origins of the envelope. This said, 'enquiries were made amongst the men but none could be found who corresponded with anyone living in Spitalfields or with any persons whose address commencing [sic] "J". The pay books were examined and no signature resembled the initials on the envelope.'

But in Inspector Chandler's original report at Scotland Yard a figure *2* is written in exactly the same way as the supposed *J* in Stephen Knight's copy. The Inspector's report speaks unequivocally of 'letters' in the plural and makes no mention of numbers. But the envelope has consequently been dismissed as insignificant ... except by the Diary.

**letter M it's true*
Along with M ha ha
Will catch clever Jim

THE RINGS

Controversy also surrounds the brass rings that Annie had, according to friends, been wearing.

Inspector Abberline noted: 'The deceased was in the habit of wearing two brass rings (a wedding and a keeper); these were missing when the body was found and the fingers bore the marks of their having been removed by force.' At the time the press referred to two and three rings.

Again the Diary explains the possible motivation behind these actions. Maybrick, it claims, removed the rings because they reminded him of his wife, to whom he refers time and again in the Diary as 'the whore'.

Begin with the rings,
one ring, two rings
bitch, it took me a while before I could wrench them off.
Should have stuffed them down the whore's throat. I wish to
God I could have taken the head. Hated her for wearing them,
reminds me too much of the whore.

One ring, two rings
A farthing one and two...

*Here and throughout the book an asterisk indicates that a line in the Diary has been crossed out.

This story was changed in the telling and became a 'pile of rings and coins'. Later this was embellished by various authors and the coins became 'two new farthings'.

A journalist, Oswald Allen, wrote in the *Pall Mall Gazette* in 1888: 'A curious feature of this crime is that the murderer had pulled off some brass rings, with some trumpery articles which had been taken from her pockets and were placed carefully at her feet.' These facts were later confirmed by Inspector Edmund John James Reid who was head of CID in Whitechapel in 1888. At the inquest into Alice McKenzie, murdered in 1889, he said that he had 'held a watching brief as coins found under her body were similar to those in Annie Chapman's case.'

So what of the farthings?

THE FARTHINGS

The farthings were also reported in the press immediately after the murder but not at Annie Chapman's inquest. Martin Fido wrote to me, 'it is my speculation that the initial silence on these coins was police strategy to try to hold back information that would only be known to a guilty suspect.'

The A-Z of Jack the Ripper authors say that there 'were almost certainly two farthings...' On the other hand, Philip Sugden does not mention the farthings at all.

Newspaper reports of the pills found by Annie's body seem to have amused Maybrick, perhaps because of his own hypochondria.

> *The pills are the answer*
> *end with pills. Indeed do I always not oh what a joke... Am I not indeed a clever fellow? It makes me laugh they will never understand why I did so.*

A distinctive aspect of the second killing was the actual 'ripping' of the victim's body and the removal of her uterus. Dr George Bagster Phillips, a police surgeon who conducted or attended post-mortems on four of the women, believed the murderer must have been a doctor. Since then the medical prowess of the killer has been hotly disputed.

But most doctors agree now that although the lower end of Annie Chapman's uterus and cervix had been detached with a single, clean slash through the vaginal canal the rest of the operation was extremely inept. I wondered about the educational role of Liverpool's Museum of Anatomy!

The coroner, Wynne Baxter, put forward an ingenious theory prompted by a press report, that an American doctor had been visiting London hospitals with a plan to export preserved uteri for which he was prepared to pay a high price. Such a macabre trade could, the coroner argued, suggest a motive for the crime. But the medical press refuted this idea promptly. On October 1st the curator of the Pathological Museum gave the market price for whole and partial corpses:

For one corpse complete £3.5s.0d
For one thorax 5s.0d
For one arm, one leg, one head and
neck and abdomen net 15s.0d

It is therefore nonsense, the curator said, that large sums were being offered for complete bodies. His message was clear. There was not enough profit in such a trade to offer a motive to the Whitechapel killer. The Diary provides a credible motive for the first time and one with which, tragically, we are today all too familiar. Jack the Ripper was a cannibal.

> *I took some of it away with me. It is in front of me. I intend to fry it and eat it later* ha ha. *The very thought works up my appetite.*

Few people have tasted human flesh and fewer still would ever admit it. Whether the uterus, bladder or vagina are edible is not common knowledge. These organs could well be difficult to swallow. But

Maybrick's apparent pleasure in the idea was to be supported during the trial of the Russian Ripper, Andre Chikatilo, in 1992. 'I like to nibble on a uterus,' he testified. 'They are so pink and springy, but after nibbling them I throw them away.'

After Annie Chapman's death, 16 East End businessmen formed themselves into the Whitechapel Vigilance Committee. Under the presidency of builder George Lusk, they demanded brighter street lights and better policing of the area. On September 14th a telling letter signed JFS was printed in the *Pall Mall Gazette*:

> Yesterday at 11 a.m. a gentleman was seized and robbed of everything in Hanbury Street. At 5 p.m. an old man of 70 was attacked and served in the same manner in Chicksand Street. At 10 p.m. today a man ran into a baker's shop at the corner of Hanbury Street and King Edward Street and ran off with the till and its contents. All these occurred within 100 yards of each other and midway between the scenes of the last two horrible murders.
>
> If all this can happen now, when there is supposed to be a double police patrol in the area and where plain clothes policemen are said, literally, to jostle one another in the streets, the ease with which the murderer conducted his dissection and made his escape ceases to be at all wonderful.

Soon afterwards the *Times* suggested yet another theory: that the killer might not, after all, be a member of the working class and was lodging somewhere quite respectable in the area. The Diary tells them exactly where – Middlesex Street.

The Diary also accurately reflects with wry humour on another popular feeling, no doubt based more on bigotry than evidence, that only a foreigner could commit such crimes. In Whitechapel, foreign meant Jewish and so the police were, with reason, anxious about a growing anti-Semitism.

> *I have read all of my deeds they have done me proud. I had to laugh, they have me down as left-handed, a Doctor, a slaughterman and a Jew. Very well, if they are to insist that I am a Jew then a Jew I shall be. Why not let the Jews suffer? I have never taken to them.*

On September 22nd, the magazine *Punch* published a cartoon by Tenniel (illustrator of *Alice in Wonderland*) that amused the Diarist, with his love of word games. It showed a policeman, blindfolded and confused by four villains.

The caption: 'BLIND-MAN'S BUFF. Turn round three times and catch whom you may!'

> *I could not stop laughing when I read Punch there for all to see was the first three letters of my surname. They are blind as they say. I cannot stop laughing it amuses me so shall I write them a clue...*
>
> *May comes and goes*
> *In the dark of the night*
> *he kisses the whores*
> *then gives them a fright*
> *The Jews and the Doctors*
> *will get all the blame*
> *but its only May playing his dirty game.*

If the Diary was indeed written by Maybrick this is an intriguing entry; *Punch* would have been quite appropriate reading for a Victorian merchant.

The same rhyme contains another clue. In 1889 Florie had sent a telegram to Brierley which has never appeared in print. On May 8th she wrote: 'Recalled owing to May's critical state.' May was another nickname in family use which we found, not in a book, not in the press, not in the trial reports but hidden among the Maybrick papers at Kew!

The idea was already growing in Maybrick's mind that he could use the current anti-Semitic mood as a diversionary tactic to throw the police off the scent when he committed his next murder. Then, as so often happens in the Diary, he suddenly switches mood.

> *I am fighting a battle within me. My disire [*sic*] for revenge is overwhelming. The whore has destroyed my life. I try whenever possible to keep all sense of respectability... I miss the thrill of cutting them up. I do believe I have lost my mind.*

It is at this point that Inspector Abberline is first mentioned in the Diary.

> *Abberline says, he was never amazed*
> *I did my work with such honour*

For Maybrick, as for many people, Abberline represented the force of law. Throughout the Diary he refers to the police as 'headless chickens'. He is revelling in their fruitless attempts to find him but as the story progresses Abberline becomes the bogeyman, the hangman, haunting Maybrick's nightmares.

> *I see thousands of people chasing me, with Abberline in front dangling a rope.*

It is at these moments of heightened emotions released from inner chaos that the Diary becomes most believable. The mood swings become ever more uncontrolled – a familiar side effect of drug-taking. One moment he speaks of 'cutting' and the next he is by his parents' grave.

> *I miss Edwin. I have received but one letter from him since his arrival in the whores country. The bitch is vexing me more as each day passes. If I could I would have it over and done with. I visited my mother and father's grave. I long to be reunited with them. I*

believe they know the torture the whore is putting me through.

Apart from this moment in the Diary we have found only one other obscure written reference, buried deep in the gargantuan reports of Florie's trial, to the fact that James' mother and father are dead and buried together in Anfield Cemetery Liverpool.

Equally, the effect of drugs is beginning to concern him – he is afraid for his beloved children.

> *I am beginning to think less of the children, part of me hates me for doing so.*

But for Florie there is no compassion. He allowed her every opportunity to meet her 'whoremaster' and paradoxically revelled in thoughts of what they might be doing.

> *The whore seen her master today it did not bother me. I imagined I was with them, the very thought thrills me. I wonder if the whore has ever had such thoughts?*

That September Maybrick took out the first and larger of two insurance policies with the Mutual Reserve Fund Life Association of New York. Presumably he had fooled the company, since friends noticed a dramatic deterioration in his physique about this time. He was ageing rapidly, and John Aunspaugh even doubted that he would see out the year. Maybrick's terror of illness and death was becoming a reality.

10

To my Astonishment, I Cannot Believe I Have Not Been Caught

The night of Saturday September 29th 1888 was miserably wet. At about 11 p.m., 44-year-old, Swedish-born Elizabeth Stride, known as Long Liz, was seeking shelter from the rain outside the Bricklayers' Arms in Settles Street. She was seen by John Gardner and his friend Best, both labourers, being fondled by a respectably dressed man in a black morning suit and overcoat. A little later old Matthew Packer claimed that a man accompanying a woman who could have been Elizabeth Stride had bought some black grapes from his shop in Berner Street. Matthew Packer was just one of many unreliable witnesses whose story and description of the couple he had supposedly seen changed every time he gave new statements to the police. Even so, the story of the grapes – and the 'blood-stained' stalk found in the yard by Liz Stride's body – was widely circulated and publicised. The Diary does not mention the grapes.

The International Workingmen's Educational Club at 40 Berner Street was a socialist club largely patronised by immigrant anarchists and intellectuals. That Saturday night about 150 people had gathered on the first floor to hear a discussion, led by Morris Eagle, on 'The necessity for Socialism among Jews'. By 11.30 p.m. only a few people remained behind, and the sound of Russian folk music could be heard on the night air.

The police interviewed a number of so-called witnesses of varying reliability. One, William Marshall, who later identified Liz Stride's body, said that at about 11.45 p.m. he had seen her talking to a man in Berner Street. The man kissed the woman and Marshall overheard him say 'you would say anything but your prayers' – they then walked on towards Dutfield's Yard.

At the inquest on October 5th he described the man he had seen as about 5'6", middle-aged, rather stout, of clerkly appearance and decently dressed, wearing a round peaked cap. Marshall said that he appeared to be not a manual worker and had a mild voice with an English accent.

Constable William Smith also thought he had seen Elizabeth Stride at about 12.30 a.m. while on his beat. She was, he said, with a well-dressed man, who was wearing a black coat, hard felt hat and white collar and tie. He also noticed a flower pinned to her jacket.

After Mrs Fanny Mortimer of 36 Berner Street heard the 'heavy stamp' of Constable Smith passing outside, she went to her front door and stood there listening to the music from the club, which was three houses away.

Beside the club building, through a wicket door between a pair of wooden gateposts, was a dark passage leading to an unlit yard used by van and cart builder Arthur Dutfield. Mrs Mortimer said that during the time she was at the door she saw no one enter or leave the yard.

She did see a man carrying a black bag walk down the street but he was identified and belonged to the club. Nevertheless the image of 'the black bag' became forever linked to the legend of Jack the Ripper.

At 12.45 a.m. Israel Schwartz, a Hungarian immigrant, walked past the gateway of Dutfield's Yard. He gave a statement to the police on

Sunday, September 30th at Leman Street police station, recorded on file by Chief Inspector Swanson. Schwartz claimed that turning the corner from Commercial Road he saw a man accost a woman. She was standing in the gateway to Dutfield's Yard and he tried to pull her into the street. She screamed three times but not very loudly. Schwartz crossed to the far side of the street and saw a second man lighting his pipe. The assailant shouted 'Lipski' apparently to the second man. Lipski was a Polish Jew who had been convicted of murder the year before and his name could well have been used as a term of abuse. Schwartz told the police that at this point he escaped, followed by the second man.

The attacker Schwartz described as about 5' 5", 30 years old, with a fair complexion, full face, dark hair and a small brown moustache. He was wearing a dark jacket and trousers and an old black peaked cap. The second man was a little older – about 35, about 5'11" with light brown hair, dark overcoat and an old black hard felt hat.

The *Star* newspaper tracked Schwartz down and printed a interview with him on October 1st. This time he did not refer to the screams. The article differed in several significant details from Inspector Swanson's report. In the *Star's* report, Elizabeth Stride was thrown on to the pavement, the second man is described as having red moustaches and carrying a knife, not a pipe. In this account, the cry of 'Lipski' was made by this second witness, not the attacker, as he rushed forward to defend Stride. At this point Schwartz fled.

Despite the rain and the darkness of the night, police took Schwartz's surprisingly detailed evidence seriously and it was judged that of all people he might indeed have been the only person to have seen Jack the Ripper. However, Inspector Abberline reported to the Home Office on November 1st that Schwartz, who spoke no English, had needed an interpreter to tell his story.

Schwartz was believed as a major witness but his utter confusion graphically demonstrates the risk in attaching blind importance to contemporary records. We cannot be sure what really happened.

The Diary account is subjective – not surprisingly. It does not record any of this detail but describes only the killer's emotional recollections of the killing. For instance, clutched in Elizabeth Stride's left hand was a packet of cachous, lozenges eaten to sweeten the breath. The detail that is so poignantly recalled is not the sweets themselves but the lingering smell on Liz Stride's breath. He writes:

I could still smell her sweet scented breath

The entry is distraught and distorted.

To my astonishment I cannot believe I have not been caught. My heart felt as if it had left my body. Within my fright I imagined my heart bounding along the street with I in desperation following it.

I would have dearly loved to have cut the head of the damned horse off and stuff it as far as it would go down the whores throat. I had no time to rip the bitch wide, I curse my bad luck. I believe the thrill of being caught thrilled me more than cutting the whore herself. As I write I find it impossible to believe he did not see me, in my estimation I was less than a few feet from him. The fool panicked, it is what saved me.

The 'fool' who interrupted the murder was Louis Diemschutz, a seller of cheap jewellery. He too described in the *Star* of October 1st how he had arrived in Dutfield's Yard at 1 a.m. with his pony and cart. Although it was too late to save Liz Stride's life, his appearance clearly stopped any further butchery.

As he drove into the yard the pony veered towards the left wall to avoid an obstruction in their path. Diemschutz leant down and prodded the sodden bundle with his whip. It was the body of Elizabeth Stride. And somewhere in the shadows was her murderer.

Within minutes, several police officers and bystanders gathered in the yard, which was still so dark that a match was needed to light the gruesome scene. Elizabeth Stride was lying on her back behind the gate. The killer was gone.

* * *

At the same time as the Ripper was escaping from Dutfield's Yard, Catharine Eddowes, the 46-year-old daughter of a Wolverhampton tin worker, was being released from Bishopsgate police station in the City of London. Kate Eddowes was a 'regular jolly sort'. Earlier in the day she had pawned a pair of boots to pay for a cup of tea, sugar and food. But by 8.30 p.m. she was drunk and in custody for causing a disturbance by pretending to be a fire engine. She left the police station at 1 a.m. when it was 'too late to get any more drink', said PC George Hutt.

'Good night, old cock,' she called and then turned left in the direction of Houndsditch. About thirty minutes later she must have been by the Duke's Place entrance to a covered alley called Church Passage, leading into Mitre Square.

Was it then that her path crossed with that of her killer? If he had left Berner Street, turned left into Commercial Road and left again along Whitechapel High Street in the direction of Middlesex Street, he could have continued into Aldgate and crossed the divide between the Metropolitan Police and the City Police.

In 1965, Tom Cullen retraced the killer's steps for his book *An Autumn of Terror*. He said: 'It took me exactly ten minutes (this was without taking advantage of the short cuts which may have been known to the killer).'

At about 1.35 a.m. Catharine Eddowes was seen talking to a man at Church Passage – he identified her later by her clothes. This witness was a Jewish cigarette salesman, Joseph Lawende. He had left The Imperial Club in Duke's Place, with Harry Harris and Joseph Hyam Levy at about 1.30 a.m. In a report in the *Times* on October 2nd, he described the man as about 30 years old, 5'7", with a fair moustache and a cloth cap. He said the man had his hand on Catharine Eddowes' chest but they did not appear to be arguing. He doubted that he would recognise him again but nevertheless he was protected from the press prior to the inquest on October 4th and 11th 1888.

At 1.45 a.m. Catharine Eddowes' crumpled body was found by Police Constable Edward Watkins. The City police surgeon Dr F. Gordon Brown arrived on the scene just after 2 a.m. Once again it seems the Ripper had lured his prey into a corner and this time his 'work' was uninterrupted. Catharine Eddowes was strangled first and then when dead, her body frenziedly slashed and torn apart. The left kidney and womb were removed, although Dr Brown said that these would serve no medical purpose. Dr Brown thought that the injuries showed signs of medical knowledge but not surgical skill.

For the first time the face, too, was mutilated and two puzzling inverted V-shaped incisions made in the cheeks. But in the light of the Diary this all makes sense – the cuts on the cheeks referred to merely as triangular flaps could, in fact, have formed the *M* that was Maybrick's 'mark'.

> *The thrill she gave me was unlike the others, I cut deep deep deep. Her nose annoyed me so I cut it off, had a go at her eyes, left my mark, could not get the bitches head off. I believe now it is impossible to do so. The whore never screamed. I took all I could away with me. I am saving it for a rainy day* ha ha.

The *M* is clearly visible in a sketch made at the time. It was discovered in the basement of London Hospital and eventually published for the first time in its magazine, the *London Hospital Gazette*, in 1966 illustrating an article by Professor Francis Camps.

The police list of Catharine Eddowes' clothes is a forlorn affair. They were old and dirty. A black cloth jacket trimmed with imitation fur, a black straw bonnet, a man's white vest, a man's lace-up boots, no drawers or stays but three very old skirts and a grey stuff petticoat, all marked her out as a vagrant.

Her possessions were numerous and assorted. The police list was not published in full until 1987 when two books by Martin Fido and Donald Rumbelow appeared. That list included, among other items:

1 tin box containing tea
1 tin box containing sugar
1 small tooth comb
1 red leather cigarette case with white metal fittings
1 piece of old white apron
1 mustard tin containing pawn tickets found beside the body
1 tin match box, empty.

That single unpublished item, '1 tin match box, empty', was crucial. It is there in the Diary: 'I showed no fright and indeed no light damn it, the tin box was empty.' In 1888 no one but the murderer could have known about the empty tin box. This, more than any other piece of evidence, confirms the belief that either the Diary is a post-1987 forgery, or it is genuine.

The *Times* reported on October 6th that one of the boxes in the published list contained some cotton. Could this have been the clue referred to in the Diary by Maybrick the cotton merchant?

did I not leave him a very good clue,
Nothing is mentioned, of this I am sure,
ask clever Abberline, could tell you more.

* * *

There has always been a strong division of opinion about what happened next. All that has been known for certain is that at 2.20 a.m. on the night of Catharine Eddowes' murder, PC Alfred Long passed down Goulston Street which runs north from Whitechapel High Street, parallel to Middlesex Street. He saw nothing remarkable. But on his return at 2.55 a.m. he did notice a crumpled rag lying at the foot of the stairway leading up to 108-119 Wentworth's Model Dwellings. This was a piece of Catharine Eddowes' blood-stained apron. The murderer had, without doubt, passed that way. The stairway itself was unlit but in the gloom PC Alfred Long, of the Metropolitan Police, saw some smudged graffiti on the wall which he had not noticed before. He copied it down but admitted later at the inquest that he might have misspelt the word 'Jews'.

His note read: 'The Juwes are the men That Will not be Blamed for nothing.'

This echoes the mis-spellings, solecisms and the curiously ill-educated turns of phrase in parts of the Diary.

The City police recorded the message differently as: 'The Juwes are not The men That Will be Blamed for nothing'.

The City CID instructed that the message be photographed immediately and then obliterated. After all, it was their murder. But when the Metropolitan Police Commissioner, Sir Charles Warren, arrived on the scene at 5 a.m. he agreed with Superintendent Thomas Arnold that the anti-Semitic message could cause trouble with the Jewish tenants in the building and he personally rubbed it out.

In a report to the Home Office of November 6th 1888, Sir Charles Warren enclosed a copy of the writing on the wall. The form and layout of the words had been exactly reproduced, so it is reasonable to assume it is a good copy but it is probably wishful thinking to hope that it is an accurate reproduction of the handwriting too since it is similar to the more controlled passages of the Diary!

Crime writers have devoted a great deal of energy to the task of solving the Goulston Street mystery. Most believe that it was indeed the work of the killer. It has been taken to prove that the writer was anti-Jewish, that he was Jewish, that the words have a mystical meaning, that they are a Masonic code. But if you remember those lines in the Diary, then it was all much simpler than that.

> *I had to laugh, they have me down as left handed, a Doctor, a slaughterman and a Jew. Very well, if they are to insist that I am a Jew then a Jew I shall be.*

And then, almost naively:

> *I wonder if they enjoyed my funny Jewish joke?*

These taunting games were to be but a prelude. For the very next day, Monday October 1st, was the day the world would first hear the name of Jack the Ripper.

11

Before I am Finished all England Will Know the Name I Have Given Myself

On October 1st 1888, the *Daily News* published the text of a letter in its first edition. This letter, written in red ink, was to become perhaps the most infamous letter in the history of crime. It was either the genius of a self-publicising killer, or, as many Ripper buffs believe, the work of a practical joker.

This 'Dear Boss' letter is important to us because the Diary's author admits adopting the name of Jack the Ripper. In fact the entries on this topic are particularly convincing because originally Maybrick did not want to call himself Jack the Ripper – he preferred to be known as 'Sir Jim', using this throughout the Diary. But new evidence, recently discovered, and detailed in Sue and Andy Parlour's book *Jack the Ripper: The Whitechapel Murders*, suggests that the 'trade name' of 'Jack the Ripper' may have already been circulating around the streets of Whitechapel. In other words it seems that Maybrick did not invent the name, he merely adopted it and publicised it.

> *All whores will feel the edge of Sir Jims shining knife. I regret I did not give myself that name, curse it, I prefer it much much more than the one I have given.*

Either way, had the letter not been signed 'Jack the Ripper', the Whitechapel murders might have been relegated in time to a place alongside the many equally horrific crimes catalogued in Scotland Yard's Black Museum or on show in Madame Tussaud's Chamber of Horrors. Not until that letter, addressed to the Central News Agency, dated September 25th, did the name of 'Jack the Ripper' ricochet around the world.

> Dear Boss,
> I keep on hearing the police have caught me but they won't fix me just yet. I have laughed when they look so clever and talk about being on the *right* track. That joke about Leather Apron gave me real fits. I am down on whores and I shant quit ripping them till I do get buckled. Grand work the last job was. I gave the lady no time to squeal. How can they catch me now. I love my work and want to start again. You will soon hear of me with my funny little games. I saved some of the proper *red* stuff in a ginger beer bottle over the last job to write with but it went thick like glue and I cant use it. Red ink is fit enough I hope *ha ha*. The next job I do I shall clip the ladys ears off and send to the police officers just for jolly wouldnt you.
>
> Keep this letter back till I do a bit more work, then give it out straight. My knife's so nice and sharp I want to get to work right away if I get a chance. Good luck.
> Yours truly
> Jack the Ripper
> Dont mind me giving the trade name

A second post script in red crayon ran down the side of the letter and read:

> wasnt good enough to post this before I got all the red ink off my hands curse it. No luck yet. They say I'm a doctor now. *ha ha*.

The letter reached the Central News Agency on Thursday September 27th and was forwarded to police headquarters at Scotland Yard on Saturday September 29th. A covering letter from the editor to Chief Constable Adolphus Williamson said: 'The editor presents his compliments to Mr Williamson and begs to inform him that the enclosed was sent to the Central News [Agency] two days ago & was treated as a joke.'

The text of the letter was published in the 2 a.m. edition of the *Liverpool Daily Post* and in the 5 a.m. edition of the *Daily News* in London on Monday October 1st. (Some details of the murders had already appeared in the Sunday papers.) That same morning the Central News Agency received a postcard written in red crayon and postmarked October 1st. Its handwriting matched that of the letter. Posted in the East End of London the card referred to the two murders that had occurred within less than an hour of each other in Whitechapel early on Sunday September 30th, and said:

> I was not codding dear old Boss when I gave you the tip, youll hear about Saucy Jackys work tomorrow double event this time number one squealed a bit couldnt finish straight off. had not time to get ears for police thanks for keeping last letter back till I got to work again.
>
> Jack the Ripper

This became known as the 'Saucy Jacky' card, and its text was printed in the London *Star* in the 1 p.m. edition on October 1st.

The detail that one of the ears of the Mitre Street victim was partially severed was known to very few people on the Sunday immediately following the crime and was only widely publicised when the story made all the newspapers on Monday. Because of the references to ear-ripping – as well as the same mannerisms, handwriting and the chilling signature – it was assumed at the time that the letter and card must have been written by the same person.

The idea has taken root today that the card, too, was written by a copy-cat and that in those days of frequent and excellent postal services it would have been quite possible for a hoaxer to read the 5 a.m. newspaper and send a prank card to make the midday edition. Certainly Philip Sugden, who expresses grave doubts about the authenticity of any of the Ripper letters, says that news of the double event spread like wildfire throughout the East End in the early hours of Sunday morning. In his view it would have been easy to imitate the letter.

This may be true, but only the text of the 'Dear Boss' letter had appeared in printed form. Not until October 3rd did the police issue a facsimile poster of both letter and card, printed in red. This was then sent to every police station in the country, indicating that those in charge of the case did, indeed, view the communications seriously.

Stewart Evans and Paul Gainey say in their book *Jack the Ripper, the First American Serial Killer* that the London Chief of Police telegraphed to San Francisco asking the Hibernia Bank to supply the handwriting of one of their suspects, Dr Francis T. Tumbelty, to them. Paul Feldman rightly asks, 'why compare samples of handwriting with letters that were believed to be forgeries?' The police on the spot clearly thought they were genuine.

In hindsight, Philip Sugden feels that publishing the facsimile was a tactical mistake. Together, the letter and the card provoked a flood of about 2,000 copycat communications, most of which have never been fully investigated and remain at the centre of fierce debate.

Paul Feldman, with typical enthusiasm, hurled his research team at the letters. He scrutinised their contents more thoroughly than almost any other researcher and the results of his determination have challenged previous theories. He has made sense of some letters which appeared of little importance and unearthed some interesting new material.

He discovered that on October 10th 1888 the *Liverpool Echo* had carried an article headed 'A Liverpool Fanatic'. It concerned a postcard from Stafford Street.

Dear Sir. I beg to state that the letters published in yours

> of yesterday [these concerned a Ripper letter from Ireland] it is somebody gulling the public. I am the Whitechapel purger. On 13th at 3 p.m. I will be on Stage as am going to New York. But will have some business before I go. Yours truly Jack the Ripper (Genuine) DIEGO LAURENZ

The 'stage' was nautical jargon for the gangway up which passengers embarked. And Diego? In a lengthy article in *History Today* in May 2000, one of the latest recruits to the Ripperwatch scene, Professor William D Rubinstein, American Professor of Modern History at Aberystwyth University, wrote a ten-page feature 'The Hunt for Jack the Ripper'. In it he suggests that this is "arguably the most important clue that we have ... Diego is Spanish for James."

The value of this claim was immediately scorned by most of the Ripper world. But the Professor has a point. In *A Dictionary of Surnames* by Patricia Hanks and Flavia Hodges published by Oxford University Press in 1988 it says: the *American* [my italics] term for a South American, is a corruption of another form of James: Diego.'

I had had serious doubts myself about tackling these letters because it would be so easy to venture into such a minefield and unwittingly manipulate whatever information is there to support a favourite theory. This is known as 'affirmation bias' and Professor Canter warned me not to fall into this trap! I knew that we would be accused of attempting to compare a 'forged' Diary with 'forged' letters. The fact is that no one really knows the truth of this matter. In 2002 Keith Skinner and Stewart Evans published *Jack the Ripper: Letters from Hell*, a scholarly book which has been described as 'the best long essay that has ever been written on the Ripper letters.'

With the freedom of Scotland Yard's entire collection of correspondence they have examined the letters, in detail, from every aspect of the case but have been careful to make few assertions.

We were in a unique position, in possession of a manuscript which purported to be by the writer of at least some of the Ripper correspondence. We had an opportunity not to be missed. Careful comparison of one with the other might give us fresh insight into the Whitechapel murders through the eyes of the killer.

Of course, we were faced with a problem because the handwriting of the Diary and the original 'Dear Boss' letter did not appear to be compatible! Certainly Sue Iremonger, our document analyst, who had already begun a detailed study of the letters in the police files, did not believe they were. However, David Forshaw has suggested that the Diary could reflect the true inner feelings of its author whereas the letter and card – which he also believes *could* be in the same hand – are contrived to impress.

I was more interested and puzzled by a question that so far no one has really resolved. If the Diary is an old forgery why did its writer not attempt to emulate more closely the writing of the Dear Boss letter? And if it is a modern forgery, why claim authorship of a letter and card believed by many to be a hoax?

* * *

At 12.45, on the morning after Liz Stride and Catherine Eddowes died, a short, one inch wide, round-ended knife was found outside Mr Christmas' shop in Whitechapel Road. Police surgeon Dr George Bagster Phillips claimed that this knife might have been the murder weapon and could have belonged to Elizabeth Stride; many prostitutes carried knives for self protection.

Until now, researchers have mistakenly dated the discovery of the knife to two days before the murders but the Diary seems to have it right again.

> *My shiny knife*
> *the whore's knife*

The Diarist is making the point – now accepted by most Ripper historians – that the knife which killed Stride was not the knife that killed the other women. There were two knives, the second being found in the very same postal district from which the 'Saucy Jacky' postcard was sent later that morning.

* * *

But over 20 years later, Sir Robert Anderson stirred up a hornets' nest. As Dr Anderson, he was Assistant Commissioner, Metropolitan Police CID in charge of the investigations from October 6th. In 1910 his memoirs, *The Lighter Side of My Official Life*, were serialised in *Blackwood's Magazine*. He says: 'The Jack the Ripper letter which is preserved in the Police Museum at New Scotland Yard is the creation of an enterprising London journalist.'

This comment convinced many Ripper writers that the first 'Dear Boss' letter was a hoax. In a footnote to his memoirs Sir Robert Anderson had written: 'I should almost be tempted to disclose the identity of the murderer and of the pressman who wrote the letter.' He added, as though to protect his uncertainty, 'provided the publishers would accept all responsibility in view of a possible libel action.'

In 1914 Sir Melville Macnaghten also poured cold water on the 'Dear Boss' letter: 'In this ghastly production I have always thought I could discern the stained forefinger of the journalist.' But which journalist?

Two decades after this, in 1931, a former *Star* journalist named Best, then a spry 70 years old, told a colleague that he had indeed written many of the letters 'to keep the business alive'. A strange statement, considering the police were struggling with a monster who was all too alive and a situation that hardly needed stimulus. He claimed he had done it with a flattened Waverley nib to give the appearance of semi-literacy. Sue Iremonger says that the first Dear Boss letter was definitely *not* written with a Waverley nib.

Then in 1993, the Littlechild letter came to light, in which, in 1913, Chief Inspector Littlechild not only named Dr Tumbelty as a suspect but also named two journalists allegedly suspected by Scotland Yard at the time. They were Tom Bulling (mispelt Bullen by Littlechild), of the Central News Agency and Charles Moore, his boss. Moore was a regular guest at smart Monday night dinner parties given by Sir Melville Macnaghten.

Strangely, the Littlechild letter contradicts Paul Gainey and Stuart Evans's earlier argument. For having focused on police belief in the letter and postcard, by comparing them with the handwriting of their suspect Tumbelty, they use Littlechild's suspects, Bulling and Moore, as proof that the letters were *not* genuine.

However, for those who accept without question the role of handwriting, the *Jack the Ripper A-Z* authors note that neither that of Bulling nor Moore matches that of the 'Dear Boss' letter or 'Saucy Jacky' postcard.

So these communications, especially those initialled by Chief Inspector Swanson himself, continue to be the subject of serious research. Sue Iremonger, introduced to the letters through her contact with the Diary, has embarked on an exhaustive study of their form.

Arthur Conan Doyle, when asked how Sherlock Holmes would solve the Ripper mystery, replied that he would look for a killer with American connections. His reason was language. The Americanisms 'Dear Boss', 'fix me' and 'shan't quit' would have been familiar expressions to Maybrick from his long links with Norfolk, Virginia and from his American wife. There are other, fascinating, links between Conan Doyle and the Maybricks. Conan Doyle as a trained doctor owned a copy of *Materia Medica* which seems to have influenced the Diary writer; he was aware of Pauline Cranstoun, to whom Maybrick went for advice and had received a letter from a Liverpool merchant, "who burns to know who Jack the Ripper is"! These letters have, like so many others, been lost.

I have become intrigued by the ferment of journalistic activity and talent based around Ludgate Circus. An entire chapter in *Letters from Hell* is devoted to claims and counterclaims about various pressmen. But, as with everything else in this story, the file is open.

In 2002, Roger Palmer, an American Ripper enthusiast and regular contributor to the Internet 'Casebook' site, discovered an astonishing article in the *St Louis (Missouri) Evening Chronicle* of December 15th 1888. It revealed that over 100 years before the Maybrick diary came to light, there had been a similar confession doing the rounds of Fleet Street.

In the 5pm edition of the *Chronicle* in St Louis – the city to which British detectives were already on their way as part of their investigations into the American Connection – the headlines announced:

> Ripper's' Diary
> A Strange Parcel received
> By a New York Englishman
> Its startling enclosures are given to the world
> All theories of the Whitechapel butcheries are wrong.

The newspaper summarised 'A Wife's Wrong Doing Unseats Her Husband's Reason and in his Ravings he sells Himself to Satan.'

It is clear from the following account that this could not have been Maybrick, although there are several parallels with our story. But what were the origins of the document, and was it merely a bit of journalistic Christmas fun?

The source of the St Louis article is obscure. The newspaper quotes a letter, dated December 5th, from a Richard Walters, who gives his address as 134 ½, Ludgate Hill, London EC. Ludgate Hill runs into Ludgate Circus and from there in to Fleet Street, at that time home to most British national newspapers, foreign correspondents and press agencies. But, according to Kelly's Street Directory, 134 ½ did not exist. Richard Walters himself is just as elusive. Was he real?

He writes (note the American spellings):

> Mr. E.A.S. Sir,
>
> You will perhaps think it strange receiving a communication from one who is a total stranger to you. You will, however,

> I am sure, pardon the liberty when I explain I am simply fulfilling the request of a mutual friend who has lately, very mysteriously disappeared.
>
> He desired me to enclose the following photo and small book to you in case anything should occur to him, furnishing me with your name and address. He seemed to me, just previous to his disappearance to be laboring under a constant delusion of a vague, indefinable dread of the future. Though he appeared rational, I don't think he was in his right mind and I think he may have committed suicide.
>
> You will recognize our poor friend in the enclosed likeness. Should you hear anything further about him you will confer upon me the great favour of communicating to yours respectfully, Richard Walters, 134 ½ Ludgate Hill, London EC.

The mention of suicide could be a reference to the suspect Druitt, whose body was found in the Thames two weeks after the letter was posted, but the contents of that 1888 diary do not seem to reflect the Druitt story.

Who was Mr E.A.S? The name of the friend was not revealed nor was the photograph ever printed although it is described as that of a well-off individual of about 28 years. He has clean-cut features, a prominent Roman nose and crisp golden curly hair. He wears expensive clothes and a top hat. In the diary he refers not to his children but to 'my child'!

The diary is described as the sort presented by a leading London tailoring firm to its customers. It is in a very childish code and is melodramatic in the extreme:

> O! My wife how could you do this wrong to me, who loved you more than life itself … I am tempted at once to put an end to that which can now only be to me a burden.

Gradually the writer, like Maybrick, racked with pain, formulates revenge on his pleasure-loving wife. He talks of selling his soul and turning his madness on 'all those who have left the path of virtue.' The Devil appears and the killings begin.

However, unlike the Maybrick diary, this document offers no revealing real-life details about its writer and even the murder descriptions are far removed from the facts. There is none of the sophisticated psychology of the Maybrick diary.

* * *

We were all, by now, deeply immersed in the Ripper correspondence. My delight at the discovery that there had been a letter posted in Liverpool was dashed when I learned that, like so much of the vital evidence in this story, it had disappeared. Even so, it should not be ignored.

The Liverpool letter was, it seems, first noted in J. Hall Richardson's book *From The City to Fleet Street* published in 1927 and quoted again by Donald McCormick in 1959 and Robin Odell in *Jack the Ripper Fact and Fiction* in 1965.

> Liverpool
> 29th inst
>
> Beware I shall be at work on the 1st and 2nd Inst, in the Minories at twelve midnight, and I give the authorities a good chance, but there is never a policeman near when I am at work. Yours Jack the Ripper.

The postscript was equally important. It read:

> What fools the police are. I even give them the name of the street where I am living. Prince William Street.

Prince William Street is in one of Liverpool's poorest areas, Toxteth. In 1888 it was lined with tenement lodgings used by ladies described as 'our disillusioned sisters of the pavement'. Since Prince William Street lay a few yards from the road which runs between Battlecrease House and the city centre, Maybrick would have passed by every day on his way to the office and must have known it well.

It has been pointed out in *The Jack the Ripper A-Z* that the expression 'inst' means 'of this month' and cannot therefore be used for an event in the future. But Maybrick would not have been the first businessman to misuse such a word in a somewhat pompous attempt to sound efficient and correct. Many still do.

On October 2nd the *Evening News* was very near the mark when it reported: 'A belief is gaining ground that the murderer is not a frequenter of common lodging houses but that he occupies a single room or perhaps finds refuge in an empty warehouse. He is supposed to make his home somewhere between Middlesex Street and Brick Lane.'

The next piece of the jigsaw was detected by Paul Begg who also has a complete copy of the Ripper letters. On October 5th 1888 a letter was sent from journalist Bulling to Chief Constable A.F. Williamson.

> Dear Mr Williamson,
> At 5 minutes to 9 o'clock tonight we received the following letter, the envelope of which I enclose by which you will see it is in the same handwriting as the previous communication.
> Yours truly T.J.Bulling

> 5 Oct 1888

> Dear friend,

> In the name of God hear me I swear I did not Kill the female whose body was found at Whitehall. If she was an

honest woman I will hunt down and destroy her murderer. If she was a whore God will bless the hand that slew her. for the woman of Moab and Median shall die and their blood shall mingle with the dust. I never harm any others or the Divine power that protects and helps me in my grand work would quit for ever. Do as I do and the light of my glory shall shine upon you. I must get to work tomorrow treble event this time yes yes three must be ripped will send you a bit of face by post I promise this dear old Boss. The police now reckon my work was a practical joke well well Jacky's a very practical joker ha ha ha Keep this back till three are wiped out and you can show the cold meat.

Yours truly
Jack the Ripper

The letter refers to a headless, limbless body washed up on October 3rd at the Victoria Embankment on the Thames. The letter had never been published either in the press or in books before it appeared in Paul Feldman's text. With justifiable delight he remembered a line in the Diary which was written immediately after the double event.

Will visit the city of whores soon, very soon, I wonder if I could do three?

As far as I am aware, that letter and the Diary are the *only* places in which the dream of a triple murder is expressed!

On October 6th the *Liverpool Echo* reported anxiously beneath its headline 'The Whitechapel Murders': 'There can be no doubt that the Whitechapel murderer is not in that district and did not live there at the time of the murders.' The *Liverpool Daily Post* carried a story on October 11th with the headline: 'Alleged Liverpool Clue'. It read: 'A certain detective of the Criminal Investigation Department has recently journeyed to Liverpool and there traced the movements of a man which have been proved of a somewhat mysterious kind. The height of this person and his description are fully ascertained and amongst other things he was in possession of a black leather bag. This person suddenly left Liverpool for London and for some time occupied apartments in a well known first class hotel in the West End.' The story claimed that the man was in the habit of visiting the poorest parts of the East End and that he left behind in the hotel his black leather bag containing certain items of clothing, documents and prints 'of an obscene description. It has been suggested that the mysterious person landed in Liverpool from America'.

Stewart Evans and Paul Gainey have, understandably, used this story to point the finger once more at Tumbelty, who they say had arrived from the United States in June 1888 and was therefore likely to escape by the same route.

But they fail to mention that, according to the custom of the day, the hotel in question – The Charing Cross – had advertised in the *Times* appealing for owners of lost property to claim their belongings. Paul Feldman traced that advertisement to June 14th 1888. There, among the list of names was one that sounded all too familiar: S.E Mibrac. Mibrac is not a name that exists in any dictionary of names; it was either misread by hotel staff or it is Maybrick again playing games. We know that James Maybrick was in London in June – the Diary tells us so.

> *I will visit Michael this coming June.*

Also on October 6th a badly spelt, threatening letter was posted in London N.W. It was in a well formed hand – the signature was felt by Sue Iremonger and Anna Koren to be the same as that of the September 25th letter.

> 6 October 1888
> You though yourself very clever when you informed the police. But you made a mistake if you though I dident see

> you. Now I know you know me and I see your little game and I mean to finish you and send your ears to your wife if you show this to the police or help them if you do I will finish you. It no use your trying to get out of my way because I have you when you dont expect it and I keep my word as you soon see and rip you up. Yours truly Jack the Ripper.

The letter remained undisturbed in Home Office files at the Record Office until it was found by my publisher at the time, Robert Smith. Like the October 5th letter this too has never previously been published and could not have been seen by a forger at any time. This letter was probably intended for Schwartz, who was being kept out of harm's way by the police for his own protection, or for Lawende who was also being guarded. It was sent from the postal district of Michael Maybrick's chambers in Regent's Park.

The language of the letter is marked by exactly the same vindictive violence and clear expression of intent that appears in the Diary.

> *Damn it damn it damn it the bastard almost caught me. curse him to hell I will cut him up next time, so help me. a few minutes and I would have done, bastard, I will seek him out, teach him a lesson.*

On that day too, the *Daily Telegraph* had published two artist's impressions of the same man whom, it said, they were seeking in connection with the murders. They appeared in the *Liverpool Echo* two days later. These would seem to bear a resemblance to Maybrick reproduced in the picture section. According to the newspaper description the man was of education and means, probably about 40 years old, with dark clothes and a dark silk handkerchief around his neck. 'His hat is probably a dark stiff bowler and his appearance entirely respectable. His manner is quiet and composed and there is nothing to betray the monomaniac, except a certain mingled restlessness and cunning in the expression of the eyes.'

October 6th was a Saturday – the day which seems to be pivotal to all the murders. Did Maybrick stay with Michael after the double murder and reading the morning papers feel driven to write to one of those who said they had seen him and whose evidence could convict him?

By October 12th and 13th, various newspapers were reporting that steamers leaving Liverpool were being watched.

* * *

Back home with his family after the double murder on September 30th, Maybrick would have watched and waited. As always, thoughts of Florie both titillated and enraged him. A lonely man, sick in mind and body he turned once more for solace to his best friend George Davidson.

> *Tonight I will celebrate by wining and dining George. I am in a good mood, believe I will allow the whore the pleasure of her whore master, will remark an evening in the city will do her good, will suggest a concert. I have no doubt the carriage will take the bitch straight to him... I will go to sleep thinking about all they are doing. I cannot wait for the thrill.*

On October 12th the Manchester *Guardian* carried a disturbing story about an event that had taken place in Liverpool. 'On Wednesday evening a young woman was walking along Sheil Road, Liverpool, not far from Sheil Park. She was stopped by an elderly woman, aged about 60, who in an agitated and excited manner urged her most earnestly not to go into the park. She explained that a few minutes earlier she had been resting on one of the seats in the park when she was accosted by a respectable-looking gentleman in a black coat, light trousers and a soft felt hat, who enquired if she knew any loose women in the neighbourhood and immediately afterwards produced a knife with a long, thin blade and stated that he intended to kill as many women in Liverpool as in London, adding that he would send the ears of the first victim to the editor of a Liverpool paper. The old woman, who was trembling violently as she related this story, stated that she was so terribly frightened, she hardly knew how she got away from this man.'

On October 15th, newspapers in Leeds reported that Jack the Ripper had been seen in Chorley, a small town a few miles north of Liverpool.

The editor of *Ripperana*, Nick Warren, discovered an article in the *Daily Telegraph* of 20th October describing how a tall man aged about forty-five and six foot tall walked into the leather shop of Mr Marsh at 218 Jubilee Street, Mile End Road, on October 15th. His daughter, Emily, was behind the counter as her father was out. The stranger asked for the address of Mr Lusk whose name appeared on a vigilance committee reward bill in the shop window. Emily read out Mr Lusk's address – Alderney Road, Globe Road – and he noted it down. She was anxious about his furtive appearance – he kept his eyes on the floor – and sent the shop boy after him to see what he did. The stranger was described as wearing a black felt hat pulled over his eyes. He had a dark beard and moustache and spoke 'with what was taken to be an Irish accent.' (To a Londoner, Irish and Liverpool accents are very much alike.)

The following day, Tuesday October 16th, George Lusk, president of the Whitechapel Vigilance Committee, found a three inch cardboard box in his mail. Inside was half a human kidney preserved in spirits of wine along with a barely intelligible letter that has since disappeared.

> From hell
> Mr Lusk,
> Sor, I send you half the kidne I took from one woman prasarved it for you tother piece I fried and ate it was very nise. I may send you the bloody knif that took it out if you only wate a whil longer
> signed
> Catch me when you can Mishter Lusk.

The City pathologist, Dr Sedgwick Saunders, said at the time that the kidney did not belong to Catharine Eddowes and that it was probably a hospital specimen, while Dr Openshaw, curator of the Pathology Museum at the London Hospital, declared it to be the 'ginny' kidney of a 45-year-old woman with Bright's disease. Why only half a kidney? The Diary answers this;

Sweet sugar and tea,
Could have paid my small fee,
But instead I did flee
and by way showed my glee
By eating cold kidney for supper.

David Forshaw believes that Maybrick might, like other serial killers, have cannibalised parts of his victims to assert absolute power over them. It is possible that the Ripper believed, like some primitive cannibal tribes, that eating human remains was a magical way of gaining power, perhaps some sort of life force from the dead person. Later in the Diary, as his behaviour grew less controlled, Maybrick had nightmares of cutting up Florie and serving her to the children.

During the summer, Florie had been to see Dr Hopper herself. She expressed deep anxiety that her husband was taking some 'very strong medicine which has a bad effect on him' and that he always seemed worse after each dose. She begged the doctor to speak to him and stop him. Her concern eventually produced a backlash in October, the month of Maybrick's 50th birthday.

The whore has informed the bumbling buffoon I am in the habit of taking strong medicine. I was furious when the bitch told me. So furious I hit her. ha. The whore begged me not to do so again. It was a pleasure a great deal of pleasure. If it was not for my work I would have cut the bitch up there and then...

Maybrick was a man given to explosion under stress and if this was the first time he had actually hit Florie it was not to be the last.

Michael was by now also concerned about his dissolute brother's health and, according to the Diary, wrote several letters during October enquiring, in particular, about Maybrick's 'sleepwalking' problems.

October was not a good month for Maybrick. He was not deriving from his drugs the strength they usually gave him and which he needed to commit murder. He had temporarily lost control. There were no murders that month and so there was no reason to write in his Diary. He put aside his pen for three or four weeks. Did he go to America? At the end of the month he writes again.

> *It has been far too long since my last. I have been unwell.*

The age of 50 is for many people a watershed. For a man like James Maybrick, the reality of his declining health and sexual prowess must have been a nightmare. On his birthday, October 24th, James Maybrick reached that watershed. His morale was crumbling. During the second week in November he went to London and stayed at Michael's home in Regent's Park. He had planned to go over to Whitechapel but something went very wrong. Despite all efforts Maybrick's ordeal must have been heard all over the apartment that night.

> *I was forced to stop myself from indulging in my pleasure by taking the largest dose I have ever done. The pain that night has burnt into my mind. I vaguly recall putting a handkerchief in my mouth to stop my cries. I believe I vomited several times. The pain was intolerable, as I think I shudder. No more.*
>
> *I am convinced God placed me here to kill all whores, for he must have done so, am I still not here. Nothing will stop me now. The more I take the stronger I become. Michael was under the impression that once I had finished my business I was to return to Liverpool that very day. And indeed I did one day later. ha ha.*

So it was on Friday, November 9th, the world was sickened by the unbelievable bestiality of one of the most depraved murders ever committed.

12

God Placed me Here to Kill all Whores

Mary Jane Kelly was a young prostitute. Of uncertain origin, she was possibly born in Ireland and brought up in Wales. At about 25 years old she was almost the same age as Florence Maybrick and like Florie, but unlike the other victims of the Ripper, she was pretty. Her resemblance to Maybrick's wife may well have fuelled his anger when he spotted her walking down Commercial Street past Thrawl Street, in what the local vicar the Reverend Samuel Barnett called 'the wicked quarter mile'. In the person of Mary Jane Kelly there was even greater incentive to kill. She is the only one of the victims mentioned by name in the Diary.

Mary Jane had spent the afternoon and early evening of Thursday November 8th with friends. She was looking forward to the Lord Mayor's Show next day when all the ceremonial pageantry the City of London could muster would be on parade for the inauguration of the new Lord Mayor. But Mary Jane Kelly never reached the show.

Early that evening her young friend, Lizzie Albrook, dropped in for a chat at 13 Miller's Court, where Mary rented a tiny, 12' x 10' partitioned ground floor back room. As Lizzie left, Mary Kelly's poignant parting words to the younger girl were; 'Whatever you do, don't you do wrong and turn out as I have.' Mary's movements from then on are uncertain.

She was in musical mood that night, disturbing the neighbours by singing loudly in her room. The tune they remembered was a typically sentimental Victorian ballad, 'Only A Violet I Plucked From My Mother's Grave'.

At about 2 a.m. on November 9th George Hutchinson, a labourer, of the Victoria Home in Commercial Street, was returning from Romford in Essex. Not until the day of the inquest did Hutchinson report to the police. He told them then that on the morning of the murder he had seen a man approach Kelly, who was looking for trade. Hutchinson was probably a former client so knew her well: he sometimes gave her money, but this time he had none left.

> Just before I got to Flower and Dean Street, I met the murdered woman, Kelly... A man coming in the opposite direction to Kelly, tapped her on the shoulder and said something to her they both burst out laughing. I heard her say alright to him and the man said you will be alright for what I have told you: he then placed his right hand around her shoulders. He also had a kind of small parcel in his left hand, with a kind of strap round it. I stood against the lamp of the Queen's Head Public House, and watched him... They both then came past me and the man hung down his head with his hat over his eyes. I stooped down and looked him in the face. He looked at me stern...

The police wanted to keep the information to themselves but Hutchinson spoke to the press and immediately the whole country became aware of the new suspect. Indeed, Jack the Ripper was now international news.

He was, said Hutchinson, of a dark 'foreign' appearance, respectable, wearing a long dark coat with astrakhan collar and cuffs; a dark jacket and trousers; light waistcoat, dark felt hat 'turned down in the middle'; button-boots with spats; a linen collar; and a black tie with a horseshoe pin. A thick gold chain was displayed over his waistcoat and he carried a small package. He was 34 or 35 years old, 5' 6" tall, with a pale complexion and a slight moustache curled up at the ends.

Horseshoe tiepins and thick gold chains were popular at the time – Michael Maybrick appears in various magazine photographs dressed in such style. Hutchinson continued:

> They both went into Dorset Street. I followed them. They both stood at the corner of the court for about three minutes. He said something to her. She said alright my dear come along you will be comfortable. He then placed his arm on her shoulder and she gave him a kiss. She said she had lost her handkerchief. He then pulled his handkerchief a red one and gave it to her. They both then went up the Court together. I then went to the court to see if I could see them but I could not. I stood there for about three quarters of an hour to see if they came out. They did not so I went away.

If Hutchinson's story was correct in essence, even if not in detail, the man he saw with Mary Jane Kelly was probably her killer. Was it Maybrick?

The police were told that neighbours thought they heard the cry of 'murder' around 4 a.m. They did nothing, for such cries were common in a violent area and were usually ignored. So there is now no way of knowing what happened or why... except, again, through the Diary.

We know that, in the weeks before the butchery of Mary Kelly, Maybrick had hit his wife – a fact that can be verified by reading through the mass of evidence surrounding Florie's trial. It gave him a great deal of pleasure. His drug taking was escalating and there is a hint that brother Michael was suspicious. There have been previous references to Maybrick's euphemistic description of his murderous outings as 'sleepwalking'. Now he writes:

I have had several letters from Michael. In all he enquires about my health and asked in one if my sleepwalking had resumed... I have informed him it has not.

He again mentions his cold hands – just as earlier he spoke of his love of warmth and sunshine. This constant feeling of chill and the involuntary rubbing of clammy hands are a reminder of those little known symptoms of arsenic poisoning as described in the *Materia Medica*.

The pain of that night before the murder, spent at Michael's apartment was, as we know, unbearable. But in the Diary there is no other build up, no creative scene setting or foretaste of the terrible events about to happen. The Diary continues when James Maybrick is back in Liverpool – when the re-living and writing of Mary Kelly's last moments seem to offer the greatest thrill of all. What went before seems to have been blotted from his mind.

I have read about my latest, my God the thoughts, the very best. I left nothing of the bitch, nothing. I placed it all over the room, time was on my hands, like the other whore I cut off the bitches nose, all of it this time. I left nothing of her face to remember her by. She reminded me of the whore. So young unlike I. I thought it a joke when I cut her breasts off, kissed them for a while. The taste of blood was sweet, the pleasure was overwhelming... Left them on the table with some of the other stuff. ...she riped like a ripe peach...

Is this writing really that of a forger indulging perverted pleasures by proxy or is there not the chilling ring of truth?

When Thomas Bowyer and John McCarthy looked through the window of Mary Kelly's cramped hovel on that Friday November 9th, they saw what they described as 'more like the work of a devil than of a man'.

There was panic. Dr George Bagster Phillips and Inspector Abberline were quickly on the scene but no one forced the locked door until 1.30 p.m. when John McCarthy broke it down with a pick handle.

Even at the inquest three days later Dr Phillips spared the jury many details of what he had seen, although an official photographer recorded the nightmare for posterity. Dr Phillips' early observation that Mary Kelly was wearing a 'skimpy shift' was correct but contradicted the post-mortem report that she was naked. Not till 1987 was the full catalogue of the horror discovered. Then the police released notes, written on November 10th 1888 after the post-mortem by Dr Thomas Bond, police surgeon to A Division. These notes said that the breasts had been left, 'one under the head and the other by the right foot.'

The fact that the Diary contradicts Dr Bond has been taken by many of its critics as proof of forgery. They claim that a forger – then or now – could have scoured the newspapers and found that the *Pall Mall Gazette*, the *Times* and the *Star* of November 10th and the *Pall Mall Budget* of November 15th reported that the breasts were on the table. It is thought by some that, even in the midst of that carnage, driven by frenzy beyond belief, the murderer would have recalled exactly what he did with the mangled remains.

According to Dr Thomas Bond too, 'the viscera were found in various parts.' The Diary says:

> *I placed it all over the room... Regret I did not take any of it away with me it is supper time I could do with a kidney or two ha ha.*

The last words of Dr Bond's notes make the simple, dramatic statement: 'the Pericardium was open below and the Heart absent.' There was never any reliable explanation of where the heart could have been. Philip Sugden believes it was taken from the room.

The press issued the usual contradictory statements but most significantly Dr Phillips and Dr Roderick MacDonald the district coroner, went back to Mary Kelly's room and sifted through the ashes of the fire in which clothing had been burned. It seems they were looking for a part of the body that could not be located at the autopsy but apparently found nothing. So where was the heart and what motive did the murderer have for removing it?

Paul Feldman suggests he may have used it to write the initials on Mary Kelly's room wall.

An initial here an initial there
will tell of the whoring mother

A curious and controversial photograph was taken for the police and first appeared the following year in a book *Vacher L'Eventreur et les Crimes Sadiques* by J.A.E. Lacassagne. In 1976 Stephen Knight's *Jack the Ripper: The Final Solution* reproduced the picture with enough clarity to show that there appeared to be some initials on the wall partition behind Mary Kelly's bed, although they were not pointed out until 1988. Then, crime researcher Simon Wood mentioned them to Paul Begg.

As part of his own investigations into the Diary, Paul Feldman went to Direct Communications in Chiswick, where computer technology made possible a more detailed examination of the photograph. The initials could then be seen clearly in the grime of the partition – a large *M,* and to one side a fainter *F*.

I was sceptical about those initials, but recently I was sent a cutting from the *New York World* of November 13th 1888. It was headed 'The London Horror' and described how:

> Profiting from their previous blunders the police called a photographer to take a picture of the room before the body was removed. This gives rise to a report that there was more handwriting on the wall, though three or four people who were allowed to enter the room say they did not observe it. But possibly they were too excited to notice such details.

Judging by all the photographs – now a chilling record of Ripper history – I doubt that anyone entering Mary Kelly's room that day and seeing what lay on the bed would have remembered anything at all.

The Diary does not refer to the heart at the time of the murder. Only at the end of his life, in despair, does Maybrick utter the words that could equally be applied to Mary Kelly (the only victim for whom he shows remorse) and to his wife Florie. He offers no explanation. Only the agonised cry 'no heart no heart'.

David Forshaw says of Maybrick's frame of mind at this time:

> While we know little, so far, about Maybrick's parents, we know from studies of other serial killers that there is often deep resentment beneath superficial filial love.
>
> At this precise moment the profound sense of inadequacy which was the true inspiration of Maybrick's teasing, boastful writing as well as of the murders, came violently to the surface. Mary Jane Kelly took the place of Florie 'the whoring mother' of the Diary and perhaps, of all mothers.

* * *

After the Kelly murder, alleged sightings of the killer – and especially the evidence of George Hutchinson – had provided the most detailed description so far. Indeed, Hutchinson told press reporters that he had gone out hunting the murderer on the following Sunday November 11th and despite a choking fog was almost certain he had seen him in Middlesex Street.

Paul Feldman discovered that on November 19th, after Hutchinson's original statement, the press again threw the spotlight on Liverpool: 'The Whitechapel murderer is supposed to travel up from Manchester, Birmingham or some other town in the Midlands for the purpose of committing the crimes. Detectives have been engaged in Willesden and Euston watching the arrival of trains from the Midlands and the North.'

It is strange that of all the places and ports in Britain through which the

Ripper might have escaped, the police focused on Liverpool and London.

There had been an enormous escalation of police activity – over one hundred officers were now working on the corpse. Then, on the very day of Mary Kelly's death, the Metropolitan Police Commissioner, Sir Charles Warren, resigned. There was no direct connection, although there had been ongoing and unhelpful hostility between Sir Charles and Home Secretary Henry Matthews. He had also become increasingly unpopular with the press, following a great deal of social unrest and in particular his use of troops against the unemployed on Bloody Sunday, November 13th, 1887. He was succeeded by James Monro, former head of the CID with whom he had also quarrelled.

The burden on the police was horrendous. They received hundreds of letters. One of the later examples was published on November 19th. It said:

> Dear Boss,
> I am now in the Queen's Park Estate in the Third Avenue. I am out of red ink at present, but it won't matter for once. I intend doing another here next Tuesday night about ten o'clock. I will give you a chance to catch me. I shall have check trousers on and a black coat and vest so look out. I have done one not yet found out, so look out, so keep your eyes open. –Yours Jack the Ripper.

Queen's Park Estate is in the area of Michael Maybrick's London apartments, far from Whitechapel.

*   *   *

We were now entering an exciting period of richly unresearched material. This centred around the missing writings of Dr Thomas Dutton (1854–1935) whose practice in 1888 was listed in directories at 130 Aldgate High Street. Dr Dutton was, according to the authors of *The Jack the Ripper A-Z* a man of wide interests and considerable ability. He is said to have studied the Ripper correspondence and selected 34 letters which he believed to be in the same hand. Throughout his professional life he compiled a random, handwritten collection of notes, thoughts and impressions on all the major crimes and always claimed that he knew the identity of Jack the Ripper. These notes entitled *Chronicles of Crime* were supposedly given to a Miss Hermione Dudley before he died and both she and they vanished without trace. Research has failed to find any reference to Miss Dudley's life or death.

The only source for some of the many interesting observations allegedly arising from the *Chronicles of Crime* is the late author Donald McCormick who met Dr Dutton in 1932 when the doctor was living the life of an elderly recluse. Mr McCormick took notes from the Chronicles but put them away so that they did not see the light of day until after World War II. These notes in turn were lost.

Our interest in Dr Dutton focused on a rhyme which was published in Donald McCormick's *The Identity of Jack the Ripper* in 1959.

> Eight Little whores, with no hope of heaven,
> Gladstone may save one, then there'll be seven.
> Seven little whores begging for a shilling,
> One stays in Henage [sic] Court, then there's a killing.
>
> Six little whores glad to be alive,
> One sidles up to Jack, then there are five.
> Four and whore rhyme aright, so do three and me,
> I'll set the town alight ere there are two.
>
> Two little whores, shivering with fright,
> See a cosy doorway in the middle of the night,
> Jack's knife flashes, then there's but one,
> And the last one's ripest for Jack's idea of fun.

According to Donald McCormick's lost record, Dr Dutton copied the rhyme from one of the 34 attested letters which he had identified at Scotland Yard as belonging to the same hand.

Our diarist clearly echoes the Dutton verse in his reference to ripping his victim like a ripe peach and in his urge set fire to buildings with bad memories. In a trial rhyme (which he has scratched out) he writes:

> One whore in heaven
> Two whores side by side,
> Three whores all have died
> Four

The disputes over Dr Dutton and the work of Donald McCormick are as lively as any other part of the Ripper saga. He has been branded a fantasist who made up the entire Dutton episode and either wrote *The Chronicles of Crime* himself or, since no one else has seen them, that they simply did not exist. At the forefront of McCormick's critics is Melvin Harris who has said they were 'sheer fiction'.

However, a lengthy obituary in the *Daily Express* of November 13th 1935 spoke of the diary which the Doctor had kept faithfully for over 50 years. 'It tells not only of his medical activities but records events of importance in the lives of the Royal Family ... in his diaries Dr Dutton revealed himself as ... a keen student of crime ...'

In fact it seems that Dr Dutton was a regular visitor to the scene of the Whitechapel murders and that it had been he, with his black bag, who had once been suspected of being Jack the Ripper.

At least one of Dutton's alleged theories, as also mentioned by McCormick, is a recorded fact. There was a link between the murdered women – they had all, at one time, lodged at St Stephen's Workhouse, off the Walworth Road, Southwark. Perhaps we should be wary of dismissing the legend of Dr Dutton too lightly.

In the library I found the *Faber History of England in Verse*, edited by Kenneth Baker MP (now Lord Baker). There, in the Victorian section, I found 'Eight

Little Whores', attributed anonymously. I wrote to Mr Baker to check if his source was indeed Victorian or whether he had merely read Donald McCormick's book or any of the others that followed it. He was fighting an election at the time and was also moving house. As a consequence his reference notes had been irretrievably buried in a trunk. He could not remember whether he had, or had not, read any Ripper books.

I turned to Iona and Peter Opie's *Oxford Dictionary of Nursery Rhymes* (new edition 1997). There I found the old favourite, 'Ten Little Nigger Boys'. This begins:

> Ten little nigger boys went out to dine
> One choked his little self and then there were nine...

I learned that this rhyme first appeared in 1869. It was based on an American song by Philadelphia musician Septimus Winger (composer of 'Oh where, oh where has my little dog gone?'). It was taken up by the many minstrel groups which had arrived from America in Britain. By the late 1870s it was a very popular ditty, included in the repertoire of musical societies and ballad shows and performed by artistes, such as Michael Maybrick, throughout Victoria's reign.

There are other echoes from the poem in the Diary. There is the threat to set the town alight, reflecting Maybrick's threat to burn down St James' (presumably the church where he was married). Most curious perhaps is the mention of Henage Court. Years later – not until 1931 in fact – a retired policeman, Robert Spicer, who had been a young constable in 1888, wrote to the *Daily Express*. They sent a reporter to see him and an article appeared under the headline 'I caught Jack the Ripper'.

Mr Spicer described what happened in the early hours of one night after the double murder. He had come to Heneage Street (mispelt Henage in the *Daily Express* and in the poem) off Brick Lane. Fifty yards down is Heneage Court, at the bottom of which was a brick-built dustbin. Both Jack and a woman (Rosy) were sitting on this. 'She had 2s (10p) in her hand and followed me when I took Jack on suspicion. He turned out to be a highly respected doctor and gave a Brixton address.

His shirt cuffs still had blood on them. Jack had the proverbial bag with him (a brown one). This was not opened and he was allowed to go.'

Spicer got into trouble for his over zealous arrest and completely lost heart in police work. But was he wrong? Nobody seems to have checked on the respectable doctor. In fact, Spicer saw him again at Liverpool Street station. His appearance was always the same: high hat, black suit with silk facings and a gold watch and chain. He was about 5' 8", about 12 stone, fair moustache, high forehead and rosy cheeks. A good description of Maybrick!

We went to visit PC Spicer's granddaughter who had lived in the same house in Woodford Green for 60 years. She told us how Rosy wrote to her grandfather after the event, thanking him for saving her from murder and thereafter always sent him Christmas cards. Like so many other documents, these have now been lost. But the family remembers Mr Spicer clearly as a tall, striking figure with a big beard. He had eight children and eventually became a groundsman for Bancroft's School in Woodford and also for the cricket club but he, like Dutton, died a lonely man and his body was not discovered until a week after his death.

According to the Diary, Maybrick was now beginning to fear that he could be caught. Drugs continued to provide his escape.

> *I cannot live without my medicine. I am afraid to go to sleep for fear of my nightmares reoccuring.*

The fact that immediately after the Kelly murder Maybrick's headaches worsened was recorded in affidavits for Florie's trial. He even added yet another doctor to his already overcrowded team of medical consultants. Dr J. Drysdale was an elderly Scotsman, neat in appearance and sparing of words. Maybrick consulted him in Liverpool on November 19th, 22nd, 26th and again on December 5th and 10th, telling him that for three months he had endured pains from one side of his head to the other. This had been preceded by a pain in the right side of the head and a dull headache. He said he was never free from pain except sometimes in the morning. If he smoked or drank too much he experienced a numbness on the left side of his hand and his leg and was liable to suffer from an eruption of the skin on his hands. He said nothing concerning drugging himself.

'He seemed to be suffering from nervous dyspepsia,' was all Dr Drysdale could diagnose, which he repeated when he gave evidence at the trial. Then with masterly understatement he added: 'I should say he was hypochondriacal.'

It was perhaps natural that, with all of London on the trail of the Ripper, he should decide to return to the scene of his first confessed attempt at killing, Manchester, where brother Thomas lived.

> *My first was in Manchester so why not my next?*

At this stage the Diary is becoming increasingly confused as Jekyll and Hyde fight within him.

> *The children constantly ask what I shall be buying them for Christmas they shy away when I tell them a shiny knife not unlike Jack the Ripper's in order that I cut their tongues for peace and quiet. I do believe I am completely mad. I have never harmed the children in the years since they have been born. But now I take great delight in scaring them so. May God forgive me.*

David Forshaw says that Maybrick's fondness for his children is quite consistent with the psychology of the serial killer. He was trying to distance himself from them, unsuccessfully, and only his medicine could relieve the torment. It was a vicious downward spiral.

On December 5th a newspaper clipping was sent to Dr William Sedgwick Saunders, the City of London's Public Analyst. Written across the newspaper was the message:

> England
> Dear Boss. Look out for 7th inst. Am trying my hand at disjointing and if can manage will send you a finger. Yours
> Jack the Ripper

Saunders Esq
Police Magistrate

This letter has not been analysed by handwriting experts to be beyond doubt in the same hand as the original 'Dear Boss' letter. But it looks very similar. Is it not a strange coincidence that it is written over a story concerning three Liverpool businessmen running about naked in a public place. Here in one short item are the words 'Liverpool', 'mad' and 'businessman'.

The constant use of such provocative clues, says David Forshaw, shows the gambling criminal's way of tempting fate. He did not want to be caught, but the possibility excited him.

The handwriting in the Diary is becoming more and more uncontrolled. Frustration and rage are relieved by the violent crossing out of line after line of disconnected words. In the midst of the frenzy the pressure of trying to compose seems to become overwhelming. He is losing confidence and control.

> *So help me God my next will be far the worst, my head aches, but I will go on damn Michael for being so clever the art of verse is far from simple. I curse him so. Abberline Abberline, I shall destroy that fool yet, So help me God...*
> *I am cold curse the bastard Lowry for making me rip. I keep seeing blood pouring from the bitches. The nightmares are hideous. I cannot stop myself from wanting to eat more. God help me, damn you. No one will stop me. God be damned.*

He wants to stop but he must go on.

* * *

November was the time of the Maybrick pre-Christmas ball at Battlecrease House. Amongst the guests was Alfred Brierley. Soon after, Charles Ratcliffe, an old business colleague of Maybrick's wrote to John Aunspaugh about a cargo of poor quality corn. Tucked away in a note at the bottom of the letter is the comment 'Think Alf is getting the inside track with Mrs James' affections.'

The Diary records:

> *The bitch, the whore is not satisfied with one whore master, she now has eyes on another.*

On December 22nd Inspector Walter Andrews and a party of colleagues were sent down to New York from Montreal, where they had been on another case. According to the *Pall Mall Gazette*, Jack the Ripper had left England for America three weeks earlier. Although the New York police strongly denied the link, rumours appeared in the New York papers that this was Francis Tumbelty and that he was the man Inspector Andrews was now after.

Christmas was celebrated at Battlecrease House, as it was all over the country, with a tree, presents and cards. But there was still much talk of Jack the Ripper since the police appeared to be making no headway.

> *The children enjoyed Christmas. I did not. My mood is no longer black, although my head aches. I shall never become accustomed to the pain. I curse winter. I yearn for my favourite month, to see flowers in full bloom would please me so.*
>
> *Warmth is what I need, I shiver so. Curse this weather and the whoring bitch.*

Time and again in this story, Christmas – both in England and in America – seems to have been a time of trauma and tension for Maybrick.

Warmth was what he could no longer have from Florie. Far from it. Just before Christmas he describes a seventh, unidentified murder – once more in Manchester. Yet the old excitement is no longer there. He no longer feels 'clever'.

> *I could not cut like my last, visions of her flooded back to me as I struck. I tried to quosh all thoughts of love. I left her for dead, that*

> *I know. It did not amuse me. There was thrill.*

The experience only seems to work for him when it embraces an impersonal act of mutilation. In rage and frustration he returns to Battlecrease – and beats his wife.

> *I have showered my fury on the bitch, I struck and struck. I do not know how I stopped. I have left her penniless. I have no regrets.*

Florie wrote to her mother on the last day of 1888 but did not mention the beating. This is not surprising – it is a well known phenomenon, which would have been equally true in respectable Victorian society, that battered wives hide their hurt from the world. Often they suffer for years and they certainly do not confide in their mothers.

> In his fury he tore up his will this morning as he had made me sole legatee and trustee for the children in it. Now he proposes to settle everything he can on the children alone allowing me only the one third by law. I am sure it matters little to me as long as the children are provided for. My own income will do for me alone. A pleasant way of commencing New Year.

The Baroness described the year's end when she wrote to Home Secretary, Henry Matthews, in 1892. 'The December of 1888 was the first time during her married life she had been able to dance or had been out in society; and her health was then stronger. She was left unattended by her husband.'

Maybrick was in sombre mood. The weather matched that mood. The fog that had blanketed Liverpool at the beginning of 1888 returned on New Year's Eve and the local paper, the *Liverpool Echo*, predicted that 'There is no agreeable change of weather and to judge by appearances we are likely to experience a bad spell of mist, rain and general murkiness.'

It was a bad omen for 1889.

13

When I Have Finished my Fiendish Deeds, the Devil Himself will Praise me

The slaughter in Whitechapel had stopped but the story of Jack the Ripper had not ended with the murder of Mary Jane Kelly. During the spring of 1889, Maybrick's worsening health and the turmoil surrounding his private life created a vortex into which Florie and the family were drawn. If any of them had any suspicion that James Maybrick was the most feared man in Britain they did not reveal it. His secret was soon to be buried deep with his corpse in Anfield Cemetery. But his death would also destroy the life of his young American wife.

Why did the Maybrick family close ranks and the servants conspire against her? Why did the medical men disagree about how James Maybrick died? Why were so many crucial letters destroyed and Maybrick's prescriptions torn up? And why did Edwin and Michael suppress information about their brother's past at the trial and stand by while his widow faced the unimaginable horror of the gallows?

This much is known. In January, according to the cook, Elizabeth Humphreys, Alfred Brierley's visits increased. He was also a regular companion of the Maybricks at the race meetings they so enjoyed.

Maybrick was only too aware of Florie's flirtations – indeed, because of them seven women had already died. True to Victorian morality which applied very different rules for men and women, Maybrick's own infidelity was of no importance.

Not everyone was as captivated by Alf Brierley as was Florie. A cotton broker colleague met him in Savannah a few years previously, when he was working for the family firm of Brierley, Maitland and Dougal. Speaking later (August 20th 1889) to a reporter for the *Savannah Morning News* he observed that he 'could not conceive how Brierley could make a favourable impression on a lady as he was a raw-boned, uncouth young gentleman and anything but an Adonis.' He made very few acquaintances and was not, generally speaking, a popular man.

David Forshaw is not surprised that Brierley continued to be invited to join the family. The perverted pleasure of watching the unsuspecting couple was just part of a power game. Even as he described the pleasure of ripping he became excited by the idea of voyeurism.

> *The whore seen her master today it did not bother me. I imagined I was with them, the very thought thrills me. I wonder if the whore has ever had such thoughts? I believe she has...*

As the dismal weather wore on, Maybrick became restless.

> *It shall not be long before I strike again. I am taking more than ever. The bitch can take two, Sir Jim shall take four, a double double event* ha ha. *If I was in the city of whores I would do my fiendish deeds this very moment... Once more I will be the talk of England... When I have finished my fiendish deeds, the devil himself will praise me.*

At least there was no need for concern about a supplier for his 'medicine'. He had discovered a new source – Valentine Blake – who was a member of a team working for the manufacturing chemist

William Bryer Nation, developing the use of rhea grass, or ramie, as a substitute for cotton.

In April 1894, long after the trial was over, Valentine Blake and William Bryer Nation both gave affidavits to solicitor J.E. Harris. Astonishingly, their statements were not sent to Henry Matthews, and never published until they appeared first in 1899 in J.H. Levy's book on the case, *The Necessity for Criminal Appeal*. If the Diary is a modern forgery, its forger would have had to locate and read its learned text to find the only printed reference to a new source of medicine.

It seems that in January 1889 Blake had travelled to Liverpool to meet Maybrick. He needed help in the marketing of a new product. Maybrick casually asked Blake to tell him the chemicals used in its manufacture. 'I do not wish to obtain your trade secrets,' he reassured him. 'It is a question of price and the chemicals may be obtained more easily in Liverpool.'

One of the substances was arsenic. The two men chatted about the arsenic-eating habits of Austrian peasants and about Thomas de Quincey, author of *Confessions of an English Opium Eater*. Blake wondered 'that De Quincey could have taken such a quantity as 900 drops of laudanum in a day.'

Maybrick apparently smiled. 'One man's poison,' he said, 'is another man's meat, and there is a so-called poison which is like meat and liquor to me whenever I feel weak and depressed; it makes me stronger in mind and body at once.'

'I don't tell everybody,' he went on, 'and wouldn't tell you only you mentioned arsenic. It is arsenic. I take it when I can get it but the doctors won't put any in my medicine, except now and then a trifle that only tantalises me.'

Blake said nothing. Maybrick continued, 'Since you use arsenic can you let me have some? I find difficulty in getting it here?'

Blake recalled in the later affidavit, 'I had some by me and that since I only used it for experiments, which were now perfected, I had no further use for it and he, Maybrick, was welcome to all I had left. He then asked what it was worth and offered to pay for it in advance. I replied I had no licence to sell drugs and suggested we should make it quid pro quo, Mr Maybrick to do his best with the ramie grass product and I to make a present of the arsenic.'

When they met again in February, Blake gave Maybrick about 150 grains of arsenic in three different packets. 'I told him to be careful with it as he had almost enough to poison a regiment.'

The timing of this sudden dramatic increase of intake in drugs is reflected immediately in the Diary. The handwriting becomes wilder and the threats lurid. Maybrick returns to London where the failure of his attempted eighth killing provokes uncontrolled rage.

> *Damn it damn it the bastard almost caught me, curse him to hell. I will cut him up next time, so help me. A few minutes and I would have done* bastard. *I will seek him out, teach him a lesson. No one Will stop me. Curse his black soul. I curse myself for striking too soon, I should have waited until it was truly quiet so help me. I will take all next time and* eat it. *Will leave* nothing. *not even the head. I will boil it and eat it with freshly picked carrots.*

In March 1889, the children caught whooping cough and Dr Humphreys was called. The Diary makes an early reference to Gladys' rather fragile health.

> *My dearest Gladys is unwell yet again, she worries me so.*

This deceptively simple passing reference to Gladys strongly supports its author's intimate personal knowledge of the family.

The word 'again' is crucial. Every book on the Maybricks refers to this illness; *none* suggests Gladys was recurrently unwell. But buried deep among those thrilling Maybrick boxes at Kew was a letter from Margaret Baillie, a friend of the Baroness. It was written in April 1889 and said, 'I am sorry that your little girl has been unwell again.' The letter is referred to by Levy – but he copies it incorrectly and drops the word 'again'.

There is no other source for the information that Gladys was repeatedly sick.

While Dr Humphreys was at Battlecrease House he asked Florie about her husband's health. She told him of her fears about his use of drugs, just as she had told Dr Hopper the previous summer. She said he was now taking a white powder she thought was strychnine and asked what was likely to be the result. The doctor said that it could kill him and then with uncanny foresight added, 'If he should ever die suddenly, call me and I can say you have had some conversation about it.'

It was as though he knew the danger Florie was in.

For his part, Maybrick paid a visit to Dr Drysdale that month. He said that, although he was never free of headaches, he had been feeling better since his last visit in December. His tongue was furred however and he was still feeling a creeping numbness in his left arm and hand.

Florie wrote to Michael in London telling him of her anxiety about the white powder her husband was taking. She said that he was very irritable and complained of pains in the head. She said that Maybrick did not know she had discovered his drug addiction or that she had written to Michael.

Michael destroyed that letter but not before he questioned his brother about its contents, provoking an angry response, which he recalled at Florie's trial. His anger is recorded.

> *The bitch has written all*
> *tonight she Will fall.*

During the winter the Maybricks booked into the Palace Hotel, Birkdale, near Southport for a short break. With them were their friends the Samuelsons and Alf Brierly.

On the last night of their stay, a game of whist ended in a temperamental flare-up by Christina, who ran off shouting 'I hate you' to her husband. There were tears and, to her credit, Florie tried to smooth things over. 'You must not take any serious note of that' she reassured Charles. 'I often say "I hate you" to Jim.'

A few months later at the inquest into Maybrick's death, she told a different story and a somewhat more incriminating version of the incident. 'I had a conversation with Mrs Maybrick,' she said, 'and she told me she hated her husband.'

Some time in mid-March, Maybrick travelled to London to stay with his brother. According to Bernard Ryan in *The Poisoned Life of Mrs Maybrick* this was when Florie and Alf Brierley planned their escapade. On her husband's return Florie announced that she too wished to travel to the capital, to stay with a sick Aunt. Maybrick apparently bought her a new fur wrap for the visit, while confiding his true feelings to the Diary.

> *I shall buy the whore something for her visit. Will give the bitch the impression I consider it her duty to visit her aunt... what a joke, let the bitch believe I have no knowledge of her whoring affairs.*

Storms and floods were buffeting Liverpool when, on March 16th, Florie sent a telegram to the manager of the Flatman Hotel in Henrietta Street, London. She booked a two-room suite for 'Mr and Mrs Thomas Maybrick of Manchester' for one week. We don't know why she used her brother-in-law's name. It was seemingly stupid. When the hotel failed to confirm the reservation she wrote again, this time with a special request for a menu of soup, sole, duckling and green peas, new potatoes, cheese, celery and dessert, on arrival. The choice of the hotel itself was provocative for it was a meeting place of cotton men from Liverpool. She informed the hotel that she would be arriving first and her husband the following day. The manager accordingly arranged for bedroom nine and the adjoining sitting room sixteen to be at her disposal from Thursday March 21st.

At about the same time Florie wrote to her childhood friend, John Baillie Knight, in Holland Park, London, telling him that she was in a great deal of trouble and would like to meet him for dinner. She gave no explanation.

Florie left Battlecrease House and arrived at Flatman's at around 1 p.m. At about 6.30 p.m. John Baillie Knight called to see her and they stayed chatting in her sitting room. She explained that she had come to London to arrange a separation from her husband. She could no longer cope with his keeping a woman, she said, adding that he was cruel and hit her.

Baillie Knight agreed that a separation was best and suggested she see the solicitors, Markby, Stewart and Company, and then go to join her mother in Paris. John and Florie went to dine at the Grand Hotel and then on to the theatre, returning at about 11.30 p.m.

The next day Brierley arrived. He installed himself in Florie's suite and stayed there until 1 p.m. on Sunday when they both left, abruptly, settling the bill of £2.13s.

'He piqued my vanity and resisted my efforts to please him,' Florie said afterwards. 'Before we parted he gave me to understand he cared for someone else and could not marry me and that rather than face the disgrace of discovery he would blow his brains out. I then had such a revulsion of feeling I said we must end our intimacy at once.'

Brierley himself told the *New York Herald*, after her trial, 'We parted in London as if we were never to meet again... it was distinctly understood we were not to correspond.'

That understanding was soon forgotten – by them both.

Before leaving the capital, Florie did go to see Mr Markby, and with his help wrote a letter to her husband, asking for a separation and suggesting she remain at Battlecrease House with a yearly allowance. There is no record of whether that letter was received or even posted.

From March 24th–28th, Florie stayed with the Misses Baillie and on Wednesday March 27th, she dined with Michael. It had been a busy week for him. On the Monday he had been responsible for organising and performing in a star-studded gala concert, attended by the Prince and Princess of Wales, at the opening of his regiment's new headquarters in Euston Road. Next day, Thursday, Florie returned to Liverpool, to face the music and some of the letters from the Misses Baillie and John Baille Knight, castigating Florie.

So, ignominiously, ended her sadly inept escapade.

*　*　*

Florie had been a theatrical child. Friends recalled that she found the boundaries between fantasy and truth sometimes hard to recognise. She was about to find real life infused with more drama than she could have ever dreamed possible.

Liverpool's Cotton Exchange was already buzzing with rumours. Its members raised an eyebrow or two and it was suggested that if Maybrick were to learn of Florie's affair with Brierley he would 'fill him full of lead'.

Things came to a head the day after her return – March 29th, the day of the Grand National. It was a splendid event, attended by the Prince of Wales, to mark the 50th anniversary of the race. Brierley, of all people, had once again joined the Maybricks' charabanc party to Aintree. Maybrick was still playing the voyeur.

> *the bitch gave me the greatest pleasure of all. Did not the whore see her whore master in front of all, true the race was the fastest I have seen, but the thrill of seeing the whore with the bastard thrilled me more so than knowing his Royal Highness was but a few feet away from yours truly ha ha what a laugh, if the greedy bastard would have known he was less than a few feet away from the name all England was talking about he would have died there and then. Regret I could not tell the foolish fool. To hell with sovereignty, to hell with all whores, to hell with the bitch who rules,*

That particular National, won by Frigate, *was* the fastest then on record – information that has been confirmed after a great deal of probing in the race archives and local papers. Once again an obscure but accurate detail makes nonsense of the crude modern forgery theory.

Less than a week after their declared intention never to meet again, Florie and Brierley were photographed arm in arm when they went to see the Royal party. These photographs were apparently displayed in the window of Woollright's store during Florie's trial but have since been lost.

Maybrick was outraged and did not hide his anger. Florie was furious at her husband's outburst and left the races boasting to Christina Samuelson that when they got home she would 'give it to him hot and heavy'. But that night it was Maybrick the servants heard shouting, 'Such a scandal will be all over town tomorrow'.

What scandal? Was it Florie's indiscretion at the races or had the letter arrived from Markby's regarding the proposed separation?

A terrible scene followed. 'It began in the bedroom,' said Mary Cadwallader. 'Mr Maybrick told the maid, Bessie, to send his wife away. She came downstairs into the hall to go to the cab; he followed her and raved and stamped like a madman – waving his pocket handkerchief over his head. The button holes of Mrs Maybrick's dress were torn with the way he had pulled her about. She had on a fur cape; he told her to take it off as she was not to go away with that on. He had bought it for her to wear in London.

'I went up to the master and said: "Oh master, please don't go on like this, the neighbours will hear you.'" He answered: "Leave me alone, you don't know anything about it." I said: "Don't send the mistress away tonight. Where can she go? Let her stay till morning." Then he shouted: "By heavens, Florie, if you cross this doorstep you shall never enter it again." He became so exhausted he fell across an oak settle and went quite stiff. I did not know if he was drunk or in a fit. I sent the cab away and we got Mrs Maybrick upstairs and Mr Maybrick spent all night in the dining room.'

Next morning Florie had a black eye. She went to see Matilda Briggs to ask her advice and help in arranging a separation. They went together to see Dr Hopper. Florie confided to him that she had been up all night, her husband had beaten her and she was on her way to a solicitor. She also told him that she could not bear for her husband to come near her.

Good family doctor that he was, Dr Hopper decided to attempt to mend matters and went up to Battlecrease House later the same day. He saw Maybrick and Florie, who seemed calmer and more ready to resolve their respective differences. Florie repeated that she could not bear sleeping with her husband and did not want any more children. Despite this, it seems that Maybrick agreed to pay his wife's debts. They appeared to want to forgive and forget, so Dr Hopper left in the sincere, if naive, belief that he had effected a complete reconciliation.

* * *

Matilda Briggs joined the household the following day and there was another almighty row. The servants heard Florie shouting that she never invited anyone to the house without consulting him, so why should he do such a thing to her? There was a great deal of quarrelling and shouting and when, at 6 p.m., Mary Cadwallader took a cup of tea up to Florie, she found her lying on the sofa in a faint.

The maid rushed down to fetch Maybrick and Mrs Briggs' and together they ran upstairs. In yet another curious change of mood Maybrick knelt by his wife saying, 'Bunny, Bunny, here's your hubby.'

There was no response and for a while the servants thought Florie was dead.

It was another disturbed night. Mrs Briggs, half undressed, and wearing a dressing gown of Florie's that was far too small for her, kept disappearing into the kitchen for beer. She said she needed something 'to keep her up'.

This time, Dr Humphreys was sent for to see Florie. Confronted by the unseemly spectacle of the staggering, dishevelled Mrs Briggs, he demanded to know, 'Who is this woman?' That night the unfortunate doctor was recalled to Battlecrease House five times.

Florie remained in bed for nearly a week, during which time she confided to Elizabeth Humphreys that she and Maybrick also had money problems. She said that she was in debt and her husband's income was not enough to support them. But she still did not reveal the full story.

Many of the newspapers told of her extravagant habits but the Boston Globe in America was particularly explicit.

> Mrs Maybrick has been applying to private money lenders for small loans, paying heavy interest and repaying the principal in small sums from $5 to $15 a week. It was only a fortnight before his death that Maybrick accidentally became aware of these transactions. He came across a letter addressed to Mrs Maybrick, from a firm of money lenders, requesting the payment of a loan and, on learning the amount, which was $200 called at the office and discharged the debt.
>
> One letter that will be produced at the Trial is from Mrs Maybrick to the money lender telling him that if her husband called he was not to say how much she owed.

Maybrick also had a word with the servants. He told Mary Cadwallader not to take letters up to Florie until he had seen them. 'Your mistress sees all my letters,' he explained, 'there is no reason why I should not see hers.' On recovering, Florie contrived yet another meeting with Brierley, this time in Liverpool on April 6th. She told him that Maybrick had beaten her and dragged her around the room.

After that she wrote Brierley two more letters, apparently on the advice of Dr Hopper, telling him that she was reconciled with her husband.

Amazed, he tore the letters up.

On Saturday, April 13th, Maybrick went down to London. According to the Diary this visit was, in part, to settle Florie's debts. But the memory of that last aborted mutilation haunted him. He felt ready to strike yet again.

> *Once more the bitch is in debt, my God I will cut her... I will visit the city of whores I will pay her dues and I shall take mine, by God I will. I will rip rip rip...*

The other reason for visiting London was to see Michael's own physician Dr Fuller, who examined him for an hour when he called at

Michael's chambers on the Sunday. Maybrick complained of pains in his head and numbness. He said he was afraid of being paralysed. Dr Fuller decided there was little wrong and prescribed a nerve tonic and liver pills.

The following Saturday, Maybrick was back in London yet again. He went to Dr Fuller for a second consultation and acknowledged that he was much better. His prescription was slightly altered, the liver pills being replaced by lozenges. Whatever Dr Fuller said during those visits had a curious and dramatic effect. The handwriting in the Diary immediately becomes more controlled, the thoughts calmer and there are no further plans for murder. The thoughts now turn inward and begin to dwell on Maybrick's own death.

> *Fuller believes there is very little the matter with me. Strange, the thoughts he placed into my mind. I could not strike, I believe I am mad, completely mad. I try to fight my thoughts I walk the streets until dawn. I could not find it in my heart to strike, visions of my dear Bunny overwhelm me. I still love her, but how I hate her. She has destroyed all and yet my heart aches for her, oh how it aches. I do not know which pain is the worse my body or my mind.*

At last the idea dawns that he should throw his knife into the river which flowed only a few hundred yards from Battlecrease House.

The killing days were over.

> *I shall return to Battlecrease with the knowledge that I can no longer continue my campaign. 'Tis love that spurred me on so, 'tis love that shall put an end to it.*

On that Sunday, Florie wrote to her husband in London. The apparent about-face is a typically theatrical example of the deceit, lies and breathtaking dishonesty that surround the Maybrick story.

My own darling hubby!

...I have had a terrible night of it – and try as hard as I will to be brave and courageous because Jim thinks I may yet be of comfort to him and the children my physical weakness overcomes what remains of my mental strength. I have not sufficient self-respect left to lift me above the depth of disgrace to which I have fallen, for now that I am down I can judge better how very far above me others must be morally. I despair of ever reaching that standard again although I may recover some of your confidence by living a life of atonement for yours and the children's sakes alone. Nothing you can say can make me look at my actions but in the most degrading light and the more you impress the enormity of my crimes upon me the more hopeless I feel of ever regaining my position. I feel as though for the future I must be... a perpetual reminder of... trouble and that nothing can efface the past from your memory.

Please darling put me out of my pain as soon as you can. I have deceived and nearly ruined you but since you wish me to live tell me the worst at once – and let it be over... Darling, try and be as lenient towards me as you can for notwithstanding all your generous and tender loving kindess my burden is almost more than I can bear, my remorse and self-contempt is eating my heart out and if I did not believe my love for you and my dutifulness may prove some slight atonement for the past I should give up the struggle to keep brave! Forgive me if you can dearest and think less poorly of your loving wifesy
Bunny.

The children are well. I have been nowhere and seen no one.

This, from a woman who had recently told her doctor she could not bear to sleep with her husband and who ten days later addressed Brierley in a letter as 'dearest'. Was she truly contrite? Or could it have been, most naturally of all, that she was terrified that she could be pregnant after the Flatman escapade and needed to protect her future by once again sharing a bed with her husband?

About this time, Maybrick also commissioned his portrait in oils from a rising young Liverpudlian artist, J.T. Steadman, on the grounds that he might not live long. The *Pall Mall Gazette* later claimed that he had requested a 'Pictorial record of his bodily existence.' Sadly that picture, like so much else, has vanished without trace.

* * *

Between April 15th and 25th, Florie walked to Wokes the chemist on the corner of Aigburth and Beechwood Roads and bought a dozen fly papers. She said her kitchen was troubled by flies and asked the errand boy to deliver them to the house.

In July 1997, I was contacted by Mrs Gill Wokes, granddaughter-in-law of Arthur Siminson Wokes, who supplied Florie with those fly papers. She was researching the family tree. She told me that old Mr Wokes had two sons – one of whom, Arthur, known as Sam, was living with her when he died in 1993 at the age of 90. Sam Wokes was a prolific writer and hoarder of scraps of paper. A chemist himself, he had given lectures about the family business and its connections with the Maybricks. According to Mrs Wokes, Sam had talked a lot to her about his father's belief in Florie's innocence and his own suspicion that the Maybricks – maybe Michael – were linked to the Ripper case!

Most importantly, she sent me a copy of a scrap of paper she had found amongst Sam's possessions. In Sam's handwriting at the top (and written before publication of my book in 1993) are the words 'James Maybrick died May 11 1888.' He has the date wrong but beneath follows an excerpt from a book by Melvin Harris on Jack the Ripper published in 1989.

Soon after Florie's purchase, the housemaid, Bessie, was puzzled to find the washstand covered with a towel and peeping underneath she saw the soaking fly papers. Next morning they were in the wastepaper basket.

Also, on April 24th, Maybrick went to Clay and Abraham with Dr Fuller's prescription. His health continued to deteriorate rapidly. The same day, the much-missed Edwin returned from America.

My dear brother Edwin has returned. I wish I could tell him all.

The next day, four months after he had destroyed his Will, James made a new one. Or did he? It is on flimsy paper and is written in a strong hand. The witnesses were Maybrick's book-keeper George Smith and his great friend George Davidson. Neither mentioned the Will during the trial.

We know from Florie's letter to her mother that in December 1888 Maybrick had torn up his original Will and threatened to write a new one.

> In case I die before having made a regular proper Will in legal form I wish this to be taken as my last Will and testament.
>
> I leave and bequeath all my wordly possessions of whatever kind or description, including furniture, pictures, wines, linen, plate, Life Insurances, Cash, Shares, property, in fact everything I possess, in trust with my Brothers Michael Maybrick and Thomas Maybrick, for my two children James Chandler Maybrick and Gladys Eveleyn [sic] Maybrick. The furniture I desire to remain intact and to be used in furnishing a home which can be shared by my widow and children but the furniture is to be the children's. I further desire that all moneys be invested in the names of the above trustees (Michael and Thomas Maybrick) and the income of same used for the children's benefit and education, such education to be left to the discretion of said trustees.

> My widow will have for her portion of my estate the policies on my life, say £500 with the Scottish Widows Fund and £2,000 with the Mutual Reserve Fund Life Association of New York both Policies being made out in her name. The interest on this £2,500 together with the £125 a year which she receives from her New York property will make a provision of about £125 a year, a sum, although small, will yet be the means of keeping her respectably.
>
> It is also my desire that my widow shall live under the same roof with the Children so long as she remains my widow. If it is legally possible, I wish the £2,500 of Life Insurance on my life in my wifes name to be invested in the names of the said Trustees, but that she should have the sole use of the interest thereof during her lifetime, but at her death the principal revert to my said Children James Chandler and Gladys Eveleyn [sic] Maybrick.
>
> Witness my hand and seal this twenty fifth day of April 1889.
>
> signed James Maybrick.
>
> signed by the Testator in the presence of us who at his request in his presence and in the presence of each other have hereunto affixed our names as witnesses George R Davidson and George Smith.

Even at the time the Will became the focus of much speculation. MacDougall, in fighting form, went to see the Will in 1891 and was shocked by what he read. He wrote, in his book:

> It is absolutely inconceivable that James Maybrick could have been in his sound senses when he signed that Will.... [which] makes over and for ever every single thing James Maybrick possessed.... to the absolute, unfettered control of Michael Maybrick and Thomas Maybrick. Not only that

> but it makes over the children... to be treated by them as they like... To be educated and brought up, the boy as a chimney sweep! the girl as a seamstress if they liked... There is no provision in this Will that any of the property should come to either of these children when they come of age, or ever!
>
> Mrs Maybrick is to have neither bed nor blanket but he desires her to live in the 'home' which Michael and Thomas are to furnish and 'under the same roof' as his two children who are to be brought up and educated by Michael and Thomas Maybrick in any way they please! But this is not all! James Maybrick goes on in this Will to attempt to grab for these trustees even some life policies which belong to Mrs Maybrick herself... It is a Will which no court in any civilised country could have regarded as a Will made in his sound senses by any husband and father.

But the wording of the Will described by MacDougall is not exactly the same as that we read in London at Somerset House. For instance, in the Will that is kept at Somerset House, Maybrick's daughter's name is incorrectly spelt as 'Eveleyn'. In the MacDougall version it is not. Paul Feldman has listed ten other variations. MacDougall may have been inaccurate – rather unlikely since he was a lawyer – or he may have been looking at a different version. So what happened?

It is known that on the evening of May 10th, as Maybrick lay dying, Edwin and Michael came to the house with some papers to sign which Nurse Yapp, described as 'knowing and seeing everything', said were a Will. Yet he had, apparently, already written a Will on April 25th. Maybrick was heard calling out 'Oh Lord, if I am to die why am I to be worried like this. Let me die properly.'

On May 12th, Mrs Briggs searched the house for the keys to the safe in which she believed the missing Will was kept. On May 18th Thomas Maybrick prepared the servants for dismissal as 'the Will had left things very awkward'. The newspapers also referred to a 'curious Will'. Then, at the inquest before Florie's trial, Michael said that he would rather James' Will was not produced in evidence. It wasn't.

On July 29th, the newspapers reported that an Affidavit of Due Execution had been filed – implying that Maybrick's Will had been rejected for probate. If MacDougall's version of the Will *is* correct this would have been because there was a mistake in the wording of the attestation clause at the end. The words 'in his presence' should have been inserted after 'at his request'.

Clive Dyall, record keeper at Somerset House, offered an explanation to Paul Feldman when he wrote to him on August 17th 1993. He suggested that one Will could have been rejected by probate and the trustees told that another must be found or the testator would die intestate. A second Will was then 'found' and with an affidavit of due execution filed at the Liverpool District Probate Office. After 50 years, only the proved Will would have been sent to Somerset House, the others, said Mr Dyall would have been destroyed.

So Paul Feldman argues that there were in fact three Wills. The first, written in December after the row with Florie was 'in a large and shaky hand' as seen by MacDougall in 1891. The second Will was drafted on April 25th in order to 'redress the balance' of that written in the heat of the moment around Christmas. The brothers, realising that this left everything to Florie, persuaded James, as he lay dying, to sign the one he had drafted at Christmas. But after his death this Will is rejected because there was a mistake in the attestation clause and so the brothers 'find' a third version – in which Gladys Evelyn's name is mis-spelt and James' main insurance policy is omitted. This, says Paul, is the Will at Somerset House.

When I first heard of Paul's theories on the Will, I recalled a letter that I had received myself on June 9th 1993 – from Sue Iremonger. She wrote, 'I cannot, however, get away from the fact that both James and Michael have incredibly similar writing. Even taking into account their parallel schooling, I would not have expected to find such a similar style and weight of strokes.'

But, as with so much of this extraordinary story, that is not the end of the matter. Horns have been locked. Melvin Harris, in many pages of detailed analysis, rejects the fact that MacDougall ever saw the Will, in spite of MacDougall specifically saying he went to Liverpool to see the original. Mr Harris claims that he copied it wrongly from newspaper accounts (which were themselves inaccurate). He sums up any attempt to suggest that there was skulduggery afoot on the night of May 11th and that the Somerset House Will was not written by Maybrick as 'bluff and bluster' on the part of Paul Feldman.

The last word rests with Florie herself. In a petition to the authorities from prison she refers to the Will that 'I should have contested on the ground that "unlawful pressure had been brought to bear on the testator."'

14

I do not Know if She has the Strength to Kill me

At 8.30 a.m. on April 26th 1889, a parcel from London was delivered to Battlecrease House. Mary Cadwallader accepted it and went straight upstairs to her master. It was the medicine that Maybrick had been expecting.

The following day he was ill. He told Mary that he had vomited and his legs were numb, adding that he must have taken an overdose of the substance that had arrived the day before. Despite his condition and the dismal weather, he was determined to go later that day to the Wirral races, a great social event.

He went to the office at about 10.30 and left at about 1.30 p.m. returning home for his horse. He then rode off in the drizzle.

By the time he had arrived at the racecourse he was wet and shaking. His friend, William Thomson, noticed that he had difficulty remaining in the saddle. Maybrick's explanation was that he had taken a double dose of 'medicine' that morning.

Mrs Morden Rigg, the wife of Maybrick's old friend from America, also noticed his condition. He gave her the same explanation but this time he added that the 'medicine' was strychnine.

Although his clothes were soaked through, Maybrick decided to dine with his friends the Hobsons after the races. By this time he was so ill he could not hold a glass and, after spilling his wine twice, he left, embarrassed that his friends would think him drunk.

Next morning, Sunday April 28th, he was even worse. Florie asked the cook to prepare some mustard and water. 'Master has taken another dose of that horrid medicine,' she said. Dr Humphreys was summoned. When he arrived at Battlecrease House Florie told him she thought her husband's illness was probably due to some bad brandy he had drunk at the races. Maybrick himself said his symptoms had worsened after he had had a strong cup of tea but added that he had suffered from a headache for more than a year.

The doctor asked Maybrick about the effects of strychnine and nux vomica on him. In complete contradiction of his previous admission to Mrs Rigg that he had taken strychnine he said, 'I think I know a great deal of medicine. I cannot stand strychnine and nux vomica at all.'

Dr Humphreys recommended that he eat meat only once a day and that he take some beef tea thickened with Du Barry's Revalenta. This favourite Victorian remedy was advertised as a cure for 'indigestion, flatulency, dyspepsia, phlegm, constipation, all nervous bilious and liver complaints, dysentry, diarrhoea, acidity, palpitation, heartburn, haemorrhoids, headaches, debility, despondency, cramps, spasms, nausea, sinking fits, coughs, asthma and bronchitis, consumption and also children's complaints'! In other words the perfect medicine for a hypochondriac.

That Sunday Edwin came for lunch and during the day massaged James' legs, and stayed overnight. On Monday James wrote an astonishing letter to Michael, giving yet another version of events and hinting that Maybrick knew his end was near. Strangely, the letter was not produced at Florie's trial but a clerk made a copy and this survives. Michael's name has been crossed out and 'Blucher' substituted by the solicitor William Swift, who acted for the prosecution. A margin note in his handwriting explains that Blucher is Maybrick's pet name for his brother. Blucher was a kind of lace-up boot and was also the name of a Prussian general who fought against Napoleon at Waterloo.

Liverpool April 29th

My Dear Michael [deleted] Blucher
I have been very seedy indeed. On Saturday morning I found my legs getting stiff and useless but by sheer strength of will shook off the feeling and went down on horseback to Wirral Races and dined with the Hobsons. Yesterday morning I felt more like dying than living so much so that Florie called in another Doctor who said it was an acute attack of indigestion and gave me something to relieve the alarming symptoms, so all went on well until about 8 o'clock I went to bed and had lain there an hour by myself and was reading on my back. Many times I felt a twitching but took little notice of it thinking it would pass away but instead of doing so I got worse and worse and in trying to move round to ring the bell I found I could not do so but finally managed it but by the time Florie and Edwin could get upstairs I was stiff and for two mortal hours my legs were like bars of iron stretched out to the fullest extent but as rigid as steel. The Doctor came finally again but could not make it indigestion this time and the conclusion he came to was that the nux vomica I had been taking under Dr Fuller had poisoned me as all the symptoms warranted such a conclusion I know I am today sore from head to foot and played out completely.

What is the matter with me none of the Doctors so far can make out and I suppose never will until I am stretched out and cold and then future generations may profit by it if they hold a post mortem which I am quite willing they should do.

I don't think I shall come up to London this week as I

don't feel much like travelling and cannot go on with Fuller's physic yet a while but I shall come up and see him again shortly. Edwin does not join you just yet but he will write you himself. I suppose you go to your country quarters on Wednesday...

With love
Your affectionate brother Jim.
I have not seen Dickinson yet.

Meanwhile Florie wrote to her mother in France as though all was well.

We are asked to a bal masque which, being given in Liverpool and the people provincials, I hardly think likely to be a success. A certain amount of 'diablerie', wit and life is always required at an entertainment of this sort: and as it will be quite a novel innovation people will hardly know what is expected of them. However, we are expected to come 'in dominoes and masks' and I should like to know how the former is made and if the latter are not procurable in gauze instead of 'papier mache.'

Naturally Florie wanted to look her best for the ball, however 'provincial' her fellow guests! That day, April 29th, she went to Hanson's the chemist and bought some cosmetic tincture of benzoin and elderflowers. She also made another purchase which she was to regret for the rest of her life: more fly papers.

The next day Maybrick felt a little better and returned to work. The cook prepared some Revalenta and, since Edwin was staying at the house, Florie asked him to take the medicine to the office in Tithebarn Street for her husband's lunch. Thomas Lowry, the young clerk, left the office to buy a saucepan in which to heat up the mixture.

It was the gentle, good-looking Edwin who escorted Florie to the ball that night, presumably because James did not feel up to it. The

Top left: James Maybrick during the 1880s. Eyewitnesses claimed to have seen Mary Kelly talking to a man wearing a heavy gold chain.

Top right: The early-morning market crowd in Middlesex Street, better known as Petticoat Lane. James Maybrick rented a room here in the autumn of 1888, and the Ripper murders occurred in this exact vicinity.

Bottom left: Florence Maybrick, photographed during her marriage.

Bottom right: A never-before-published picture of Florence as a young woman.

An inoffensive looking Victorian diary. But the pages within contain the horrific confessions of James Maybrick, aka Jack the Ripper.

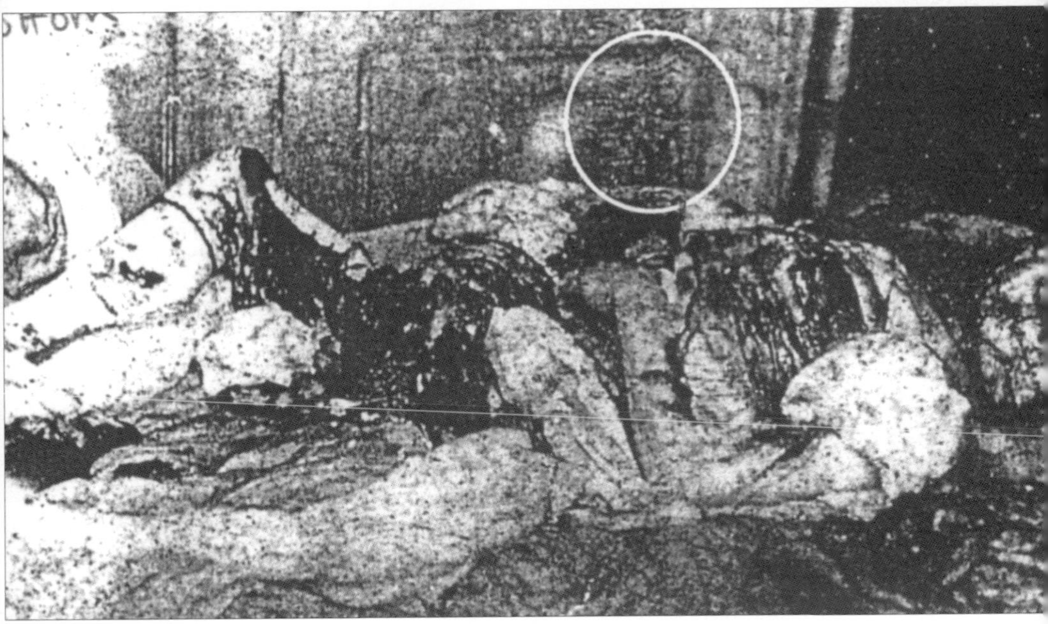

Top left: Battlecrease House, the Maybricks' Liverpool residence.

Top right: The house James Maybrick kept in Norfolk, Virginia, USA has been destroyed. This is its twin in the adjacent road. Recent evidence suggests that he could have committed his horrific deeds in America as well as England.

Bottom: The horrifically mutilated remains of Jack the Ripper's final victim, Mary Kelly. On the wall behind her are FM, Florence Maybrick's initials.

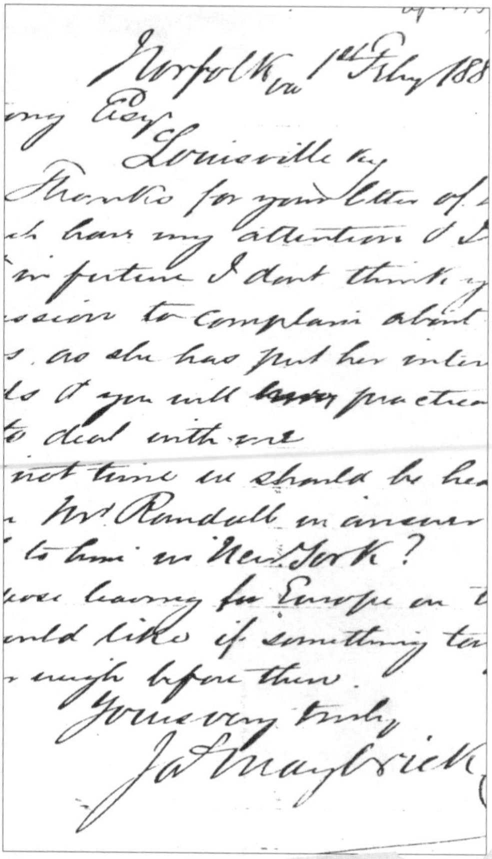

Norfolk Va 1st Feby 188
...ny Esq
Louisville Ky
Thanks for your letter of ...
...h have my attention I ...
...r future I dont think y...
...ssion to complain about
...s. as she has put her inter...
...ls & you will ~~[illegible]~~ practica...
to deal with me
not time we should be hea...
... Mr Randall in answer
to him in New York?
...pose leaving for Europe on t...
...uld like if something ter...
...rough before then.
Yours very truly
Jas Maybrick

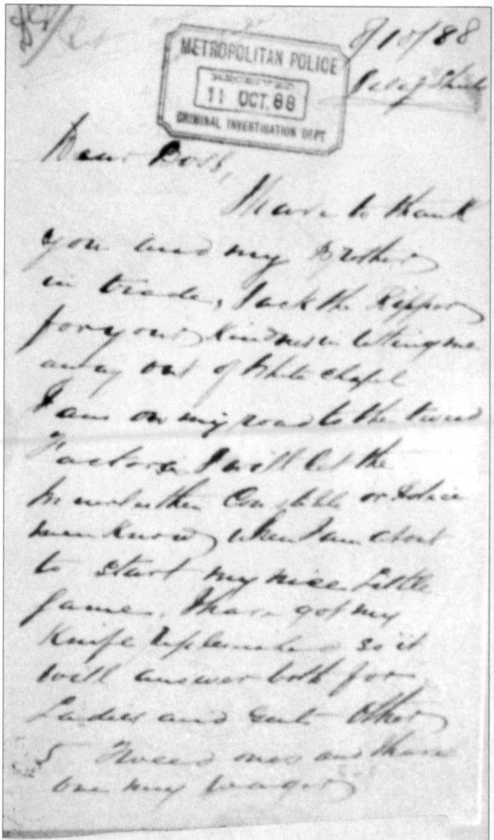

METROPOLITAN POLICE
11 OCT. 88
CRIMINAL INVESTIGATION DEPT

8/10/88
Gala Shiels

Dear Boss,
I have to thank you and my brother in trade, Jack the Ripper for your kindness in letting me away out of Whitechapel I am on my road to the Tweed Factories I will let the [illegible] Constables or Police men know when I am about to start my nice little game. I have got my knife replenished so it will answer both for Ladies and Gents other 5 [illegible]

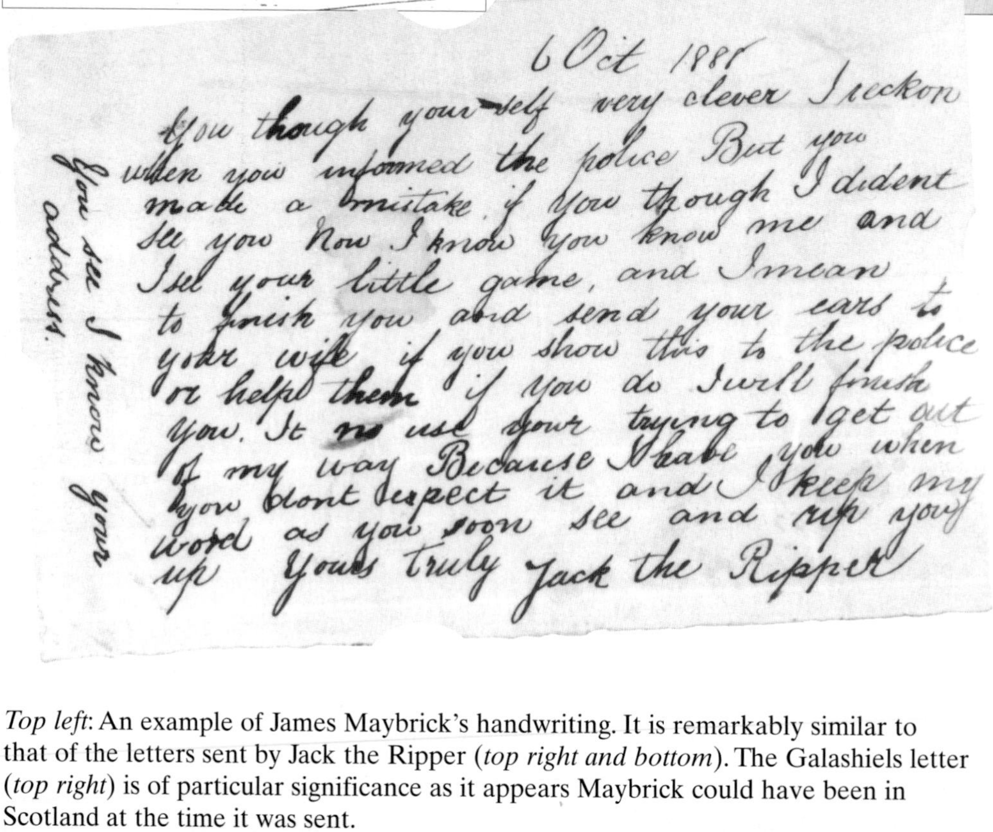

6 Oct 1888

You though your-self very clever I reckon when you informed the police But you made a mistake if you though I dident see you Now I know you know me and I see your little game, and I mean to finish you and send your ears to your wife if you show this to the police or helpe them if you do I will finish you. It no use your trying to get out of my way Because I have you when you dont expect it and I keep my word as you soon see and rip you up Yours truly Jack the Ripper

You see I know your address.

Top left: An example of James Maybrick's handwriting. It is remarkably similar to that of the letters sent by Jack the Ripper (*top right and bottom*). The Galashiels letter (*top right*) is of particular significance as it appears Maybrick could have been in Scotland at the time it was sent.

Top: The Cotton Exchange in Liverpool.

Bottom: Drawings of the International Cotton Exposition in New Orleans which opened Christmas 1884. It is inconceivable that Maybrick would not have been at this event. On December 30 1884, the mutilated body of a black cook, Mollie Smith, was discovered in Austin, Texas... Could it be that Jack the Ripper had struck in America?

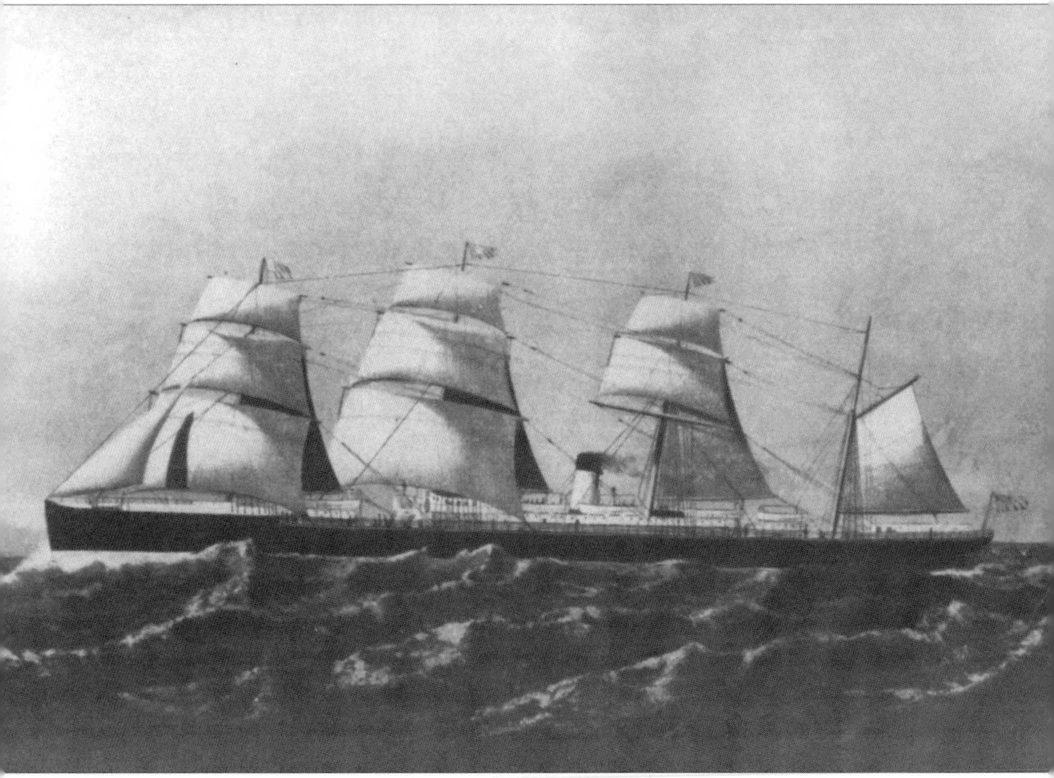

Top: The house in Mobile, USA, where Maybrick's wife Florie was born.

Bottom: The trans-Atlantic ship on board which James and Florie met.

Top left: Anne and Michael Barrett with their daughter Caroline in happier days – before the contents of an inconspicuous looking diary ripped their lives apart.

Top right: Alfred Brierley, who became Florie's lover. The behaviour of the couple provoked murderous rages in James Maybrick.

Bottom: A recently discovered gold watch, hall-marked in 1846, and made by Henry Verity of Lancaster. Scratched on the inside cover (*right*) are the signature of J. Maybrick, the words 'I am Jack' and the initials of the five Whitechapel victims: MK, ES, CE, MN and AC.

Eula Phillips, the final victim of the Austin murderer. But could it be that this is the face of a hitherto unknown victim of Jack the Ripper?

following day, May 1st, Captain Irving of the White Star Line met the two brothers at the office. While they were talking he recalled, in a later affidavit, Maybrick pulled out a small packet, the contents of which he emptied into a glass of water. Captain Irving noticed him take two doses in 15 minutes. 'Everybody knew Jim was always taking some medicine or other'. When the Captain returned with them to Battlecrease House, Maybrick was unable to sit at the table. Captain Irving subsequently met Edwin in town and asked him 'What on earth is the matter with Jim?'

'He is killing himself with that damned strychnine,' said Edwin.

When a newspaper later printed Captain Irving's account of these events, Edwin categorically denied everything. 'Statement absolutely and entirely untrue in every respect,' he said in a telegram to the press. 'Never saw my brother use any white powder in wine or otherwise in my life.' And at Florie's trial, Edwin claimed that he had no knowledge of his brother's drug habit.

On Thursday May 2nd, Maybrick again took his lunch to the office but returned home feeling ill. The diary records:

> *I no longer take the dreaded stuff for fear I will harm my dear Bunny, worse still the children.*

If what he wrote was true – if Maybrick had indeed stopped taking drugs – a sudden withdrawal would have been almost unbearable. In 1885, *Chambers Journal of Popular Literature, Science and Art* had reported on a conference that included the topic of arsenic eating.

> When a man has once begun to indulge in it he must continue to indulge or, as it is popularly expressed, the last dose kills him.
>
> Indeed, the arsenic eater must not only continue his indulgence, he must also increase the quantity of the drug, so that it is extraordinarily difficult to stop the habit for, as the sudden cessation causes death, the gradual cessation

produces such a terrible heart gnawing that it may probably be said that no genuine arsenic eater ever ceased to eat arsenic while life lasted.

From the last entries in the diary, until his death, Maybrick would have been in agony. And indeed, it is in these entries that he expresses remorse and begs for release from the torment of living.

I do not have the courage to take my life. I pray each night I will find the strength to do so, but the courage alludes me. I pray constantly all will forgive. I deeply regret striking her, I have found it in my heart to forgive her for her lovers. I believe I will tell her all, ask her to forgive me as I have forgiven her. I pray to God she will understand what she has done to me.

On May 3rd Maybrick saw Dr Humphreys and complained that the medicine was doing him no good. Florie observed, tartly, that he said the same about any medicine after two or three days. After seeing the Doctor, Maybrick went to his office for the last time. That afternoon, with the Doctor's approval, he went to the Turkish baths. This was also the day on which he made his final emotional entry in the diary.

The pain is unbearable. My dear Bunny knows all. I do not know if she has the strength to kill me. I pray to God she finds it. It would be simple, she knows of my medicine, and for an extra dose or two it would all be over. No one will know I have seen to that. George knows of my habit and I trust soon it will come to the attention of Michael. In truth I believe he is aware of the fact. Michael will know how to act he is the most sensible amongst us all I do not believe I will see this June, my favourite of all months. Have begged Bunny to act soon. I curse myself for the coward I am.

During the evening Maybrick became very ill with a 'gnawing pain from the hips down to the knees'. At midnight Dr Humphreys once again made his way to Battlecrease House. He decided the pains were the result of hard towelling at the baths and, ignoring the fact that his patient had also vomited twice, he administered a morphine suppository.

The following morning Maybrick was worse. He was vomiting violently. Dr Humphreys made an early visit and gave instructions that the patient was to drink nothing at all: he could quench his thirst by washing out his mouth with water or sucking ice or a damp cloth. Some medicine was delivered by the chemist and taken straight up to Maybrick's room by Mary Cadwallader.

'Nothing must be taken to his bedroom without my seeing it first', Florie ordered. Recovering the medicine she emptied it all down the sink and explained later to Cadwallader that the tiniest bit more would have killed her husband. In such circumstances the simplest actions with straightforward explanations can become tainted by innuendo and rumour. There was a deepening air of prurient excitement at Battlecrease House which was infecting the atmosphere like a fever. There is no doubt that the case against Florie was built on gossip and malicious misunderstanding.

Trevor Christie refers to 'the deadly cabal' of Nurse Yapp, and the three sisters – Mrs Briggs, Mrs Hughes and Gertrude Janion – who stirred up a witches' brew of hatred and suspicion.

Alexander MacDougall described the bizarre events at Battlecrease in the last few hours of James Maybrick's life but included in that cabal Maybrick's brothers Michael and Edwin. It was his belief that, for reasons we can only guess, they had conspired together in James Maybrick's death. In other words it was a plot which went wrong. Michael, in particular, certainly had so much to lose. He was at the peak of his career, mixing in elevated circles and making a great deal of money; his life would have been shattered if a whisper of James' secret life in London were to leak to the press. Edwin was in love with Florie.

Independent support for this suspicion came from the most unexpected place – Burma.

With astonishing speed, immediately after Florie's trial, a missionary,

Mrs Frederick Mason, widow of the Reverend Dr Frederick Mason, wrote a book entitled *The Secret to the Maybrick Poisoning*. It was published as a 45-page limited edition in Rangoon by the D'Vauz Press, in February 1890 – and in 2003 an original copy was sold to a collector in Cheadle, Cheshire for £1,000.

Like that of Alexander McDougall, the following year, it is an indignant treatise, ferociously, if somewhat naively defensive of Florie, with a curiously stimulating way of thinking laterally about the evidence produced at the trial. Mrs Mason has a different perspective on almost everything that happened. Any profits from the sale of her book were to be sent to Florie's solicitors to help pay the costs of her trial.

There are three main thrusts to Mrs Mason's argument.

1. The trial was a pre-determined gladiatorial fight to the death. Florie owed her sentence and imprisonment to the eminent position of her defence and to politics. 'When it became known that Sir Charles Russell was to be pitted against Mr Justice Fitzjames Stephen, it put that latter functionary, holding the scale, upon his mettle, and it was secretly vowed that he should come off the victor.' Florie never had a chance, she was a pawn in a power game.

2. Maybrick did not die of arsenic poisoning. He died from lack of arsenic. 'His disease was clearly and unmistakably ... induced by the erosion of the Indian Ringworm ... This initially produces a small watery pustule and is attended by great irritation, inflammation, intense thirst and restlessness ... It sometimes attacks the mouth and if not stopped will ... go all over the tongue ... and up into the head. One young gentleman died here with a sensation of creeping inside his head.

'Dr Drysdale says at the Trial: "He complained of creeping all over the head, causing pain and the tongue was furred ..." Mr Maybrick must have contracted the disease from the negroes of Virginia or perhaps from handling cotton which had been handled with diseased hands.'

Arsenic, she says is the only cure. She was supported by a letter in the *Times* on August 16th 1889 from David Cumming of Liverpool, who admitted that he had been similarly cured of chronic eczema by taking large quantities of arsenic, mostly in Fowler's Solution

Mrs Mason rails against the ineptitude of the doctors and then turns her venom on the brothers.

3. Michael and Edwin, she says, showed 'only the subtlety of the cobra and the ferocity of the tiger'. She refers to Michael's 'hatred' of Florie's nationality – supported at the trial by Elizabeth Humphreys' statement. She even accuses them of behind-the-scenes undermining of Florie to the jurors and, like MacDougall, interfering with Maybrick's 'dreadful' will. She does not believe that this emanated from Maybrick, or was signed by him in his right mind. 'If James Maybrick lived,' she thundered 'his brothers would get nothing at all, but if he died they would grasp at one bound more than 50,000 Rs (rupees). She is sensorious and extreme but it does contain some food for thought and certainly confirms widespread unease that there was something very nasty afoot during Florie's trial.

*   *   *

On the morning of Saturday May 4th, Florie sent Mary Cadwallader to Wokes to collect some medicine on prescription. James Grant, the gardener, told Alice Yapp that Mr Wokes had refused to give it to her on the grounds that it contained a deadly poison. Alice then passed this juicy information on to Mrs Briggs and Mrs Hughes.

But on August 21st, three months after James' death, Mary Cadwallader told the *Liverpool Post*: 'I don't know how she could have dared tell such a story.' Mary said that Dr Humphreys started to write a prescription that he did not complete. He laid it to one side. In her agitation Florie had suddenly picked this up so Mary went to the chemist with the wrong prescription – Mr Wokes explained that the doctor's signature was needed and suggested that the doctor should call in himself. Mary denied that there was ever any mention of poison.

She went home, explained the mistake and returned to Mr Wokes, who then gave her the meat juice. Dr Humphreys later called to give Mr Wokes the necessary information for the original prescription.

Dr Humphreys' account of the event makes no mention of the prescription containing poison. Nevertheless, that innocent visit, like so many other things, assumed sinister proportions in the servants' quarters.

On Sunday May 5th, Elizabeth Humphreys went up to see her master, who begged for some lemonade with a little sugar, saying, 'I want you to make it as you would for any poor man, dying of thirst.'

Florie was in the room and said, 'You cannot have it except as a gargle'. She was following Dr Humphreys' instructions.

That afternoon, Edwin turned up at the house and disobeying doctor's orders, gave his brother a brandy and soda which Maybrick promptly vomited.

On Monday May 6th, the doctor called at about 8.30 a.m. He reminded Maybrick not to take his usual Valentine's Meat Juice or prussic acid since they were making him vomit. He prescribed Fowler's Solution, which contained arsenic.

While Florie went shopping, Nurse Yapp was left behind with Maybrick. He was moaning and hot; she rubbed his hands, which he again said were numb. When Florie came back Yapp suggested calling the Doctor but Florie rejected the idea on the grounds that her husband would not do what he said anyway.

Battlecrease House was by now crowded with family, staff and visitors, all bustling about, whispering and watching each other and, in particular, Florie. In the midst of all this, a letter from Brierley arrived in which he said he was afraid their secret was about to be exploded and that he was off abroad – out of harm's way.

During the evening of May 6th Dr Humphreys paid yet another visit and applied a 'blister' – a dressing intended to ease Maybrick's stomach pains.

As the illness wore on, the atmosphere of mistrust increased. So, when Alice Yapp spotted Florie pouring something from one bottle to another, she was decidedly suspicious. She remembered the fly papers that Bessie told her she had discovered soaking under a towel in the washbasin.

In the early afternoon of May 7th, Florie sent a telegram to Edwin's office in Liverpool asking him to find someone who could offer a second medical opinion. So it was that Dr William Carter, a self-described 'physician of considerable experience, including cases of overdosing medicinally with arsenic', joined the medical team. He met Dr Humphreys at the house at 5.30 p.m. and together they examined the restless patient. By now Maybrick was also complaining of a 'hair' in his throat.

The Doctors decided he was suffering from dyspepsia and this time prescribed small doses of antipyrine to relieve his painful throat and tincture of jaborandi plus diluted chlorodyne to relieve the foul taste in his mouth. That night Maybrick vomited continuously and was still bothered by the 'hair'.

On Wednesday May 8th, he was unable to get out of bed and told Dr Humphreys he thought he was going to die. Edwin saw his brother before leaving early for work. Maybrick suggested that a nurse be brought in to help Florie, who was exhausted. Florie telegraphed her mother in Paris with a terse message that bore a sharply different tone from her previous breezy letter: 'Jim very ill again'.

Through the upstairs window, Nurse Yapp, who was agog with all she had seen or imagined, spotted the sisters Mrs Briggs and Mrs Hughes hurrying up the drive. She accosted them in the yard with the shocking declaration, 'Thank God you have come, for the mistress is poisoning the master'. She led them immediately up to see James.

Florie was understandably put out when she discovered that the sisters were already in her husband's room. She called them down to the sitting room where it was eventually agreed that a nurse should be hired. Mrs Briggs and Mrs Hughes left about noon but immediately telegraphed Michael in London. 'Come at once,' said the message. 'Strange goings on here.' This was one of two portentous telegrams sent to Michael that day. The second was from Edwin who also urged his brother to come to Battlecrease House.

Nurse Gore, from the Nurses' Institution in Liverpool, arrived at the house at about 2.15 p.m. With the Nurse there to relieve her, Florie made a critical mistake. She wrote a reply to Brierley. She followed this with a second mistake. She asked Alice Yapp to post the letter.

Alice took the letter and admitted later at Florie's trial that that she gave it to little Gladys to carry as they walked to catch the 3.45 p.m. post. On the way Gladys 'dropped it'. 'I went into the post office and asked for a clean envelope to readdress it. I opened it as I was going into the post office,' she testified.

What Alice Yapp read so shocked her that she put the letter in her pocket. It was never posted.

> *Dearest*
>
> *...I cannot answer your letter fully today, my darling, but relieve your mind of all* fear of discovery *now and in the future. M has been delirious since Sunday, and I now know that he is* perfectly ignorant *of everything, even* to the name of the street*, and also* that he has not been making any inquiries whatever*! The tale he told me was pure fabrication, and only intended to frighten the truth out of me. In fact,* he believes *my statement, although he will not* admit it.*You need not therefore go abroad on that account, dearest; but, in any case, please don't* leave England until I have seen you once again*! You must feel that those two letters of mine were written under circumstances which must even excuse their injustice in your eyes.*
>
> *Do you suppose that I could act as I am doing if I really felt and meant what I inferred then? If you wish to write to me about anything do so* now*, as all the letters pass through my hands at present. Excuse this scrawl, my own darling, but I dare not leave the room for a moment, and I do not know when I shall be able to write to you again. In haste, yours ever, Florie.*

When Edwin returned at about five o'clock, Nurse Yapp was at her customary look-out post, watching for him in the yard, and she intercepted him. As they sat on a seat in the garden she disclosed her startling find. But he took no action.

Michael arrived at Edge Hill Station just before nine and was met by his brother in a cab. When Edwin told him about the letter Michael took charge of the situation. Back at the house the two men read the Brierley letter and after Michael had seen their now half-conscious brother, he spoke sharply to Florie. He still did not tell her that they had read the letter but criticised her rather for not having brought in a professional nurse and a second Doctor earlier. Then he left to see Dr Humphreys at his house, arriving at 10.30 p.m. The doctor acknowledged that he was not satisfied with Maybrick's condition and Michael informed him of Nurse Yapp's suspicions. The doctor did nothing either. He merely said, 'Your brother has told me he is going to die.'

Everyone had a restless night. Nurse Gore had been instructed that she alone was to give Maybrick his food and medicine. A new bottle of Valentine's Meat Juice was supplied by Edwin and given to a relief Nurse who, by that time, had taken over from the exhausted Nurse Gore.

Dr Carter was back at Battlecrease House the following afternoon and persisted in his diagnosis of 'acute dyspepsia'. Michael, extremely agitated, objected. Since April, he claimed, his brother had been ill when at home and perfectly well when away. He added that the rift between Maybrick and his wife was serious and that Florie had been buying fly papers. What was Dr Humphreys going to do?

Now that suspicion of Florie had been discussed with the doctor, Michael decided to step up the safeguards surrounding the patient. Florie was by now virtually dispossessed in her own house. She wandered from room to room in a tearful state. She went up to the night nursery where Nurse Yapp was tending to the children and said, 'Do you know I am blamed for this?'

Nurse Yapp answered disingenuously, 'For what?'

Florie replied, 'For Mr Maybrick's illness.'

Everything was against her. She knew that Dr Humphreys had not been in favour of calling a second doctor and that Dr Carter had said there was no need for a nurse. She had ultimately defied them and asked for both but Michael was accusing her of delay. She was confused and upset.

Florie had only two loyal friends in the house. One was Mary Cadwallader, who found some old fly papers in the butler's pantry and burnt them. The other was the cook, Elizabeth Humphreys, who watched in the servants' hall as Florie collapsed and sobbed for fifteen minutes. Since Michael's arrival, Florie told her, she had not been allowed in Maybrick's room. 'My position is not worth anything in this house.' Michael hated her, she said, and if James got better she would not have Michael there again. But Florie's vow would never be put to the test.

On Thursday May 9th, Maybrick was too ill to be examined. The doctors gave him double doses of bismuth with some brandy as a stomach sedative. For the first time they took samples of urine and faeces, which Dr Carter took back to his surgery for analysis. Michael with some zealousness turned over a small bottle of Neaves Food, with which Florie was suspected of tampering, to the doctor. A bottle of brandy of which Michael was also suspicious was tested. All proved negative, a fact that was never mentioned at Florie's trial.

During the evening, Maybrick grew still worse. Against Doctors' instructions, Nurse Gore took the unopened bottle of Valentine's Meat Juice which Edwin had produced from a table on the landing and gave him two teaspoonsful in water. Florie was there and protested in vain that the Doctors had told Maybrick to discontinue the juice which always made him sick.

Just after midnight, Nurse Gore gave Maybrick some champagne, perhaps to calm his stomach, and noticed that Florie took the remaining bottle of meat juice into the dressing room. According to the nurse, Florie returned after two minutes and 'surreptitiously' replaced the bottle on the bedside table. Nurse Callery, who was also attending Maybrick, said afterwards that Michael later removed the bottle without any of the meat juice having been given to the patient since Florie had returned it. Later on Friday Michael handed a bottle of meat juice to Dr Carter for analysis. It proved to contain half a grain of arsenic.

This bottle was produced in evidence at Florie's trial.

On Friday Maybrick was even worse. Nurse Wilson, a relief nurse, said she overheard Maybrick calling repeatedly to Florie, 'Oh Bunny, Bunny, how could you do it? I did not think it of you.' Florie replied, 'You silly old darling, don't trouble your head about things.'

Later, when Thomas Lowry and George Smith delivered the papers to the house to be signed, they heard the shouted protestations from James to Michael and Edwin that he wanted to die in peace.

At 4 a.m. on Saturday May 11th, Florie sent Mary Cadwallader to collect Mrs Hughes and Mrs Briggs. The children were taken in to see their father for the last time. During the morning Florie herself was carried from the sickroom to the spare bedroom, where she lay in a mysterious 'swoon' for 24 hours, totally unaware of what was happening. Dr Carter arrived and warned Michael that he had found some arsenic in the bottle of meat juice and that he and Humphreys could therefore not give the cause of death as 'natural'.

At 8.40 p.m. – in the arms of his most intimate friend, George Davidson – James Maybrick died.

The next day Dr Hopper was called up to the house. In a supplemental statement at the trial he recalled that visit and his words point, for the first time, to the possibility that Florie could have been pregnant. 'I found that she was suffering from a sanguinous discharge, which might have been a threatened miscarriage and she told me that she had not had her monthly period since March 7th. I was unable then to tell whether she was pregnant or not but I think it could be ascertained now by examination.'

If Florie was indeed pregnant it seems unlikely that the baby would have been James'.

* * *

Where, amid all this uproar, was the Diary? Did Maybrick leave it at the office or was it hidden somewhere in Battlecrease House? Was it found by Michael and Edwin, who would have had every reason to protect the family name, or was it in the trunk of Florie's possessions which was lost; or, more likely, was it discovered by the servants when they ransacked the house and smuggled secretly away as a memento? Wherever it was, the Diary is specific about Maybrick's own hopes.

> *I place this now in a place where it shall be found. I pray whoever should read this will find it in their heart to forgive me. Remind all, whoever you may be, that I was once a gentle man...dated this 3rd day of May 1889*

15

I Place This Now in a Place Where it Shall be Found

Maybrick was dead. The last page of the Diary was closed. But the dark shadows of conspiracy surrounding Florie's trial – the lying, the suspicions and the suppression of evidence – confirm my belief that much, much more was known than ever saw the light of day.

Two days after Maybrick's death, on May 13th, Drs Humphreys, Carter and Barron carried out a post-mortem in the presence of Superintendent Bryning. The police had already begun to investigate the circumstances of the death, because Doctors Carter and Humphreys had refused to issue a death certificate and decided instead to refer the case to the coroner.

Michael took charge of everything after his brother's death, including his ailing widow, who found herself being tended by a strange nurse. Florie recalled that Michael told the nurse, 'Mrs Maybrick is no longer mistress of this house. As one of the executors I forbid you to allow her to leave this room.'

She was a prisoner even before she was formally charged. Although suspicions of arsenic poisoning had been rumbling around for some days, no search was made until after Maybrick had died. Then, with Florie locked out of the way, Michael, Edwin, Mrs Briggs, Mrs Hughes and all the servants ransacked Battlecrease House. They said at Florie's trial that in a linen chest on the landing they found a bottle of morphia, a bottle of vanilla essence and a packet of harmless yellow powder, none of which Bessie, the housemaid who was in charge of the chest, said she had noticed before.

But the discovery most sinister to the prying eyes of Florie's adversaries was a packet on which was written, in red ink: 'Arsenic. Poison for Cats'. On the other side was a printed label saying 'poison'. Inside was a mixture of arsenic and charcoal. Michael wrapped the packet in paper and affixed the family seal. Florie was devoted to cats and her supporters believed that the label, which was not in her handwriting, must have been a joke by Nurse Yapp and her friend Alice Grant, the gardener's wife.

An 'Important Statement' appeared in the *Pall Mall Gazette* of June 15th, stating that 'the probable explanation of the package found labelled "Poison for Cats", may be found in the fact that a kennel of dogs near to Battlecrease House – which caused great annoyance to the deceased – were poisoned and arsenic found in their bodies upon examination. It is alleged that the deceased was suspected, after his death, of poisoning the dogs.'

How strange that, as happened so often during Florie's trial, this evidence – albeit rumour – was never produced, when its inclusion could have provided useful support for her case and some further insight into the terrible truth about James Maybrick's other life. But at the time the full significance of this story was not understood. Nobody had appreciated, as the Diary had shown, how James Maybrick's sometimes sadistic sense of humour could have turned on Florie.

The haul of medicines gathered from all over the house was then turned over to the police. The list that was handed later to the chemical analyst is truly astonishing – not for the finger it points at the unhappy wife, but for the picture it paints of a man enslaved by drugs. Everyone in that house had access to huge quantities of drugs.

It was an outrage that Florie, alone, should be charged with administering poison. She was a victim of whispered gossip.

The analyst, Mr Edward Davies, said at Florie's trial that he had found enough arsenic to 'kill two or three people'. His evidence was so technical that it was quite beyond the comprehension of witnesses, the jury or even the judge himself. In the end, it seems only six items contained any arsenic and that these were not in a form suitable for murder! For example, the arsenic stain found in Florie's dressing gown pocket could well have come from the handkerchief with which she wiped her face after using arsenical products. Such explanations were not forthcoming at the trial.

Alexander MacDougall is scathing in his attack on Davies' unreliability and the inaccuracy of his methods and results. Of all the things in the list which did contain arsenic, 'the whole of them might have been swallowed together and all would not have contained sufficient to kill anybody.'

Years later, Florie Maybrick wrote her autobiography, *My Fifteen Lost Years*, in which she described those terrible days after her husband's death:

> Slowly consciousness returned, I opened my eyes. The room was in darkness. All was still. Suddenly the silence was broken by the bang of a closing door which startled me out of my stupor. Where was I? Why was I alone? What awful thing had happened? A flash of memory. My husband was dead. I drifted once more away from the things of sense. Then a voice, as if a long way off, spoke. A feeling of pain and distress shot through my body. I opened my eyes in terror. My brother-in-law, Edwin Maybrick, was bending over me as I lay upon my bed. He had my arms tightly gripped and was shaking me violently. 'I want your keys. Do you hear? Where are your keys?' he exclaimed harshly. I tried to form a reply but the words choked me and once more I passed into unconsciousness.

The day after Maybrick's death, Florie told her nurse-cum-jailer that she wanted to see her children. 'You cannot see Master James or Miss Gladys,' she recalled the nurse answering in a cold, deliberate voice. 'Mr Michael Maybrick gave orders that they were to leave the house without seeing you.'

'I fell back upon my pillow, dazed and stricken, weak, helpless and impotent,' Florie wrote. 'Why was I being treated like this?... my soul cried out to God to let me die... the yearning for my little children was becoming unbearable.'

Bobo and Gladys were sent away temporarily with Nurse Yapp to friends, and eventually went to stay with their former nanny, Emma Parker, who had married and was now Mrs John Over. Within days, they had lost both parents as well as the familiar comfort of the nursery at Battlecrease House. Their mother, the former Southern Belle who had fallen in love as a girl and exchanged her affluent cosmopolitan circle in America for the secure claustrophobia of middle-class Victorian Liverpool, was now a widow and a prisoner in her own home. She was suspected by family and friends of her husband's murder.

On May 14th, three days after her husband's death, the rumours surrounding Florie were to become formal allegations. As she herself described it:

> Suddenly the door opened and Dr. Humphreys entered. He walked silently to my bedside, felt my pulse and without a word left the room. A few minutes later I heard the tramp of many feet coming upstairs. They stopped at the door. The nurse advanced and a crowd of men entered. One of them stepped to the foot of the bed and said to me: 'Mrs Maybrick, I am the Superintendent of Police and I am about to say something to you. After I have said what I intend to say be careful how you reply because whatever you say may be used as evidence against you. Mrs Maybrick, you are in custody on a suspicion of causing the

> death of your late husband, James Maybrick, on the eleventh instant.'

Earlier that day the coroner had decided that 'poison was found in the stomach of the deceased in such quantities as to justify further proceedings.' A policeman was stationed in Florie's room, although there was no likelihood of her escaping. The officer would not even let her close the door night or day. On the day of Maybrick's funeral, Thursday May 16th, Florie awoke to the sound of muffled voices and hurrying footsteps. She was told abruptly by the nurse 'the funeral starts in half an hour.'

At first, Florie found herself barred from the bedroom where her husband's coffin, covered with white flowers, had already been closed. She wrote in her book:

> I turned to the policeman and nurse. 'Leave me alone with the dead.' They refused. I knelt by the bedside and was able to cry the first tears which many days of suffering had failed to bring... Calmed, I returned to my room and sat near a window, still weeping.
>
> Suddenly the harsh voice of the nurse broke on my ears. 'If you wish to see the last of the husband you murdered you had better stand up.' I stumbled to my feet and clutched at the window sill, where I stood, rigid and tearless until the hearse had passed from sight. Then I fainted.

* * *

The Baroness, in her bombazine best, burst on Battlecrease House the following day in response to a grudging telegram from Michael. 'Florie ill and in awful trouble' it read, without bothering to mention Maybrick's death.

'Edwin met me in the vestibule and took me into the morning room,' wrote the Baroness later. 'He was much agitated...he then went on to tell me in a broken way that Michael had suspected, and the doctor thought, that something was wrong... the nurse said Florie put something in the meat juice.'

The Baroness stormed upstairs and tried to speak to Florie in French. When Florie told her mother that she was suspected of poisoning Maybrick, the Baroness replied, 'If he is poisoned, he poisoned himself. He made a perfect apothecary's shop of himself.'

On Saturday morning, May 18th, the Baroness consulted Florie's solicitors, the brothers Arnold and William Cleaver, of the firm of Cleaver, Holden, Garnett and Cleaver. While she was in their office a telegram arrived announcing that Florie was about to be removed from the house. Thirteen legal and medical men had arrived by train and gathered around Florie's bed. Both Arnold and William Cleaver arrived before the Baroness and were already among the assembled party. There had been a huddled consultation in the drive beforehand, watched eagerly by a crowd of reporters and onlookers. The Cleavers agreed not to object to a remand.

The Baroness arrived as Florie was being led away. 'I went up to my bedroom which looked out on the front,' she recalled, 'to try and see her face as they put my child into the cab and they turned the key and locked me in ... they hurried her away in so unseemly a manner that even her handbag with toilet articles was left behind... The nurse snatched up my cloak and hat and put them on her and they hustled her into an armchair, she being too weak to stand, and she was carried to the cab.'

* * *

A few weeks after Maybrick's death, his friend Charles Ratcliffe wrote a long letter to John Aunspaugh in Atlanta, Georgia. This letter is recalled in Trevor Christie's book *Etched in Arsenic* and formed a part of Florence Aunspaugh's personal collection of memorabilia.

The letter shows a dramatic personal view of events leading up to Maybrick's death, especially as Ratcliffe was a long-standing friend of the family and a reliable witness. It is a harsh, but most likely a true assessment of the trap set to catch Florie.

> This was a great shock to me. I had been expecting a tragedy within the family but was looking for it from the other party. James had gotten wise to the Flatman hotel affair and I was expecting him to plug Brierley at any time.

Ratcliffe explains how Maybrick came home from the Wirral races on April 27th and began dosing himself 'as usual'. He talks in the letter of 'female serpents' – mistakenly he says 'old lady' Briggs showed the Brierley letter to Edwin, whereas we know it was Nurse Yapp who spilt the beans. He then says that Edwin, '*Deep in the mire himself,*' paid no attention to it:

> Old Dr Humphreys made a jackass of himself. After James died he and Dr Carter expected to make out the death certificate as acute inflammation of the stomach. After Humphreys had a conversation with Michael he refused to make a certificate to that effect but said there were strong symptoms of arsenical poisoning... Now wouldn't that cork you. A musical composer instructing a physician how to diagnose his case. Michael, the son of a bitch, should have his throat cut. Mrs Maybrick was sick in bed when James died. He had only been dead a few hours when Michael... searched the house and in her [Florie's] room they claimed to have found quantities of arsenic, thirteen love letters from Edwin, seven from Brierley and five from Williams [a solicitor]... I always thought the madam was dumb, but I must frankly admit that I did not consider her that dumb as to leave her affairs accessible to anyone... Edwin is in bed with nervous prostration, Tom and Michael are seeing to it that he leaves England and

Michael says Edwin's letters will never be produced in court...

During those same weeks following Maybrick's death, the newspapers in Liverpool began their own trial, carrying a torrent of abusive, hysterical articles in which they presented evidence and formed judgements, even before Florie had been charged formally. The *Liverpool Echo* ran a regular column entitled 'Maybrickmania'. As the *Liverpool Review* acknowledged, 'The Maybrick case is a stroke of good fortune for the papers.'

On May 28th, lawyers, witnesses, spectators and a battery of journalists jammed into the old police court in Wellington Road. The acoustics were terrible and for 12 hours the journalists took their notes, as the *Liverpool Echo* described, 'standing up between serried ranks of policemen, on their knees, sometimes on the backs of learned counsel and in various other awkward positions, for it was found impossible to hear at tables assigned to them.' They had gathered for the Coroner's Inquest and the sensation it caused was only the beginning.

The unholy muddle of contradictory evidence, lies and mistakes that followed has proved impossible to disentangle. In Britain, such an inquest is *not* a trial; its task is to establish only the cause of death. But, in 1889, it could also apportion blame and in the Maybrick case there were many anxious to hear the verdict. The foreman of the jury, Mr Dalgleish, who turned out to be a friend of the deceased, admitted that on the day of the Grand National Maybrick had told him he took strychnine. He was immediately dismissed, and the evidence he had about Maybrick's drug habit forgotten. Mr Fletcher Rogers then became foreman and impressed everyone with the way he discharged his duties.

Florie was still too ill to attend the inquest, so she did not hear witness after witness restate the whispered gossip of her domestic staff. They talked about the fly papers, the meat juice and the 'poison for cats' and, above all, the letter to Brierley. Florie's adultery was offered as the prime motive for the murder. In Victorian eyes, a woman's adultery was a crime worse than all others.

The actual cause of Maybrick's death seemed to be of secondary interest. And in any case, despite what the coroner had asserted immediately after the the post-mortem, no measurable amount of arsenic had been found in his body. Nevertheless, the coroner insisted that the inquest be adjourned in order that the stomach and its contents might be chemically analysed. As a result, on May 30th, the torch-lit exhumation of James Maybrick took place in Anfield cemetery.

* * *

Florie made her first appearance at the coroner's court on June 5th. Hissed at by the women, who outnumbered men by two to one, she sat in the anteroom while the remaining evidence was given. Brierley was sitting at the back of the court with his father but he and Florie did not meet and he was never asked to give evidence.

This was to be the day of the doctors, and one by one they gave their preliminary findings. They were followed by Mr Flatman, proprietor of Flatman's, in Covent Garden, where Florie and Brierley had stayed. Then came Alfred Schweisso, a waiter at the hotel, who identified Florie and Brierley. He later recanted his testimony in a letter to MacDougall on January 18th 1890, in which he said, 'With regard to Mr Brierley. Of course I should not have recognised him at all if it had not been for the police; but as I was for the prosecution I went by their orders which I am sorry for now for they acted in a very shameful manner… I could not recognise him when he came; but a policeman came up and showed me where Mr Brierley was… it was a regular got up job.'

Next to appear in the box was Thomas Lowry, the clerk who had been sent out of the office to buy a saucepan, basin and spoon for Maybrick's Revalenta tonic. He was followed by the charwoman, Mrs Busher, who washed the utensils, and Mrs Briggs, who led the search of the house. Next day the court heard from Edwin, from Frederick Tozer, the assistant at Clay and Abrahams, one of the dispensing chemists who supplied medicine to James, and the police.

Finally, the analyst Edward Davies reported that as a result of the exhumation, he had found unweighable amounts of arsenic in Maybrick's intestines, an estimated one-thousandth of a grain in his kidneys, an estimated one-eighth of a grain in his liver and nothing anywhere else in his body.

When I sought an opinion on this from Dr Glyn Volans of Guy's Hospital, London, he told me, 'Although a man may have been dosing himself on arsenic and strychnine for years they simply did not have the forensic techniques to detect it accurately. It is quite understandable that so little arsenic was found in Maybrick's body. It is equally understandable that they did not pinpoint the true cause of death.'

Then, Mrs Hughes was called in to identify the infamous letter from Florie to Brierley. Despite the lack of evidence, the jury – most of whom, said the local press, had been guests of the Maybricks at one time or another – decided that James Maybrick died 'from the effects of an irritant poison administered to him by Florence Elizabeth Maybrick and that the said Florence Elizabeth Maybrick did wilfully, feloniously and with malice aforethought kill and murder the said James Maybrick.'

On June 8th 1889, a truly shocking death certificate was issued for James, by the registrar James McGuire. Florie had not yet been put on trial and had not been accused in court. Yet the cause of death was given as 'irritant poison administered by Florence Elizabeth Maybrick. Wilful murder'!

* * *

To avoid the long drive back to Walton Jail, on the edge of the city, the authorities sent Florie to the tiny Lark Lane Lock-Up. There she was kindly treated and fed with food brought in from a local hotel.

The wives of cotton merchants and brokers rallied to her support and kept her clean and clothed. A reporter from the *Liverpool Post*, who called to see her, wrote:

> She is supplied with a little table which is placed close to the entrance of her cell. She is allowed to take as much exercise as she pleases in the corridor and when tired sits at the table which is covered with a snow white cloth. On it were two books, one with crimson binding, the other in less conspicuous colours. She reads the comments on her case with the liveliest interest and indulges occasionally in sarcastic references to anything which does not please her, She is somewhat wayward in her manner.

The spark was still there.

On June 13th Florie, in heavy mourning, was taken to the magisterial inquiry (rather like a magistrates' court today) in Liverpool's Islington courthouse to hear the evidence against her for the very first time. She listened as one by one, her servants, brothers-in-law and doctors testified.

Even at this stage the doctors did not agree with each other about the cause of death and admitted to having insufficient understanding of Maybrick's condition. Moreover the proceedings were remarkable for what they left out. In particular, no one mentioned that no trace of arsenic had been found in faeces and urine samples taken from James only days before his death. Equally remarkable was the fact that, of all the wealth of material that was submitted, in the end all that remained beyond dispute was that in March, Florie and Brierley had spent two nights at Flatman's Hotel in London. But that, it seemed, was enough for a capital charge!

Florie was committed for trial on July 26th and removed to Walton Jail. Crowds ran booing after her carriage as it pulled away from the court. Local photographers were quick to capitalise on the story. Shops carried huge window displays of the Maybricks, including that sensational photograph (long since lost) of Florie and Brierley together at the Grand National. Battlecrease House became a tourist attraction, with dozens of rubber neckers pointing ghoulishly to the windows of the room where Maybrick died.

The prosecution received a letter from Brierley's solicitors, Banks and Kendall, on July 6th. They protested that their client had never received the letter of May 8th and requested that he should not be subpoenaed as he was booked for a holiday. The request must have been refused.

On July 8th, not seven weeks after Florie's arrest, Michael flagrantly disregarded the instructions in his brother's will. Claiming it was with her consent, he auctioned the entire contents of the house. It was as though he was sure Florie would never return. While Florie waited in her prison cell, Michael and Thomas disposed of every single item from the young widow's home in a sale that took place in the showrooms of Messrs Branch and Leete.

Opening the proceedings, Mr Leete was greeted from the packed room with a murmur of approval. He explained that he knew both the dead and the living and he hoped they would all withhold their judgement in this sad case as all Englishmen should. Bidding was brisk and many items sold for more than their expected price. A burnished French bedstead fetched 10 guineas, and a suite of American walnut from the best bedroom fetched 36 guineas. There were numerous, not very distinguished, paintings and a library of books described as 'the usual commonplace books'. Poignant among the shattering of this family home were the toys – the child's saddle with girths and a child's tricycle horse. Florie's beautiful clothes were bundled into trunks marked with the initials FEC and sent to storage at Woollright's. What happened to them nobody knows but the store eventually became a branch of John Lewis and in 1938 was sold to become a gas showroom.

There was also a gold watch, mentioned in the auction preview which did not arrive at the auction itself. It was not the only item that went missing. The *Liverpool Post* commented that Alice Yapp arrived for

Florie's trial brazenly carrying one of her umbrellas. The *New York Herald* London edition, of August 9th, commented, 'the other servants do not hesitate to say that she has made good use of her position to possess herself of many of Florence Maybrick's dresses and suchlike.'

What happened to the money from the auction? At one point Michael claimed that he spent half to help pay for Florie's counsel. Later he said that since he was to be a witness for the prosecution he would not fund Florie's defence. It was one more contradiction.

At least the Mutual Reserve Fund Life Association of New York waived its three-month embargo after a person's death and sent the sum of $1,000 to Florie. Florie needed every penny since the terms of Maybrick's new will were extremely stringent.

Florie was very anxious that her trial should not take place in Liverpool. She wrote again to her mother:

> I sincerely hope the Cleavers will arrange for my trial to take place in London. I shall receive an impartial verdict there which I cannot expect from a jury in Liverpool whose minds have come to a 'moral conviction', en attendant, which must influence their decision to a certain extent. The tittle-tattle of servants, the public, friends and enemies and from a thousand by-currents, besides their personal feeling for Jim, must leave their traces and prejudice their minds, no matter what the defence is.

It was not to be. Florie's advisers believed she would have a stronger case if she stood firm on home ground, and she accepted their counsel.

Arnold Cleaver set off for America to rally support and witnesses. There, the newspapers were wildly excited by the image of the forlorn and friendless expatriate, married to a debauched foreigner, in a distant land. It was the beginning of a groundswell of support.

But at Madame Tussaud's, in London, they were already designing her waxwork for the Chamber of Horrors.

16

The Whore will Suffer Unlike She has Ever Suffered

St George's Hall, Liverpool, opened in 1854, is one of those magnificent Victorian monuments to a time of confident pride and commercial exuberance. Standing Acropolis-like above the centre of the city, it is said to be one of the finest neo-classical buildings in the world and a favourite of the present Prince of Wales. Inside, the 169-foot-long Great Hall is breathtaking, with its polished porphyry columns, richly panelled vaulting, gaudy stained glass and glorious Minton mosaic floor. The small circular concert room, encircled by graceful sculptures, reflecting mirrors and illusion of space, has been described as the most beautiful of all early Victorian interiors. Today, the Hall is still the scene of many a social gathering as it was in Florie's day. No doubt Michael Maybrick performed there on the organ which, until the building of a larger version in the Royal Albert Hall in 1871, was the best in Britain.

It was here that Florie was to stand trial in what was anticipated to be the greatest show Liverpool had staged in years. Already scores of requests for seats were being received from people who, as the Southport *Guardian* put it, 'like flowers in Spring had nothing to do with the case.'

Outside, the city was overrun with thousands of American tourists, passing through on their way to the Paris Exhibition. 'I feel so lonely', Florie wrote to a friend at that time. 'As if every hand were against me. To think that I must be unveiled before all those uncharitable eyes... the darkest days of my life are now to be lived through. I trust in God's justice, whatever I may be in the sight of man.'

Florie had already been through the inquest and the magisterial inquiry, which delivered the magistrates' ruling that she could be tried on a charge of murder. There was one more proceeding before she could be called into the dock to answer the charge against her – the Grand Jury.

The function of the Grand Jury was to stand between the crown and the accused and decide if a person committed for trial by magistrates should be so tried. Unless the Grand Jury agreed, by returning a 'true bill', there could be no trial. The Grand Jury had the last word. Its members were selected not at random, but for their rank and intelligence. They were deemed to be free of local influence and constraint by the Crown. If the Grand Jury thus represented the people, the judge at the proceedings represented the Crown.

The judge for Florie's trial, Mr Justice (better known as Mr 'Injustice') Fitzjames Stephen, was at the end of a very distinguished career. The *Liverpool Review* described him as a 'big burly brainy man', adding, 'His mind is like one of those very wonderful and exact machines that one sees in manufacturing districts. It does its work with remarkable precision and laborious and untiring exactness, but unless it is carefully watched by the attendant and occasionally set in the right direction, it is liable to go all wrong.'

At the time of the Maybrick trial it seemed clear that Mr Justice Stephen had already gone 'all wrong'. Reason was sliding away, and this once great man no longer seemed capable of sustained concentration. In correspondence with Lord Lytton in 1889, he had revealed, 'I do still now and then smoke an opium pipe as my nose requires one occasionally and is comforted by it.'

On July 26th, the day of the Grand Jury, several thousand people jostled for a sight of the prisoner outside the courthouse. Inside, the sunshine poured through the glass roof and lit the judge, who sat in his scarlet and ermine robes beneath a gold and crimson canopy. In his address to the Grand Jury, Mr Justice Stephen set out the details, injecting them with innuendo and failing to master the basic facts. His opening words were an outrage. He referred to James Maybrick as a man 'unhappy enough to have an unfaithful wife.'

'If the prisoner is guilty of the crime alleged to her in the charge,' he continued, 'it is the most cruel and horrible murder that could be committed.' His words were reported in full, so that, before the end of the trial, the world knew the judge's opinions on adultery. Unfortunately for Florie, his strictures applied only to women. There was no discussion of James' extramarital cavortings.

Two questions were at the heart of the case against Florie. Was arsenic the cause of death and, if so, had it been administered by Mrs Maybrick with felonious intent?

It was open to the Crown to add other counts to the charge of murder, and to do so was quite common. However, in Florie's case the sole charge was to be that of murder, despite the fact that there was absolutely no evidence to connect the defendant with any of the arsenic found at Battlecrease House, apart from the fly papers. The Grand Jury's deliberations finished: Florie's trial was scheduled to begin on July 31st.

* * *

Florie's counsel, Sir Charles Russell QC, was a persuasive, flamboyant Irishman, who habitually sported in his breast pocket a bandana, which he waved to emphasise his views. He was also a Member of Parliament and a former Attorney General who had been one of Britain's most respected lawyers. His title greatly impressed the Baroness, and everyone deemed Florie fortunate to have so famous a man to defend her. With hindsight, she could have done better.

Sir Charles had recently had a bad record with murder cases. In 1883, he had defended a man named O'Donnell for murder.

O'Donnell was executed. Three years later he prosecuted Mrs Adelaide Bartlett for poisoning her husband with chloroform. She got off. But most recently, Russell had been leading counsel for Charles Stewart Parnell, the Irish MP, who had been charged with sedition. The trial, which took place in 1888/9, required Russell to listen to 340 witnesses and make a six-day speech. Parnell was not convicted but by July 31st, the day Florie's trial was due to begin, the barrister was exhausted.

About 8 a.m. on that day, Florie was bundled into a prison van with a number of male prisoners and driven to St George's Hall, where a crowd of several thousand had gathered in the already blistering heat. Florie could not help but observe the carnival atmosphere. 'During all the days of my trial, I am told, Liverpool society fought for tickets. Ladies were attired as for a matinee, and some had brought their luncheons that they might retain their seats. Many of them carried opera glasses, which they did not hesitate to level at me.'

Among the attractions was an itinerant street singer who had drawn a huge crowd by rendering songs based on the Maybrick case.

> Oh! Naughty Mrs Maybrick what have you been and done
> Your goings on are bad I must confess
> To get mashed on Mr Brierley you know was very wrong
> And get yourself in such a blooming mess.

The Crown Court is quite small and appropriately sombre, closed in by dark wood-lined walls and lit from above by a glass roof. It remains exactly as it was in 1889 when, just before ten o'clock, the handsome Sir Charles Russell appeared, flourishing his bandana. Counsel for the prosecution was the jovial John Addison QC. The jury consisted of twelve Lancashire men, at least one of whom could neither read nor write, while another had been recently convicted of beating his wife. They were a mix of tradesmen and labourers who could not have been expected to understand the technicalities of this particular case.

At ten o'clock, to a fanfare of trumpets, the court rose and Mr Justice Stephen appeared, unsmiling, in a full-bottomed wig, his sideburns bristling below. After a few preliminaries, the clerk called out 'Put up Florence Elizabeth Maybrick.' Downstairs, in the tiny holding cell, sat case number 24. The cell, too, remains unchanged today, a cold memorial to her tragic story. There is no light, a single candle still flickers on the stone walls above the bench where Florie waited to know her destiny.

She climbed the steep narrow stairs into the dock, a small figure in a black dress, a crepe jacket and bonnet with black streamers. A thin black veil covered her face. Then, to the charge against her, she answered clearly and firmly, 'Not guilty'.

* * *

After the trial, Alexander MacDougall became Florie's champion, believing her to be the victim of a complete travesty of justice. His book recounts the inconsistencies and inaccuracies in the case against her. Among the medical men who testified there was general agreement that the cause of Maybrick's death was gastroenteritis. They could not agree, however, on whether this was the result of bad food or poison, or, if the latter, whether the poison was arsenic.

DR RICHARD HUMPHREYS

Dr Richard Humphreys, who had treated Maybrick for the first time during his illness, was one of those who attributed the death to arsenic. But at the magisterial inquiry he acknowledged that he had never treated anyone who had died of arsenic poisoning, nor had he assisted at any such post-mortem examination.

DR WILLIAM CARTER

Dr William Carter had treated Maybrick just four times. Moreover, he acknowledged under cross-examination that he, too, had never assisted at a case involving death by arsenic, nor at a post-mortem examination involving arsenic. Dr Carter had, on May 9th, diagnosed Maybrick with acute dyspepsia due to 'indiscretion of food or drink.' Two days later, after a conversation in which Michael Maybrick mentioned his own suspicion of arsenic poisoning, he changed his mind. At the trial he agreed with Dr Humphreys.

DR ALEXANDER BARRON

Dr Alexander Barron, professor of pathology at Liverpool's University College, was present at Maybrick's post-mortem and exhumation but had never treated him. He concluded that death was due to 'acute inflammation of the stomach, probably caused by some irritant poison.'

Under cross-examination by Sir Charles, Dr Barron was asked, 'Is it possible to differentiate the symptoms of arsenical poisoning or poisoning from impure food?'

'I should not be able to do so myself,' he replied.

DR CHARLES MEYMOTT TIDY

Dr Charles Meymott Tidy, for two decades a Home Office analyst and examiner in forensic medicine at the London Hospital and whose experience of poisons ranged back to 1862, declared, 'The symptoms of the post-mortem distinctly point away from arsenic.'

DR CHARLES FULLER

Dr Charles Fuller, who had 30 years of experience as a medical practitioner and homoeopath, said he had no reason to believe Maybrick was taking arsenic. The symptoms which accompany the habitual taking of arsenic were not present in this case.

DR RAWDON MACNAMARA

Dr Rawdon Macnamara, Fellow of the Royal College of Surgeons of Ireland and Doctor of Medicine at the University of London, had administered arsenic in 'a very large number of cases'. When asked if Maybrick died of arsenic poisoning he replied, 'Certainly not.'

DR FRANK THOMAS PAUL

Dr Frank Thomas Paul was a pathologist with some 3,000 post-mortems to his credit and Professor of Medical Jurisprudence at University College, Liverpool. His verdict was that the symptoms described in the case 'agree with cases of gastronenteritis pure and simple… I presume that he died of exhaustion produced by gastroenteritis'.

DR THOMAS STEVENSON

Dr Thomas Stevenson, lecturer in forensic medicine at Guy's Hospital, London, and Home Office analyst, was called in to examine Maybrick's viscera. After a lengthy cross-examination, he testified, to the contrary, that he had 'no doubt' death was due to arsenical poisoning.

* * *

Incidentally, Dr Hopper, who had been the family doctor from 1881, gave evidence about Maybrick's drug taking but was not asked for his opinion on his patient's final illness.

Dr Glyn Volans, of Guy's Hospital, at our request, read the contemporary 'Toxicological Report' on the case of James Maybrick and was 'not at all convinced' that he died from arsenic poisoning. 'The lowest recorded lethal dose is two grains,' he said, 'yet only one-tenth of a grain of arsenic was found in James Maybrick's body. The evidence that Florence Maybrick administered poison is just not there. It is more likely that he died from the accumulative effect of all the stuff that was being pumped into him by the doctors in the last weeks, plus the results of a lifetime of drug abuse – in addition to which, he no longer had access to his poisons so was suffering withdrawal symptoms. Renal failure is a more likely cause of death.'

* * *

If the jurors were unperturbed by the confusion of the medical evidence, it was perhaps because they had testimony far more scintillating on which to focus. By the end of the first week of the trial, Florie had heard witness after witness reconstructing her life with Maybrick and the events of 1888/9. One of these was Mollie Hogwood who gave a deposition to the State Department in Washington in which she said:

> I knew the late James Maybrick for several years, and that up to the time of his marriage [to Florie] he called at my house, when in Norfolk, at least two or three times a week, and that I saw him frequently in his different moods and fancies. It was a common thing for him to take arsenic two or three times during an evening. He would always say, before taking it: 'Well, I am going to take my evening dose.' He would pull from his pocket a small vial in which he carried his arsenic and, putting a small quantity on his tongue, he would wash it down with a sip of wine. In fact, so often did he repeat this that I became afraid he would die suddenly in my house, and then some of us would be suspected of his murder. When drunk, Mr James Maybrick would pour the powder into the palm of his hand and lick it up with his tongue. I often cautioned him but he answered 'Oh, I am used to it. It will not harm me.'

She also gave an interview to a reporter from the *New York World* and issued a 1,500-word statement which ended: '... I am not at all surprised at his sudden death ... I regret to hear that his poor wife is charged with his murder and knowing Maybrick as well as I did, I do not hesitate to say that, in my opinion, had nothing more to do with his death than I did.' Florie then weakened her defence by requesting that, for the sake of their children, no mention be made of her husband's own indiscretions.

Then there was the matter of the meat juice. Against Dr Carter's orders it was given by Edwin to Nurse Gore and the bottle stood, new and unopened, by Maybrick's bed on the night of May 9th. Nurse Gore knew Florie was under suspicion. Shortly after 11 p.m. Gore gave him one or two spoonfuls in water, despite Florie's warning that it made him sick. About midnight, she watched Florie remove the bottle for a few moments, take it in to the dressing room, returning it to the bedside a few seconds later. She also noted that Florie moved the bottle out of reach to a dressing table after Maybrick had woken up. He did not drink the meat juice.

The bottle then passed from Nurse Gore to Michael to Dr Carter, before it was sent for analysis. Mr Edward Davies reported that there was half a grain of arsenic in solution in the bottle, a finding that was fuel for the prosecution. When Florie first told her story to the solicitor before the inquest, she admitted freely, but perhaps naively, to having put some powder into the meat extract but at her husband's request. This information was suppressed in her own interest but formed part of a statement she insisted on reading, against her counsel's advice, at the end of the trial. She told the court:

> On Thursday night, the 9th May, after Nurse Gore had given my husband beef tea, I went and sat on the bed beside him. He complained to me of being very sick and very depressed and again implored me to give him this powder which he had referred to earlier in the evening, and which I declined to give him. I was overwrought, terribly anxious, miserably unhappy and his evident distress utterly unnerved me. He had told me the powder would not harm him and I could put it in his food. I then consented. My Lord, I had not one true or honest friend in the house. I had no one to consult, no one to advise me. I was deposed from my position as mistress in my own house and from the position of attending on my husband, notwithstanding that he was so ill. Notwithstanding the evidence of nurses and servants I may say that he wished to have me with him; he missed me whenever I was not with him; whenever I went out of the room he asked for me and, for four days before he died I was not allowed to give him a piece of ice without its being taken

> out of my hand. When I found the powder I took it to the inner room with the beef juice, and in pushing through the door, I upset the bottle and, in order to make up the quantity of fluid spilled I added a considerable quantity of water. On returning to the room I found my husband asleep, and I placed the bottle on the table by the window. When he awoke he had a choking sensation in his throat and vomited; after that he appeared a little better, and as he did not ask for the powder again and as I was not anxious to give it to him, I removed the bottle from the small table where it would attract attention, to the top of the washstand where he could not see it. There I left it, my Lord, until, I believe Mr Michael Maybrick took possession of it. Until Tuesday 14th May, the Tuesday after my husband's death and until a few minutes before Mr Bryning made this terrible charge against me, no one in that house had informed me of the fact that a death certificate had been refused, or that a post-mortem examination had taken place; or that there was any reason to suppose that my husband had died from other than natural causes. It was only when Mrs Briggs alluded to the presence of arsenic in the meat juice that I was made aware of the nature of the powder my husband had asked me to give him.

What Florie did not realise was that powdered white arsenic does not dissolve easily. The arsenic found in the bottle of meat juice must have been in solution and could not have been added in the way that Florie described. So what was the powder that Maybrick had begged her to give him? Could it have been strychnine? According to the Diary, he had written ten days before of his intention to ask Florie to kill him, wondering if she had the strength to do so. If she had poisoned him with strychnine, the tests for arsenic applied by the analysts would not have revealed it.

Much was made of the fly papers. Only five years earlier, two married sisters from Liverpool named Flanagan and Higgins had been hanged for using arsenic extracted from fly papers to kill three people. Florie's defence argued that the fly papers could not have been responsible for Maybrick's death, since no fibres from them had been found in any of the contaminated bottles in the house. Of this, Florie said in her statement:

> The fly papers were bought with the intention of using as a cosmetic. Before my marriage, and since, for many years, I have been in the habit of using a face wash, prescribed for me by Dr Greggs of Brooklyn. It consisted principally of arsenic, tincture of benzoin, elderflower water and some other ingredients. This prescription I lost or mislaid last April and, as at the time I was suffering from a slight eruption of the face, I thought I should like to try to make a substitute myself. I was anxious to get rid of this eruption before I went to a ball on the 30th of that month. When I had been in Germany many of my young friends there I had seen using a solution derived from fly papers, elder water, lavender water and other things mixed, and then applied to the face with a handkerchief well soaked in the solution. I used the fly papers in the same manner. But to avoid the evaporation of the scent it was necessary to exclude the air as much as possible, and for that purpose I put a plate over the fly papers, and put a folded towel over that, and another towel over that. My mother has been aware for a great many years that I use an arsenical cosmetic in solution.

It sounded harmless enough. But because the statement had not been made at the magisterial inquiry, Judge Stephen interpreted it as a lie, made up for the occasion – and said so.

Many months after the trial, the Baroness von Roques was turning the pages of the Chandler family Bible – one of the few items that had been saved from auction. There she found the lost presciption, written on the back of a New York chemist's label and dated 1878. Florie had not been lying. And the year after the trial, 1890 – too late for Florie – E. Godwin Clayton, a consulting chemist and Member of the Society of Public Analysts, carried out a test in which he attempted to extract arsenic from two fly papers. His verdict was that 'It is next to impossible for any person without opportunities for and knowledge of chemical manipulation to make or procure an aqueous infusion of fly papers which could be added to Valentine's Meat Juice in sufficient quanity to introduce half a grain of arsenic.'

* * *

The trial ended after seven days. The judge's summing-up took an interminable twelve hours, spread over two days. 'For a person to go deliberately administering poison to a poor, helpless sick man upon whom she has already inflicted a dreadful injury – an injury fatal to married life – the person who could do such a thing as that must indeed be destitute of the least trace of human feeling.'

By the end of the summing-up, everyone was in utter confusion. (A witness to the proceedings said that he 'had never in a court of law heard such a pathetic exhibition of incompetence and inaccuracy.')

The judge ranted on. 'The circumstances indicated in the evidence are very varied and the witnesses go backwards and forwards in a way which makes the evidence somewhat confusing from beginning to end. I am sorry to say I shall not be able to arrange it before you exactly as I would wish…'

Journalists, spectators and the thousands of people thronging the square outside St George's Hall were confident that Florie would be acquitted. There had been a huge surge of public opinion in her favour. After all, there was no evidence linking Florie with any of the arsenic found in the house; none to prove that she had consciously administered arsenic, or even that arsenic had killed James Maybrick.

Still, the jury took just 35 minutes to record their verdict: 'Guilty'.

The *Boston Globe* reported: 'Gasping and trembling she [Florie] arose with a respectful bow and addressed his lordship in these words: "My lord, evidence has been kept back from the jury which, had it been known, would have altered their verdict. I am not guilty of this crime.'

The only telephone in St George's Hall had been booked in advance by the *Evening Express* and the *Morning Courier*, eager for a scoop. Equally enterprising, the *Daily Post and Echo* organised a system of semaphores between a reporter in the court and a string of correspondents stationed on the way to the newspaper office. But in the turmoil, the confused journalist in court waved the wrong flag and 5,000 copies of the newspaper flooded on to the streets carrying banner headlines announcing that Florie was free.

Mr Justice Stephen put on his black cap. The silence in court was broken only by a gasp. Men were in tears. Women fainted.

The *Globe* continued: 'At this moment there was an awful hush upon the court and a pin could have been heard to drop amid the painful stillness. Women were in tears, great strong men were seen stealthily wiping their eyes ... as Mrs Maybrick rose to walk from the fated dock she tottered and almost fell. Kindly warders put their hands to steady her. It was her strength, not her courage that failed.'

Should not James Maybrick, who was lying in Anfield cemetery, have been in that dock, to stand trial? Instead, it was Florie, his widow and last victim, who stiffened, stumbled and then, after sentence of death had been passed, walked from the court, unaided and alone.

* * *

The Maybrick case was to be Mr Justice Stephen's last. Within two years he was sent to a private asylum for the insane in Ipswich, where he died in 1894.

As Florie's scaffold was being noisily hammered into place within earshot of the condemned cell, she was granted a reprieve. The Home Secretary, Mr Henry Matthews, who had worked so hard and so unsuccessfully the year before to catch the Whitechapel killer, commuted the sentence to one of penal servitude for life.

So many questions about the case are unanswered still.

In 1899 J.H. Levy edited a major 609 page book on the case *The Necessity for Criminal Appeal*. In this he referred to Florie's trial as 'one of the most extraordinary miscarriages of justice of modern times' and talked of a 'deep blush of shame'. He wrote his book in order to help repair the 'defective working of the machinery of justice'. Even the judge admitted later that this was the one case in his career in which 'there could be any doubt about the facts'.

In America, lawyer and campaigner for Florie, Andrew H.H. Dawson was also compiling a book on the case. On the whole the American press was less hysterical than the British, but despite the almost unanimous concern for Florie and condemnation of Maybrick himself, no one at any time linked him to the Whitechapel murders.

The *Virginian* described how Florie 'almost unceasingly moans and calls for her children. She weeps copiously and welcomes the visits of the prison chaplain whose ministrations she fully appreciates.'

There were also a number of tit bits that appeared in the regional papers that were not seen in Britain. The *Virginian* of May 22nd 1889 claimed: 'A safe which belonged to him [Maybrick] while he was in Norfolk is now owned by Messrs W.H.H. Trice and Co. who purchased it from a second hand party some time after he gave up business in Norfolk.' Trice and Co are an old family firm of realtors (estate agents) founded in 1875.

The first report of that possible pregnancy had also appeared in America as early as May 31st 1889, after Florie had been too ill to attend the inquest on her husband. The report alleged that the child was Alfred Brierley's and that their intimacy had been going on for two years. This was followed on June 2nd, in the *Boston Globe*, by an interview with the Baroness. 'The solicitors for the defence have positively interdicted the Baroness from making any statement to the press so she was very cautious about what she had to say.'

Nevertheless the Baroness blamed Edwin and Michael for interfering in her daughter's marriage. The interview continued: 'The Baroness admits that her daughter is enceinte and says there had been loving, conjugal relations with her husband up to the time of his recent illness. The Baroness says her daughter assures her that the story that these relations were not maintained for nearly two years is untrue.'

Dr Hopper himself had hinted at a pregnancy and the *Liverpool Weekly Times and Echo* was not alone in its inference that there were hidden reasons why Florie had been granted a reprieve. 'It is believed there has been no instance of the execution of a woman who, at the time of her trial, was in Mrs Maybrick's supposed condition, since the execution of Margaret Waters nineteen years ago.'

There is, so far, no record of such a birth although the American papers did note that Florie was to be placed in solitary confinement for nine months. Prison records no longer exist and, since there is no way of knowing the name given to the baby, his story is almost impossible to verify.

On the afternoon of August 20th – nine days before Florie was removed from Liverpool and taken by train (3rd class) to carry out her sentence in Woking Prison, the United States Circuit Court met in Louisville, Kentucky. Among the business of the day, reported the *United Press*, was the filing of papers by the well known lawyer David Armstrong. They related to the disposal of Florie Maybrick's estate should she be hanged.

> Mrs Maybrick, the principal petitioner and her two children, ask the court to compel Wm. H Gardner of New York and John T. Ingraham of Missouri to act as Trustees of the estate of a Dennis Maybrick, whose will was filed for probate in 1858. Mrs Maybrick's petition was signed in Liverpool where she is in jail, under death sentence. The petition states that there is some property belonging to her in Kentucky and this is one of the reasons why the case was filed in the Circuit Court of the United States here.

The suggestion that there could have been Maybrick land in America is curious. Florie's grandfather Darius Holbrook died in New York in 1858 and I am inclined to think there is the usual journalistic confusion between two names.

What of the behaviour of Michael and Edwin, who it was said would not tie his shoes without instruction from his older brother? Even before Maybrick's death the two had discussed with Mrs Briggs, Mrs Hughes and even Nurse Yapp the possibility that he was being poisoned. Yet the search of Battlecrease House was not made until it was too late. Then the entire premises were blitzed in a frenzied search – for what? Compromising love letters were found from Edwin to Florie – and destroyed.

Edwin had discussed Maybrick's habit of taking 'that damned strychnine' with friends and yet denied it at the trial. Michael also knew of his brother's use of drugs and denied it. So why did the analysts search only for arsenic? And why, between Maybrick's death and the trial, did Dr Hopper destroy all his prescriptions?

Michael managed to prevent James' latest will being used in court, for it gave him and Thomas enormous powers and Florie nothing. So why did Florie's solicitors not stop Michael's sale of contents from Battlecrease?

Much was made of Florie's debts; nothing was said of her husband's. Maybrick's lifetime of infidelity was ignored; Florie's lapse was enough to see her convicted.

Why were so many important witnesses not called to testify? Where were the Baroness, Maybrick's other brothers, Alfred Brierley himself, John Baillie Knight (Florie's friend and supporter), Mrs Christina Samuelson or the Hobsons, with whom Maybrick dined on the night of the Wirral Races?

What was the suppressed evidence which both the Baroness and solicitor Jonathan Harris referred to in correspondence with Henry Matthews and later with the Rt Hon H.H. Asquith?

Maybrick moved in the shadowy fringes of his brother Michael's world, a world of bright lights, high society, masonic brotherhood and military manoeuvres. But if he was Jack the Ripper he was a threat to that world and I believe that it is very likely he was the victim of a plot that went wrong and for which Florie suffered.

I doubt that Florie herself was aware of the dark secrets of his London life, although the Diary does confess 'My dear Bunny knows all'. I am deeply suspicious of Edwin and Michael. One day their undoubtedly sinister role in the tragedy of Florence Maybrick may be revealed.

*　　*　　*

On the same day that Florie was reprieved, August 18th 1889, Alfred Brierley sailed with his brother on board the Cunard liner *Scythia* for Boston, in the vain hope that he could avoid the press.

There had been an international outcry for Florie's release – especially and understandably in America, where a Maybrick Committee was formed. 100,000 signatures were petitioned in Liverpool alone.

The indefatigable *Boston Globe* was waiting when Alfred Brierley arrived, on September 2nd. They described the cigar-smoking Brierley as 'an ordinary type of Englishman whose gentility and breeding would be admitted at sight but whose attractiveness was beneath the surface.'

His unnaturally flushed face paled on questioning. He claimed that he had paid £6,500 towards Florie's defence costs and, equally incorrectly, that he had never before been in America.

On August 22nd, while the Brierley brothers were still at sea, the *St Louis Chronicle* carried a report from their New York correspondent. It confirmed, from a presumably reliable source, the rumour that had been circulating in Liverpool.

ANTICIPATED MATERNITY WILL SAVE HER NECK
FOR A TIME AT LEAST.

> Mr Macklin, one of the New York attorneys of Mrs Maybrick, says the firm is in momentary expectation of receiving a cable despatch from London relative to the result of the appeals to the Home Secretary for a pardon or commutation of sentence.

'In any event,' said Mr Macklin, 'it is pretty definitely settled now that Mrs Maybrick will not be hanged next Monday. Her condition precludes that. We were aware of this fact two months ago, but the matter was kept secret precisely to meet the present state of affairs. There is not any question about the paternity of the unborn child. She did not criminally associate with Brierley – certainly not until the latter part of April and the child will be born in three months from the present time …'

Levy believed, as did many others, that Florie should have been released. Instead she was kept in prison for 15 years for attempting to murder her husband – a crime for which she had not been tried or found guilty and which in any case carried a maximum sentence of 10 years.

Ironically, history has several times linked the name of Florence Maybrick, not James, with that of Jack the Ripper. The judge's son, J.K. Stephen, was tutor to the Duke of Clarence and was himself named as a suspect by Michael Harrison, in his book *Clarence*. Stewart Evans, co-author of *Jack the Ripper, the First American Serial Killer* discovered a cartoon which had appeared in a journal called *St Stephen's Review* in August 1889. It depicted the Home Secretary with Jack the Ripper on his right and Florence on his left. The caption read 'Attempted murder of Florence Maybrick – save her Mr Matthews'!

The names of Chandler, Leipzig and Liverpool all appear in *The Lodger*, the novel by Marie Belloc Lowndes based on the Whitechapel murders, which was published in 1913. This is one of the books which Melvin Harris names as an inspirational source reference for the 'forgers' although there is only a veiled reference to the Maybrick case.

Even more bizarre was the case of the Maybrick diary. On September 16th 1889, the *Liverpool Echo* carried a story headed 'Mrs Maybrick's Diary.' It told how the three volumes had been found in a case of Florie's effects at Battlecrease House and offered for sale by a relative to a London publisher, Triscler and Co. They were, said the story, tied with blue silk cord and were each in a different handwriting, though by the same person and seemed to describe Mrs Maybrick's childhood, youth and married life.

The article related that the publisher was uncertain of the diaries' authenticity and recommended that they be taken to a Mr Stuart Cumberland. Why Mr Cumberland? Keith Skinner, on behalf of Paul Feldman, went on the trail of Stuart Cumberland and discovered that his quarry was the editor of the *Illustrated Mirror*. Mr Cumberland himself wrote an article on September 17th 1889, doubting the authenticity of the diaries and complaining that they were being offered for publication as 'a shilling shocker'.

Although Paul Feldman had drawn a line under the story, I was intrigued and decided to pick it up again when I began assembling information for this edition. I looked at some copies of Stuart Cumberland's *Illustrated Mirror*, whose first issue was published on June 16th 1889, and discovered it to be heavily biased towards occult and psychic interests. Mr Cumberland, whose real name was Charles Garner, was keenly involved, as was Sir Arthur Conan Doyle, with Stanstead Hall, Essex, today still the headquarters of the Spiritualists' National Union. He wrote a number of books such as *A Fatal Affinity* described as a 'weird story' about the Whitechapel murderer and the *Times* described on September 12th 1889 how he had 'worked his way' into the inquest on a woman's torso found dismembered in Pinchin Street, Whitechapel – 'For what purpose is not known.' That murder was generally agreed not to be the work of Jack the Ripper.

Was it a coincidence that Stuart Cumberland's lawyers, the prestigious international firm of Lumley and Lumley, were also engaged by the Baroness Von Roques?

The *Illustrated Mirror* is uniquely overloaded with colourfully intemperate articles, not only about Jack the Ripper but also the Maybrick trial.

On July 29th 1899, Cumberland claimed to have had a vision of the Ripper and reproduced an entertainingly Maybrick-like portrait of his visitor. This produced a response from Liverpool. 'You call yourself a thought-reader and claim to know all about that blood-thirsty scoundrel Jack the Ripper; but up to the present I have seen no sign from you respecting the innocent woman who lies in agonized suspense in Walton gaol.

'You can have visions about the Whitechapel murderer but poor Mrs Maybrick is apparently unworthy of a dream. It ought all to be clear to you but perhaps you don't want it to be so.'

What should be clear? Was there an implied link between the case of Florence Maybrick and that of the Ripper.

Stuart Cumberland was no supporter of Florie. 'Wild eyed strangers,' he said, 'and sober minded acquaintances, temporarily deranged under the influence of the craze of the hour, waylay me in the street ... When, I would like to know is this epidemic of Maybrickism likely to end?'

In 1889 the bars of Fleet Street served all the newspapers and agencies of the surrounding area. Men like Cumberland, George R Sims, Tom Bulling, Best and perhaps even the elusive 'Richard Walters' mingled and competed in those bars. Yet as far as I know no one, apart from Cumberland, ever ran the story of the diaries and they were never heard of again.

17

My Campaign is Far From Over Yet …

James Maybrick's legacy to his family was sombre enough, but in the years that followed, his shadow was to darken so many lives – and it still does.

Florie Maybrick was a survivor. After the trial she was transferred to the grim, gloomy labyrinth of the half-empty Woking Prison where, as prisoner LP29, she endured solitary confinement, hard labour and illness, locked into a tiny, unlit cell. Huge efforts were made for her release or a re-trial, especially in America. There was a far greater transatlantic uproar over Florie's conviction and a far more militant campaign for her freedom than had ever been experienced before. In America, the Women's International Maybrick Society was founded, with many leading suffragettes on its committee. The *New York Herald* reported that the Committee was planning to apply for a writ of habeas corpus and was appealing for funds to help them overturn the verdict since the case was ultra vires (being conducted away from home) and should be quashed.

The Baroness eventually sold her flat in Paris and moved to Windsor, from where she mounted a noisy campaign to obtain Florie a re-trial or release and visited her daughter, as permitted, every three months.

Florie later recalled, 'At these visits she would tell me as best she could of the noble, unwearied efforts of my countrymen and countrywomen in my cause; of the sympathy and support of my own Government; of the earnest efforts of the different American ambassadors in my behalf... The knowledge of their belief in my innocence, and of their sympathy comforted, cheered, and strengthened me to tread bravely the thorny path of my daily life.'

These visits took their toll on the Baroness. 'Almost before we had time to compose ourselves there would come a silent sign from the mute matron in the chair – the thirty minutes had passed. "Goodbye" we would say, with a lingering look and then turn our backs upon each other ... no one will ever know what my mother suffered.'

At the time of Florie's trial and the emergence of her alleged diaries in 1889, Stuart Cumberland's *Illustrated Mirror* had run a profile of Theodore Lumley, 'a tall, handsome, striking man whose face would attract attention in any crowd.'

In 1892, the Baroness asked Lumley and Lumley to fight Florie's case. Their report set out concisely all the arguments in her favour but it was all useless.

Florie's Counsel, Sir Charles, later Lord, Russell, continued to express his support for his infamous client and never lost confidence that she would be freed. He died in 1900 before Florie was to see his belief vindicated.

For the entire fifteen years of her incarceration Florie remained the focus of an international campaign to clear her name. Three American Presidents registered pleas for mercy. Cardinal Gibbons, Secretary of State James G. Blaine and the Ambassador to Britain, Robert Lincoln, added appeals on her behalf. Not until 1904, after the death of Queen Victoria in 1901, was Florie finally a free woman. On January 25th aged 41 she was taken into the kindly care of nuns at the Community of the Epiphany, a convent in Truro, Cornwall. Six months later, according to the local press, she left the convent using the name 'Graham' – a truncated form of her family name 'Ingraham'. She then rejoined her mother in France before sailing home to a new world in America, lit by electricity, over-populated and noisy with the march to industrialisation. The change was hard. Never pardoned, she was free from prison but not from her past.

'A time will come when the world will acknowledge that the verdict which was passed on me is absolutely untenable,' she wrote in her autobiography. 'But what then? Who shall give back the years I have spent within prison walls; the friends by whom I am forgotten; the children to whom I am dead; the sunshine; the winds of heaven; my woman's life, and all I have lost by this terrible injustice?'

Florie's repeated attempts at appeal may have been in vain as far as her early release was concerned but her prison sentence produced an ultimate irony: Britain's Court of Criminal Appeal was set up in 1907 as a direct result of her case. In future, defendants would face a more equitable system of justice. Previously, there was no Court of Appeal to which the verdict could be referred on any grounds, and a defendant could not give evidence in his or her own defence. Indirectly the change could be said to have been brought about by James Maybrick, whose other life as Jack the Ripper led to her downfall.

Florie wanted privacy. But the public wanted her story. In need of money and with the encouragement of her American supporters she wrote about her experiences in prison and toured the country lecturing on the need for penal reform. She never once discussed the events of 1889 that had taken her to the shadow of the gallows. This public life, however, made it impossible for her to escape the curiosity of her audience, and she abandoned the lecture circuit after two years.

In 1910, the Baroness returned to France after an extended visit to see Florie and she died there a few months later. She was buried beside her son in the cemetery at Passy.

When attempts to reclaim family land failed, Florie was in dire need of money. She worked briefly for a publishing company, then her health broke down and in 1910 she moved to Moraine, near Chicago. There she stayed for five years in the care of Frederick W. Cushing, proprietor of the elegant Moraine Hotel. But she became ill, she ran up debts and eventually was taken in to the protection of the Salvation Army, homeless. In 1918 she contacted a friend, Cora Griffin, asking about employment opportunities. Miss Griffin had a friend in Gaylordsville, Connecticut, Genevieve Austin, who was looking for a housekeeper on her poultry farm. Florie was hired. The following year, she bought a tract of land in Gaylordsville and had a small three-roomed cottage built. Before moving there she had decided to revert to her maiden name and thereafter was known as Florence Elizabeth Chandler. Mrs Maybrick ceased to exist.

While Florie served her prison term, many of those who had figured so prominently in her life were also trying, in their own ways, to escape what fate had dealt them.

* * *

When Alexander MacDougall published his study of the case after Florie's conviction, he addressed the preface emotionally to Bobo and Gladys.

> This work is dedicated to James Chandler Maybrick aged 8 years and Gladys Evelyn Maybrick aged 4 years by the author, with the sincere hope that it will enable them to feel during their lives that the word 'MOTHER' is not a 'sound unfit to be heard or uttered' by them AND that when they are old enough to be able to understand this record of the facts and circumstances connected with the charge put upon, and the trial of Florence Elizabeth Maybrick aged 27, her children may have, throughout their lives, the comfort of feeling that their mother was not proved to be guilty of the murder of their father JAMES MAYBRICK.

It did not work. Florie never saw her children again. James and Gladys went to live in London – not with Uncle Michael at first but with Dr Fuller and his wife, who were paid £100 a year to care for them. For the first few years that Florie was in prison, Thomas annually posted photographs of her children to her. But when James was old enough to be told about the tragedy of his parents he reacted badly. He adopted the name 'Fuller' and instructed Uncle Thomas to send no more pictures to the prison. This broke Florie's heart; she felt as though her children had died.

'The innocents – my children – one a baby of three years, the other a boy of seven, I had left behind in the world,' she wrote in her autobiography. 'They had been taught to believe that their mother was guilty and, like their father, was to them dead. They have grown up to years of understanding under another name. I know nothing about them. When the pathos of all this touches the reader's heart he will realize the tragedy of my case.'

In March 1893, Michael Maybrick decided to break totally with the memories of his past – although he was at the peak of his professional career. He married his housekeeper, butcher's daughter Laura Withers, at Marylebone Register Office and retired to live on the Isle of Wight. It was not a love match, they had nothing in common and never even took holidays together. But Laura was happy enough, driving around in her monogrammed carriage to Ryde's main street, in order to give the shopkeepers the pleasure of saying they had served her.

Eventually, when the children were older, first James and then Gladys joined the Maybricks at Lynthorpe in Ryde. In November 1900, Michael was elected Mayor. Speeches at the inauguration referred to his ability to 'produce grand harmonies from discordant notes'. It was an honour to which he was re-elected five times. He visited Osborne when Queen Victoria was there, he welcomed King Alfonso of Spain and represented the island at Westminster Abbey for the Coronation of George V. He undoubtedly worked hard to promote the island's image – and his own.

His funeral in 1913 was the largest the island had ever seen. But he is remembered, nonetheless, with some amusement there today. Solicitor John Matthews says, 'he was a chameleon type of man. He had no deep emotions and no close relationships. He dabbled in every committee possible but participated very little. At his funeral, among the astonishing array of wreaths was one from the Temperance Movement (but he drank), several from the churches (but he didn't go to church), and from the cycling club (but he had no bicycle). His one-time world of international music was hardly represented.'

In December 1892, three months before his own wedding, Michael had persuaded his brother Edwin to abandon bachelor life. Edwin married Amy Tyrer and they had a daughter, also called Amy. Many years later, daughter Amy described her father as 'absolutely a bachelor at heart. All his friends were bachelors. Some came over from America and they were all bachelors. Father used to invite them to dinner in the evening but there were never any women with them. At Easter, he would go off motoring with his men friends. He made me feel I was an unwanted child. He was never loving. I got my ears boxed on many occasions.'

Amy Maybrick sometimes spent summers on the Isle of Wight. She dreaded these visits when bored Aunt Laura fell asleep, while Uncle Michael played his gramophone interminably and the children were left to their own devices. 'All the Maybricks were cold, very formal and they didn't understand children at all,' she said.

Her father, Edwin, died in 1928, leaving only £39 1s.8d. His funeral cost £5 7s.8d.

* * *

In 1911, James Fuller was 29 and working as a mining engineer in the Le Roi gold mine in British Columbia. He was engaged to a local girl and apparently free from the shadow that had clouded his childhood. On April 10th he telephoned his fiancée. That was the last time she spoke to him. James was later found dead alone in his laboratory. He had apparently mistaken a glass of cyanide for water. The verdict was accidental death. The Maybrick curse had taken its toll again.

In 1912, at the parish church of St Mary the Virgin, Hampstead, Gladys Maybrick married Frederick James Corbyn, known as 'Jim'. Her guardian, Mrs Fuller, signed the register and when Michael died in 1913, Gladys' name does not appear among the mourners nor do the newspapers record her sending a wreath. Was this the whiff of a family feud? Jim Corbyn's family immediately cut off his inheritance because of Gladys' notorious name.

During World War I Jim, a navy lieutenant, was awarded the OBE for his shore-based services but, on Gladys' insistence, resigned when it was over and went into business. The Corbyns chose not to have children – Gladys was ashamed of being a Maybrick. In 1957, they built themselves a retirement bungalow not far from the sea, overlooking a beautiful isolated valley in South Wales. There, Gladys was a somewhat formidable and demanding neighbour. She didn't like children at all, and members of the family still recall the dread with which, as youngsters, they had awaited the 'state visits' from Aunty Gladys and Uncle Jim. These were occasions for best clothes and formal behaviour.

Sally and I went to see the place in which the tragic little daughter of James and Florie chose to end her days. As we drove in through the gate I felt a shiver of disbelief. From the time of the trial Florie had had no contact at all with her daughter; there had been no exchange of photographs or letters. And yet the house in which Gladys died was a modest cedar bungalow, larger but otherwise similar in every way to the place in which her mother was found dead in 1941.

Just as extraordinary was yet another coincidence; when Gladys died in 1971 and the bungalow was cleared, relatives found medicines and pills in every pocket, every drawer, every cupboard. Like her father, she too was a hypochondriac.

What of Alfred Brierley? The history books tell different stories. Some say he emigrated to North Africa, others that he died in South America. Years after she was released from prison Florie gave an exclusive and painful interview to the *Liverpool Post and Echo* in which she admitted that during the years in prison she was buoyed up by the memories of Alfred. 'I was foolish enough to think that I could find happiness with the man who offered me the love my husband denied me... bitter, bitter was my disappointment. The man for whom I had sacrificed everything had forgotten me during the years I had been trying to keep my heart young, in prison, for his sake.'

The truth about Brierley makes Florie's words even more poignant. He did go to South America. There is a letter from him when in Venezuela, written to John Aunspaugh, in which he reflects ruefully, 'The women surely can kick up a devil of a dust with us men and a pretty face can sure lead a man to hell.' In fact, Brierley returned to England, married twice, had a son and died in a nursing home in Hove, Sussex. He had been living in the beautiful Poynters Farmhouse in the village of Newick, East Sussex and is buried there in the shelter of St Mary's Church at the foot of the South Downs. On his tombstone are the now moss-covered words: 'And a sower went forth'.

George Davidson, Maybrick's closest friend, hailed from an eminently respectable Scottish Free Church family. He was found, drowned, on a bleak stretch of the coast at Silecroft near Whitehaven, Cumbria, in March 1893. According to the *Whitehaven News* of March 16th, 'For about two or three weeks he had complained of being unable to sleep. He frequently got up during the night and went for a walk and a smoke around the square. On the morning of February 10th at about 10 a.m. he was found to be missing and has not been heard of since.' A reward of £10 had been offered for news of his whereabouts.

He died, penniless and intestate, but left behind a gold watch, placed beneath his pillow. Was it Albert Johnson's watch? Was the burden of such knowledge too much for Maybrick's dearest friend? We shall probably never know.

And in 1927, Sarah Ann Maybrick was certified dead of senile dementia in Tooting Bec Hospital, London. Paul Feldman found, among Trevor Christie's papers, a copy of an article that had appeared in the American *Brooklyn Eagle* of July 27th 1894. It was headed 'There are no flies on her', and said, 'Mrs Sarah Maybrick of Brooklyn asks that her daughter, Hester, be removed to an insane asylum. She imagines she has been deserted by her lover and flies whisper in her ear that he is faithless.'

If this was, indeed, James Maybrick's Sarah Ann, how ironic that Hester who could, from her age, have been his daughter, was haunted by the twin nightmare of the Maybricks – faithlessness and flies.

* * *

Florie returned to England at least twice. The first time was in 1911 after she heard of Bobo's death in Canada. Her remarks, also reported in the *Brooklyn Eagle*, on May 10th, are moving;

> The past is dead. The boy has been dead to me for more than 20 years. Before the death of my husband ... he provided that the children be brought up and educated and required to live in England until of age and if, then, they wished to continue under the patronage of his estate they must continue to reside on British soil. They were taken in charge by some of Mr Maybrick's relatives and I never made any effort to communicate with them.

In 1927, she returned for what she hoped would be a family reconciliation. But according to Amy, Edwin's daughter, he was 'out' at the time. Could there have also been a link between that visit and the death of Sarah Ann?

> It is bitterness worse than death. I have longed for my children who were but babes at the time and the mother hunger in my heart was so strong that I felt I must make this journey now in the hope of seeing them ... It seems terrible that the children I risked my life to bring into the world should think their mother guilty of the crime that left them fatherless. But that is the only construction I can put upon their attitude towards me now.

Who is Florie talking about? Bobo had been dead for 16 years. She had previously spoken of her feelings about his death. So who are the children she had come to see?

There had been so many rumours at the time of her trial that Florie was pregnant. Dr Hopper himself had mentioned the possibility. The *Weekly Times and Echo* was not alone in its inference that there were hidden reasons why Florie had been granted a reprieve.

These stories were denied both in the press and later, contradicting her earlier statement in June 1889, by the Baroness, but the rumours lingered. If Florie had given birth in prison, he or she would have been thirty seven.

In 1995, Paul Feldman lobbed another bombshell theory into the arena. His relentless search for Maybrick descendants has been chronicled in his book, *Jack the Ripper: The Final Chapter*. He believes he has discovered the truth about Florie's 'other child', born, not in prison but, he says, in West Hartlepool when she was just 15 years old. This baby – a boy – was adopted but what Paul Feldman believes may have happened next belongs later in the story.

Florie spent the rest of her old age in the small Connecticut town where she had gone to work as a housekeeper. The job did not last long and when the small income she received ceased to be enough she finally found the kindness that had eluded her through so much of her life. Neighbours and students from the nearby South Kent School for Boys saw to it that she always had groceries and other supplies.

As the years wore on, Florie became more and more reclusive, and as passers-by would note, ever more eccentric. Her odd little house had five small doors let into its sides to allow easy access for her cats, which according to the local newspaper, numbered anything from 17 to 75. When she could barely afford to feed herself she made sure she had over two litres of milk a day to feed her hungry companions. Hardly the care one would expect from a woman who, so many years before, had been damned by a package labelled 'Arsenic. Poison for Cats'.

The 'Cat Lady', as she became known locally, managed to live out the last few decades of her life in Gaylordsville in anonymity. No one knew who she was, though they may have guessed from her bearing that she was a lady. And Florie never told a soul – not in words, anyway. When she gave a black lace dress to Genevieve Austin, she inadvertently left on a cleaning tag that read 'Mrs Florence E. Maybrick'. For nearly 20 years Mrs Austin kept Florie's secret. Only on the death of her neighbour did she alert the newspapers to the truth.

It was a tragic end. In October 1941 Florie was found in the garden having suffered a mild stroke. She refused hospital treatment and next day her neighbour, Mrs Conkrite the milkman's wife, called with a hot meal. Early the following morning when Howard Conkrite himself arrived with her daily milk, he found Florie dead on the sofa. Beside her was the Bible in which she had preserved the face wash prescription, two rosaries and a tattered address book – with all the 'G's torn out. The mattress in her bedroom was alive with bugs, her last remaining teeth were held together by string.

One of her dresses is now cherished in the Richmond Museum. A curious and unexplained little hand-drawn card was also found and is among Trevor Christie's Collection. It is a rather childish drawing of a cat and underneath – a chilling echo from Whitechapel – are the words 'Ha! Ha!'

The South Kent pupils who had cared so well for their eccentric friend attended her funeral and bore her coffin to the grave in the school grounds. The plain wooden cross said simply 'FECM 1862-1941'. Among the mourners was a well known journalist whose life had by chance followed Florie's footsteps. He was J.C O'Connell who, as a young cub reporter in Liverpool, had covered her trial. He went to America – to Mobile and eventually joined the *New York Times* but he stood by her grave not as a journalist but as a sympathetic supporter.

In 1999, largely as a result of the limelight into which Florie had posthumously been thrust by the discovery of the Maybrick Diary, that wooden cross was replaced by a headstone at a ceremony re-consecrating the graveyard, her name inscribed in full. It has become a place of pilgrimage.

* * *

18

The Pain is Unbearable

In 1992, Michael Barrett too had felt the shadow of James Maybrick fall across his life. Once the Diary had found its way into his house, nothing was ever to be the same again. No one, least of all an invalid as he was, could withstand the battering to which he was subjected, especially after publication of the hardback. He suffered phone calls in the night, the press camped on his doorstep and he was interviewed by Scotland Yard – an experience his former wife, Anne, will never forget. Yet he stuck convincingly to his story.

Sally and I had coffee with Tony Devereux's three daughters in Liverpool at the beginning of our researches but, because of the confidentiality statement we were all trying to protect, we could not tell them then that the Diary had anything to do with the Ripper. We described it only as 'James Maybrick's Diary'. They have been very distressed since at the suggestion by the Diary's disbelievers that their father was part of the forgery plot. Understandably they were angry with us all and insisted that they would have known if he had ever had the Diary in his house.

So we still had no idea of the origins of the Diary and because I knew there would be a need to update the paperback version of my book in October 1994 research continued.

1994 was a crazy year. By this time two research 'camps' had evolved, each believing fervently in the authenticity of the Diary. Paul Feldman was a man with a mission and although I admired his energy I was extremely concerned that he might be causing distress to ordinary folk. Behind the scenes, legal and political wrangles meant that there was virtually no contact between us. This complicated research and added to the sense of confusion.

We pressed Michael for more details; we spoke with his family and friends. We checked his handwriting and also that of Tony Devereux and Anne. Michael Barrett had always said he was convinced that Maybrick left the Diary in his office in Tithebarn Street on May 3rd 1889. So there was momentary excitement when I discovered that this office had only been demolished in the late 1960s to make way for a prestigious office block, Silk House Court. Amusingly, among the tenants of Silk House Court was a reputable firm of laywers descended by way of mergers and new partnerships from Cleaver Holden Garnett and Cleaver, Florie's solicitors. But, sadly, they said that they had never been put in charge of the Diary and so the trail went cold.

I hoped that if we could find some more of Maybrick's handwriting our problems might be over. The Reference Library in Norfolk, Virginia, sent us wads of papers detailing his attendance and responsibilities at Cotton Exchange meetings. There was even a mention of letters. But they had long since vanished. Cotton Exchange records in Liverpool had also been destroyed.

Paul Feldman's team unearthed a cache of correspondence in the Richmond, Virginia Chancery Office. It was voluminous and often forthright, between Maybrick and various American solicitors dealing with the many tortuous land claims of Florie and her mother, and the fortune which James could see slipping through his fingers. The handwriting itself is variable and sometimes deteriorates, but it appears much more closely related to that of the will to the Diary, although it is very like some of the Ripper letters.

We hunted down the family of George Davidson and I talked to descendants of Sir Thomas Clark, his brother-in-law, whose family publishing firm still thrives in Edinburgh. They knew nothing. 'To have a possible suicide in a prominent Free Church family would have been such a scandal it would have been hushed up.'

We had elevenses with Peggy Martin, Mary Cadwallader's grand-daughter, living comfortably with her husband in a bungalow near Dover. She told us of a gold watch once owned by Mary which they all believed had come from Battlecrease House. It was pawned years ago, so we shall never know. We sipped sherry in the beamed 18th century home where Alice Yapp's great niece, Jo Brooks, lives with her husband. She placed on the table a silver locket and monogrammed teaspoon that, she said with a wry smile, Alice claimed Florie had 'given' her. Jo also told us that there was a 'whisper' in her family that Alice Yapp was rather more than a servant to James even before he employed her.

We had several meetings with chartered surveyor Gerard Brierley, great-great nephew of the now notorious Alfred Brierley. He admitted his family, too, had closed ranks in silence.

Quite by chance, we were introduced to David Fletcher Rogers whose great grandfather had been foreman of the Coroner's Court jury preceding Florie's trial. Fletcher Rogers took out a lease on Battlecrease House after the Maybricks but died in 1891. New people moved in, found the Fletcher Rogers family Bible and gave it to neighbours for safe keeping. In 1978, David Fletcher Rogers returned to take photographs of Battlecrease House, called next door and was to his astonishment, handed the Bible. Like our Diary it had emerged after several decades.

A Maybrick family Bible, which belonged to James' Uncle Charles, is now the treasured possession of Edith Stonehouse who was living in one of Liverpool's most depressed areas. We thumbed its pages hopefully looking for clues. There were none.

Back in Liverpool, we called on Helen Blanchard, descended from Abrahams the chemist. She lent us an exciting box of family letters which contained a prescription for James Maybrick and a letter from Alexander MacDougall. But nothing relating to our quest.

From America, I had a call from Mrs Gay Steinbach, who told me proudly that her grandmother had grown up in the Maybrick household in Ryde. Her name was then Laura Quinn – and she had always claimed to be the daughter of an Irish Customs clerk, Patrick Quinn ('although,' says Mrs Steinbach, 'the family wondered if she was Michael's daughter.') She went to live with the Maybricks at the age of ten – and hated it there. When Laura Maybrick died, she left Michael's royalties to Laura Trussle – as she had by then become.

We listened to a delightful tape recording of Edwin Maybrick's daughter Amy Main, chuckling through her reminiscences of life at Lynthorpe on the Isle of Wight, where she spent many miserable summer holidays as a little girl.

We ferreted among the archives of Ryde, eager to find a late-in-life confession from Michael that there were dark secrets he had never revealed. All we found was the very Victorian epitaph on his monumental gravestone, which, in the circumstances, seemed laden with significance. 'THERE SHALL BE NO MORE DEATH'.

Meanwhile, Paul Feldman was ploughing his own furrow. Keith Skinner had, by now, joined his team as an independent consultant and was being as fastidious as ever. Birth, death and marriage certificates on almost every member of the 'cast' were hoovered up, contacts were made with record offices and solicitors around the world; trips were made to America, to Cornwall, to Scotland and even the Isle of Man in a gallant attempt to trace the movements and families of anyone who might be harbouring the secret of the Diary.

Behind the scenes, a personal tragedy was unfolding. On January 2nd 1994 Anne Barrett could no longer cope with her husband's drinking, which had become increasingly out of control. She left him, taking his beloved Caroline with her. Michael responded by telephoning all of us, at any time of the day or night, sometimes using up an entire tape on the answerphone. Those calls were heartbreaking. He repeatedly said he was dying and wouldn't last the night. He was lonely, hurt and desperate to see his daughter. We all felt anguish for him. But it was clear that when he drank he lost his grasp on reality.

In early June 1994, Paul Feldman had discovered a nest of hitherto unknown Maybricks in Peterborough. He was sure that these were the illegitimate descendants of James Maybrick. He began a ferocious crusade, relentlessly pursuing anyone in Liverpool who might unravel what he began to see as a gigantic cover-up. Men in parked cars watched and waited, there were mysterious phone calls. No one, thought Paul, was who they said they were. He even suspected a national security matter.

It was not surprising that Michael Barrett became even more confused and bewildered. His emotional and financial world was collapsing. He too now employed Alan Gray, the local detective who worked in turn for Stanley Dangar, Melvin Harris and the *Sunday Times*! (However, when we made an appointment to visit Mr Gray in Liverpool in January 1995, we arrived to find a note pinned to the door saying that he had been 'advised' there was a conflict of interests and he would not now see us!)

On June 21st 1994, Sally and I went to see Michael in a new home, where he was living with a lady who had taken him under her wing. He led me into the garden and with much emotion poured out the story of how he had forged the Diary. He was bitter and angry that he had not seen his daughter and threatened to tell everything to the national press. His reasons for such actions were also confused. He kept repeating that all he wanted was to see Caroline, but he then pursued a course of action that made this less and less likely.

On June 24th 1994, he succumbed and gave an exclusive interview to Harold Brough of the *Liverpool Daily Post*. This appeared on June 27th under the heading: 'How I faked Ripper Diary' and quoted him saying 'Yes I am a forger, the greatest in history.' The photograph of a dishevelled Michael standing by Maybrick's grave, bore an uncanny resemblance to one of James Maybrick beneath it!

Harold Brough was sensibly doubtful about the reliability of Michael's admissions. This was no case of *in vino veritas*. He traced Anne and called to see her only to have the door firmly shut with a forthright, 'This is bullshit. He is trying to get back at me because I have left him.' I did not understand why forging the Diary would get back at Anne – unless of course Michael was implying that she was involved.

Michael's solicitor, Richard Bark Jones, immediately issued a rebuttal: 'With regard to the statement (confession) recently made by Michael Barrett that he had, himself, written the *Diary of Jack the Ripper*, I am in a position to say that my client was not in full control of his faculties when he made that statement which was totally incorrect and without foundation. Mr Barrett is now in the Windsor Clinic, where he is receiving treatment.'

Mr Bark Jones no longer acts for Michael, and has also told me that he would never have agreed to work for him if for one moment he thought that he *had* forged the Diary. The *Sunday Times* published the story but did not print the solicitor's denial.

Meanwhile, from January 1994, Paul Feldman had been scooping up contacts and information. Wherever I went, Paul seemed to have been there before. At the time I was aware of some of the fantastic flights of fancy he pursued and not a little puzzled by the number of the times he had 'cracked it'. But his boundless optimism did serve to keep the rest of us on our toes. Keith Skinner noted at the time, somewhat ruefully, that 'Paul bases a theory upon a hypothesis, sinks it deep in speculation and confounds it with mystery.'

Michael Barrett is no fool. Like Winnie the Pooh, his spelling is 'wobbly' in the extreme, but he has a taste for quoting Latin phrases culled from a classical dictionary and a knack of collecting unexpected snippets of knowledge from the library. I was therefore shocked but not altogether surprised when on September 30th, Michael apparently discovered the answer to a problem that had been facing us all.

There is a phrase in the Diary which I was sure must be a quotation.

Oh costly intercourse of death.

Without success we had hunted high and low in anthologies to find it. I asked Michael to look in the Liverpool library. He badgered the staff there for help and sure enough he rang me within a few days and told me, 'You will find it in the Sphere *History of English Literature*. Volume 2. It is by Richard Crashaw.'

He was right. A quick foray into the life of Crashaw revealed that he was an obscure, baroque poet (1613-1649) whose religious fervour fired his verse and inspired many other poets such as Milton and Shelley. His father was the Reverend William Crashaw (1572-1626), the most famous rector of St Mary Matfellon, the original White Chapel, in the heart of Jack the Ripper's London. Crashaw himself spent many hours there writing poetry but there is no way of knowing now if any of that poetry found its way onto the walls or tombs of the church. St Mary Matfellon, the most important in Whitechapel and renowned for its monuments, was destroyed in 1941.

The line in question occurs in a poem from a collection of religious verse entitled *Steps to the Temple: Delights of the Muses*. The poem is called 'Sancta Maria Dolorum or The Mother of Sorrows.' The correct wording is:

> O costly intercourse
> Of deaths & worse,
> Divided loves. While son & mother
> Discourse alternate wounds to one another;
> Quick Deaths that grow
> And gather, as they come & goe:
> His Nailes write swords in her, which soon her heart
> Payes back, with more than their own smart;
> Her SWORDS, still growin(g) with his pain,
> Turn SPEARES, & straight come home again.

This is obscure stuff and difficult to understand. If the Diary is a modern forgery, its author must have possessed extraordinary luck to find the poem and uncanny sensitivity to use it, as he has, to such poignant effect.

I wrote to the British Library to ask if a Victorian merchant would have known of Crashaw. R.J. Goulden replied on 25 March 1998: 'Several editions of Crashaw's poetry were in fact published between 1857 and 1887: a library edition of the poets in 1857, the works of Crashaw by John Russell Smith in 1858, a privately printed edition in 1872–3, the general Cassell's library edition of British poets in 1881 and another private edition in 1887. James Maybrick could have picked up secondhand copies of any of these works or else he could have subscribed to a circulating library and come across Crashaw's works in it.

There is yet another possibility that Stephen Adams (your 'singer of ballads') knew Crashaw's poems and Maybrick heard of Crashaw through Adams.'

Crashaw's works were much better known in 1888/9 than they are today and might possibly have found their way into the private home, especially if there was some religious influence. Just around the corner from his childhood home, there was a nationally famous second-hand book shop from which Gladstone used to order by post. It was known as The Temple of the Muses. So it is feasible that Maybrick could have, for instance, inherited such books from his parish clerk father. But the sophisticated use of the quotation puzzled me.

Then, to my dismay, Michael Barrett announced that he had a copy of the book at home. He had forgotten it was in his attic! His explanation was typically plausible and utterly baffling. 'After the Hillsborough disaster in 1989,' he said, 'I had worked hard to raise money for the fund. I wrote to a lot of publishers and asked them to contribute out-of-print books for a sale I was organising. Amongst the many volumes that arrived from Sphere were twelve volumes of their *History of English Literature*.' Michael says that he couldn't sell them and put it in the attic with others and forgot them, until finding the quotation in the library reminded him of their existence.

I was extremely suspicious. The Diary's critics were jubilant. This was proof positive of Michael Barrett's guilt. Despite this damning discovery, I was still confident that Michael Barrett could never have used these lines to such sensitive effect in the Diary. Even had Michael Barrett found that poem and inserted it in the Diary, how did he discover that Crashaw was so closely linked to Whitechapel. For me this was pushing the bounds of even my readiness to believe too far. There had to be a different explanation.

* * *

I have now seen some of Keith's records – every verbatim conversation, every phone call minuted and literally hundreds of pages of debate with Paul Begg and Martin Fido. It would be very difficult for anyone who has not read these records to make sense of what happened at that time – by explaining the context and the nuances of what was said, they make some sense of what happened next.

Anne has also written her own memories of the 'nightmare' of that time. The details of all she remembers are so precise and accurate because Keith Skinner had already taken her painstakingly through every emotion and every event leading to her eventual confession.

> After a few months I received a note from Paul Feldman. I showed it to my father and he told me to contact him. But I refused – I was sick of the Diary. In August I moved from the flat into a house.
>
> Paul Feldman eventually found out where I was living. He was ringing everyone: my best friend Audrey, all the Barretts – everyone. Then one night Michael's sister rang me – she was furious and dreadfully upset that Robert Smith, Shirley and Paul had all been phoning her. She was terribly distressed about Michael, and I was really embarrassed and worried. I felt a strong sense of guilt because I knew the true story about the Diary.

> So at about 11 p.m. on July 19th 1994, in a blind fury, I picked up the phone and called Paul's home in Middlesex.[sic] We were both screeching and shouting at each other. I told him to back off. The Diary had nothing to do with the Barretts. I was on that phone for four hours. From what I could make out he thought I wasn't Anne Graham/Barrett, Michael wasn't Michael – his sisters' birth certificates were wrong and my background had been destroyed by the Government. I thought he was mad! In fact I was very frightened. Paul appeared to believe that I knew more than I had been telling and was determined to get it out of me by fair means or foul. I thought 'I've got to get this man off their backs.'

In her notes Anne referred to Paul as 'the enemy' and on other occasions 'that bloody lunatic.' However, at her suggestion, Paul went up to Liverpool on July 30th. In the meantime Keith Skinner had drawn his attention to the page in Nigel Morland's book *The Friendless Lady*, which said that when Florie Maybrick left the Convent for France she was using the name Graham! This was checked and confirmed by local newspaper coverage. In Paul's mind a new theory was growing. It was Anne – not Michael – who was a Maybrick descendant.

She would not let him into her house and he took her to a city hotel where they sat together in an almost empty bar, armed with photographs and other family memorabilia which would prove his theories were wrong.

> I felt as though I had come up against a brick wall. I was at the end of my tether. So I told him in no uncertain terms that Michael knew nothing about the origins of the Diary. It had been given to me by my father. It was me who had given it to Tony Devereux to give to Michael and that when my father died the truth would all come out. My

> main worry at that time was my father. I was trying to get a decent home so that he could live with us... as he was very close to needing 24-hour care. By now I was also being hounded by Michael and I never knew what he would say or do next.

So it was that Paul persuaded Anne and Caroline to go down to his home and try to sort things out. They walked in the garden in the pitch dark because Anne was afraid the house was 'bugged'.

Little by little, a degree of confidence grew and she says she began to tell him what she knew about the origins of the Diary. 'I wasn't interested in the bloody Diary and I wanted nothing to do with it. I just wanted my father to be happy for his remaining months of life. Paul said he would protect me from the media and from Ripperologists if I told the true story. He said he could send Caroline and me away for a holiday to be out of reach.'

Keith Skinner recalled the confusion of this period in a letter to Martin Fido on June 2nd 1996.

> April to July 1994
>
> Focus is now on Anne and her background. Feldy becomes convinced that the only reason none of the certificates tie up with his theories is because wrong information has been deliberately fed into the system by the government, in order to protect the identitites of all the illegitimate children of James Maybrick aka Jack the Ripper. Thus Anne is not Anne, Michael is not Michael, Billy is not Billy and the Barrett family are not the Barrett family. Michael, now hopelessly lost but reasonably confident he is Michael Barrett, decides to put an end to the nightmare by confessing he forged the journal, which – and this is speculation – he now wonders whether Anne forged and for some perverse reason foisted on him. It is important to

> understand that Michael's confession came before anybody knew of Anne's involvement ... Feldy is by now convinced he has uncovered one of the greatest cover-ups of the 19th/20th century...This was the point (July) when Anne contacted Feldy...

* * *

Anne eventually gave Paul permission to meet her father. She moved from the flat in to a house and decided to revert to her maiden name – Graham. At this stage Paul was still convinced that Billy Graham was descended from James' illegitimate offspring. The first of two, long, animated conversations was recorded on July 30th. On August 12th Keith Skinner was also present and noticed a copy of my book on top of the wardrobe, new and unread. These two conversations are partially transcribed in Paul's book.

Billy Graham, then 80 years old, was a down-to-earth, former soldier in the Cheshire Regiment with a youthful reputation for rebelliousness and several medals for 'services to his country' in France, Germany and Africa. He was far more interested in the British Legion than he was in Jack the Ripper and Paul's visit was a somewhat irritating delay in his regular visit to the 'Legion'.

During these spontaneous exchanges about his childhood and background, Paul mentioned that when Florie came out of prison she had used the name Graham. Billy responded 'dirty ol' cow'. He then became very thoughtful and then very quietly handed Paul a golden nugget. He implied, on tape, that he thought it was possible that his own Dad could have been Florie's son. Billy seemed to be aware that in his far distant memory he had heard from within the family that Florie may indeed even have had a baby before she married James. Anne was clearly flabbergasted. Later she confirmed, 'I'm still in a state of shock. I thought the thing had been nicked from the house but I certainly didn't expect this.'

Caroline asked, 'Does this mean we are descended from him?' to which Paul said, triumphantly, 'No you are descended from her,' meaning Florence.

* * *

I was puzzled. Paul's research seemed to indicate that Billy Graham was descended from Florie through the paternal line. Yet the Diary, he claimed, had been passed down the maternal line. This was a coincidence too far.

There was another gap in the story. If Florence was, indeed, Billy Graham's grandmother, then who was his grandfather – Florie's lover? Anne remembered that, as a child, her Dad used to take her to Croxteth to see a grave he said was 'family'. She could not recall the name on the tombstone but she returned there much later, by which time she too had become fascinated by the story of the Maybricks. She took a photograph which shows that this is the grave of Henry Flinn – born 1858, died 1927, the year that Florie returned to England. Henry would have been 21 in 1879 – the year that Paul believed Florie may have had a baby.

* * *

Anne's guilt that her secret had caused such confusion brought about a change of heart and so on Sunday July 31st, about three weeks before the publishing deadline for my paperback, she recorded a message to Doreen Montgomery, Robert Smith and me over the telephone to Paul. He in turn contacted us and invited us to hear it in his office. As I wrote afterwards, 'We sat in stunned silence.' Anne's voice was brisk and rather tense. I guess she was nervous.

> Dear Doreen, Shirley, Robert and Paul
>
> I suppose I knew it was inevitable that one day the truth about the Ripper Diary would be revealed. I apologise

most sincerely that it has taken so long, but I felt I had justifiable reasons.

I realised some time ago that the snow-ball effect had intruded so deeply into your lives and this has been a heavy burden for me to carry. The Diary was never meant for publication, not by me.

First, I would like to confirm that I have not taken any money from Paul Feldman, nor has my father, nor has Paul offered anything more than his protection. The following part of this letter is the story in its entirety. I leave you all to work out the best way to present it to the press, with as little harm to us all as possible. That also includes Mike. I do not want to hurt him any more than he has been already.

I think it was in 1968/69 I seen [sic] the Diary for the first time. I was living with my father and my maternal grandmother and we were leaving the house as my father was about to re-marry after being widowed some years ago.

My grandmother was going to live with her son. In my bedroom was a fitted cupboard. I discovered the diary in a large metal trunk at the back of the cupboard. I read the first page and put it away to read when I was not so busy.

Some time later, after reading most of the Diary, I took it to my father and asked what he knew about it, if anything. He was doing his pools at the time and was not very interested. He said his Granny's friend had given it to her and his mother had given it to him. I asked him if he had read it and he said he had started to but the writing was too small – I left it at that.

For the sake of clarity I will tell you the story he eventually pieced together from different things he told me.

My father's step-grandmother, whose name was

Formby, was a great friend of the nurse who worked at Battlecrease. Granny Formby accompanied the nurse when she gave evidence at the trial.

On Christmas Day 1950, just after I was born, my father's step-mother, Edith, had come for Christmas dinner; she brought a suitcase with various books and documents my father had entrusted to her care during the war and in it was the Diary. She told my father his grandmother had left it to him.

After my step-mother's death we bought the house in Goldie Street to be near my father. It must have been around that time he gave me the Diary amongst lots of other things he no longer wanted. I never showed it to Mike – why, I honestly don't know. I didn't like having the Diary in my house and jammed it behind the cupboard in the spare room.

Sometime later, I can't remember how long, Mike started drinking. He was desperately trying to write but didn't seem to be getting anywhere. It was all very frustrating and was making things difficult between us.

I thought of giving him the diary then so that he could use it as the basis of a book. I was hoping he would write a fictional story about the Diary. I knew if I gave it to him and told him its history he would be badgering my dad for details and by this time he and my father were beginning to irritate each other.

So I came up with the idea of giving Mike the Diary via someone else. That way he would not connect it with me or my family. My only motive was to give Mike something of interest to do without it coming from me. I found some brown paper which had been lining the drawer and wrapped the Diary with it and tied it with string.

I took the parcel to Tony Devereux and asked him to give it to Mike and tell him to do something with it. This he faithfully did. What he thought about it all I have no idea. I never seen [sic] Tony again. I apologise to the Devereux family for being brought into this but then I never realised what would happen.

I suppose I was very naïve because far from using it as a basis for a story Mike started to investigate it. When he said he wanted to get the Diary published I panicked and we had a big argument and I tried to destroy the Diary. I don't mean I destroyed any of the pages – I just wanted to burn the Diary in its entirety. Anyway, he contacted Doreen just the way he said he did and I just hoped the Diary would live or die on its own merits – so I just let everyone get on with it. I never realised the problems it would cause.

The reason I am making this statement to Paul is so that I don't have to repeat it again and again to twenty different people. I also have no intention of allowing my father to be hounded to death. He has an inoperable tumour and a heart problem and is 80 years old. I seen [sic] Paul the other day simply to clear up the problems caused by his investigating the Barrett family and my friends. I realised then how out of hand everything had gone and reluctantly came to the decision that things had to be sorted out one way or another.

I hope you can understand why I did not in the end come to you Doreen. If I had, the whole machinery would have gone round and round and I could not cope with it. I have a great respect for you and everything you have tried to do in the past. As far as breaking contracts is concerned I suppose you will have to do whatever you think is right. I know nothing about contracts. I just signed what Michael told me.

In conclusion can I just say that I have never been interested or cared who Jack the Ripper was. Neither has my father. All these people who are obsessed by a 100 year old sex murderer seem to me to be most pitiful. Since 1889 there has been two world wars, the threat of nuclear annihilation, the break down of the ozone layer and the scourge of Aids. I am afraid the identity of a man who wouldn't even be thought of today if his nom-de-plume hadn't captured the public's imagination comes very low on my list of priorities.

Anyway this is my story. Do with it what you will. I hope it makes up in some ways the secrecy I took on to protect my father and his family....

Robert, I give you your paperback. Shirley I give you your story. Paul I give you your film. Doreen I hope I give you back the occasional night's sleep.

19

I am Tired of Keeping up the Pretence

ANNE'S STORY

To be honest, my first reaction to Anne's tape was one of disbelief and exasperation. I felt let down. I did not feel that Anne had lied. She had simply evaded the truth. But there were others, notably Martin Fido, who claimed that because she had never revealed what she knew about the Diary, everything she said was automatically suspect. Doreen, Sally, Robert Smith and I were understandably, I think, angry that Anne had not confided in us first. We felt that the truth should have been given to us first, as her contractual publishing partners, and could not understand the need for the secrecy.

We had suffered horrendous anxiety and loss at the hands of Scotland Yard and the *Sunday Times*. Doreen, as she always does, had fiercely protected her clients' concerns and taken a personal interest in their welfare. If the Diary had come through Anne's family what was the point in pretending otherwise? Knowing the importance of provenance why complicate the issue? Why not end the agony?

Anne has explained her actions now many times. She wrote to me with obvious distress in July 1997 saying that from the time the contracts were signed our contact had always been with Michael. So far as she was concerned we were just 'the people in London'. She certainly didn't think of us as friends or even colleagues at that stage. Her life was in turmoil: as a Catholic the concept of divorce was horrific and she could not share her problems with anyone, certainly not with us.

I also worried that the research waters had been muddied, but I was extremely relieved to learn later how closely Keith had been involved with the unravelling of the plot because I trust his integrity implicitly. Keith has said to me on many occasions, 'I was involved from the very first and I was present at most of the meetings of Paul and Billy. If the story had been forced I would have detected it by now. If I had detected it I would have exposed it.

'Those who believe Anne is lying, or that she has been bought by Paul must include me in the plot as well,' he claims. In his inimitable, pernickety way he has, at times, tested Anne's patience with his minute cross-examinations of every second of the journey that led her to make the confession. Keith's honesty and fervour is very persuasive. Anne's defection and seeming obliviousness to her professional and personal responsibility to us and indeed to the Devereux family distressed me, but on balance I see now how it could have happened.

All through our dealings with Michael he had always been to the fore; he it was who telephoned (at great length) and wrote. So far as we were concerned Michael and the Diary were synonymous – of her own volition Anne had remained very much on the 'outside'. I suppose, with hindsight, that the Diary swamped everything – we did not know the full extent of Anne's sufferings behind the scenes and she was not aware of all that was happening to us. London was remote and unreal to her and besides, like so many people, she thought the police were investigating the authenticity of the Diary not the suspected fraud of the publishers.

Over the following years, we have spent more time with Anne. She has made me very welcome in her home. She has been hospitable and welcoming. I have not enjoyed 'questioning' her honesty.

Anne is a very private person, a characteristic seen by her detractors as a 'convenient' fall-back position. She is bright, bustling and humorous and during the time she was the family breadwinner, she was a secretary in Liverpool. She is also a 'scouser' with a fiery temper when roused, and not given to suffering fools gladly. I knew I had to give Anne a chance to re-establish the confidence I had lost. If her story was true, I could at last prove that the Diary is not a modern forgery. If she was lying, it was equally important that I was not duped and continued to establish the provenance of this baffling journal.

It was also obvious to me that the doubters would jump on Anne's story as yet another 'convenient' ploy and that if I did eventually decide that Anne was honest I would myself be accused of believing what I wanted to believe.

From these various meetings, sitting on her floor, chatting over lunch, looking at family holiday snapshots, she has told us with considerable reticence about the events that led to her confession that night in Paul Feldman's garden.

Since then she admits she has been fascinated by Paul's growing evidence about her complicated background and possible lineage.

I understand why she did not spill the beans when the police visited her home. She was frightened then and fear froze her. On the other hand, when Paul Feldman approached her friends, she was very, very angry. Anne is a person who responds to feeling angry with action.

The story in brief, as pieced together from the Billy Graham tapes, for his daughter's information as much as for Paul Feldman, is this. Billy's father William Graham, who was probably born in Hartlepool, married twice. His second wife was Edith Formby and, according to an old family tradition her mother, Elizabeth, had been a friend of one of the servants at Battlecrease House: 'the skivvy' was how Billy Graham described her. Granny Formby could neither read nor write and signed her marriage certificate with an *X* so presumably never understood the contents of the diary. She worked later at the Hillside Laundry. This still exists but in 1889 was not far from Battlecrease

House, in Peel Street. Billy remembered her as a lovely old lady – he used to run errands and fetch her pension for her.

He also recalled, on tape, that as a lad living in Liverpool, he and his pals played a game in which they ran up and down outside Battlecrease House, pretending to be on horseback, slapping their thighs and calling 'Look out, look out, Jack the Ripper's about'.

In 1933 Billy Graham joined the army and did not return until 1943, by which time his 'ganny' had died (in 1939). It was then he remembered seeing a black tin box with the three white letters on it. (Remember Florie Maybrick's trunk?) In 1946, Billy married Anne's mother, Irene Bromilow. Anne takes up the story.

> My mother's father, Grandfather Bromilow, was a professional footballer and he had a decent income when other people didn't so my mother was privately educated. She'd had two babies who died before me and I was so precious that she insisted I was convent educated too, although my Dad was a manual worker. I was just so different from the other girls. I was in a different class; I had no friends. I hardly saw my father because he was working all the time and then my mother got TB and was in and out of sanatoriums. My Granny Bromilow lived with us but she was a hypochondriac and had taken to her bed. It was a very strange set up. When I was about 12 my mother started drinking, then she had an accident and was bed-ridden so I was running up and down looking after them both. My Dad was lovely, sweet as water but I only found out what a rotten time he had at the end of his life. My Mum died in 1964 when I was 14 years old.
>
> When I was about 18 years old, my father married Maggie Grimes and we moved house. It was then, as I said in the statement, that I first saw the Diary – about 1968 or 9. There was a big walk-in cupboard – I was terrified of it and never went in; there was a Dansette and a Virgin in

> front and lots of stuff from the war – gas-masks and so on. At the back was this trunk full of tropical gear and a first-aid box. The Diary was at the bottom. I looked through it quickly – I thought it looked interesting and we packed it to move to the new house in Dorrington Street.
>
> Maggie had three sons but they weren't around much and I was still very lonely. When I did ask Dad about the Diary he was doing his pools and wasn't interested. People have asked me since why on earth I didn't do something with it then. But I was just a kid – times were hard in Liverpool – no one was the slightest bit interested in Jack the Ripper. It didn't mean a thing. It got put away in a wardrobe with lots of bits and pieces.

Later Billy said, 'If I'd known what it was worth I'd have cashed it years ago. Blimey, I wouldn't have been slaving away in Dunlops – 12 hour shifts – on dirty big tyres if I'd known… I could have been lying on a beach now with a couple of strippers…'

Although she thought Maggie was a wonderful woman, in 1970 Anne decided to emigrate to Australia as a nurse. She loved it there. Australians make no emotional demands and that suited her fine. During the entire five years she was in Australia, Anne had not a word from her Dad. 'He could hardly write,' she says. 'In fact Caroline remembers how she always used to write all his Christmas cards for him in later years – including her own! Anyone who suggests that *he* wrote the Diary is plain daft.'

Anne worked for six months with a market research company in Sydney and then went to Canberra to train as a nurse. In 1972 she returned to Sydney to work as a nurse.

The Australian connection was to provide us much later with another headache. In August 1999 an Australian impresario, Steve Powell, contacted Andy Ayliff, then working for the BBC on a completely different matter. He mentioned in passing an astonishing memory of Anne in Australia. Andy then kindly passed the information on to me. The story Steve told was exciting. Even so I was suspicious that, although his original contact with Andy had been on a totally different subject, and Anne's story was coincidental, here could be another media man with an eye on the theatrical potential of the Diary. However, if Steve's memory was correct then we would have proof that Anne did, indeed, know about the Diary in 1968. It was worth investigating.

I made email contact with Steve Powell myself but decided to say nothing to Anne. I did not want her to corroborate Steve's memory of events 30 years ago, as a superbly convenient support for her own story.

He confirmed that, as a member of a rock band called The Mint, he and various other young friends had met an English nurse called Anne who was working at Caringbah Hospital, near Sydney. The facts of what happened all that time ago changed somewhat with each telling. This did not surprise me, since I can't, myself, recall the detail of anything that happened in 1968. I was more suspicious of the amount of detail recalled. But finally, on July 3rd 2000, Steve put his final version on the Internet Message Boards. He said, 'Try as I could, as I sat beside her in my old blue bandwagon, I just could not believe her story.'

According to Steve, he was on chauffeur duty one night and collected some nurses who needed taking back to the hospital from a party. They were talking about another nurse who had a diary of Jack the Ripper. In fact, the girls told Steve they had had a pyjama party at the hospital and were telling 'scary stories'. 'Anne' said she had a scary tale of her own and went to fetch a book from which she proceeded to read. It was so horrific that one of the nurses had to leave the room.

Steve was then staying in Cronulla, south of Sydney, with an English family from Sheffield – the Daltons – since the three boys Michael, David and Edward were in the band. He arranged to meet Anne himself and, sitting in his old blue bandwagon, she told him the story that we had already heard.

He passed on to me a number of names in addition to the Daltons.

I contacted David Dalton, without giving him any information that would lead him in the direction I hoped to hear. He agreed to phone me the following week during a trip to London, but he never did and I was not able to make contact again. Stephen Park(e), and David McLean I failed to find. The key witness according to Steve was a Victoria Courtney whose father was in Sydney police. I was still curious because I knew that Anne had shared a room with a girl she called Vicky.

I eventually tracked Victoria down in 2000 in Wahroonga where she is married; she was friendly and helpful but, unfortunately, all-too-honestly vague about events so long ago. She was not a nurse (that tallied with Anne's memory of her flat-mate) and could not recall what Anne looked like. She thought she had a dim memory of diary talk among the Caringbah nurses but not enough for me to cry 'Eureka!' She agreed to send me a photograph.

At this stage, in June 2000, Keith Skinner decided to tell Anne about the Australian link and recorded a long 'phone conversation with her. This could have been her golden opportunity to clinch a lie – if, indeed, what she had told us was a lie. But she didn't. She laughed. 'I wish it was true,' she said. When I spoke to Anne myself she was astonished that anyone would think that a teenager, as she was then, would attach any interest to the diary. 'It was no big deal,' she told me. 'I just wasn't interested and never gave it a thought. I certainly didn't take it to Australia with me. It was the last thing on my mind at the time.' Anne's memory of the girl she called 'Vicky' was that she was diabetic and had a slightly troublesome skin. She thought she was a hairdresser or maybe an air hostess. Victoria Vickery, as she now is, does not have diabetes.

When the picture arrived I sent it to Anne and asked, 'Does this mean anything to you?' I pretended I'd found it in a file and wanted identification. She said, 'No, it means nothing,' but when I explained that it was Vicky from Australia she said, 'Well she could have dyed her hair since I knew her. It's far too far back to be sure.' I sent Anne's picture, as a nurse in Australia, to Vicky (who had not read my book or

Paul Feldman's). She did not recognise Anne.

None of the ends tied up. Regretfully, this is another story in the 'unsolved' file.

Anne returned to Liverpool in 1976, went to the Irish Centre and there met the youthful, persistent Michael Barrett. She was flattered by his attentions, fell in love and on December 4th, within weeks, they were married by special licence, though her family warned her against it. Michael had been involved in a terrible car accident when he was 14; he'd been given the last rites and wasn't sure he could have children. But Caroline arrived when Anne was 30.

'Michael was an absolutely brilliant dad. I was at work and he did everything for her, changed her nappies, cleaned the house, had my tea on the table when I came home. He was so proud of her achievements at school.' I remembered, sadly, how, when I first visited the Barretts apparently happy home in 1992, Michael persuaded Caroline to play to us on the piano and showed us the pictures of her playing the Last Post on the trumpet on Remembrance Sunday.

> Caroline knew he had started drinking long before I did. I blame myself for that. I would come home from work and find that he hadn't done the shopping but there was no money left either.
>
> In 1989 my step-mother, Maggie, died. I began to get really close to my Dad after that. It was like a fusion of two souls – incredible. Caroline's birth taught me what parental love was like. I adored him.
>
> We moved to Goldie Street to be near him. That was an absolute bloody disaster. Michael didn't want to live there. Dad and he were getting on each other's nerves and so I would pop in to see Dad for five minutes after work and Michael was jealous. When he was eventually due to move into sheltered accommodation Dad began clearing out and he kept giving me stuff. It was then that he handed over the Diary.

> I hid it behind a cupboard which we had bought from the Salvation Army. This was in the small room which we had meant for Caroline, but she preferred the larger bedroom. So the pink room became a rubbish dump.
>
> Michael had always had an idea he wanted to write. Dad had lent him some money to buy a word processor in 1985 (sic) and he had started sending puzzles and short star interviews to the magazine *Look-In*. I wanted so much to be proud of him.

Anne continued. 'I was desperate for money – I knew things were going well for me at work but nothing was happening for Michael – he was on an invalidity pension. I had met Tony Devereux a couple of times – once at the Saddle pub. I popped in there after a garden fête at Caroline's school one Saturday afternoon because my back was killing me. But I could have walked past the man in the street and would never have recognised him.'

The landlord of the Saddle, Bob Lee, recalled that visit. 'She seemed a nice lady. Tony used to come here regularly, long before he ever met Michael… Michael used to come in every day and sometime he'd run errands for Tony when he was ill but I don't think they got on particularly well. He didn't have friends. Tony's daughters used to come in too – nice ladies, they looked after their Dad. We never discussed the Diary in the pub afterwards… Tony was very quiet, he'd have never said a word. Tony'd never have given Michael anything he thought was valuable. I never saw the Diary – I didn't know anything about the Maybricks… I wasn't interested. You never ask questions in this job… I haven't even read your book…'

So Anne described how, one evening, on the spur of the moment, she wrapped the Diary in some brown paper and carrying it in a plastic bag she told Michael she was off to get a bottle of wine. But instead she went down to Tony's house.

Anne goes on:

> You have to understand I was terribly depressed – we had such financial problems, I was very, very low and often thinking about leaving. But it felt like the absolute pits to do something like that. What was the alternative? I needed to feel proud of him again… He needed to gain some self respect without my help but more important, I didn't want him pestering my Dad, as I knew he would. I was so nervous. Tony couldn't walk very well and took so long to answer the door I nearly chickened out. I gave him the bag – said it was a book (I had read it by then) and asked him to give it to Michael – with instructions to tell him to 'do something' with it, I don't think he knew who I was from Adam at first. I made him promise not to tell Michael where it came from so that he could have some self-respect.

After that everything happened much as Michael has described it. 'I never dreamed that things would turn out the way they did. When Michael said he was going to take the Diary to London I really thought that Doreen Montgomery would send him packing,' Anne recalls, with some regret.

Caroline remembers, all too well, the day her dad opened the Diary. When he saw what it was he rang Tony over and over again. He borrowed books from the library, read up about the Ripper and made lots of notes. Sometimes he tried to discuss the Diary with Tony but he wasn't interested.

In January 1991, just as Michael had described, Tony fell and broke his hip. After he came home from hospital, he could no longer walk so much and eventually died in Walton Hospital that August. Perhaps because he is no longer there to answer questions, those who insist the Diary is a forgery have added Tony Devereux to their list of suspects.

* * *

Anne's friend Audrey Johnson was receptionist at Rensburgh's where they worked together. She was shy about being disloyal and would only see us with Anne's agreement. Sally, Keith and I went out to see her in the countryside near Southport on February 12th 1997. She was a friendly, easy-going lady who made us lunch while we watched red squirrels in the garden.

> Anne never talked to anyone at work, she was such a private person. But we started chatting about books; I knew she was unhappy but she never said a word.
>
> One day she was obviously upset and she did say that her husband was writing a book... but she couldn't talk about it. I remember calling into Goldie Street one day; Anne had had to give up work for a while with a bad back and Caroline was at school. But things were frenetic, Michael was in the front room and you could hear him pacing around, the phone kept going and the beer cans kept going but I had the strong feeling Anne just wanted to keep her head down.
>
> When the story broke I didn't like it at all – the idea that people were making money out of the deaths of some poor souls but I was very glad for Anne because she would have some money. When her confession came out I was absolutely astounded. I knew her father. He was a very throw away sort of bloke; if he had something fantastic in a box and he wasn't interested he wouldn't have been bothered with it. If people say he wrote it, I say, 'Don't be daft!'

* * *

In November 1994, Paul Feldman called a 'conference' of all the Peterborough Maybricks, which was also attended by Brian Maybrick, Albert Johnson and me. I had to admit that I was utterly confused by the mass of genealogical evidence and dozens of photographs Paul displayed with such pride, apparently linking everyone with everyone else. However, with more research I became aware of the chaos that is Victorian birth, death and marriage certificates. So often there are extraordinary coincidences, unexpected family links and clerical errors. But perhaps Paul had, despite this, begun to unravel the hitherto unknown Maybrick web. Certainly, the descendants gathered that day were enthralled.

There seemed to be an unmistakeable Maybrick face. Albert Johnson even offered to take a blood test. Brian Maybrick too was enjoying every minute and was, by now, himself convinced of the Diary's pedigree.

But sadness was to overshadow that gathering, for Anne Graham took a call to say that her father was dying and Paul arranged for her to rush home to Liverpool by taxi. Billy was already dead when she arrived. Even then the critics were relentless, observing that the Diary's provenance was once more, conveniently, untraceable and implying that Anne had chosen just the right moment to break her story.

I went, with Keith, to Billy's funeral; it was a moving and very emotional event, with a gathering back at the Legion afterwards. Billy was clearly a much liked man and dearly loved by his family. I felt sad that I never had the opportunity to meet him.

There were to be other sadnesses. For on April 9th 1996 Brian Maybrick also died – he had kept the news that he had cancer from everyone. His funeral on April 18th was a eulogy to a man whose open good-heartedness had enriched his parish and his family life. The hymn they poignantly chose to end the ceremony was by Michael Maybrick – 'The Holy City', sung by the BBC Welsh Choir with Aled Jones, as soloist. His son, David, has inherited his father's interest and continuesto help us whenever asked.

* * *

Since that time we have carried on playing Devil's advocate. Well aware that Anne's story would be treated with derision by Diaryphobes, we could not ignore any new information that might expand our understanding of the facts – even if it did not support what Anne had told us.

One such lead came, out of the blue, in the summer of 1997. Its source was impeccable – a London lawyer, Stephen Shotnes of Simons, Muirhead and Burton, had been told the story by Tim Martin-Wright, Managing Director of A1 Security and Electrical Ltd., a large international security firm based in Liverpool. The tale he told had echoes of an earlier rumour which Paul Feldman and I had pursued, that the Diary had, in fact, been found by builders or electricians working at Battlecrease House. One version claimed that it had been removed from behind window panelling, another from under the floor boards of Maybrick's study. Various dates had been given – 1982, 1989 and 1991. But these stories had foundered. This time it seemed different.

Knowing of publisher Robert Smith's professional interest in the Diary, Mr Shotnes persuaded Tim Martin-Wright to meet them both in Liverpool. On their arrival he took them to his retail outlet near Bootle, which sells domestic alarm systems. There they spoke with one of his employees. He recalled that, at the end of 1991, a customer, identified as Alan Davies, an electrician working for Portus and Rhodes, told him how a colleague, doing a re-wiring job at Battlecrease House, had found a biscuit tin under the floorboards. It contained a leather-bound diary and a gold ring.

The shop assistant suggested to Mr Davies that he show the Diary to Tim Martin-Wright, as he was a collector of antique books. A purchase price of £25 was mentioned. Alan Davies, however, was not working in the house at the time and the Diary never surfaced. Later the shop assistant heard that it had been sold 'in a pub in Anfield'. (This is the area of Liverpool where Michael Barrett and Tony Devereux drank at The Saddle).

Mr Martin-Wright confirmed that the above events occurred 'a month or two' after his shop opened in October 1991, which appeared to fit conveniently with April 1992, the month that Michael Barrett brought the Diary to London.

Armed with this information, I went with Robert Smith and Sally

Evemy to see Alan and his wife – a hard-working couple with a 17-year-old son. He recounted the story of his colleague at Portus and Rhodes, Brian Rawes. At the end of one day, Mr Rawes had been picking up two other employees from Battlecrease House in the firm's van. He recalls one of them coming to the driver's window saying, 'I've found something under the floor boards. I think it could be important.' Mr Rawes advised him to tell his boss, Colin Rhodes, about it.

Mr Rawes has confirmed this account, but, disconcertingly, was certain (by reference to an old daily memo book) that the above events took place in June 1992. So if something was found it was not our Diary.

And there the trail went cold. Mr Rawes' colleagues working in the house in June 1992 declined to be interviewed by me, having apparently been scared by the police investigation of the Diary's authenticity after my book was first published in 1993.

We made a return visit to Battlecrease House in June 1997 and sat in James Maybrick's bedroom, now Paul Dodd's living room. It was an eerie experience.

Paul was adamant. The house was originally gaslit and converted to electricity in the 1920s. It was re-wired when his father bought it in 1946 and again in 1977 when Paul himself had gutted the place and lifted the floor boards. Had anything been hidden, he was sure that he would have found it then.

Work was done on the cellars in 1989 and in 1991 there were repairs to the roof but the workmen had no access to the house for this. Storage heaters were installed in two phases – in Maybrick's bedroom in the late summer of 1991 and in the downstairs flat in 1993. Paul had again undertaken the initial preparation himself.

But once we started pinning down the dates, none of the people whose names we had been given appeared to have been in the right place at the right time. The key characters didn't want to talk. It was all very mysterious. Something might indeed have been found at Battlecrease House, but, whatever it was, it was seemingly not our Diary and whatever it was had vanished – at least temporarily!

20

The Man I have Become was Not the Man I was Born

There was a great deal of anger and frustration expressed at this time – not least by Michael Barrett himself. When the paperback version of my book appeared in October 1994, Anne's statement was, for him, the final straw. He had lost Caroline, his claim to fame as the man who found the Diary of Jack the Ripper was destroyed, and Anne had also deprived him of his newly declared wish to be 'the greatest forger in the world.' So he changed tack and began to say that he 'created' the Diary but it was in Anne's handwriting.

Anne has described their already crumbling relationship in those years before the Diary came to London and has said, sadly, that the idea that she and Michael could, by then, have collaborated over anything was absolute rubbish.

In January 1995, Sally, Keith and I decided we must go to Liverpool and give him the opportunity to tell us in detail exactly *how* he had achieved this extraordinary work that had fooled us all! He agreed that he would tell us everything. We arrived in Goldie Street accompanied (with Michael's agreement) by a former Detective Superintendent, Kenneth Forshaw, with 32 years' experience in Liverpool CID. He was to be an independent observer to what we suspected might be a tricky meeting and Michael was unaware of his full identity.

We taped that five-hour interview. 45 pages of typescript with Michael in varying moods, pleading with us to go off and get a bottle of Scotch (which we refused). Ken Forshaw reprimanded him for compromising his visitors. He denied that he had ever forged the Diary and swore on the Bible, on Caroline's life and his own life that Tony Devereux gave it to him and that Anne was lying. He showed us his arm, badly lacerated and where he had severed an artery 'accidentally' pushing his fist through Anne's front door. We taped everything (with his co-operation), hardly said a word and left, saddened and exhausted.

Almost immediately, Michael dictated a new statement to Alan Gray in which he said he had been intimidated and frightened by us. He also prepared a 6-page statement, in which he describes himself as an author, sworn in the presence of the ubiquitous Alan Gray at the office of D.P. Hardy and Co, solicitors in Liverpool.

This statement was very soon in general circulation and finally in 1996 appeared on the Internet in its entirety. For legal reasons I am unable to quote it in full. I have extracted the sections dealing with Michael's alleged 'forgery' of the Diary.

> I Michael Barrett was the author of the original Diary of Jack the Ripper and my wife Anne Barrett, hand wrote it from my typed notes and on occasions at my dictation…
>
> About January 1990 Anne purchased a diary, a red leather back diary for £25… through a firm in the *1986 Writers and Artists Yearbook*… when it arrived it was of no use, it was too small… At about the same time I spoke to William Graham about our idea…
>
> At the end of January 1990 I went to the Auctioneer Outhwaite and Litherland, Fontenoy Street.
>
> It was about 11.30 a.m… I found a photograph album which contained approximately 125 pages of

photographs… to do with the 1918 war. This album was part of lot 126 which was for auction with a brass compass… it looked to me like a seaman's compass… and I particularly noticed that the compass had no fingers.

When the bidding started I noticed another man who was interested… he was smartly dressed… I think he was a Military man. This man bid up to £45 and then I bid £50 and the other man dropped out… I was given a ticket on which was marked the item number and the price I had bid. This ticket was stamped… I gave my name as P. Williams, Allerton Street… When I got home I noticed inside the front cover the maker's stamp mark, dated 1908/9… to remove this without trace I soaked the whole of the front cover in Linseed Oil… which took about two days to dry out. I even used heat from the gas oven to assist.

I removed the maker's seal. I then took a Stanley knife and removed all the photographs and quite a few pages… Anne and I went to town in Liverpool and in Bold Street I bought three pens that would hold nibs… I bought 22 brass nibs… from the Medico art gallery… We then decided… to make our way to Bluecoat Chambers… and purchased a small bottle of Diamine Manuscript Ink…

I sat in the living room by the rear lounge window with my word processor… Anne sat with her back to me as she wrote the manuscript… All in all it took us 11 days…

During this period we were writing the Diary Tony Devereux was housebound and in fact after we completed the Diary we left it for a while… He died in May 1990.

During the time I was dictating to Anne mistakes occurred from time to time… page 6… 2nd paragraph line nine starts with an ink blot, this blot covers a mistake I made when I told Anne to write down James instead of Thomas. The mistake was covered with an ink blot.

> Page 226 of the book, page 20... Turn Round Three Times and catch whom you may. This was from Punch magazine 3rd week in September 1888. The journalist was PW Wenn...

He then goes on to describe how his discs, photographs, compass, pens and ink were taken to a member of his family who destroyed them to protect him. This has been strenuously denied in a formal statement and legal action threatened.

> There is little doubt in my mind I have been hoodwinked... My inexperience in the publishing game has been my downfall while all around me are making money. I have even had bills to cover expenses incurred by the author of the book, Shirley Harrison...
>
> I give my name so that history do tell what love can do to a gentleman born, Yours truly Michael Barrett.

All this was a gift from the Gods to those who challenged the Diary. It was so convincing – on the face of it. But the facts are these.

1. The red diary was in fact purchased after the Diary had been brought to London. (Anne has the receipt.)

2. Tony Devereux died in August 1991.

3. On January 30th 1997 Doreen Montgomery received the following statement from Kevin Whay, director of Outhwaite and Litherland: 'Having searched through our files and archives on either side of the alleged sale dates I can confirm that no such description or lot number corresponding with his statement exists. Furthermore we do not and have never conducted our sales in the manner in which he describes...'

4. The former chief chemist for Diamine ink, Alec Voller, says that the Diary ink is not Diamine.

5. The *Punch* cartoon is by Tenniel. The name PW Wenn does not appear.

6. The word under the blot is not 'James' but 'regards'.

7. The Diary is not in Anne Barrett's handwriting.

8. Michael Barrett and Anne Barrett between them have earned exactly the same from the book *The Diary of Jack the Ripper* as I have, although since their separation, by virtue of the terms of the collaboration agreement, Anne Graham has received 25% of the gross sums payable to us. But Michael consistently failed to honour his contractual share of research expenses despite receiving regular invoices, and I long ago gave up hope.

Since that first affidavit, Michael Barrett claimed to be a member of MI5, to have foiled an IRA attack and been awarded the Queen's medal for gallantry, to be dying (within the next hour), to be re-married and expecting a baby, to be impotent, to have cancer and to be going to live in Russia and America. He also inserted an advertisement in *Loot* magazine for illustrators to send him drawings for a children's story which he then told entrants was to be published by Smith Gryphon. Copies of illustrations submitted then turned up in art shop windows in Southport and the originals returned 'not accepted by the publisher.' Smith Gryphon did not publish children's books and had no knowledge of all this! He also claimed to have a gun.

Interestingly, in 1997 a letter came into my possession. It had been sent from Alan Gray to Michael on October 15th 1996.

Be assured that if we can possibley [sic] prove without

doubt where you brought the Diary from I can almost guarantee you will make 'money'. I have a National Newspaper ready to do business BUT we must get the evidence that will support you.

Then watch them jump because your credibility will then be 100%. Feldman is about to release a new book. The time is right to pay these terrible people back. So let's do it.

Phone me...'

But the most effective demolition of the 'Great Forger' theory has been done by Michael himself. In 1992 Michael had given me all his notes, re-typed and 'tidied up' by Anne from his researches. They are a record of his forays to Liverpool Library before he brought the Diary to London when he was desperately trying to make sense of it all. I quote:

> Check for copy of *Punch* around Sept.1888... nothing to date... Where was Knowsley Buildings? To date cannot find... Question. Who else other than the Ripper would have known that he was almost caught..? Answer: Not sure but if the Diary is genuine and written at that time these facts could only have been known by the Ripper.

These are not the notes of a man who knows. They are the simple notes of a man who is seeking information. The man who was the first to be caught in the web of this Diary. Not the man who was writing a master forgery.

Nevertheless, the rumour reverberated around the Ripperology world and was burnished through 1995-6 until it shone like truth. To the sceptics behind the scenes, Michael Barrett had forged the Diary and they re-doubled their efforts to expose it – and us. An unseemly slanging match developed, throughout which I largely maintained a low profile.

Eventually, in exasperation, I sent a contribution to the Internet from which I quote.

> The Diary has generated its own momentum. It has not been kept alive by the publishers and myself but remains because so many knowledgeable people have been captivated and refused to let it die. It has revealed much new historical material, especially about the Maybricks. It has also been a catalyst for a great deal of good, providing opportunities for original research in a great variety of disciplines.
>
> Over three years, Mr Harris has consistently claimed to know the names of those who forged the Diary. In the [London] *Evening Standard* of December 8th 1994, he says, 'the identities of the three people involved in the forgery will soon be made known.'... I challenge him to name these forgers so that the appropriate action can be taken.

Mr Harris's reply appeared as part of an article for the Internet Casebook, in March 1997.

> Mrs Harrison's 'challenge' to me to name the forgers of the Diary is sheer hogwash and an excuse for yet more evasions! (Now, there's a chance to yell, 'abuse'). She already knows my answer. There are good legal and logical reasons why I choose to remain silent; I have, in fact, taken legal advice on this score. But I am quite willing to present my papers to any neutral solicitor and he, or she, will confirm that there are sound and logical reasons for my silence. But this is a petty diversion. My case against the Diary rests on the text and the handwriting of that document and is independent of the identities of the forgers. Thus anyone can review this evidence, here and now, and see just where the jiggery pokery lies...

The July 1997 edition of *Ripperana* summarises a letter from Keith Skinner, Paul Begg and Martin Fido. 'Despite our stated respect for much of Mr Harris's work... his persistent tone of superior self-confidence and patronising view of other writers may mislead the casual reader to believe he is always reliable...'

Finally when Mr Harris placed a 30-page document on the Internet entitled *The Maybrick Hoax – a Fact File for the Perplexed* I decided, reluctantly, to respond.

> I was heartened at the positive reactions from readers weary of the aggressive and destructive wind that was blowing.
>
> I have no intention of dissecting this latest analysis of the case against the Ripper Diary. In the five years since Paul Feldman and I have been, independently, searching for the truth about this enigmatic document we have become all too familiar with Mr Harris' trenchant views...
>
> Mr Harris' argument is based entirely on his assumption that the Maybrick Diary and watch are modern forgeries, perpetrated by a small group of people in Liverpool. But I would like to remind Casebook readers that there is another, equally honourable and genuine view: that the Diary and the watch are *not* modern hoaxes.
>
> If the Diary is old, then it is an historical document, either the work of a forger many years ago (possibly a Ripper contemporary) or – as I believe – genuine. Ripper research in the past has leaned a great deal on unreliable witnesses (see Philip Sugden's *The Complete History of Jack the Ripper* for examples). But should the Diary be proved to be old or the work of James Maybrick it could throw a totally new light on Ripper history. Then Mr Harris' thesis will be left without substance.
>
> In the past, Mr Harris has called me 'a practised evader'. I am, indeed, someone who dislikes confrontation and I am all too aware of the dangers of extremism. Is it not a shame

that a hitherto respected writer is so determined to vilify the Diary, that he relentlessly reads sinister and underhand motives into every action of those with whom he disagrees? He is entitled to an opinion. So are we.

Parts of Mr Harris's contribution are impressive and stand by themselves. Others are just as impressive *unless* you are in possession, as we are, of all the facts relating to the writing, publishing and promotion of my own book *The Diary of Jack the Ripper*. He bases his opinion here on often unreliable and partially informed secondary sources.

For example, Mr Harris' picture of Michael Barrett's character when he first came to London is a figment of his imagination. Was Mr Harris present at those meetings? Doreen Montgomery and I had natural reservations but in turn Michael Barrett was suspicious of us. The suggestion that at that stage we knew he was a 'braggart and a drunkard' and there was a convenient cover-up for commercial reasons, is a typical distortion of the truth. At first we did not appreciate the extent of Michael's troubles and felt duty bound to protect him as far as possible. He was nervous and vulnerable. The deterioration of Michael's health accelerated when his wife left and became a tragic and erratic process which is honestly documented in the paperback edition of my book...

Some of Mr Harris' observations about the historical background to the Diary appear fair at first, but are tainted by his insistence that any viewpoint other than his own, arises only from malintent and commercial greed.

Does Mr Harris have grounds or evidence for such defamatory comments? He has met none of the original team involved with the Diary research. More importantly, he has not discussed his accusations face to face with those whom, he implies, had a hand in the affair.

It is facile for him to claim that all the forgers' information was culled from a number of books – one of which, a novel by Michael Dibden, *The Last Sherlock Holmes Case*, is obscure and not easy to locate. This in itself would have called for considerable pre-knowledge and even erudition, such as his own. Such a feat might well seem easy to Mr Harris.

I have Michael Barrett's 'research notes' in my possession. They were typed and collated for him by Anne, his then wife, while he was trying to make sense of the Diary, before he brought it to us. Where he can't find what he wants, he writes, 'nothing to date'. Or 'not known'. Interestingly, there is a remark about the Diary reference to the Punch cartoon 'Catch whom you May'. Mr Harris implies that the forger had only to look at the cover of Martin Fido's hardback *The Crimes Detection and Death of Jack the Ripper* to see this reproduced. But Michael Barrett had never heard of Martin Fido at that time. He relied on Paul Harrison, Colin Wilson and Robin Odell. His research note says simply: 'check for copy of *Punch* around September 1888.'

This is not the strategic, forward-looking plan of a forger embarking on research! It reflects the uncertainties of a man struggling to understand material that has already been written.

Had Mr Harris spent more time with his 'nest of forgers', he would realise just how unlikely his theory is!

The amount of bad temper generated by the Diary has so often obscured its complexity. As believers and non-believers alike try to prove or disprove its authenticity, it throws up new possibilities and new challenges at every twist and turn.

The Internet debates have raged on and moved from the Maybrick diary to a number of related disagreements. At one stage these were so abusive that the Message Boards were briefly closed down. They have now been reinstated, more civilised and less aggressive. It has amused me to see what fires have been fuelled by the Diary over the last ten years and how many hours of entertainment and intense aggravation it has given to such a wide variety of people.

There is a postscript. For nine years, since the *Evening Standard* of December 8th 1994 quoted Melvin Harris as saying, 'The identities of the three people involved in the forgery will soon be made,' the 'outing' of the alleged forgers has been a running theme and occupied an astonishing amount of space on the Message Boards.

In February 1995, Nick Warren, editor of *Ripperana*, went a little further. He wrote that the three supposed forgers comprise:

a) someone who composes a text on a WP
b) an amanuensis
c) a man so embittered against an ex-wife that he always referred to her as 'the whore'

By 1999 Stanley Dangar was assuring me that no forgers could be named 'because there is absolutely no proof that this is a modern forgery.'

In September 1999 Nick Warren wrote to Keith Skinner naming the names of 'the three guilty men' (although they were not, by this time, exactly the same three previously identified). However, one name – a friend of Tony Devereux – was consistently on the list as the alleged penman.

In *The Maybrick Diary: The Inside Story* by Seth Linder, Keith Skinner and Caroline Morris, a line is finally drawn under those suspected forgers. Following the allegations from the outset, with carefully documented support, the authors confirm that, like Scotland Yard, they had found 'no evidence whatsoever to support the theory that [...] is responsible for the handwriting in the diary of Jack the Ripper.'

Doreen, Robert, Paul and I had given the authors free access to all our files. We trusted their objectivity. They were not making a case for or against the Diary, merely recording the events that had surrounded it since 1992. Their book, launched at the Ripper conference in 2003, is the first record drawn from archives of what really happened.

21

Am I not Indeed a Clever Fellow?

In August 1889, the *Liverpool Citizen* printed an editorial comment:

> My own observation – and it is purely personal – is that experts are not particularly large minded men. They appear to grow so absorbed in their own experiments that broader outside considerations – considerations which influence journalists, lawyers, and statesmen – do not greatly affect these gentlemen. They seem to be like experts in handwriting, only in a more scientific and elevated degree, but there is a good deal of the same kind of conjecture and uncertainty in their conclusions.

* * *

For a long time we had been strangers in a foreign field and somewhat in awe of experts. Despite the continually increasing amount of circumstantial evidence supporting my belief in Maybrick's guilt, I knew that there were material questions which would have to be further addressed – in particular, the handwriting of the Diary, the date when the ink went on the paper and the internal historical evidence it presented. I guessed there would be a need, too, for more laboratory tests, psychological profiling, and a dictionary search for anachronistic words or phrases not generally in use in 1888, and I was worried about the cost of such investigations on my limited budget.

The ongoing research has straddled many years and, throughout this time, I have listened to all opinions and been ready to adapt or revise the text as new information or insights were brought to my attention. This is why some observations have been modified or expanded from edition to edition. In order to simplify the reports from our expert witnesses, I have brought their various conclusions together so that they can be interpreted in context. In the case of the scientific tests, I have not included tables and data which are unintelligible for the layman, but they are all available in full for those with the knowledge and interest to examine them. Equally, space does not permit the publishing of entire reports which run to several thousand words but they can be seen at any time by serious researchers. There is absolutely nothing to hide.

THE HANDWRITING

The investigation of handwriting falls into two categories. We asked for a forensic comparison of the Diary with the writing of Maybrick and the chosen Ripper letters. We also asked for character analysis and a graphological report: many people are sceptical about the use of handwriting analysis and graphology, although they are both used in police detection work.

Paul Feldman arranged for Anna Koren to fly to London from Israel. With an international reputation, Anna is the director of the Graphology Centre in Haifa, London and Sydney. She is also a member of the American Association of Graphologists and a Forensic Document Examiner for the Israeli Ministry of Justice and Social Security Services.

We first met her in Paul's office, just two hours after she had arrived to see the Diary in late December 1992. Her spoken English was basic.

We sat in total silence round the table while she pored over a few of the centre pages of the Diary. She did not absorb the words themselves or see the signature at the end. We learned afterwards that, in any case, she had not heard of Jack the Ripper and knew nothing about the Diary. She had not had time to read it. 'I do not need to understand the words themselves,' she told us.

After 20 minutes her off-the-cuff assessment stunned us. She later confirmed it in writing:

> The Diary shows an unstable personality. Inner conflicts lack of social adaptability and a tendency to schizophrenia.
>
> The author's feelings of inferiority, emotional repression and lack of inner confidence may cause him to lose control every now and then and he may explode very violently.
>
> Tendencies to despotism, irascibility and brutality are clearly discernible. He is affected by unconscious instincts and aggression is the constant companion of his instincts.
>
> A tendency towards hypochondria and a use of drugs or alcohol is evident.
>
> Any impulsive activity is carried out in secrecy, giving vent to his revenge and aggression fighting against an authoritative hostile figure in his childhood.
>
> A psychotic disease impedes his ability to distinguish between good or evil, forbidden or permissible and may lead to criminal activity.
>
> His behaviour is unusually bizarre. His disturbed thinking leads to strange ideas, paranoic suspicions and magic beliefs. His mode of thinking is circular, clouded, stereotyped and metaphoric. His disease can in all likelihood be termed chronic and persistent, with a tendency to get worse.
>
> He shows an identity disorder, with confusion as to his sexual identity and distorted image of his masculinity, as

> well as an absence of a stable system of values. There are clear cracks in the super ego and an inability to persevere in matters involving a choice of career, long term targets, establishing friendships, loyalty.
>
> Behind the violent outbursts lie deep-rooted feelings of loneliness, emptiness and insecurity which lead to depression and the partial withdrawal from contact with reality. Egocentric traits along with vanity and exhibitionism, childishness, a tendency to dramatise, a constant search for attention and lack of consideration for others in the pursuit of his own interests.
>
> His perception of sexuality and mating is distracted to the point of a tendency to sadism. His lack of trust in others and his paranoid feelings of being tormented are apparent. He is unable to form relationships of equality.
>
> He suffers from psychological disorders, which produce illogical, obsessive, destructive and aggressive behaviour. An inner feeling of compulsion causes this behaviour to repeat itself in cycles.

It was an impressive performance! Moreover, Anna said later that any suggestion that the Diary was a forgery was 'impossible'! On the other hand, our euphoria at Anna's uncanny insight was well and truly dented by the later observations of Sue Iremonger, to whom I had been introduced at the outset as a fairly new but 'impressive' document analyst (not a graphologist). She had been called in on a number of police fraud investigations and was an expert on false signatures, anonymous notes and poison pen letters. Sue was trained in Chicago and the United Kingdom and is a member of the World Association of Document Examiners. She is also a qualified psychotherapist specialising in the psychopathic personality.

So, armed with her camera and microscope, Sue began her examination of a facsimile of the Diary (the original was, by this time, securely safeguarded in the bank).

Both Sue and Anna were faced with the problem that, apart from the signature on Maybrick's marriage certificate and his will, we had, at that time, discovered few examples of his handwriting with which to compare the Diary.

We, too, were faced with a dilemma – Sue and Anna each worked from a completely different principle.

Sue believes that an individual's writing always contains unconscious, identifiable, characteristics. 'Handwriting is as revealing as fingerprints,' she told me. 'It doesn't matter if a person is young or old, or switches from right to left hand after an accident – the style may appear to change but the components of every individual's handwriting remain consistent.'

Anna, however, produced examples of the handwriting of a woman with a multiple personality disorder and sixteen distinct styles to support her contention that one person may exhibit many handwritings.

Sue Iremonger did not link the writing in the Diary with either the Dear Boss letter, or with Maybrick's alleged will. She looked at over two hundred of the original Jack the Ripper letters at the Public Record Office but could find none which she felt matched the Diary. She explained in a letter to me on June 25th 1993:

> If we look at the comparisons of the capital letter I in the Diary and the letter, the formation is completely different. In the Diary the formation of the I is a similar formation to a lower case g. In the Dear Boss letter it has a narrow initial loop which starts approximately half way up the stem. The tail of the stroke ends in a similar way to a thick full stop whereas in the Diary the ending is a small circular loop. The punctuation in the two documents is totally different and generally the differences between them far outweigh any slight similarities. A couple of the similarities include the left hand margin and the weight (thickness of stroke) of some of the letters.

For me, these reports showed an interesting new way of looking at the formation of letters. But I was uncertain of the absolute, unshakable reliability of handwritng analysis. On the other hand I was aware of the dangerous road down which rejecting such advice could lead us. It would be all too easy to make possibly superficial assumptions on the rapidly increasing number of handwriting samples in our files.

We noted that one of the 'Dear Boss' letters had been posted in Scotland and that it was believed to be in the same hand as the Liverpool letters. It said, 'Think I'll quite using my nice sharp knife. Too good for the whores. Have come here to buy a Scotch Dirk. ha. ha. that will tickle up their ovaries.' We also recalled James and Michael Maybrick had on occasion visited Scotland together.

So when Paul Feldman's team discovered, in 1996, a hitherto unremarkable letter in the Scotland Yard files – from Galashiels in Scotland – there was a feeling of great excitement. The letter itself was dramatic.

> Dear Boss,
>
> I have to thank you and my brother in trade, Jack the Ripper for your kindness in letting me away out of Whitechapel.
> I am now on my road to the tweed Factories I will let the Innerleithen Constable or Police men know when I am about to start my nice Little game. I have got my knife replenished so it will answer both for ladies and gents other tweed ones and I have won my wager.
>
> I am yours
> truly
> The Ripper.

Innerleithen was then a small border town, famous for its tweed making. Some forms of inferior tweed were, in those days, made with a blend of cotton. Maybrick, like most Liverpool cotton merchants, visited the area both commercially and for pleasure. He had, only recently, been there with Michael.

More than this, the handwriting of the Galashiels letter bears a striking likeness to that in a letter written by James Maybrick. This was found by Paul Feldman in America and was penned aboard *The Baltic* in March 1881. This letter in turn is also, to my mind, not unlike the hand that wrote the Diary. The jury is out.

The conflicting opinions are bemusing. There appears, to my untrained eye, a clear relationship between the Galashiels letter and Maybrick's will. Bill Waddell, former curator of the Scotland Yard Black Museum, has a lifetime's experience of forgery and is convinced they are one and the same.

As I was preparing copy for this new edition I came across confirmation of my doubts about handwriting analysis from a most unexpected – and welcome – source. Former policeman, Donald Rumbelow, no less, had written in the 1988 edition of his much respected book *The Complete Jack the Ripper*:

> ...very little reliance can be placed on handwriting comparison. The handwriting of the German murderer, Peter Kurten, who was known as the Dusseldorf Ripper because of the way he imitated his notorious predecessor, changed completely after each murder, so much so, indeed, that he used to point out to his wife the anonymous letters that he wrote to the police and which were reproduced in the newspapers, so confident was he that she would never recognise them – nor did she...

*   *   *

THE ASTROLOGICAL EVIDENCE

Nicholas Campion is President of the British Astrological Association and when he heard about the Diary he offered to prepare a chart on

James Maybrick. I was curious, although wary of the scorn that I knew could be poured on such projections. I include Nicholas' report, not as evidence but out of interest – for the many readers (including some world leaders) who do set store by astrology.

Like Anna Koren, he had read none of the books on James Maybrick or on Florie's trial and knew as little about the Ripper. He prefaced his profile with an insistence that astrology should *never* be used to pinpoint guilt in the absence of other evidence. 'I am always very alarmed by amateur astrologers who go around accusing people of something purely on the basis of their charts.' But it cannot be ignored that, despite living thousands of miles apart, Anna and he produced almost identical profiles. This is the report of Nicholas Campion:

> James Maybrick was born in Liverpool on October 24 1838 with the Sun in Scorpio, an intense and secretive sign and the Moon in Capricorn, indicating broadly conservative tendencies. Unfortunately we have no record of his time of birth and we are therefore unable to calculate Maybrick's rising sign. So, although we can tell a certain amount about Maybrick's character we are lacking much important information which could tell us, for certain, if Maybrick was Jack the Ripper. However we still have much valuable information.
>
> Venus and Mercury together in Libra tell us that Maybrick was capable of being extremely charming, and was able to hide his deeper feelings behind a perfectly acceptable public face. We may even imagine him having his dandyish side, although within the respect for formal manners appropriate to the Moon in Capricorn and the reserve typical of the Sun in Scorpio.
>
> As Maybrick is suspected of committing some of the most gruesome ever sexual murders, it makes sense to examine planets of sexual attraction, Venus and Mars. Intriguingly, both are making powerful alignments, Mars is

in a square (a 90 degree angle with Saturn), indicating the threat of violence. However, this alignment alone is not sufficiently powerful to suggest that Maybrick was a perpetrator of violent crimes.

Venus, however, is very striking, being in a tight opposition (a 180 degree alignment) with Pluto. Venus is the symbol of the maiden, while Pluto, in classical mythology was the underworld god who abducted Persephone, a goddess closely associated with Venus. There could be no more powerful evocation than this of the Ripper myth within Maybrick's horoscope, and here we find one of the key astrological symbols of sexual violence. It is well worth quoting extensively on the matter from *The Astrology of Fate* by the Jungian analyst, Liz Greene. Dr. Greene writes that:

'Whenever the myth protrays his (Pluto's) entry into the upper world, he is shown persistently acting out one scenario: rape ... Its (Pluto's) intrusion into consciousness feels like a violation, and we, like Persephone, the maiden of the myth, are powerless to resist. Where Pluto is encountered there is often a sense of violent penetration, unwished for yet unavoidable.'

Later, Dr. Greene discusses the psychological complexes indicated by the astrological alignment of Venus and Pluto at birth. These offer a fascinating insight into Maybrick's personality and the pressures which may have compelled him towards his violent actions. Describing Pluto as the 'destroyer rapist', she discusses the dilemmas which occur when it brings its emotional power to the subtle femininity represented by Venus:

'Something or someone is *trying to dismember* the very thing one values and cherishes the most ... *Here fate often intrudes upon love, frequently in the form of an obsessive sexual passion or the breakdown of the sexual relationship between two people.*' [My italics.]

The psychological complex represented by Venus and Pluto indicates an individual who cannot tolerate imperfection. If the object of their desire is found to be flawed, there is only one option: to destroy it. Maybrick may have believed that women were essentially ideal and perfect creatures, in effect, goddesses. It is not impossible that, when confronted with the reality of ordinary flesh and blood mortals he reacted by recreating his own version of the underworld, taking to the dark, narrow streets of Whitechapel and committing there the most horrible murders.

The essence of any astrological investigation is timing, and if Maybrick is to be accused of the Ripper murders it is necessary that his Mars–Saturn and Venus–Pluto alignments were themselves powerfully aspected by the planets on the night of the first murder. The Ripper's first victim, Mary Ann Nichols, was murdered at 3.00am on August 31 1888. Intriguingly, at this moment, Maybrick's Mars–Saturn alignment was indeed extremely powerfully aspected.

Maybrick's Venus–Pluto alignment was strongly connected with Uranus. Uranus destabilises already uncertain situations and is closely associated with erratic and uncontrollable events. We may therefore conclude that Maybrick's psychological obsession with death and sexual initiation was likely to be expressed in a shocking manner. Combine this with the violence of his Mars–Saturn alignment and we have powerful evidence that, on the night of Mary Ann Nichols' murder, Maybrick was poised to commit a violent act. The circumstantial evidence of the horoscopes for his birth and the first murder offer powerful testimony in support of Maybrick's guilt.

There was one other important alignment at Nichols' murder which, at first sight, bore little relationship to

Maybrick's horoscope. This was a 90 degree square alignment between the Moon at 25 degrees in Gemini and Venus at 22 degrees in Virgo. Psychologically this pattern is indicative of extremely unstable emotions, bordering on hysteria. However, both Gemini and Virgo are analytical signs which find it difficult to express feelings. They are most likely to conceive a practical and apparently rational plan via which pent up emotions may be expressed. Symbolically, Venus in Virgo represents the maiden, while the Moon represents the mother, both the female planets. The alignment between them was separating, and therefore growing weaker, but would have been exact around 9.00pm on the previous evening, perhaps around the time when the Ripper was preparing his first murder.

Whether Maybrick was the Ripper or not, his horoscope repeatedly describes psychological complexes appropriate to the Ripper.

Yet the strangest coincidences occur when we enter the realms of metaphysical speculation for it's here that we begin to come closest to the undying mythology of the Ripper, the ultimate male murderer of women. From a 20th century perspective Jack the Ripper is no longer a flesh and blood man but larger than large, a being of demonic myth, capable still of inspiring fascination and fear.

It is particularly strange then that the significant violent alignments in Maybrick's horoscope recurred on October 30 1975, the date of the first murder committed by Peter Sutcliffe, the Yorkshire Ripper. We find a number of planetary coincidences. For example, on the date of Sutcliffe's first murder Venus and Mars were both repeating the positions they occupied in Maybrick's horoscope at Nichols' murder.

This is a truly astonishing coincidence, as if Maybrick's horoscope were that not only for the first Ripper but for the second. It is almost as if the spirit of the Ripper was alive in Sutcliffe when he savaged his victims. Perhaps, to take a different approach, both Sutcliffe and Maybrick were locked into the same psychological archetype via common astrological configurations. If Maybrick was not the original Ripper, he certainly possessed a sufficient streak of viciousness to have committed acts of violence against women. It is also an interesting fact that the sun at Maybrick's birth occupied exactly the degree of the zodiac to that occupied by Hitler's Sun. This is not in itself unusual, although the coincidence develops if we cast Maybrick's horoscope for noon, which is the custom in cases of uncertain birth time. In this case, we find that the moon occupied the same degree of the zodiac as at Hitler's birth. At Nichols' murder, Saturn, considered by ancient astrologers the most unfortunate of all possible influences, had reached exactly the same degree of the zodiac as that which it occupied at Hitler's birth. Such coincidences do not tell us that Maybrick was Jack the Ripper. They do suggest however, that there may be a common mythology of evil, indicated by certain identical planetary positions which connected the Ripper murders to Hitler's holocaust.

This connection between the serial killer and the mass murderer offers a symbolic clue that we are on the right track in our suspicions that James Maybrick may have been Jack the Ripper.

Maybrick's horoscope confirms that he may, reasonably, be considered a prime suspect.

As if this were not in itself an extraordinary report I also spoke with a Sussex author and astrologer of long experience – John Astrop. John specialises in criminal astrology and has a huge library of associated horoscopes. He had written Florence Maybrick's some years ago and sent it to me. Summarising his report, he concluded:

> The attraction factor between them both (Florence and James) would have been immediate and impulsive... it would have been a compulsive but uncomfortable relationship when they were not showing a dignified face to the world... She would have been a person who could easily believe her own lies. He would have been emotionally manipulative and a bully... Scorpios are traditionally the worst sign to battle against – they always play dirty.

* * *

THE PSYCHOLOGY

In 1993, Paul Feldman and scriptwriter/author Martin Howells, who were working on the video of my book, called a meeting which was attended by Paul Begg, Sally Evemy, Martin Fido, Don Rumbelow, Keith Skinner, Robert Smith and Bill Waddell, former curator of Scotland Yard's Black Museum. Special guest was Dr David Canter, then a professor at Surrey University but now professor of Psychology at Liverpool University and Britain's leading specialist in psychological profiling.

In 1994, Professor Canter wrote *Criminal Shadows*, in which the 'psychological traces surrounding the crime, the tell tale patterns of behaviour indicate the personality of the offender right down to his hobbies, job and address... these subtle and ambiguous shadows lead to an understanding of the serial killer's mind and ultimately to an "inner narrative" that exposes the identity of the criminal.'

Professor Canter confirmed with professional authority many of my own instincts about the Diary. He was impressed with the subtle banality and creative weaving. Serial killers do, he said, write about themselves in such a banal way, and their preoccupations are amazingly trivial to anyone else. They want to re-enact and enjoy what they have done and to publicise their deeds.

'This is not really a Diary at all,' he told me. 'It's more of a log of things significant to him and as such I would expect to find inconsistencies. It would be much more likely to be a forgery were it perfect and completely without flaws. I was worried about the end at first – it is a bit too stage-managed but on the other hand the wrapping up of a life is typical of a man who knows he is dying.'

Professor Canter does not dismiss the Diary. Far from it. He has included it in two books and a television documentary. For him it is most likely to be either a modern forgery making use of Freudian techniques – or it is real, using these techniques naturally, from experience and not as an intellectual exercise.

But I knew that before Michael Barrett showed the Diary to Doreen Montgomery and me in 1992 no present day Ripperologists were aware of its existence.

Piece by piece our jigsaw profile of the Ripper was appearing compatible with what we knew of Maybrick. He was a child-loving, genial host of a man, particular about his appearance and anxious to improve his status in society. William Stead, the journalist, wrote later, 'Friends would say Maybrick was a very good kind of fellow'. Indeed, when Maybrick's business colleague and friend wrote to the Home Secretary in 1889, he proclaimed, 'I can state that I have known Mr Maybrick for more than 25 years on the most intimate terms as an exceedingly good natured, amiable and generous nature, who, tho' after his marriage did not lead a happy life at home, was always trying to take a generous view of his wife's shortcomings and was devotedly fond of his children...'

But behind the well-groomed facade there was a darker side. Rumours were spread during Florie's trial that he had killed his neighbour's dogs; there was the strange packet marked 'poison for cats' and the known outbursts of violent temper resulting in blows.

David Forshaw, like Professor Canter, has a special interest in the mind of the serial killer and has kept closely in touch with developments on the Diary throughout the life of my book. I met him first at Maudsley Hospital and later, in 1997, at Broadmoor Hospital for the Criminally Insane, now the home of Peter Sutcliffe, the Yorkshire Ripper.

Dr Forshaw offered to study the Diary and report on the mind of the man who wrote it. He was *not* asked 'Is the writer of this Diary, Jack the Ripper?' His report had two aims:

1. To explain the psychopathology of serial killers alongside what is known about Jack the Ripper.
2. To compare the above findings with the psychopathology of the Diary.

> The Jack the Ripper Diary represents the serial recording of the Ripper's thoughts or feelings, or more accurately, his expressing and working through his emotional and intellectual turmoil. It is an integral part of his psychopathology.
>
> Of course, the Whitechapel murders were not the first serial killings. Such crimes have occurred throughout history. There are recorded cases of serial killings dating back to classical times. In fact, in their book *Perverse Crimes in History*, Masters and Lea describe a plague of stabbers and rippers in the 19th century that reached a peak in the 1880s and 1890s. So, Jack the Ripper, monster that he was, was one among many. He might have been just another murderer were it not for the self-determined nick-name.
>
> Often these serial killers seem, like James Maybrick, to be quiet men, men with families, men who go to work each day and tend the garden at week-ends.

David Forshaw cited the example of Andre Chikatilo, who lived in the coal mining town of Shakhty in the former Soviet Union. He was a 42-year-old former Communist Party member with a wife, two children and a good job as a teacher in a school of mining. Then, one day in 1978, he took nine-year-old Lena Zakotnova to a tumbledown shack on the edge of the town and strangled, stabbed and slashed her.

The pleasure was immense and his newly discovered blood-lust unstoppable. So he went on, over a dozen years, to slaughter and eat women and some 53 children, tearing their insides out with his bare hands. Like Maybrick, he left taunting little jokes at the scene to tease the police.

Chikatilo is said to have never raised a hand to his own children and had made great strides in life, rising from peasant roots to the intelligentsia. But he yearned to be a brave soldier and a romantic lover. He longed for the kind of respect that would have made school children stand up as he entered a room. He believed the real Chikatilo didn't match up to this self picture and he felt a failure.

When he was finally captured in 1991, he wrote to his wife: 'Why did God send me to this earth? Me, a person so affectionate, tender and thoughtful but so totally defenceless against my own weakness.'

Chikatilo's words reflect the tormented message of painful inadequacy which fills the Maybrick Diary. They also recall his image of himself as gentle and at the same time given to extreme violence. 'The gentle man with gentle thoughts will strike again soon.'

Another such figure was Peter Kürten, the Düsseldorf murderer who was hanged in 1937 for killing nine people and attempting to kill seven more. Yet he was living and sleeping with his wife throughout the killings. So was Peter Sutcliffe, whose mission was, in his own words 'to rid the streets of prostitutes'.

In 1997, the national press reported how the fiancée of triple killer Alan Reeve described him as friendly, caring and dependable as well as loving and said she would trust her life in his hands. She was engaged to him from 1995 until he was arrested in April 1997. He had escaped from Broadmoor Hospital seventeen years earlier, after he had been assessed as a dangerous psychopath who should be detained indefinitely under the Mental Health Act.

Finally, in 1999, came the terrible story of Dr Harold Shipman, who was despatching one by one the innocent, elderly patients who adored him, without friends or family suspecting a thing. He was described as a 'godsend' by his partner in the Todmorden practice to which he went in 1974 as a newly qualified, 28-year-old GP. 'He had brilliant potential.' But he was already a drug addict, injecting himself with pethidine. In 1975 three of his patients died on the same day – and no one suspected a thing.

He married 17-year-old Primrose in 1966 and she remained, to the end, utterly innocent of his double life. By then his work colleagues were describing him as 'volatile'. There are photographs of the couple at parties, weddings and barbecues, in fancy dress, playing with their four children – and all the time he was killing at least 15 patients a year. Sometimes his victims were the relatives of his party-going friends. He is known to have murdered about 345 people before anyone began to doubt their genial GP.

Maybrick, like Kürten, Chikatilo, Sutcliffe, Reeve and Shipman was the man next door, an ordinary and unremarkable neighbour – at least on the surface. In other ways, too, Maybrick exhibits traits of the typical serial killer – who, Dr Forshaw says, are nearly always male, and often obsessional and hypochondriacal. Serial killers are usually mild-mannered too, although deep down they seethe with pent-up anger. They also have rich fantasy lives which they find preferable to reality. They dream of power and are preoccupied with their masculinity and sexual potency. It was fear of losing the latter that drove Maybrick to strychnine and arsenic.

In 1965, Eugene Revitch, author of *Sex, Murder and the Potential Sex Murderer*, studied reports on unprovoked attacks by men on women, dividing offenders into groups of those above and below the age of eighteen. He found that '...the older the attacker the more the primary motive reflected anger or hatred.'

'The unattractive nature of the Ripper's killings leads to the conclusion that the killings reflected hostility rather than a need for sexual gratification,' says David Forshaw. 'The killer was, therefore, probably *not* a young man.'

Maybrick had his 50th birthday on October 24th, not long before the murder of Mary Jane Kelly.

'Seminal fluid is not mentioned in the post-mortem reports so it is not known if the assailant had sex or if he masturbated at the scene of the crime,' Forshaw goes on. 'It seems improbable since hatred not sex is likely to have been the motive. In any case, the known time available to the killer would hardly have allowed such indulgence. It may be that the killer selected victims as anti-symbols of sex, chosen to thwart even the possibility of intercourse. However it may be their very depravity that appealed to a perverted sexuality.'

There was no doubt that the Ripper's choice of target – prostitutes – had practical advantages too. Since there is little to link them with their clients, and they work in isolation, prostitutes are easy victims for sex attackers. Moreover, a serial killer who selects prostitutes may genuinely feel he is performing a service to society.

I am convinced God placed me here to kill all whores.

But at the same time it is likely that the hapless ladies of Whitechapel represented something far more personal to Maybrick: his adulterous wife. 'Prostitutes represent to the attacker, consciously or unconsciously, despised and unfaithful loved ones who through circumstances are relatively safe from attack,' says David Forshaw. 'Women of easy virtue were the symbols of his wife's infidelity.'

Forshaw believes that the Ripper probably obtained satisfaction only from the process of killing, from feeling or seeing his victim die, even from their mutilation afterwards – not from putting them through prolonged suffering.

There was also another motivation for murder. The 'Son of Sam' killer, David Berkovitz, who terrorised New York for a year in the mid-1970s talked about 'the desire to do it, to kill', which, he said 'filled me up to such explosive proportions, it caused me such turmoil inside that when it released itself it was like a volcano erupting and the pressure was over, for a while, at least.' The American psychiatrist, David Abrahamsen, who has written about Jack the Ripper, agrees that the Whitechapel killer probably felt this tension.

I need more thrills, cannot live without my thrills. I will go on. I will go on nothing will stop me nothing.

Maybrick had a mistress, identified in the Diary only as 'mine', to whom he seemed to turn when the pressure becomes too great.

The eyes will come out of the next. I will stuff them in the whores mouth. That will certainly give me pleasure, it does so as I write. Tonight I will see mine, she will be pleased as I will be gentle with her as indeed I always am.

Maybrick, like the Ripper, enjoyed the thrill of the chase. He revelled in the excitement of possible capture – even more than ripping.

I believe the thrill of being caught thrilled me
more than cutting the whore herself.

'Serial killers,' says David Forshaw, 'typically feel inferior, except when writing or thinking about their crimes. That is the reason for a diary.' Maybrick used the journal to boost his self esteem, bestowing on himself the titles Sir Jim and Sir Jack. The Diary also enabled him to use one set of pleasant thoughts to drive away distressing ideas and feelings.

I will force myself to think of something more pleasant.

'In the Diary he used this method of thought manipulation fairly often, like a screen between himself and the real world,' explains David Forshaw. 'He therefore allowed himself to remain outwardly calm and in control. It may have also distanced him from reality.

Maybrick used sex to take his mind off reality. After his first killing he wrote:

I will take the bitch tonight. I need to take my mind off the night's events.

From the beginning his fantasies of his wife and her lover together gave him a morbid sense of pleasure.

> *The thought of him taking her is beginning to thrill me*

The entries suggest he was sexually aroused and derived some sort of sadomasochistic pleasure when actually writing the Diary.

'One very striking visual aspect of the Diary is the way in which the handwriting changes to reflect the changing emotions of the writer. It is clearly written by the same person but moves from the fairly neat school-taught hand to a much larger, uncontrolled scrawl which corresponds to mental deterioration.'

David Forshaw selected seven samples of handwriting from the Diary and examined them chronologically. He explains, 'At the beginning, before any killing has taken place, the writing is neat, undemonstrative, restrained even. But it becomes larger, more flamboyant, less controlled and certainly more confident, as he pursues what he called his "campaign" of murders. Now the handwriting is clearly laden with a mix of emotions. Then, having built up to fever pitch, towards the end of the Diary it reverts dramatically to the calm, controlled style before the killings began. This last, marked shift occurred shortly after Maybrick is known (from trial statements) to have returned from a visit to Dr Fuller in London.'

> *Fuller believes there is very little the matter with me. Strange, the thoughts he placed into my mind.*

What those thoughts were we do not know, but from this moment in the Diary there is an increased yearning for release from torment and even talk of suicide.

'Modern studies of serial killers have led to a better understanding than existed in the 19th century. Psychiatrist Malcolm MacCulloch, of Liverpool University and his team noticed a clear pattern in thirteen of sixteen offenders studied in a special hospital. The men had been preoccupied with sadistic sexual fantasies over a period of time, which became more extreme, leading to "behavioural try-outs" such as following potential victims. These "try-outs" were then incorporated into the fantasy, moving inexorably towards a climax. Increasingly, each patient became less able to distinguish between reality and his fantasy world.'

The team speculated that inflicting suffering was the route to control. Control was at the centre of the behaviour. In one sense, the ultimate possible control over anyone is when they are dead, or unconscious. Both Maybrick's Diary and the Ripper killings show a clear escalation of viciousness from one victim to the next.

'It is almost as though he was habituating the behaviour and developing a tolerance towards it,' says Dr Forshaw. 'This is a phenomenon akin to urban joyriding where offenders very often achieve their thrills from being in control, driving fast and taking ever more risks.'

As for the Ripper's cannibalism, Forshaw says, 'Very often body parts are removed in order for the killer to have some kind of memento. The Hungarian, Elizabeth Bathory, who died in 1614 aged 54, used to bathe in the blood of her victims to keep her young and attractive. Christie, who was hanged in 1953, collected pubic hair from his victims. The Ripper could have been convinced that by eating a womb he would achieve eternal youth.'

Other macabre hoarders include the American serial killer Ed Kemper who, in 1972, collected internal organs and sometimes heads, which he kept in his wardrobe. The murderer Dennis Nilsen, who was active between 1978 to 1983, stored the dismembered remains of his victims in cupboards and under the floorboards of his London homes.

Dr Forshaw continues, 'If limited information is known about a person's past, or mental state, it is difficult to distinguish the sadistic serial sex-killer with progressive sadism syndrome from multi-victim killers who kill as a result of mental illness, such as schizophrenia.' From his reading of the Diary, Dr Forshaw sees no evidence that the writer suffered from mental illness. 'He did not have delusions. James Maybrick of the Diary was mentally disordered, but whether sufficiently enough to diminish his legal responsibility is a matter for discussion. Was he mad or was he bad?'

Simon Andrae wrote of serial killers in the *Observer* in 1993: 'They are not born bad. They are rarely found mad... their behaviours develop through a complex interaction of biochemical, psychological and cultural factors, catalysed in different degrees and at different points in their lives... A small percentage of people are born with genes which make them naturally inclined towards anti-social or aggressive behaviour... Combined with predisposition, childhood trauma is the second major factor common about serial killers...'

In the case of James Maybrick there is an intriguing, if unscientific, answer to Dr Forshaw's question. It is that Maybrick was bad but Jack the Ripper was mad. Merge the two and you have a powerful force for evil.

In conclusion Dr Forshaw writes:

> If the journal is genuine then it tells a tragic tale. It makes sense. This is an encouraging sign for its authenticity. However, there are other possibilities... it would seem that the most likely options are that it is either genuine or an extremely good modern fake. If it is a fake then it is as remarkable as if it were genuine. It would be very hard to fake... a considerable amount of work would have to be done, even by someone or a team already familiar with serial killers and the Maybrick and Ripper cases. The faker would have had to work hard to mimic the thoughts and feelings portrayed in the journal, though it might be easier if they had a similar psychopathology to begin with.
>
> A thorough examination of the journal and its provenance are essential components of deciding if it is authentic. If such an examination proves indecisive and all falls back on the content, then I would argue in that case, on the balance of probabilities from a psychiatric perspective, it is authentic.

THE LANGUAGE

Yet another hurdle for the Diary to overcome was that of the language used by its writer. There are one or two phrases which leap out of the page – they feel too modern for Victorian composition.

John Simpson, co-editor of the *Oxford English Dictionary*, wrote to me:

> The *Oxford English Dictionary* seeks to document the history and development of English from the early Middle Ages to the present day. Its analysis is based upon the record of the language obtained by reading as wide a range of texts as possible and excerpting from these texts examples of usage for our quotation files. The earliest use of any term occuring in the Dictionary represents the earliest written use available to the Dictionary's editors when a particular entry is compiled.
>
> I would expect first instances to represent a useful guide to when a given term entered the language, but earlier attestations, (some of which are substantial pre-datings) are continually being brought to our notice. Language is spoken before it is written down and in some areas (such as dialect slang and local crafts) there may well be some time lag between the introduction of a term and its appearance in print. I would be surprised but not dumbfounded, if its first appearance was found to pre-date the Dictionary's first recorded example by as much as half a century.

I also spoke with Mark Agnes, a member of the editorial team of Webster's *New World Dictionary*, in America. He agreed with John Simpson. 'Even today there are phrases we all know and use but which can't be found in any dictionary. It can take a very long time indeed, especially in technical areas for the oral tradition to be recorded in the written word.'

Listeners to BBC's addictive Radio 4 programme *Countdown* will know that, time and again, contestants produce a word that we all know is in common use and yet, not being in the *Oxford English Dictionary*, is not allowed.

Dictionary searches for words that had worried me, such as 'top myself' and 'gathering momentum' were found to be in use in late Victorian times. I was more anxious about the phrase 'one off'.

Webster's gives its first written appearance as 1925. But it was in the building world that I found what I consider the real answer to my problem. I telephoned Traynors, a long-established building company in Kent, who discovered the phrase lurking in their archives. In 1860, they said, it was used when a new building material was being ordered as a 'special'. A 'one off' was also an ornamental brick used in Victorian canals and referred to a unique example or prototype. As I did not have this in writing at the time, I tried to double-check the information for this edition but the firm was no longer in existence and I have been unable to trace their archives.

MAYBRICK'S ADDICTION

I consulted doctors from the Poisons Unit at Guy's Hospital, London, for their views on whether the symptoms of arsenic abuse as they appear in the Diary are accurate. They told me that there was a dearth of reliable information available about addictions in 1888 and that, even today, a hoaxer would be severely taxed to know where to find facts upon which he could build such a very realistic portrait.

Arsenic, when taken over years, leads to an accumulation of pyruvate in the blood. This substance is important in the body's metabolism of Coenzyme-A, an essential enzyme of energy-giving carbohydrates. In acute arsenic poisoning, gastro-intestinal symptoms of the kind that Maybrick suffered predominate. In the last century, chronic poisoning was believed to be indicated by such gastric complaints. Today, however, we recognise the prominence of neurological symptoms. Most Victorians wrongly believed that chronic arsenic eating over 20 or 30 years could result in paralysis. There was – and is – almost nowhere the diarist could have learned these facts, which leads one to suspect that he could, indeed, be writing from experience.

The Victorians did understand, however, that the sudden withdrawal of arsenic could result in agonising pains, such as Maybrick is known to have experienced after he could no longer get to his office or have access to his supplies.

Dr Forshaw also tackled the question of addicition. Maybrick liked alcohol and used arsenic – both of which can produce a chronic disorder of the nerves of the limbs and gastro-intestinal problems. He explains:

> An underactive thyroid, the gland in the neck that helps regulate the general level of metabolic activity in the body, can also produce a disorder with similar symptoms to those Maybrick described: tiredness, lethargy, constipation, intolerance of cold, aching muscles. There may be deafness and hallucinations, the face looks expressionless, broad and bloated, the memory is poor and the patient may be depressed. This illness known as hypothyroidism or moxoedema, can only be confirmed by a blood test which was not available in Maybrick's day.
>
> Von Ziemenssen's 13 volume *Cyclopedia of Medicine*, in its chapter on chronic poisoning by heavy metals, says: 'the mild form of chronic poisoning can arise from the therapeutic use of Fowler's Solution.' Dr C. Binz who wrote, *Lectures on Pharmacology* in 1897, explained: 'a stimulus if frequently repeated, must be exhibited in increasing doses in order each time to produce a certain effect. In other words, an addict must, over time, take more and more of a drug in order to sustain the effect.'

In December 1994, Nick Warren, a practising surgeon and editor of *Ripperologist*, wrote an article for the journal *Criminologist*. He suggested that Maybrick was not a victim of arsenic poisoning at all. His theory is that the 'irritant poison' which killed him was potassium. 'All James Maybrick's terminal symptoms can be attributed to the excessive ingestion of potassium. Administered by the oral route, this poison causes asthesia (weakness), mental confusion, hypotension (tingling in the extremities), dyspepsia, diarrhoea and vomiting with ultimate cardiac arrest. The features which would be manifest in a post-mortem examination were all present in this case – redness, haemorrhage or frank ulceration of the upper gastro-intestinal tract from the gullet to the small bowel.'

Mr Warren recalls that Maybrick had indeed taken a very large dose of potassium salts by mouth. He took hydrate of potash on a regular basis (probably potassium bicarbonate). He had also drunk a bottle of anaphrodisiac potassium bromide in half the time prescribed and in his last few days was also prescribed the favourite Victorian remedy, Fowler's Solution – a mixture of arsenic and potassium carbonate.

It was Florie's innocent compliance with doctors' orders that may well, says Mr Warren, have provided the *coup de grâce*. 'It is quite clear that the correct verdict at the inquest into James Maybrick's death should have been one of "Misadventure".'

22

Sir Jim Will Give Nothing Away, Nothing

THE INK

Pinpointing the date when the writer of the Diary put pen to paper was the first and most obvious test of its authenticity. This has proved to be an unbelievably difficult task. It is one which has, again, generated an unpleasant amount of bad feeling and confusing uncertainty among specialists. I am not a scientist and very soon found myself out of my depth.

To the fore, once again, was Mr Harris who contributed some impressive, well-informed and very long postings to the Message Boards. In 1995 he claimed in a letter to the American handwriting analyst Reed Hayes, 'You are being deceived and deceived mightily. You are also being fed deliberate lies.'

So here is the story so far. This is a layman's summary of the tests that have been carried out and the results of some of the ensuing correspondence.

In October 1992, Dr Eastaugh prefaced his report with a warning.

> In the now famous Hitler Diaries debacle it was the materials of the documents – the paper and the ink –

> which ultimately exposed the hoax. When something as potentially important as the Jack the Ripper Diary suddenly appears there should naturally enough be great caution and it is only prudent to examine the physical composition of the document with forensic-style tests with the aim of assessing the age.
>
> There is as yet no single test which will clearly, precisely and unambiguously determine the age of written documents like the Diary. The only widely known dating technique which might conceivably be used – radiocarbon dating of the paper – is not applicable because of its accuracy and certain technical problems with materials more recent than about AD 1500. Some relative assessments of ink age are possible, but these are for testing writing within a document (such as to see whether pages have been added or swapped) and are therefore of little use here.
>
> Moreover, if we could effectively determine the age of the ink and the paper, this would be insufficient to 'authenticate' the document since we would still not know when the ink and paper were combined and the Diary actually written.
>
> In fact it is just such a document as the Diary which highlights the fact that scientists and historians lack any way of directly assessing the absolute chronological age of such items. [my underlining]

How I wish, with hindsight, that I had realised the importance of those words. I wonder, looking back, whether I would have had the courage to act on them and so save the weeks of time and enormous expense that I later incurred in my anxiety to be thorough and, as far as finances permitted, to leave no avenues of research unexplored!

As Dr. Eastaugh explained:

We can only infer when the document was created by looking at the composition of the component parts, when these constituents were available and the frequency of their use. We can also draw some general inferences about the apparent age from the appearance (for example, we might be suspicious if the writing passed over obviously recent damage to the paper). The situation is not uncommon and historic document examination just happens to be a relatively understudied, newly emergent field.

To 'date' the ink and paper we have to compare what they are made of with what we know of ink and paper composition over the past 100 years.

For example, various coloured dyes used in inks have only been invented since the time of Jack the Ripper, and if the ink were to contain any of these then it must be a later forgery.

In practice (and simplifying) this means that we must apply a series of increasingly detailed tests looking for faults: the more tests the document 'passes' the more likely it is that we are dealing with a very sophisticated forgery or the genuine article. So what are we looking for?

Historically a major change took place in inks during the 19th century because of the introduction of mass-produced steel pen nibs. Around the beginning of the 1830s a number of factors combined to make possible the large scale manufacture of such nibs. However it was soon discovered that the traditional acidic inks based on iron-gall rapidly corroded them and in consequence new inks had to be developed. Hence we find companies such as Stephens setting up new factories around this time (1834) to produce inks based on dyes and a carefully controlled iron gall-ink recipe that were non-corrosive to the steel. Innovation was not to stop there however; specific needs of fountain pens and the appearance of synthetic dyes during the second half of the century led to the development of what we may call fountain-pen type inks which have remained largely unchanged to the present.

Fortunately, we know when various dyes and other compounds used in inks were discovered, so that it is potentially possible to determine a date after which an ink must have been produced. Before the discovery of synthetic dyes various natural dyes such as indigo madder and logwood were used; in the later 19th century synthetic dyes such as nigrosine (patented in 1867 in patent number 50415) became widely used. More recently, other synthetic dyestuffs have been substituted into formulations depending on availability, cost and suitability. We might also note that ball-point and felt-tip pens, so familiar today, are 20th century inventions which again required new inks to make them possible. Their ink and marks are easy to distinguish from fountain-pen writing and it is reassuring to know that the Diary is undoubtedly in a traditional pen-type ink.

There are in fact basically two types of pen ink from the 19th century. One form is based on historical iron-gall compositions (iron gallotannate type) while the other contains primarily dyes (synthetic dye type) dissolved in water. With the iron gallotannate inks the main component is colourless until it oxidises to a permanent black colour on the paper; hence a dye is generally added to provide an immediate colour. These are the blue-black inks and their composition is broadly unchanged though details vary. The synthetic dye type inks are currently the most popular since they have a bright colour and produce attractive writing. However, they tend to fade and are sensitive to water. Recent versions of this type of ink contain modern stable pigments (such as those known as phtalocyanines) to add permanence.

Analysis of the ink in the Diary followed along the lines of a conventional forensic examination, although for various practical reasons we chose to pursue certain forms of analysis rather than others. The ink is a permanent blue-black type such as might (without more detailed knowledge of its composition) have been used from Victorian times to the present day. Naturally we want a more accurate idea of when the ink was produced and to do this we have to look at the more detailed composition of the ink and compare it to reference samples of Victorian and modern inks.

To obtain a fingerprint of the ink we looked at what elements we could detect in it using a scanning electron microscope equipped with energy dispersive X-ray spectrometry (SEM/EDS) and an instrument called a proton microprobe. It is not necessary to understand the operation of either of these instruments to appreciate how we used the results; basically all one needs to know is that both machines are capable of measuring the presence of a wide range of chemical elements: the SEM/EDS system measures down to about half a percent and the proton microprobe down to just a few parts per million of the composition. By assessing what elements are present and in what quantities with the aid of these instruments we can then determine a characteristic profile for the Diary ink and compare this with the same information for our reference examples. Using a technique essentially similar to this, American researchers looking at the Gutenberg Bible could work out that six crews using at first two and then four presses were employed in the printing!

For our research we looked at a number of 'permanent blue-black' modern inks such as Quink, Stephens and Watermans, as well as samples of writing inks dated to the late 19th century. Profiles from the (less detailed)

SEM/EDS analysis showed that there were major similarities and minor differences even between known Victorian and modern inks. This is as we would expect since the basic chemistry of these inks has not changed substantially during this time and only the details give clues as to differences. For example, we found that Quink contains relatively little iron (and, according to the manufacturers, has done so for some years) while the ink of the Diary contains significant amounts. SEM/EDS analysis also suggested that the ink used to write James Maybrick's will is different from that in the Diary.

Preliminary results from the proton microprobe were also encouraging, fitting in with and potentially extending the SEM results. However a much wider range of samples needs to be looked at with this technique to give us the data for an accurate interpretation.

To complement the elemental analysis of the inks some dye analysis was also carried out to learn more about the colouring agents used. The method we used is known as thin-layer chromatography (TLC). TLC works by the fact that different compounds within the dyes behave in a dissimilar manner chemically. In practice TLC involves separating out the dyes in the form of characteristic patterns on a sort of sophisticated blotting paper with the aid of organic solvents: the resulting patterns can be compared with patterns of known dyes and an identification made. Using the technique we found clear differences between the modern inks examined and the Diary.

Ultimately, however, the reliability of these analyses for distinguishing between a modern and a Victorian ink will depend upon the level of detail and the range of reference samples. As we look at an increasing number of dated samples with a wider range of techniques, the degree of confidence in placing the ink of the Diary as of a particular time will rise. Nonetheless, no component has thus far been detected in the Diary ink which precludes a Victorian date and it has clearly not matched any of the modern inks tested either.

As with ink, so changes have taken place in paper. Paper is made from fibres which are treated so that they split and fray: these can be 'felted' into sheets which can be further processed by adding other materials to give different qualities of paper. By looking at the types of fibres used and the composition of the other materials present in a sheet of paper, we may infer dates as we do for ink. For example, the paper used for the 'Hitler diaries' contained fibre of Nylon 6 and a particular chemical used to increase the whiteness (a derivative of a compound called stilbene) neither of which should be found in papers manufacturered before the mid-1950s. Analysis of the paper fibres of the Diary has shown only cotton and wood-pulp fibres, both of which were used in late Victorian times. No modern fibres or fluorescent brightening agents like those mentioned before were detected.

To summarise, the results of the various analyses of ink and paper in the Diary performed so far have not given rise to any conflict with the date of 1888/9. If the Diary is a modern forgery then it has 'passed' a range of tests which would have shown up many materials now used in ink and paper manufacture. However, we must be aware that we cannot as yet wholly rule out on the evidence as it stands a sophisticated modern forgery: although it is very specialist knowledge, someone just might have been able to synthesise a convincing ink or located a bottle of ink of sufficient age that was still useable (though these seem to be quite rare).

To address these possibilities there are various analyses

> which we could – and should – pursue notably increasing the range of reference material and the level of detail that we are examining. With more reference data we can aim to place the Diary precisely among other documents, perhaps even identify the manufacturer of the ink or paper. My professional response to the Diary is and must be entirely neutral. I cannot prejudge the document on the basis of what it does or does not purport to be other than in terms of the hypothetical date. Whether it is actually by Jack the Ripper is immaterial to the analysis of the ink and paper. The project does, however, raise a number of important issues and highlights the fact that historical document analysis is a field where much work remains to be done.

Dr Eastaugh also thought it possible that the black dust found in the gutter of the Diary was purified animal charcoal – *carbo animalis purificatus* – better known in the 19th century as bone black. This was sometimes used as a drying agent but also, we read with some amusement, in Squire's *Companion to the British Pharmacopoeia* (1886) 'has the property of counteracting the poisonous effects of Morphine, Strychnine and Aconite... These poisons may be swallowed with impunity if mixed in due proportion with purified animal charcoal.'

* * *

At the heart of it all, eventually, was the search for a tiny trace of that preservative called chloroacetamide.

The first mention of Diamine Ink appeared in the *Liverpool Echo*, in June 1994 after Mike Barrett claimed that this was the ink he had used to write the Diary. Despite Mike having retracted his 'confession', two days later Nick Warren contacted the Chief Research Chemist of Diamine, who was then Alec Voller (he has since retired). Mr Voller wrote to Nick on July 12th: 'The only way in which it [Diamine Manuscript Ink] differed from a genuine late Victorian manuscript ink was in the use of chloroacetamide as a preservative, whereas in a genuine Victorian ink the preservative would almost certainly have been phenol.'

Mr Harris, having obtained some samples of the diary ink from Robert Kurantz in America, then decided (without our knowledge) to send them for testing himself. He and Nick Warren commissioned Dr Simpson of Analysis for Industry, a well-established laboratory in Essex, to examine six unused dots of the Diary ink contained in an unopened, small, sterile gelatine capsule. In their report in October 1994 they stated that they had found chloroacetamide.

Chloroacetamide was first cited in the Merck Index in 1857 but according to Melvin Harris not used commercially in ink until 1972 and, as far as he was concerned, that was that.

On the basis that, when asking for professional quotations, two are safer than one, I decided to take the Diary to the Department of Dyeing and Colour Chemistry, Leeds on November 19th 1994. The department is supported by scholarships given by Courtaulds and Parker Pens.

In some ways the results from Leeds muddied the waters. We asked them to use their most modern methods including thin layer chromatography, SEM/EDX and gas liquid chromatography as performed by Dr Simpson. We also asked them to test the Diary ink against that of some documents of 1889 which had been kept in similar conditions. They knew nothing of the controversy.

The first test, which the Leeds chemists admitted had unfortunately been contaminated, did show a tiny amount of Chloroacetamide which they attributed to contamination from the control. I did not know of this until after they had, of their own volition, conducted a second test. That time they found none at all. It was very confusing and there followed a voluminous amount of criticism and correspondence from the usual sources.

Finally, I decided to ask Dr Simpson if she would test the paper itself for chloroacetamide, in case there had been some contamination into the ink. She agreed and I met her, Diary under arm, on April 19th 1996 at the Royal Society of Chemistry building next to Burlington House, Piccadilly. I was taken aback that she proposed to take samples from the book using an (admittedly brand new) paper punch. I protested and she went off to find a more suitable implement but it was not until half-way through the extractions that I could see the second tool was in fact, an unravelled paper clip. This surprised me.

Dr Simpson's test found no trace of the chemical in the paper.

Still in pursuit of some truth, I wrote in September 1995 to Dow Chemicals in the United States. They manufacture chloroacetamide today. Dr Earl Morris told me then that he had found the substance in preparations as early as 1857, 1871 and 1885. He added later: 'You may find the first large-scale commercial use of chloroacetamide in ink was in 19XX [sic] but that does not rule out the possibility that some small shop made its own ink and tried various additives.'

What follows is a layman's summary of the scientific tests that have been performed on the Diary ink.

BAXENDALE July/August 1992
Technique: Thin Layer Chromatography
Result:
The Diary ink is soluble. The Diary ink contains a synthetic dye of the nigrosine type that was not available in Victorian times. There is no iron.

EASTAUGH October 1992
Technique: Thin Layer Chromatography and SEM/EDS. Also scanning electron microscopy. Dr Eastaugh also used various brand name inks as control.
Result:
Nothing in the Diary ink inconsistent with 1888. There was a clear difference between the modern inks and the Diary. The Diary ink contains iron. The Diary ink contains some sodium. There is no nigrosine.

IN AMERICA. September and November 1993
Technique: Thin Layer Chromotography
Result:
Research ink chemist Robert Kuranz said that there was nothing in the Diary ink inconsistent with the Victorian period. Rod McNeil carried out his ion migration analysis which measures, with a scanning auger microscope, the migration of ions from the ink into the paper. He put the date of the ink-on-paper around 1921 plus or minus 12 years but later added that this could depend on the amount of exposure to light.

BRISTOL UNIVERSITY January 1994
Technique: Thin Layer Chromotography
Result:
Dr Eastaugh and I took the Diary to the Interface Analysis Centre of Bristol University where Dr Robert Wild ran a test on equipment similar to that used by McNeil. He concluded that such a test could not be carried out as claimed. He also said that not enough had been published about this particular test.

ROD McNEIL October 1993
Result:
Rod McNeil made a statement in October 1993 which somewhat diminished that which he had given to Kenneth Rendell in September: 'It is my strong opinion based on the Auger Sims results that the document was... created prior to 1970... as with any scientific test there is always the possibility of error associated either with the operator or the techniques itself...'

DIAMINE INK pre 1992
The formula of Diamine ink as it was made prior to 1992

(and if Michael Barrett forged the Diary would have been the ink sold to him) is as follows:

Gallic Acid	0.84%
Tannic Acid	0.42%
Anhydrous sulphate	1.26%
Nigrosine	0.42%
Dextrine	1.88%
Oxalic Acid	0.52%
Chloroacetamide	0.26%
Artilene Black	2.32%

(Artilene black is a proprietary pigment dispersion from Clariant (formerly Sandoz U.K.) containing 40% of Carbon Black. Its other constituents are not relevant as they form no part of the dry ink residue.)

Water	92.08%
TOTAL	100%

ANALYSIS FOR INDUSTRY October 1994

Technique: Gas liquid chromatography

Six small black dots of ink from the Diary were examined. Together these weighed 0.000583g. 'Probably in excess of 90% of this comprised the paper of the same size to which the ink dot was attached.'

Result: Chloroacetamide was present at a level of 6.5 parts per million.

LEEDS UNIVERSITY November 1994

On November 19th 1994 Keith Skinner and I took the Diary to Leeds where samples of the ink were scraped from various parts of the Diary. We also took some indisputably Victorian documents dated 1881 and 1887.

Technique: SEM/EDX

Thin layer chromatography

Optical microscopy

Result: The first test indicated the presence of a minute amount of chloroacetamide – which Leeds attributed to contamination from the control. I was unaware of this at the time and did *not* request, as has been suggested, a second test.

The laboratory, of their own volition, conducted a second test. This then showed: No chloroacetamide. The Diary ink is *not* easily soluble. It is of the iron gallotannate type. There is no sodium. The Diary ink is the same as that on the Victorian documents.

* * *

These results were loudly rejected by the anti-Diary consortium. A quite unparalleled amount of paper flew from office to office and between laboratories. I was urged to do more tests, to ask Analysis and Leeds to re-stage their experiments on exactly the same footing. I wrote to every ink expert and scientific group I could find. Typical of the response was another letter from Dr Morris of Dow Chemicals. 'You may find that the first large scale commercial use of chloroacetamide in ink was in 19XX [*sic*] but that does not rule out the possibility that some small shop made its own ink and tried various additives.'

This was all very confusing.

I asked for estimates for new tests from a range of laboratories and was quoted anything from £50 a hour to £400 per day or a total cost of about £2,000. These are apparently standard charges but were way beyond my reach. At the suggestion of Leeds University I contacted ICI at Wilton Research Centre, where was housed the finest equipment in Europe for looking at ink. Dr David Briggs replied: 'All this amounts to several days' work at the cost of £1,000 a day. I have to stress once again that this is not a simple standard test, far from it ... Given the great uncertainties I therefore do not recommend that you pursue this approach.'

I felt, in all honesty, I could do no more. There was one more line of action from which I felt we all might learn. I invited Alec Voller to see the Diary in London. He was, I knew, a man who lived and breathed ink. He had told me 'we are a dying breed'. He is – he did not want to be paid!

ALEC VOLLER Bsc October 1995

On Friday October 30th 1995 Alec Voller came to the offices of Smith Gryphon where he met Sally Evemy, Robert Smith, Keith Skinner, Martin Howells and me. These notes are taken from the tape recording of that meeting. The full transcript is available on request.

> Mr Voller was handed the Diary and looked at it for less than two minutes before saying:
>
> 'That is not Diamine ink. What is conclusive is the physical appearance. If this were Diamine Manuscript ink or at least Diamine ink of recent manufacture, that is to say within the last 20 or 30 years, it would be blacker and more opaque than this. The opacity of this is very much poorer than one would have from Diamine Manuscript ink even if it were diluted. You see dilution would simply not produce this sort of effect.
>
> 'Assuming this staining is glue... there you see a dot of ink which is beneath the glue so it's been there a very very long time. The glue does not have the feel of modern synthetic glue...'
>
> At this point Mr Voller is studying the writing closely;
>
> 'The colour isn't right... From your point of view this is good news actually. As far as the dyestuff is concerned there have always been three possibilities. One was nigrosine; the other two were acid blue 93... and the third possibility which would have been distinctly bad news for you, naphthol blue-black which wasn't discovered till 1891. This is definitely nigrosine. This means it is not a registrar's ink, it is definitely a manuscript ink. And since

Diamine Manuscript ink is the only one of its kind for many a long year and this is definitely not Diamine Manuscript ink, it puts the penmanship some considerable distance in the past.

'The fading that's occurred is quite characteristic of permanent manuscript inks of some considerable age. They don't fade evenly; you get two consecutive lines of writing, one of which remains quite legible and one fades badly.

'You see this sort of thing is very characteristic. He says *"I am tired, very tired"*. Obviously the pen has not been dipped in the ink again until he reaches the first word of the second sentence *'I'* and yet the early words of the sentence have faded more than the next two words, despite the fact there was presumably more ink on the nib at this point…

'Now with a modern ink the effect you would get in the early part of the sentence would be a more opaque and denser appearance than the end of the sentence… but the reverse is true here. 'You see the same thing here *"The devil take the Bastard I am cold curse the bastard Lowry for making me rip…"* He has obviously dipped his pen in the ink at the *'I'* and if you proceed along the sentence you can see the way the ink has faded very badly… you can see the irregular fading… with a modern ink you would get a regular fade-out along that line.

The critical point here is the length of time the ink has been on the paper… you mention powdered inks… I daresay one can find them… we have 7,000 sachets tucked away in some cobwebby corner of Diamine. But if you add the appropriate quantity of water to the powder it would still look like new ink on the paper…'

Keith notices a strong line through *'shiny knife'*:

'It is this sort of thing that rules out a modern diluted ink… you simply wouldn't get as bold a line as that.

'Here is a line with very little fading.' [*'tis love that will finish me'*] This last line is quite badly faded except for the beginning [*'tis love that I regret'*]

At this point Mr Voller took the Diary to the window.

'This is as I thought… it's barely visible… in one or two places there is some very slight bronzing …tilted to the light it can just be seen… *'the children they distract me so I ripped OPEN'*… the bronzing is in the last word… There is some more visible on the words *'building up'*. This tells me that it is genuinely old… This bronzing effect is a chemical process which is not fully understood… you only get pronounced bronzing where the ink is a blue-black that is to say when the ink is not nigrosine. With a nigrosine base the bronzing is usually less obvious. The dyestuff here is clearly nigrosine… I have seen a considerable number of documents like that where there has been very little bronzing…

'If you made up the ink in the way it is supposed to have been made up (as a modern forgery) it simply wouldn't have faded to the extent that parts of the Diary have faded… To create this document as a modern fake you would have to start with a person of at least my experience of ink… you would have to produce a convincing effect of ageing. At the very start you need the right ink and where are you going to get the right ink….

'This is where a forger would run into difficulties. There has never been a lot of literature on the subject of writing inks … this kind of literature tends to be written by experts for other experts and a certain amount of knowledge is assumed… very often, for example, literature of that sort does not always give complete formulations…This brings us neatly to the last point… Even if you can find something that gives you a complete formulation I have yet to see one that tells you how to put it together… it's like making a cake… to make a proper ferro-gallic ink takes a week of doing things at the right time and in the right order... there would have to be a preservative in the ink. If one assumes the ink is genuinely old, as I do, you are left only with phenol. Phenol is not too difficult to test for... the problem is quantity... you are talking about very, very minute amounts.

'In Diamine you have 92% water 7.91% is the constituent parts of Diamine and of that 0.26% is the preservative chloroacetamide... Professor Roberts of UMIST [University of Manchester Science and Technology Department] has mentioned that chloroacetamide was used as a preservative in cotton, rag and wool products and paper was commonly made from rag in those days... How one would produce the irregular fading that occurs in the Diary I simply don't know... If I were going to try and forge something I wouldn't use a pseudo old ink at all. I could formulate an ink that would give you the right appearance... but of course it wouldn't stand up to chemical analysis.'

Would finding phenol as the preservative in the ink be pretty conclusive?

'You could get phenol in a Victorian powdered ink... you could have it analysed... then you would have to ask... did it come from the ink or the paper? Phenol may be derived from the paper, which is an incredibly complex bag of chemical substances... even finding phenol wouldn't be conclusive because whilst its use as an ink preservative has virtually ceased it was used between the wars.

'The relevant British Standard (BS3484) demands the use of Phenol in Blue Black ink, even today.'

Mr Voller has since considered the suggestion that the Diary fading might have been produced by an accelerated fading apparatus or even a hand-held sun ray lamp. But the Diary fading is irregular and such an effect cannot be achieved artificially. 'Besides,' he says, 'any exposure to U.V. radiation that was harsh enough to simulate a century's worth of natural fading would also have a savage bleaching effect on the paper. There was nothing about the appearance of the Diary, as I recall, to suggest this.

'It's hard to be dogmatic because the rate at which fading occurs is variable but... certainly the ink did not go on the paper within recent years... you are looking at a document which in my opinion is at least 90 years old and may be older... I came with an open mind and if I thought it was a modern ink I would have said so.'

THE PAPER

Patricia Cornwell's book *Portrait of a Killer* was published in 2002. She stated that 'Peter Bower, one of the most respected paper experts in the world ... best known for his work on papers used by artists as various as Michelangelo, JMW Turner, Constable and others – as well as for determining that the notorious Jack the Ripper diary was a fraud.'

At his request I have never before mentioned my meeting with Peter Bower but I knew the Ripper world would assume I had conveniently forgotten this staggering piece of information.

The truth is different. Peter Bower, Sally Evemy and I met in Robert Smith's office. He asked us not to report his responses – it was a friendly, informal meeting and so I respected that request. When we met seven years later he told me he had been very suspicious of the paper and the binding and his on-the-spot instinct was that there was something wrong. But this is not at all what he said at the time and he conducted no tests. I wrote to him to confirm the gist of our original discussion.

He did not reply.

In March 1998 there was yet another informal meeting at Robert Smith's office. Crime writer, former police sergeant, doyen of the Ripper fraternity and Maybrick sceptic Donald Rumbelow told me that he thought the unused album had been assembled in recent years. He asked that a friend of his, whose family had been professional bookbinders for four generations, should be allowed to examine the Diary. We had some reservations because Robert Smith, himself a man with many years' experience in antique books and bookbinding, had spent many hours examining the pages and did not agree with Don. However, we agreed to the examination.

'Bill', who prefers to remain in the background, came with Don and, within two minutes scrutinising the Diary, said 'there is nothing iffy about this scrapbook.' He claimed that it showed no signs of any tampering and was typical of a medium- to lower-quality Victorian guard book for photos and more probably newspaper cuttings. He also commented that the missing pages had been 'hacked by a barbarian'.

In 2002 there was a new initiative. One of the Message Boards' most prolific correspondents, academic John Omlor, indicated that funds might be raised in America were the Diary ink to be tested at the prestigious McCrone Group laboratories. Their best-known claim to fame was, once again, the Turin Shroud. They were said to have the very latest state-of-the-art equipment. Paul Begg was asked to co-ordinate arrangements and wrote to Dr Joseph Barabe early in 2003 to establish a basis upon which to proceed. He and Robert Smith had agreed with John Omlor that it was naturally essential to understand exactly what the laboratory could undertake and whether the results would bring us confidently nearer to knowing when the Diary was written, within a reasonable margin of error. The document had already suffered damage from its many testings and clear parameters for its protection were needed before it could again be subject to analysis, especially abroad. It was also clear, from experience, that whatever the results, someone, somewhere was bound to contest them.

Paul had no reply to his letter and there was a lull in the proceedings. I had played no part in these discussions but by the time I was working on the new edition of my book I decided to contact McCrone myself. In April 2003 I spoke first to Dr Barabe and then to Dr Kenneth J Smith, senior research assistant at McCrone. This was his written response to my call:

> As we spoke yesterday the analysis is certainly challenging. We are often successful in comparing ink samples on one document and determining if the inks are consistent or inconsistent over a document. The analysis of an ink which

may be from a certain period is more difficult. Our laboratory does not have access to historical ink libraries which would be helpful in examining components of an ink from that era. There is a concern that someone could prepare an ink with a recipe from an era (an iron gall ink for example) and apply it to papers also from that era, which you pointed out are easily available.

If McCrone Associates were to perform this analysis we would want to look at the document as a whole. This would involved examining the ink, the paper, glue and dust or other particulate material associated with the document in order to get a better overall picture of the history of the document. We can attempt to analyze the ink on the document for the presence of chloroacetamide, however we have no reference information at this point about the historical application of this compound in the formulation of inks. The examination of the document as a whole often provides better insight into the overall consistency of a document with its reported history.

Please keep in mind that a definitive answer about the age of the document may not be possible. There are numerous examples of forgers who very studiously prepared documents or works of art using materials from a period that render the final product almost imperceptively different from the authentic works from a period.

But it did not end there. An abusive onslaught had broken out on the Internet, in which the words 'con' and 'lies' were hurled into space. The outrageous accusations from America were that, once again, all those in Britain interested in the Diary were blocking any offers to re-test it for purely commercial reasons and fear of exposure. Eventually conributors to the Message Boards were sternly advised to 'take this conversation to Email … it is going nowhere and serves only to increase the personal antagonism between those involved.' So that seemed to be that. We were no further forward.

23

I Pray Whoever Should Read this will Find it in Their Heart to Forgive me

We are still on the yellow brick road to the end of the rainbow but despite the many allegations, no crocks of gold have been found, no fortunes made. The Diary continues to have an astonishingly powerful hold on all those who have responded to the challenge of interpreting its contents, whatever their final conclusions. Its influence has frequently been far from benign and the vitriol it has attracted from those convinced it is the product of a clumsy plot has been beyond belief.

On the other hand, the Diary has drawn the interest of a great many men and women of considerable integrity and status, from widely differing areas of expertise. They have willingly, often unpaid, spent hours of time and reams of paper dissecting its content. It will not go away. Investigating the Diary has become a labour of love.

It was gratifying to discover that in the 1997 *Reader's Digest Encyclopaedia of Essential Knowledge*, James Maybrick is mentioned as a leading Ripper suspect.

If, as Billy Graham claimed, the Diary existed in his family, at least as far back as 1943, it poses many questions. Before this date there were very few source books for Ripper material and access to archives was more difficult. The creation of a forgery at that date would have been extremely complicated.

It is, of course, possible that Billy was lying and his daughter Anne continues to propagate the lie. Anne's story has been likened to that of the Cottingley Fairies and the schoolgirl cousins, Elsie Wright and Frances Griffiths. In 1918, their controversial photographs of real life fairies at the bottom of their garden cast a spell whose magic was to captivate the public. Sir Arthur Conan Doyle was one of many who were utterly taken in. Despite Frances' confessions before she died, in 1986, that they had faked the photographs all that time ago, there were many who did not accept her admission. The Cottingley Fairies have not yet fluttered out of sight.

Bill Waddell is one of those who have spent many hours talking with Anne and he told me, 'If Anne Graham is lying she is making a far better job of it than any of the professional criminals I have met in my life.' He should know.

If Anne *is* lying, then she is also jeopardising everything she has built since the collapse of her marriage, including her daughter's future. She is harming people she has learned to trust. She has so far profited little from the Diary – certainly not financially. She is looking forward to a new life, has become a student at Liverpool University and her book on Florence Maybrick was published by Headline in 1999. Anne is not convinced herself that she is a descendant of Florie, but the tragedy of Florence's life has become a genuine interest. Has she done all this in the shadow of the knowledge that one day, if she has deceived us all, the truth will out.

Ask yourself: if Michael and Anne forged the Diary how did they find the necessary time or money to visit the archives in London and Liverpool; to make their way to the University of Wyoming in America, where the unpublished Christie material is lodged; to pore over hundreds of pages of microfilm of national and local press in London and Liverpool; to read and understand obscure medical literature, to locate the Grand National archives as well as read the massive literature on the Ripper and the mountain of indigestible Maybrick trial material? Besides, do they possess the necessary literary skill to create a 'script' which holds the attention of two of Britain's leading psychologists?

As it was, the strain of supporting Michael's efforts to understand the Diary and transcribing his notes on to a word processor was more than enough for Anne. She was near suicidal at a time when her long term marriage problems were also coming to a head and her father was dying of cancer.

It is true that the Barretts needed money and this could have provided them with a motive. But during the most terrible row they ever had, Caroline remembers, all too well, how the couple fought, physically, on the floor – because Anne did *not* want Michael to get the Diary published.

Diaryphobes should not forget that Anne was in full time work, and exhausted at the end of the day; Michael was on an invalidity pension and their domestic life was foundering. Remember too, that they lived in a typical Liverpool terraced house and would have also had to conceal all such activities from their, much-loved ll-year-old daughter, Caroline, so that there was no danger of her spilling the beans to her pals at school.

And what about the watch? The watch, which must have caused the Diary 'forgers' a headache when it appeared, luckily passes the examinations of two scientists.

A nest of forgers? Who were their accomplices? Tony Devereux, former print worker who didn't read and had no books? Billy Graham, who could hardly write and was a respected member of the British Legion? Albert Johnson, the deeply religious family man, who had never met the Barretts and knew nothing of the Maybrick story? Were these the people who conspired to write the Diary in which the historical events and text dovetail unfailingly as the plot unfolds? To home in on Maybrick himself as the villain of the piece and make him Jack the Ripper was inspired but risky casting. There are, of course, problems still unresolved. This is why I would like to open the case and, emulating the BBC television programme *Crimewatch*, invite readers who think they can shed light on any part of the mystery to contact me. In America and in Britain we need artefacts, documents, photographs and memories from anyone with any connection to any part of the Maybrick saga.

There are so many questions, both here and in America, which remain unanswered.

AMERICA

Are there any living Maybricks in America?

Are there any descendants of James Maybrick's friends or employees such as the Nevison Wallers and the Aunspaughs, General Hazard, Andrew H. H. Dawson, Mollie Hogwood, Nicholas Bateson, the Seguins?

What happened to the book on Florie's trial being written by Andrew H. H. Dawson?

Where are the records of the Brooklyn Asylum?

Who was the Sarah Ann Maybrick who tried to commit her daughter Hester in 1894 and what happened to Hester?

Can anyone throw any light on the extent of British involvement in the Cotton Exposition in New Orleans in 1884/5?

Who was Dennis Maybrick who allegedly died in 1858?

Where is the alleged 'diary' of Jack the Ripper which emerged in New York in 1888?

Where did Michael Maybrick tour in America in 1884?

Where is the scrapbook found with Florie after her death?

Where are the descendants of J. C. O'Connell, born in Liverpool, who covered Florie's trial as a cub reporter, later became Managing Editor of *Mobile Register* and eventually joined the *New York Times*? He attended Florie's funeral and died in 1945.

ENGLAND

Are there any descendants of the Hamilton family of Prescot or the 'Hammersmiths' from Liverpool?

Can anyone shed light on the naming of The Poste House? Was there another hostelry known as The Poste House? Or is there a record that the Cumberland Street Poste House was, indeed, called that in 1888?

Between 1990-1992 did Mike Barrett tell anyone in Liverpool of a Ripper Diary. Or were rumours of a diary circulating at that time?

Is there information about the business links between Liverpool cotton merchants and the Border mills?

Are there any descendants of the Janions or Martha Briggs?

Are there descendants of ship owner Henry Flinn?

Where are the Conconis?

Where is the family of Dr Dutton?

Where are *The Chronicles of Crime*?

Where are the descendants of Dr Fuller?

Where is the Baroness's will?

What happened to Triscler and Co?

Where are the papers of Lumley and Lumley?

Where are Florie's 'diaries'?

Who can throw more light on Charles Garner, alias Stuart Cumberland?

Where are the records of Traynors builders in Kent?

* * *

Perhaps James Maybrick himself should have the last word.

In 2000, my former publisher Robert Smith was exploring the area around Bromley Street, Stepney, a district bordering Whitechapel, where Maybrick stayed with Sarah Ann and the Conconis. The church at the top of Bromley Street is St Dunstan's and All Saints, known as the Sailors' Church. Maybrick must have been familiar with it.

In the south aisle there is a stone, taken from the walls of Carthage, and on the stone is carved an epitaph.

Of Carthage wall I see a Stone
Oh Mortals Read with pity
Time consumes all it spareth none

Man, mountain town nor city.

There is a strange irony in the words of this verse. In 1881, two weeks before his wedding to Florence, Maybrick commissioned a Coat of Arms from the College of Heralds. It cost him £76.10d, the approximate equivalent of £3,200 today. The armorial bearings depict a sparrowhawk, which in heraldic terms symbolises power. In its beak is a sprig of hawthorn – more commonly known as 'may' – and beneath is a block, or 'brick'.

Of all the prophecies that Maybrick the riddler could have chosen, the spine-tingling motto beneath, emblazoned across the years, was:

TEMPUS OMNIA REVELAT

Time Reveals All

Ha Ha.

A Facsimile of the Diary of Jack the Ripper

what they have in store for them they would stop this instant. But do I desire that? my answer is no. They will suffer just as I. I will see to that. Received a letter from Michael perhaps I will visit him. Will have to come to some sort of decision regards the children. I long for peace of mind but I sincerely believe that that will not come until I have sought my revenge on the whore and the whore master.

Foolish bitch, I know for certain she has arranged a rendezvous with him in Whitechapel. So be it, my mind is firmly made. I took refreshment at the Poste House it was there I finally decided London it shall be. And why not, is it not an ideal location? Indeed do I not frequently visit the Capitol and indeed do I not have legitimate reason for doing so. All who sell their dirty wares shall pay, of that I have no doubt. But shall I pay? I think not I am too clever for that.

As usual my hands are cold, my heart I do believe is colder still. My dearest Gladys is unwell yet again, she worries me so. I am convinced a dark shadow lays over the house, it is evil. I am becoming increasingly weary of people who constantly enquire regards the state of my health. True my head and arms pain me at times but I am not duly worried, although I am quite certain Hopper believes to the contrary. I have him down as a bumbling buffoon. Thomas has requested that we meet as soon as possible. Business is flourishing so I have no inclination as regards the matter he describes as most urgent. Never the less I shall endeavour to meet his request.

June is passing much too slowly, I still have to work up the courage to begin my campaign. I have thought long and hard over the matter and still I cannot come to a decision to when I should begin. Opportunity is there, of that fact I am certain. The bitch has no inclination.

The thought of her taking her is beginning to thrill me, perhaps I will allow her to continue, some of my thoughts are indeed beginning to give me pleasure. Yes I will visit Michael for a few weeks, and allow her to take all she can from the whoring master. Tonight I shall see Sarah. I may return to Battlecrease and take the unfaithful bitch. Two in a night, indeed pleasure. My medicine is doing me good, in fact, I am sure I can take more than any other person alive. My mind is clear I will put whore through pain tonight.

I am begining to believe it is unwise to continue writing, If I am to down a whore then nothing shall lead the police back to me, and yet there are times when I feel an overwhelming compulsion to place my thoughts to paper. It is dangerous, that I know. If Smith should find this then I am done before my campaign begins. However, the pleasure of writing all all that lays ahead of me, and indeed the pleasure of thoughts of deeds that lay ahead of me, thrills me so. And oh what deeds I shall commit. For how could one suspect that I could be capable of such things, for am I not, as all believe, a mild man, who it has been said would never hurt a fly. Indeed only the other day did not Edwin say of me I was the most gentlest of men he had encountered. A compliment from my dear brother which I found exceedingly flattering.

Have decided my potions is wearing thin. The bitch has made a fool of me. Tomorrow I travel to Manchester. Will take some of my medicine and think hard on the matter. I believe I could do so, though I shake with fear of capture. A fear I will have to overcome. I believe I have the strength. I will force myself not to think of the children. The whore, that is all that shall be in my mind. My head aches.

My dear God my mind is in a fog. The whore is now with her maker and he is welcome to her. There was no pleasure as I squeezed, I felt nothing. Do not know if I have the courage to go back to my original idea. Manchester was cold and damp very much like this hell hole. Next time I will throw acid over them. The thought of them withering and screaming while the acid burns deep thrills me.

I believe I have caught a chill I cannot ~~stop~~ shaking, my body aches. There are times when I pray to God that the pain and ~~torment~~ will stop. Summer is near the warm weather will do me good. I long for peace but my work is only beginning. I will have a long ~~wait~~ for peace. All whores must suffer first and my God how I will make ~~them~~ suffer as she has made me. Edwin asked Thomas and business, I informed him that Thomas was well and business was flourishing, both true. I have it in my mind that I should write to Michael, perhaps not, my hands are far too cold, another day. I will take the bitch tonight. I need to take my mind off the nights events. The children are well.

Strolled by the drive, encountered Mrs Hammersmith, she enquired of Bobo and Gladys and much to my astonishment about my health. What has that whore said? Mrs Hammersmith is a bitch. The fresh air and stroll did me good. For a while I succeeded in forgetting the bitch and her whoring master. Felt completely refreshed when I returned to my office. I will visit Michael this coming June. June is such a pleasant month, the flowers are in full bud, the air is sweeter and life is almost certainly much easier. I look forward to its coming with pleasure. A great deal of pleasure. I feel compelled to write to Michael if not obliged. My mind is clear, my hands are not cold.

I am vexed. I am trying to quell my anger. The whore has suggested she accompany me on my trip to Michael. I need time to put my mind in order. Under no circumstances can I let the bitch accompany me, all my hard work and plans will be destroyed if she were to do so. The pain was bad today. I believe the bitch has found one of my bottles, it had been moved. I am tired and need sleep the pain kept me awake for most of last night. Will return early avoid the bitch altogether.

Frequented my club. George stated that he had never seen me in better health. I believe the bitch has changed her mind. My thoughts are becoming increasingly more daring, I have imagined doing all manner of things. Could I eat part of one? Perhaps it would taste of fresh fried bacon ha ha. My dear God it thrills me so.

Michael is expecting me towards the end of June, henceforth from July my campaign will gather momentum. I will take each and everyone before I return them to their maker, damaged of course, severely damaged.

I try to repel all thoughts of the children from my mind. I feel strong, stronger than I have ever felt. My thoughts keep returning to Manchester, next time it will thrill me. I know in my heart it will. I cannot understand why William will not accept my offer to dine. He is not unlike me, he hates the bitch. I believe if chance prevails I will burn St. James's to the ground. Tomorrow I will make a substantial wager. I feel lucky.

If I could have killed the bastard Lowry with my bare hands there and then I would have done so. How dare he question me on any matter, it is I that should question him. Damn him damn him damn him should I replace the missing items? No that would be too much of a risk. Should I destroy this? My God I will kill him. Give him no reason and order him posthaste to drop the matter, that I believe is the only course of action I can take. I will force myself to think of something more pleasant. The whore will suffer more than she has ever done so tonight, that thought revitalizes me. June is drawing to a close I shake with anticipation.

I have taken too much my thoughts are not where they should be. I recall little of the events of yesterday. Thank God I stopped myself in time. I will show my wrath towards the Crossword in such a manner that he will wish he had never brought up the subject. No one, not even God himself will deny the pleasure of writing my thoughts. I will take the first whore I encounter and show her what hell is really like. I think I will ram a cane into the whoring Bitches mouth and leave it there for them to see how much she could take. My head aches, God has no right to do this to me the devil take him.

How I succeeded in controlling myself I do not know. I have not allowed for the red stuff, gallons of it in my estimation. Some of it is bound to spill onto me. I cannot allow my clothes to be blood drenched, this I could not explain to anyone least of all Michael. Why did I not think of this before? I curse myself. The struggle to stop myself was overwhelming, and if I had not asked Michael to lock me in my bedroom for fear of sleepwalking, to which I had said I had been prone to do recently, was that not clever? I would have done my dirty deeds that very night.

I have taken a small room in Middlesex Street that in itself is a joke. I have paid well and I believe no questions will be asked. It is indeed an ideal location. I have walked the streets and have become more than familiar with them. I said Whitechapel it will be and Whitechapel it shall. The bitch and her whoring master will rue the day I first saw them together. I said I am clever, very clever. Whitechapel Liverpool, Whitechapel London, ha ha. No one could possibly place it together. And indeed for there is no reason for anyone to do so.

The next time I travel to London I shall begin. I have no doubts, my confidence is most high. I am thrilled writing this, life is sweet, and my disappointment has vanished. Next time for sure. I have no doubts, not any longer, no doubts. No one will ever suspect. Tomorrow

I will purchase the finest knife money can buy, nothing shall be too good for my whores, I will treat them to the finest, the very finest, they deserve that at least from I.

I have shown all that I mean business, the pleasure was far better than I imagined. The whore was only too willing to do her business. I recall all and it thrills me. There was no scream when I cut. I was more than vexed when the head would not come off. I believe I will need more strength next time. I struck deep into her. I regret I never had the cane, it would have been a delight to have rammed it hard into her. The bitch opened like a ripe peach. I have decided next time I will rip all out. My medicine will give me strength and the thought of the whore and her whoring master will spur me on no end.

The wait to hear about my triumph seemed long, although it was not. I am not disappointed, they have all written well. The next time they will have a great deal more to write, of that fact I have no doubt ha ha. I will remain calm and show no interest in my deed, if anyone should mention it so, but I will laugh inside, oh how I will laugh.

I will not allow too much time to pass before my next. Indeed I need to repeat my pleasure as soon as possible. The whoring Master can have her with pleasure and I shall have my pleasure with my thoughts and deeds. I will be clever. I will not call on Michael on my next visit. My brothers would be horrified if they knew, particularly Edwin after all did he not say I was one of the most gentlest of men he had ever encountered. I hope he is enjoying the fruits of America. Unlike I. For do I not have a sour fruit.

I could not resist mentioning my deed to George. I was clever and brought up the subject by way of how fortunate we were not having murders of that kind in the city. He agreed with me completely. Indeed he went on to say, that he believed we had the finest police force in the land, and although we have our fair share of troubles the women folk can walk the streets in safety. And indeed they can for I will not play my funny little games on my own doorstep ha ha.

The gentle man with gentle thoughts will strike again soon. I have never felt better, in fact, I am taking more than ever and I can feel the strength building up within me. The head will come off next time, also the whores hands. Shall I leave them in various places around Whitechapel? Hunt the head and hands instead of the thimble ha ha. Maybe I will take some part away with me to see if it does taste of like fresh fried bacon. The whore seen her master today it did not bother me. I imagined I was with them, the very thought thrills me. I wonder if the whore has ever had such thoughts? I believe she has, has she not cried out when I demand she takes another. The bitch. She will suffer but not as yet. Tomorrow I travel to London. I have decided I cannot wait any longer. I look forward to tomorrow nights work, it will do me good, a great deal of good.

One dirty whore was looking for some gain.
Another dirty whore was looking for the same,

Am I not clever? I thought of my funny little rhyme,
on my travel to the City of whores. I was vexed
with myself when I realised I had forgotten the
chalk. So vexed infact, that I returned to the bitch
and cut out more. I took some of it away with
me. It is in front of me. I intend to fry it and
eat it later ha ha. The very thought works up
my appetite I cannot stop the thrill of writing. I ripped
open my God I will have to stop laughing of the
children they distract me so I ripped open

It has taken me three days to recover, I will not feel
guilty it is the whoring bitch to blame not I.
I ate all of it, it did not taste like fresh fried
bacon but I enjoyed it never the less. She was
so sweet and pleasurable. I have left the
stupid fools a clue which I am sure they will
not solve. Once again I have been clever, very clever.

~~In my pocket I will leave the clue~~

~~One pill that's true~~

I ~~will catch Sir Jim with~~ no pills
~~eight two~~

two farthings,
two pills
the whores M
rings.

Think

It shall come, if Michael can succeed in rhyming verse then I can do better, a great deal better he shall not outdo me. Think you fool, think. I curse Michael for being so clever, I shall outwit him, I will see to that. A funny little rhyme shall come forth. Patience is needed patience. The night is long, time is on my hand:

The pills are the answer
and with pills. Indeed do I always not oh what a joke.

Begin with the rings,

One ring, two rings

bitch, it took me a while before I could wrench them off. Should have stuffed them down the whores throat. I wish to God I could have taken the head. Stupid bitch for wearing them, reminds me too much of the whore. Next time I will select a whore who has none. The bitch was not worth the farthings. Return, return, essential to return. Prove you are no fool.

One ring, two rings,
a farthing one and two
~~Sir Jim will do time~~
~~better M its true~~
Along with M ha ha
Will catch clever Jim,
its true.
~~left two~~
No pill, left but two

One ring, two rings,
a farthing, one and two,
Along with M ha ha
Will catch clever Jim
its true
No pill, left but two

Am I not indeed a clever fellow? It makes me laugh they will never understand why I did so. Next time I will remember the chalk and write my funny little rhyme. The eyes will come out of the next. I will stuff them in the whores mouth, That will certainly give me pleasure, it does so as I write. Tonight I will see mine, she will be pleased as I will be gentle with her as indeed I always am.

I am still thinking of burning St. James's to the ground I may do so on my next visit. That will give the fools something more to think on I am begining to think less of the children, part of me hates me for doing so. One day God will answer to me, so help me Michael would be proud of my funny little rhyme for he knows only too well the art of verse. Have I not proven I can write better than he. I feel like Celebrating, the night has been long and I shall award myself with the pleasures of the flesh, but I shall not be cutting ha ha I will save ~~that thrill~~ for another day.

The whore is in debt. Very well I shall honour the letter notes but the whores are going to pay more than ever. I have read all of my deeds they have done me proud, I had to laugh, they have me down as left handed, a Doctor, a slaughterman and a Jew. Very well, if they are to insist that I am a Jew then a Jew I shall be. Why not let the Jews suffer? I have never taken to them, far too many of them on the Exchange for my liking: I could not stop laughing when I read Punch there for all to see was the first three letters of my surname. They are blind as they say.

"Turn round three times, And catch whom you

MAY"

ha ha ha ha ha ha

I cannot stop laughing it amuses me so shall I write them a clue?

May comes and goes,
~~this May pleases~~ with a ~~knife in his hand~~
In the dark of the night
~~He does please~~
When he comes and goes.

with a ring on my finger
and a knife in my hand
~~This May comes and goes~~

May comes and goes
In the dark of the night
~~he does please the whores~~ he kisses
~~and gives them a fright~~
he kisse the whores
then gives them a fright

May comes and goes
in the dark of the night
he kisses the whores
then gives them a fright

With a ring on my finger
and a knife in my hand
This May spreads May-hem
~~all through the land~~
throughout this fair land

~~The Jews and slaughtermen~~
~~The Jews and Dators~~
The Dators and Jews.
~~May~~
will get all the blame – blame – tame
same – game
his dirty game.
May playing
~~The Dators~~ [illegible]

The Jews and the Dators
Will get all the blame
but its only May
playing his dirty game

~~He will not shed a tear~~
He will kill all the whores
and not shed a tear
~~He will give them a clue~~
I will give them a clue
but nothing too clear
I will kill all the whores
and not shed a tear.

May comes and goes
in the dark of the night
He kisses the whores
and gives them a fright

The Jews and the Doctors
will get all the blame
but its only May playing
his dirty game

I will give them a clue
but nothing too clear
I will kill all the whores
and not shed a tear

With a ring on my finger
and a knife in my hand.
This May spreads Mayhem
throughout this fair land!

They remind me of chickens with their heads cut off running fools with no heads, ha ha. It is nice to laugh at bastards and fools and indeed they are fools. I need much more pleasure than I have had. Strange my hands feel colder than they have ever done so.

I am fighting a battle within me. My desire for revenge is overwhelming. The whore has destroyed my life. I try whenever possible to keep all sense of respectability. I worry so over Bobo and Gladys, no others matter. Tonight I will take more than ever. I miss the thrill of cutting them up. I do believe I have lost my mind. All the bastards will pay for the pain. Before I am finished all of England will know the name I have given myself. It is indeed a name to remember. It shall be, before long, on every persons lips within the land. Perhaps her gracious Majesty will become acquainted with it. I wonder if she will honour me with a knighthood ha ha.

Abberline says, he was never amazed,
I did my work with such honour
For his decree

he had to agree,
I deserve at least an honour
so all for a whim,

I can now rise Sir Jim — I cannot think of another word to accompany Jim I like my words to rhyme damn it. It is late, mine is waiting, I will enjoy this evening. I will be gentle and not give anything away.

I miss Edwin, I have received but one letter from him since his arrival in the whores country. The bitch is riving me worse as each day passes. If I could I would have it over and done with. I visited my mother and fathers grave. I long to be united with them. I believe they know the torture the whore is putting me through. I enjoy the thrill of thinking of all I have done. But there has been, but once, regret for my deeds. I dispelled my remorse instantly The whore still believes I have no knowledge of her whoring master. I have considered killing him, but if I was to do so. I would surely be caught. I have no desire for that, curse him and the whore their time will come

---

To my astonishment I cannot believe I have not been caught. My heart felt as if it had left my body. Within my fright I imagined my heart bouncing along the street with I in desperation following it. I would have dearly loved to have cut the head of the damned horse off and stuff it as far as it would go down the whores throat. I had no time to rip the bitch wide, I curse my bad luck. I believe the thrill of being caught thrilled me more than cutting the whore herself. As I write I find it impossible to believe he did not see me, in my estimation I was less than a few feet from him. The fool panicked, it is what saved me. My satisfaction was far from complete, damn the bastard, I cursed him and cursed him, but I was clever, they could not out do me. No one ever will. Within the quarter of the hour I found another dirty bitch willing to sell her wares. The whore like all the rest was only too willing. The thrill she gave me was unlike the others, I cut deep deep deep. Her nose annoyed me so I cut it off, had a go at her eyes, left my mark, could not get the bitches head off. I believe now it is impossible to do so. The whore never screamed. I took all I could away with me. I am saving it for a rainy day. ha ha.

Perhaps I will send Abberline and Warren a sample or two, it goes down well with an after dinner Port. I wonder how long it will keep? Perhaps next time I will keep some of the red stuff and send it courtesy of yours truly. I wonder if they enjoyed my funny Jewish Joke? Curse my bad luck had no time to write a funny little rhyme before my next will send Central another to remember me by. My God life is sweet. Will give them something to know its is me.

Red-head
horse,
cryed
smelt breath

~~A rose matched the red~~
~~I did cut the head~~
~~damn it I cried, henceforth I did hide,~~
~~The horse went and shied~~

With a rose to match the red
I tried to cut off the head.
Damn it I cried,
The horse went and shied
But I could still smell her sweet scented breath

I

Sir Jim,
~~tin match box empty~~
~~cigarette case~~
~~make haste~~
~~my shiny knife~~
~~the whores knife~~
first whore no good

One whore no good,
decided Sir Jim strike another.
I showed no fright and indeed no light,
damn it, the tin box was empty

II

tea and sugar
~~sugar, sage,~~ did say
me, plea, be
~~tea and sugar paid my fee~~

Sweet sugar and tea could have paid my small
fee he he
~~then I did flee~~

Showed ~~my~~ glee
a kidneys for supper

Sweet sugar and tea,
could have paid my small fee.
But instead I did flee
and by way showed my glee
By eating cold kidney for supper

III

bastard
Abberline
~~bonnett~~
hides all
clue
clever
will tell you more

~~Mr Abberline is a funny little man~~

Oh Mr Abberline, he is a clever little man
he keeps back all that he can.
~~But I know better~~
For do I know better, indeed I do
did I not leave him a very good clue
Nothing is mentioned, of this I know sure
ask clever Abberline, ~~he does know more~~

Oh Mr Abberline, he is a clever little man
he keeps back all that he can.
For do I not ~~know better~~, Indeed I do.
did I not leave him a very good clue.
Nothing is mentioned; of this I am sure;
ask clever Abberline, could tell you more

IV

Gin Gin trips over
fear
have it near
redium it near
ioo1
Rotte [illegible]

He believes I will try over
but I have no fear
~~I cannot redeem it here~~
For I could not possibly redeem it here.
Of this certain fact, I could send him postecote
if he requests that be the case.

Am I not a clever fellow

That should give the fools a laugh, it has done so for me, wonder if they have enjoyed the name I have given? I said it would be on the lips of all, and indeed it is. I believe I will send another. Include my funny little rhyme. That will convince them that it is the truth I tell. Tonight I will celebrate by wining and dining George. I am in a good mood, I believe I will allow the whore the pleasure of her whore master, will ... an evening in the city will do her good, will suggest a concert. I have no doubt the carriage will take the bitch straight to him. ~~I will go~~ [illegible] I will go to sleep thinking about all they are doing. I cannot wait for the thrill.

With a rose to match the red
I tried to cut off the head.
Damn it I cried,
the horse went and shied
hence forth I did hide,
but I could still smell
her sweet scented breath.

One whore no good, decided Sir Jim strikes another.
I showed no fright, and indeed no light.
Damn it, the tin box was empty.

Sweet sugar and tea
could have paid my small fee
But instead I did flee and by way showed my glee
by eating cold kidney for supper.

Oh, Mr Abberline he is a clever little man,
he keeps back all that he can.
For do I not know better, indeed I do,
did I not leave him a very good clue
Nothing is mentioned of this I know sure,
ask clever Abberline, could tell you more.

He believes I will trip over,
but I have no fear.
For I could not possibly
redeem it here.
Of this certain fact I could send them postcards
If he requested that be the case

It has been far too long since my last, I have been unwell. The whole of my body has pained. Hopper did not believe me. One day I will take revenge on him. The whore has informed the bumbling buffoon I am in the habit of taking strong medicine. I was furious when the bitch told me. So furious I hit her hard. The whore begged me not to do so again. It was a pleasure, a great deal of pleasure. If it was not for my work, I would have cut the bitch up there and then. But I am clever. Although the gentle man has turned, I did not show my hand true. I apologised, a one off instance, I said, which I regretted and I assured the whore it would never happen again. The stupid bitch believed me.

I have received several letters from Michael. In all he enquires about my health and asked in one if my sleepwalking has resumed. Poor Michael he is so easily fooled. I have informed him it has not. My hands still remain cold. I shall be dining tonight. I hope kidneys are on the move, ha ha. Will put me in the mood for another little escapade. Will visit the city of whores soon, very soon. I wonder if I could do three?

If it were not for Michael insisting that we take dinner I would have tried my hand that very night. I cursed my brother as I have never cursed him before. I cursed my own stupidity, had I not informed Michael that I no longer sleepwalked I was forced to stop myself from indulging in my pleasure by taking the largest dose I have ever done. The pain that night has burnt into my mind. I vaguely recall putting a handkerchief in my mouth to stop my cries. I believe I vomited several times. The pain was intolerable, as I think I shudder. No more.

I am convinced God placed me here to kill all whores, for he must have done so, am I still not here. Nothing will stop me now. The more I take the stronger I become.

Michael was under the impression that once I had finished my business I was to return to Liverpool that very day. And indeed I did one day later ha ha. I fear not for the fact will not come to his attention as he addresses all letters to me

I have read about my latest, my God the thoughts, the very best. I left nothing of the bitch, nothing. I placed it all over the room, time was on my hands, like the other whore I cut off the bitches nose, all of it this time. I left nothing of her face to remember her by. She reminded me of the whore. So young unlike I. I thought it a joke when I cut her breasts off, kissed them for a while. The taste of blood was sweet, the pleasure was overwhelming, will have to do it again, it thrilled me so. Left them on the table with some of the other stuff. Thought they belonged there. They wanted a slaughterman so I stripped what I could, laughed while I was doing so. Like the other bitches she ripped like a ripe peach. One of these days I will take the head away with me. I will boil it and serve it up for my supper. The key and burnt clothes puzzle them ha ha.

key	rip
pipe	initial
hat	whore mother
handkerchief	back to the whore
whore	light
mother	fire
father	

~~with the key I did flee~~
I had the key,
and with it I did flee
~~the clothes I burnt~~
~~along with the hat~~
The hat I did burn
for light I did yearn
~~For the sake of the whore mother~~
And I ~~thought~~ of the whoring mother

I had the key,
And with it I did flee.
The hat I did burn
for light I did yearn.
And I thought of the
whoring mother.

I

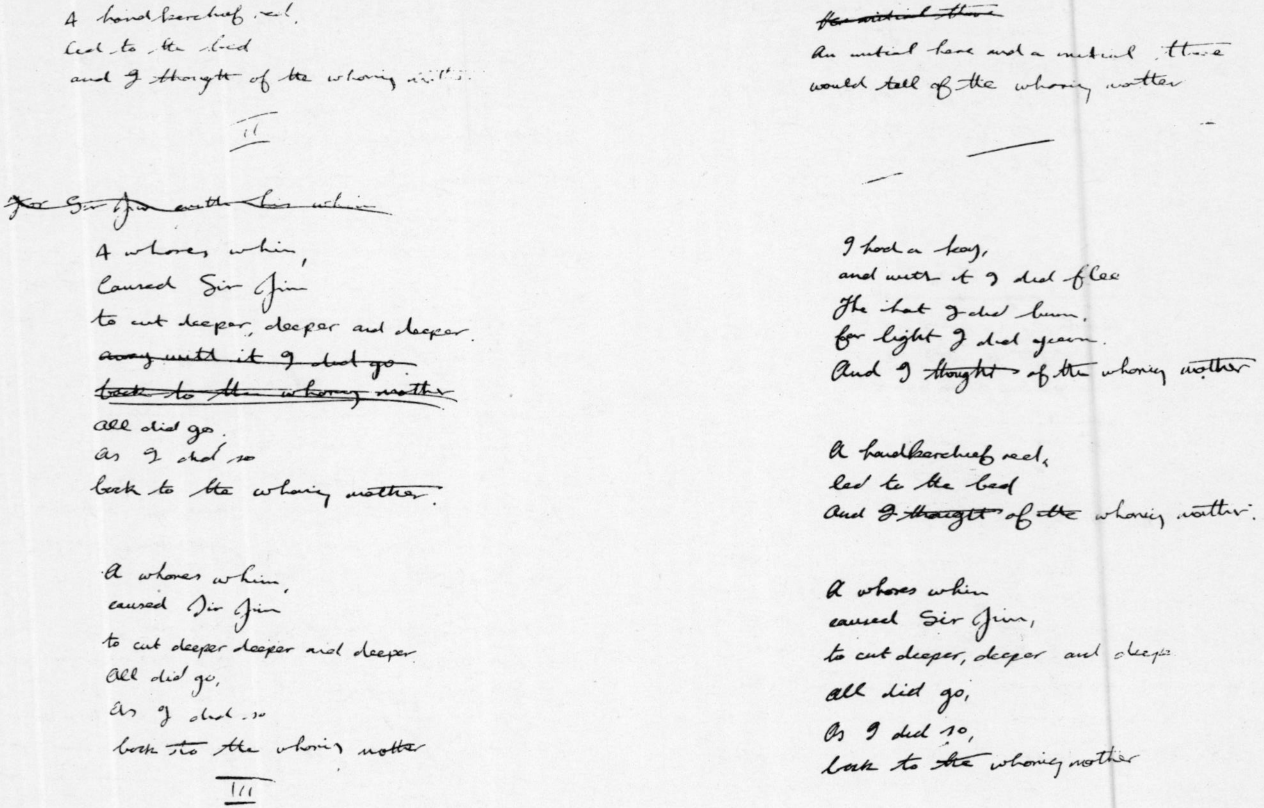

A handkerchief red,
led to the bed
and I thought of the whoring mother.

II

~~For Sir Jim with his whim~~

A whores whim,
Caused Sir Jim
to cut deeper, deeper and deeper.
~~away with it I did go.~~
~~back to the whoring mother~~
All did go.
As I did so
back to the whoring mother.

A whores whim,
caused Sir Jim
to cut deeper deeper and deeper.
All did go,
As I did so
back to the whoring mother

III

An initial here and an initial there
would tell of the whoring mother

I had a key,
and with it I did flee
The hat I did burn,
for light I did yearn.
And I ~~thought~~ of the whoring mother

A handkerchief red,
led to the bed
And I ~~thought~~ of ~~the~~ whoring mother.

A whores whim
caused Sir Jim,
to cut deeper, deeper and deeper
All did go,
As I did so,
back to ~~the~~ whoring mother

An initial here and an initial there will tell of the whoring mother.

I left it there for the fools but they will never find it I was too clever. Left it in front for all eyes to see. Shall I write and tell them? That amuses me.

I wonder if next time I can carve my funny little rhyme on the whores flesh? I believe I will give it a try. It amuses me if nothing else. Life is sweet, very sweet. Regret I did not take any of it away with me. It is supper time, I could do with a kidney or two ha ha.

I cannot live without my medicine. I am afraid to go to sleep for fear of my nightmares reoccurring. I see thousands of people chasing me, with Abberline in front dangling a rope. I will not be stopped of that fact I am certain. It has been far too long since my last, I still desire revenge on the whore and the whore master, but less than the desire to repeat my last performance. The thoughts still thrill me so. I am tired and I fear the city of whores has become too dangerous for I to return. Christmas is approaching - and Thomas has invited me to visit him. I know him well. I have decided to accept his offer, although I know the motive behind it will strictly be business. Thomas thinks of nothing else except money unlike me, ha ha.

My first was in Manchester so why not my next? If I was to do the same as the last, that would throw the fools into a panic, especially that fool Abberline. The children constantly ask what I shall be buying them for Christmas, they shy away when I tell them a shiny knife not unlike Jack the Rippers in order that I cut their tongues for peace and quiet. I do believe I am completely mad. I have never harmed the children - the years since they have been born. But now I take great delight in scaring them so. May God forgive me. I have lost my bottle and shall go on until I am caught. Perhaps I should stop myself and save the hangman a job. At this moment I have no feeling in my body, none at all. I keep missing

myself I have done no wrong. It is the whore
who has done so, not I. Will peace of mind ever
come? I have visited Hopper too often this month.
I will have to stop, for I fear he may begin
to suspect. I talk to him like no other

———— – – –

Sir Jim still,
Am I insane?
Come, gain
Sir Jim with his fancy cane
will soon strike again

One whore in heaven, –
two whores side by side,
three whores all have died.
four

Sir Jim he cuts them first
damn it

Abberline says he is now amazed,
Sir Jim has not struck another.
He waits patiently
to ... bastely

Christmas soul the whores mole bonnett
damn the Batchelor damn Michael
Give Sir Jim his due
He detests all the Jews
For he has no favourite men
As he runs away to his den.

He likes to write with his pen

Give Sir Jim his due
He detests all the Jews
and makes way it not a rule

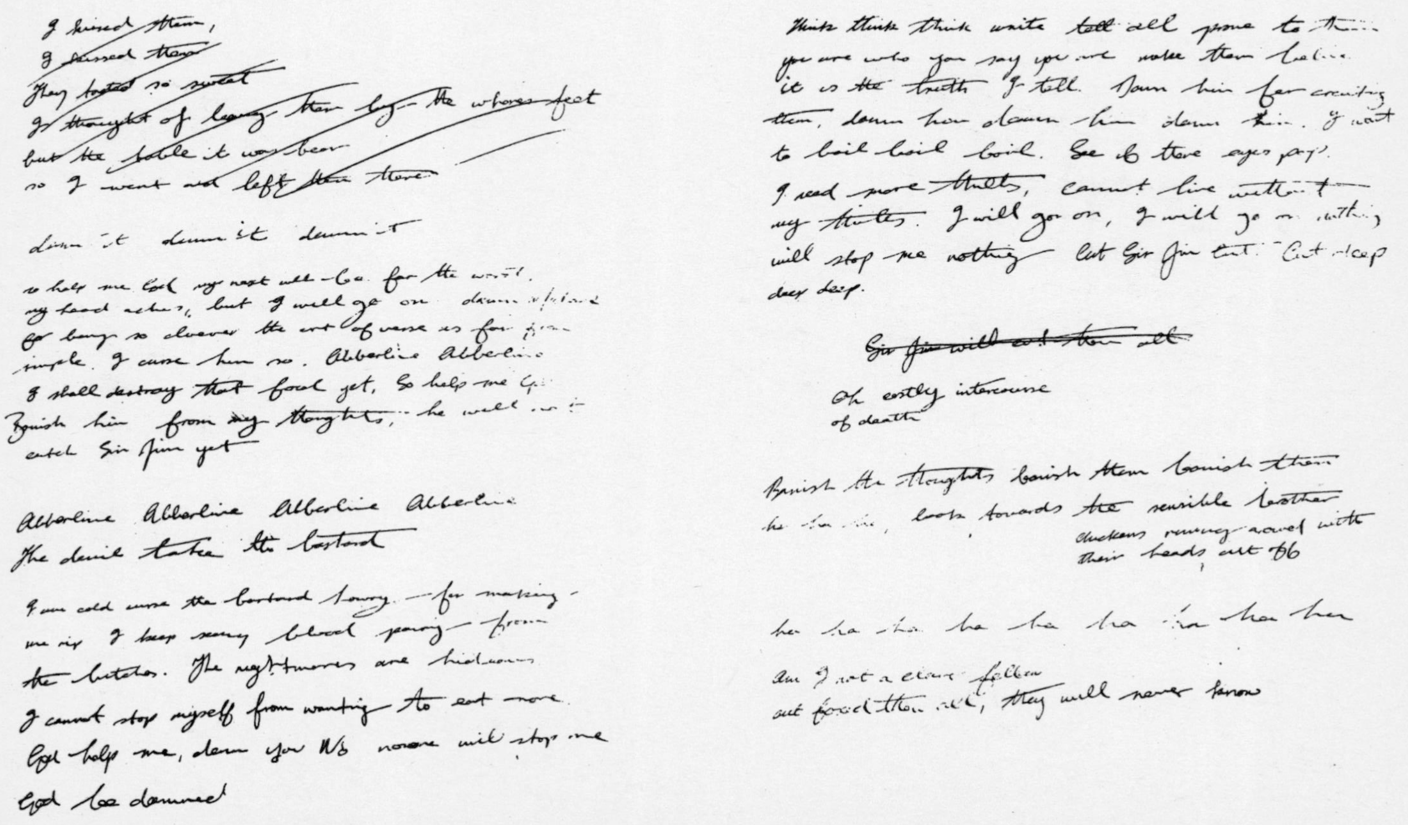

I kissed them,
~~I kissed them~~
~~They tasted so sweet~~
~~I thought of leaving them by the whores feet~~
~~but the table it was bear~~
~~so I went and left them there~~

damn it damn it damn it

so help me God my next will be far the worst.
my head aches, but I will go on damn Spring
for being so clever the art of verse is far from
simple. I curse him so. Abberline Abberline
I shall destroy that fool yet, So help me God
Banish him from ~~my~~ thoughts, he will not
catch Sir Jim yet

Abberline Abberline Abberline Abberline
The devil take the bastard

I am cold curse the bastard Lowry for making
me rip I keep seeing blood pouring from
the bitches. The nightmares are hideous
I cannot stop myself from wanting to eat more
God help me, damn you W/s no one will stop me
God be damned

Think think think write ~~tell~~ all prove to them
you are who you say you are make them believe
it is the ~~truth~~ I tell. Damn him for creating
them, damn him damn him damn him. I want
to boil boil boil. See if there eyes pop.
I need more ~~thrills~~, cannot live without
my ~~thrills~~. I will go on, I will go on, nothing
will stop me nothing let Sir Jim tell. Cut deep
deep deep.

~~Sir Jim will cut them all~~

Oh costly intercourse
of death

Banish the ~~thoughts~~ banish them banish them
he ha ha, look towards the sensible brother
chickens running around with
their heads cut off

ha ha ha ha ha ha ha ha ha

Am I not a clever fellow
out foxed them all, they will never know

~~Sir Jim will cut them all,~~
Sir Jim he does so ~~well~~

Sir Jim makes his call
he gets them all.
with his knife in his bag.

will have to take up lodgings on my return Middlesex Street that was a joke. The fools, several times they could have caught me if they had looked good and proper. My God am I not clever? Quickest I am. My head spins will save for have to find the strength for my journey home. The devil take this city it is too cold for me. Tomorrow I will make bunny suffer. The thought will ~~thrill~~ see on my journey home.

I cannot bring myself to look back, all I have written scares me so. George visited me today. I believe he knows what I am going through, although he says nothing I can see it in his eyes. Poor George, he is such a good friend. Michael is well, he writes a many time. In my heart I cannot blame him for doing so. I regret I shall not see him this Christmas.

Encountered an old friend on the Exchange floor. I felt regret for was he not Jewish. I had forgotten how many Jewish friends I have. My revenge is on whores not Jews I do believe I am truly sorry for the scare I have thrown amongst them. I believe that is the reason I am unable to write my funny little rhymes. I thank God I have had the courage to stop sending them. I am convinced they will be my undoing.

I am tired, very tired. I yearn for peace, but I know in my heart I will go on. I will be in Manchester within a few days. I believe I will feel a great deal better when I have repeated on my last performance I wonder if I can improve on my fiendish deeds. Will wait and see, no doubt I will think of something. The day is drawing to a close, however was in fine spirits. I am pleased. I regret, as with my Jewish friends I have shown my wrath. This coming Christmas I will make amends.

the bitch, the whore is not satisfied with one whore master, she now has eyes on another. I could not cut like my cat, visions of her flooded back as I struck. I tried to quell all thoughts of love. I left her for dead, that I know. It did not amuse me. There was thrill. I have showered my fury on the bitch. I struck and struck. I do not know how I stopped. I have left her penniless, I have no regrets. The whore will suffer unlike she has ever suffered. May God have mercy on her, for I shall not, so help me.

Thomas was in fine health. The children enjoyed Christmas. I did not. My mood is no longer black, although my head aches. I shall never become accustomed to the pain. I curse winter. I yearn for my favourite month, to see flowers in full bloom would please me so. Warmth is what I need, I shiver so. Curse this weather and the whoring bitch. My heart has been soft. All whores will feel the edge of Sir Jim's shining knife. I regret I did not give myself that name, curse it, I made it much much more than the one I have given.

Sir Jim with his shining knife,
cuts through the night,
and by God,
does he not show his might ha ha.

It shall not be long before I strike again. I am taking more than ever. The bitch can take two, Sir Jim shall take four, a double double event ha ha. If I was in the city of whores, I would do my fiendish deeds this very moment. By God I would.

I curse myself for the fool I have been, I shall have no more regrets, damn them all. Beware Mr Abberline I will return with a vengeance. Once more I will be the talk of England. What pleasure my thoughts do give me. I wonder if the whore will take the bastard? The bitch is welcome to him. I shall think about these deeds, what pleasure. Tonight I shall reward myself, I will visit mine, but I will not be gentle. I will show my whore what I am capable of. Sir Jim needs to wet his appetite, all whores be damned. A friend has turned, so be it, Sir Jim will turn once more. When I have finished my fiendish deeds, the devil himself will praise me but he will have a long wait before I shake hands with him. I have work to do a great deal of work to do. kidneys for supper

I am tired of keeping up this pretence of respectability. I am finding it increasingly difficult to do so. I believe I am a lucky fellow. Have I not found a new source for my medicine. I relish the thoughts that it will bring me I enjoy thinking of the whores waiting for my nice shiny knife. Tonight I write to Michael. Inform him I shall be visiting the city of whores soon. very soon. I cannot wait. The whore may take as many whore masters as she wishes. I no longer worry. I have my thoughts and pleasure of deeds to come, and oh what deeds I shall commit. Much much finer than my last. Life is indeed sweet, very very sweet.

Dear Mr Abberline,
I am a lucky man
Next time I will do all that I ~~[illegible]~~
~~[illegible]~~
~~[illegible]~~
with a little cut here,
and a little cut there
I will go laughing
away to my lair

Dear Mr Abberline,
I am a lucky man
Next time I will do
all that I can.
With a little cut here
and a little cut there
I will go laughing
away to my lair.

Damn it damn it damn it the bastard almost caught me, curse him to hell, I will cut him up next time, so help me. A few minutes and I would have done, bastard. I will seek him out, teach him a lesson. No one will stop me. Curse his black soul. I curse myself for striking too soon, I should have waited until it was truly quiet so help me I will take all next time and eat it. Will leave nothing not even the head. I will boil it and eat it with freshly picked carrots, I shall think about Abberline as I am doing so, that will give me a laugh ha ha the whore will suffer tonight for the deed she has done.

The bitch has written all,
tonight she will fall.

So help me God I will cut the bitch up and serve her up to the children. How dare the whore write to Michael. The damn bitch had no right to inform him of my medicine. If I have my funny little way the whore will be served up this very night. I stood my ground and informed Michael it was a damn lie.

The bitch visits the city of whores soon, I have decided I will wait until the time is ripe then I will strike with all my might. I shall buy the whore something for her visit. Will give the bitch the impression I consider it her duty to visit her aunt. She can nurse the sick bitch and see her whoring master ha ha.

Ha, what a joke, let the bitch believe I have no knowledge of her whoring affairs. When she returns the whore will pay. I relish the thoughts of striking the bitch once more. Am I not a clever fellow. I pride myself no one knows how clever I am. I do believe if George was to read this, he would say — I am the cleverest man alive. I yearn to tell him how clever I have been, but I shall not, my campaign is far from over yet. Sir Jim will give nothing away, nothing. How can they stop me now. Sir Jim may live for ever. I feel strong, very strong, strong enough to strike in this damn old city, believe I will!

why not, nobody does suspect the gentle
man born. will see how I will feel on my
journey home, if the whim takes me then
so be it. Will have to be careful not to
get too much of the red stuff on me.
Perhaps I will just cut the one, fool the fools,
oh what a joke, more chickens running around with
their heads cut off. ha ha. I feel clever.

This clever Sir Jim,
he loves his whims,
tonight he will call
and take away all. ha ha ha ha

Sir Jimmy
live
forever

ha ha ha ha ha

Am I not a clever fellow, the bitch gave me the greatest pleasure
of all. Did not the whore see her whore poster in front of all.
true the race was the finest I have seen, but ~~to think~~ of
seeing the whore with the bastard ~~thrilled~~ me more so than knowing
his Royal Highness was but a few feet away from yours truly ha ha
what a sight if the greedy bastard would have known he was less
than a few feet away from the name all England was talking about
he would have died there and then. Regret I could not ~~kill~~
the foolish fool. To hell with sovereignty, to hell with all whores.
to hell with the bitch who rules.

~~Victoria the bitch~~
~~Queen fool Sir Jack knows all~~
~~The queen she knows all~~

Victoria, Victoria
The queen of them all
When it comes to Sir Jack
She knows nothing at all

I

~~She knows one day~~

who knows,
perhaps one day,
I will give her a call

II

~~Shining knife~~
~~my life~~
~~honour my knife~~
Show her my knife
and she will honour me for life

III

~~Come Sir Jack she will say~~
Arise Sir Jack she will say,
and now you can go,
as you may ~~ha ha ha~~

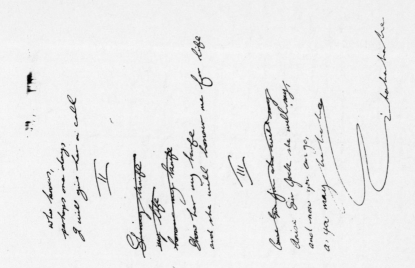

ha ha ha ha

Victoria, Victoria –
the queen of them all.
When it comes to Sir Jack
she knows nothing at all.

Who knows,
Perhaps one day;
I will give her a call

Show her my knife
and she will honour me for life.

Arise Sir Jack she will say
and now you can go
as you may

Jim, Jack Jack Jim ha ha ha

I was clever. George would be proud of me, told the bitch in my position I could not afford a scandal. I struck her several times an eye for an eye, he he too many interfering servants, damn the bitches. Hopper will soon feel the edge of my shiny knife, damn the meddling buffoon, damn all. Once more the bitch is in debt. my God I will cut her. Oh how I will cut her. I will visit the city of whores I will pay her dues and I shall ~~take~~ mine, by God I will. I will rip rip rip. May seek the Bastard out who stopped my funny little games and rip him to. I said he would pay I will make sure he damn will. I feel a numbness in my body, the tablets will pay for that. I wonder if Edwin is well. I long for him to return. I have decided ~~that~~ next time I will take the whores eyes out and send them to that fool Abberline.

Bastard

Bastard

take the eyes,
take the head,
leave them all for dead

It does not amuse me. Curse that bastard Abberline, curse him to hell I will not dangle from any rope of his. I have thought often about the whore and her whoring master The thoughts still thrill me Perhaps one day the bitch will allow me to participate. Why not? All have taken her. Have I no right to the whore. I wish to do so

The bitch
The bitch
The bitch

Fuller believes there is very little the matter with me. Strange, the thoughts he placed into my mind. I could not strike, I believe I am mad, completely mad. I try to fight my thoughts. I walk the streets until dawn. I could not find it in my heart to strike, visions of my dear Bunny overwhelm me. I still love her, but how I hate her. She has destroyed all and yet my heart aches for her, oh how it aches. I do not know which pain is the worse my body or my mind

My God I am tired, I do not know if I can go on. Bunny and the children are all that matter. No regrets, no regrets. I shall not allow such thoughts to enter my head. Tonight I will take my shining knife and be rid of it. Throw it deep within the river. I shall return to Battlecrease with the knowledge that I can no longer continue my campaign. 'Tis love that spurned me so, 'tis love that shall put an end to it.

I am afraid to look back on all I have written. Perhaps it would be wiser to destroy this, but in my heart I cannot bring myself to do so. I have tried once before, but like the coward I am, I could not. Perhaps in my tormented mind I wish for someone to read this and understand that the man I have become was not the man I was born.

My dear brother Edwin has returned. I wish I could tell him all. No more funny little rhymes. Tonight I write of love.

tis love that spurned me so,
tis love that does destroy
tis love that I yearn for
tis love that she spurned
tis love that will finish me
tis love that I regret.

May God help me. I pray each night he will take me, the disappointment when I awake is difficult to describe. I no longer take the dreaded stuff for fear I will harm my dear Bunny, worse still the children.

I do not have the courage to take my life. I pray each night I will find the strength to do so, but the courage alludes me. I pray constantly all will forgive. I deeply regret striking her, I have found it in my heart to forgive her for her lovers.

I believe I will tell her all, ask her to forgive me as I have forgiven her. I pray to God she will understand what she has done to me. Tonight I will pray for the women I have slaughtered. May God forgive me for the deeds I committed on Kelly, no heart no heart.

The pain is unbearable. My dear Bunny knows all. I do not know if she has the strength to kill me. I pray to God she finds it. It would be simple, she knows of my medicine, and for an extra dose or two it would be all over. No one will know I have seen to that. George knows of my habit and I trust soon it will come to the attention of Michael. In truth I believe he is aware of the fact. Michael will know how to act, he is the most sensible amongst us all. I do not believe I will see this June, my favourite of all months. Have begged Bunny to act soon. I curse myself for the coward I am. I have redressed the balance of my previous will. Bunny and the children are well cared for and I trust Michael and Thomas will carry out my wishes.

Soon, I trust I shall be laid beside my dear mother and father. I shall seek their forgiveness when we are reunited. God I pray will allow me at least that privilege, although I know only too well I do not deserve it. My thoughts will remain in tact, for a reminder to all how love does destroy. I place this now in a place were it shall be found. I pray whoever should read this will find it in their heart to forgive me. Remind all, whoever you may be, that I was once a gentle man. May the good Lord have mercy on my soul, and forgive me for all I have done.

I give my name that all know of me, so history do tell, what love can do to a gentle man born.

Yours truly

Jack the Ripper

Dated this third day of May 1889.

A Transcript of the Diary of Jack the Ripper

what they have in store for them they would stop this instant. But do I desire that? 358
my answer is no. They will suffer just as I. I will see to that. Received a letter from Michael perhaps I will visit him. Will have to come to some sort of decision regards the children. I long for peace of mind but I sincerely believe that that will not come until I have sought my revenge on the whore and the whore master.

Foolish bitch, I know for certain she has arranged a rondaveau with him in Whitechapel. So be it, my mind is firmly made. I took refreshment at the Poste House it was there I finally decided London it shall be. And why not, is it not an ideal location? Indeed do I not frequently visit the Capital and indeed do I not have legitimate reason for doing so. All who sell their dirty wares shall pay, of that I have no doubt. But shall I pay? I think not I am too clever for that.

As usual my hands are cold, my heart I do believe is colder still. My dearest Gladys is unwell yet again, she worries me so. I am convinced a dark shadow lays over the house, it is evil. I am becoming increasingly weary of people who constantly enquire regards the state of my health. True my head and arms pain me at times, but I am not duly worried, although I am quite certain Hopper believes to the contrary. I have him down as a bumbling buffoon. Thomas has requested that we meet as soon as possible. Business is flourishing so I have no inclination as regards the matter he describes as most urgent. Never the less I shall endeavour to meet his request.

Time is passing much too slowly, I still have to work up the courage to begin my campaign. I have thought long and hard over the matter and still I cannot come to a decision to when I should begin. Opportunity is there, of that fact I am certain. The bitch has no inclination.

The thought of him taking her is beginning to thrill me, perhaps I will allow her to continue, some of my thoughts are indeed beginning to give me pleasure. Yes I will visit Michael for a few weeks, and allow her to take all she can from the whoring master. Tonight I shall see mine. I may return to Battlecrease and take the unfaithfull bitch. Two in a night, indeed pleasure. My medicine is doing me good, in fact, I am sure I can take more than any other person alive. My mind is clear I will put whore through pain tonight.

--- 359

I am beginning to believe it is unwise to continue writing, If I am to down a whore then nothing shall lead the persuers back to me, and yet there are times when I feel an overwhelming compulsion to place my thoughts to paper. It is dangerous, that I know. If Smith should find this then I am done before my campaign begins. However, the pleasure of writing off all that lays ahead of me, and indeed the pleasure of thoughts of deeds that lay ahead of me, thrills me so. And oh what deeds I shall comit. For how could one suspect that I could be capable of such things, for am I not, as all believe, a mild man, who it has been said would never hurt a fly. Indeed only the other day did not Edwin say of me I was the most gentlest of men he had encountered. A compliment from my dear brother which I found exceedingly flattering.

Have decided my patience is wearing thin. The bitch has made a fool of me.

Tomorrow I travel to Manchester. Will take some of my medicine and think hard on the matter. I believe I could do so, though I shake with fear of capture. A fear I will have to overcome. I believe I have the strength. I will force myself not to think of the children. The whore, that is all that shall be in my mind. My head aches.

My dear God my mind is in a fog. The whore is now with her maker and he is welcome to her. There was no pleasure as I squeezed, I felt nothing. Do not know if I have the courage to go back to my original idea. Manchester was cold and damp very much like this hell hole. Next time I will throw acid over them. The thought of them ridling and screaming while the acid burns deep thrills me. ha, what a joke it would be if I could gorge an eye out and leave it by the whores body for all to see, to see, ha, ha.

360 I believe I have caught a chill. I cannot stop shaking, my body aches. There are times when I pray to God that the pain and torment will stop. Summer is near the warm weather will do me good. I long for peace but my work is only beginning. I will have a long wait for peace. All whores must suffer first and my God how I will make them suffer as she has made me. Edwin asked regards Thomas and business, I informed him that Thomas was well and business was flourishing, both true. I have it in my mind that I should write to Michael, perhaps not, my hands are far too cold, another day. I will take the bitch tonight. I need to take my mind off the night's events. The children are well.

Strolled by the drive, encountered Mrs Hamersmith, she enquired of Bobo and Gladys and much to my astonishment about my health. What has that whore said? Mrs Hammersmith is a bitch. The fresh air and stroll did me good. For a while I succeeded in forgetting the bitch and her whoring master. Felt completely refreshed when I returned to my office. I will visit Michael this coming June. June is such a pleasant month, the flowers are in full bud the air is sweeter and life is almost certainly much rosier I look forward to its coming with pleasure. A great deal of pleasure. I feel compelled to write to Michael if not obliged. My mind is clear, my hands are not cold.

---

361 I am vexed. I am trying to quell my anger. The whore has suggested she accompany me on my trip to Michael. I need time to put my mind in order. Under no circumstances can I let the bitch accompany me, all my hard work and plans will be destroyed if she were to do so. The pain was bad today. I believe the bitch has found one of my bottles, it had been moved. I am tired and need sleep the pain kept me awake for most of last night. Will return early avoid the bitch altogether.

Frequented my club. George stated that he had never seen me in better health. I believe the bitch has changed her mind. My thoughts are becoming increasingly more daring, I have imagined doing all manner of things. Could I eat part of one? Perhaps it would taste of fresh fried bacon ha ha. My dear God it thrills me so.

Michael is expecting me towards the end of June, henceforth from July mycampaign will gather momentum. I will take each and everyone before I return them to their maker, damaged of course, severely damaged.

I try to repel all thoughts of the children from my mind. I feel strong, stronger than I have ever felt. My thoughts keep returning to Manchester, next time it will thrill me. I know in my heart it will. I cannot understand why William will not accept my offer to dine. He is not unlike me, he hates the bitch. I believe if chance prevails I will burn St. James's to the ground. tomorrow I will make a substantial wager. I feel lucky.

If I could have killed the bastard Lowry with my bare hands there and then I would have done so. How dare he question me on any matter, it is I that should question him. Damn him damn him damn him should I replace the missing items? No that would be too much of a risk. Should I destroy this? My God I will kill him. Give him no reason to order him poste haste to drop the matter, that I believe is the only course of action I can take. I will force myself to think of something more pleasant. The whore will suffer more than she has ever done so tonight, that thought revitalizes me. June is drawing to a close I shake with anticipation.

I have taken too much my thoughts are not where they should be. I recall little of 362
the events of yesterday. Thank God I stopped myself in time. I will show my wrath towards the bastard in such a manner that he will wish he had never brought up the subject. No one, not even God himself will away the pleasure of writing my thoughts. I will take the first whore I encounter and show her what hell is really like. I think I will ram a cane into the whoring bitches mound and leave it there for them to see how much she could take. My head aches, God has no right to do this to me the devil take him.

How I succeeded in controlling myself I do not know. I have not allowed for the red stuff, gallons of it in my estimation. Some of it is bound to spill onto me. I cannot allow my clothes to be blood drenched, this I could not explain to anyone least of all Michael. Why did I not think of this before? I curse myself. The struggle to stop myself was overwhelming, and if I had not asked Michael to lock me in my bedroom for fear of sleepwalking, to which I had said I had been prone to do recently, was that not clever? I would have done my dirty deeds that very night.

I have taken a small room in Middlesex Street, that in itself is a joke. I have paid well and I believe no questions will be asked. It is indeed an ideal location. I have walked the streets and have become more than familiar with them. I said Whitechapel it will be and Whitechapel it shall. The bitch and her whoring master will rue the day I first saw them together. I said I am clever, very clever. Whitechapel Liverpool, Whitechapel London, ha ha. No one could possibly place it together. And indeed for there is no reason for anyone to do so.

The next time I travel to London I shall begin. I have no doubts, my confidence is most high. I am thrilled writing this, life is sweet, and my disappointment has vanished. Next time for sure. I have no doubts, not any longer,
no doubts. No one will ever suspect. Tomorrow I will purchase the finest knife 363
money can buy, nothing shall be too good for my whores, I will treat them to the finest, the very finest, they deserve that at least from I.

I have shown all that I mean business, the pleasure was far better than I imagined. The whore was only too willing to do her business. I recall all and it thrills me. There was no scream when I cut. I was more than vexed when the head would not come off. I believe I will need more strength next time. I struck deep into her. I regret I never had the cane, it would have been a delight to have rammed it hard into her. The bitch opened like a ripe peach. I have decided next time I will rip all out. My medicine will give me strength and the thought of the whore and her whoring master will spur me on no end.

The wait to read about my triumph seemed long, although it was not. I am not disappointed, they have all written well. The next time they will have a great deal more to write, of that fact I have no doubt ha ha. I will remain calm and show no interest in my deed, if anyone should mention it so, but I will laugh inside, oh how I will laugh.

I will not allow too much time to pass before my next. Indeed I need to repeat my pleasure as soon as possible. The whoring Master can have her with pleasure and I shall have my pleasure with my thoughts and deeds. I will be clever. I will not call on Michael on my next visit. My brothers would be horrified if they knew, particularly Edwin after all did he not say I was one of the most gentlest of men he had ever encountered. I hope he is enjoying the fruits of America. Unlike I, for do I not have a sour fruit.

---

364 I could not resist mentioning my deed to George. I was clever and brought up the subject by way of how fortunate we were not having murders of that kind in this city. He agreed with me completely. Indeed he went on to say, that he believed we had the finest police force in the land, and although we have our fair share of troubles the women folk can walk the streets in safety. And indeed they can for I will not play my funny little games on my own doorstep ha ha.

The gentle man with gentle thoughts will strike again soon. I have never felt better, in fact, I am taking more than ever and I can feel the strength building up within me. The head will come off next time, also the whores hands. Shall I leave them in various places around Whitechapel? Hunt the head and hands instead of the thimble ha ha. Maybe I will take some part away with me to see if it does taste of like fresh fried bacon. The whore seen her master today it did not bother me. I imagined I was with them, the very thought thrills me. I wonder if the whore has ever had such thoughts? I believe she has, has she not cried out when I demand she takes another. The bitch. She will suffer but not as yet. Tomorrow I travel to London. I have decided I cannot wait any longer. I look forward to tomorrow nights work, it will do me good, a great deal of good.

One dirty whore was looking for some gain
Another dirty whore was looking for the same.

---

365 Am I not clever? I thought of my funny little rhyme on my travel to the City of Whores. I was vexed with myself when I realised I had forgotten the chalk. So vexed in fact that I returned to the bitch and cut out more. I took some of it away with me. It is in front of me. I intend to fry it and eat it later ha ha. The very thought works up my appetite. I cannot stop the thrill of writing. I ripped open my God I will have to stop thinking of the children they distract me so I ripped open

---

It has taken me three days to recover. I will not feel guilty it is the whoring bitch to blame not I. I ate all off it, it did not taste like fresh fried bacon but I enjoyed it never the less. She was so sweet and pleasurable. I have left the stupid fools a clue which I am sure they will not solve. Once again I have been clever, very clever.

~~A ring or two will leave this clue~~
~~One pill thats true~~
~~M will catch Sir Jim with no pills~~
~~left two~~

two farthings,
two pills
the whores M
rings

Think

It shall come, if Michael can succeed in rhyming verse then I can do better, a great 366
deal better he shall not outdo me. Think you fool, think. I curse Michael for being so clever, I shall outdo him, I will see to that. A funny little rhyme shall come forth. Patience is needed patience. The night is long, time is on my hands.

The pills are the answer
end with pills. Indeed do I always not oh what a joke.
Begin with the rings,
one ring, two rings
bitch, it took me a while before I could wrench them off. Should have stuffed them down the whores throat. I wish to God I could have taken the head. Hated her for wearing them, reminds me too much of the whore. Next time I will select a whore who has none. The bitch was not worth the farthings. Return, return, essential to return. Prove you are no fool.

One ring, two rings,
A farthing one and two
~~Sir Jim will do true~~
~~Letter M its true~~
Along with M ha ha
Will catch clever Jim,
Its true
~~Left two~~
No pill, left but two

One ring, two rings,
a farthing, one and two,
Along with M ha ha
Will catch clever Jim
its true.
No pill, left but two

Am I not indeed a clever fellow? It makes me laugh they will never understand why 367
I did so. Next time I will remember the chalk and write my funny little rhyme. The eyes will come out of the next. I will stuff them in the whores mouth. That will certainly give me pleasure, it does so as I write. Tonight I will see mine, she will be

pleased as I will be gentle with her as indeed I always am.

I am still thinking of burning St. James's to the ground. I may do so on my next visit. That will give the fools something more to think on. I am beginning to think less of the children, part of me hates me for doing so. One day God will answer to me, so help me. Michael would be proud of my funny little rhyme for he knows only too well the art of verse. Have I not proven I can write better than he. Feel like Celebrating, the night has been long and I shall award myself with the pleasures of the flesh, but I shall not be cutting ha ha. I will save that thrill for another day.

The whore is in debt. Very well I shall honour the bitches notes but the whores are going to pay more than ever. I have read all of my deeds they have done me proud, I had to laugh, they have me down as left handed, a Doctor, a slaughterman and a Jew. Very well, if they are to insist that I am a Jew then a Jew I shall be. Why not let the Jews suffer? I have never taken to them, far too many of them on the Exchange for my liking. I could not stop laughing when I read Punch there for all to see was the first three letters of my surname. They are blind as they say.

'Turn round three times, And catch whom you
MAY'
ha ha ha ha ha ha

I cannot stop laughing it amuses me so shall I write them a clue?

May comes and goes,
~~this May pleases with a knife in his hand~~
In the dark of the night
~~He does please~~
When he comes and goes
368 With a ring on my finger
and a knife in my hand
~~This May comes and goes~~

May comes and goes
In the dark of the night
~~he does please the whores he kisses~~
~~and gives them a fright~~
he kisses the whores
then gives them a fright

May comes and goes
in the dark of the night
he kisses the whores
then gives them a fright
With a ring on my finger
and a knife in my hand
This May spreads Mayhem
~~all through the land~~
throughout this fair land.

~~The Jews and slaughtermen~~

~~The Jews and Doctors~~
The Doctors and jews
~~my~~
will get all the blame – blame – tame
same – game
his dirty game
May playing
~~The Doctors~~
The Jews and the Doctors
Will get all the blame
but its only May
playing his dirty game

~~He will not shed a tear~~
He will kill all the whores
and not shed a tear
~~He will give them a clue~~
I will give them a clue
but nothing too clear
I will kill all the whores
and not shed a tear. 369
May comes and goes
in the dark of the night
He kisses the whores
and gives them a fright

The Jews and the Doctors
will get all the blame
but its only May playing
his dirty game

I will give them a clue
but nothing too clear
I will kill all the whores
and not shed a tear

With a ring on my finger
and a knife in my hand
This May spreads Mayhem
throughout this fair land.

They remind me of chickens with their heads cut off running fools with no heads, ha ha. It is nice to laugh at bastards and fools and indeed they are fools. I need much more pleasure than I have had. Strange my hands feel colder than they have ever done so.

I am fighting a battle within me. My disire for revenge is overwhelming. The whore has destroyed my life. I try whenever possible to keep all sense of respectability. I worry so over Bobo and Gladys, no others matter. Tonight I will take more than ever. I miss the thrill of cutting them up. I do believe I have lost my mind. All the bitches will pay for the pain. Before I am finished all of England will know the name I have given myself. It is indeed a name to remember. It shall be, before long, on every persons lips within the land. Perhaps her gracious Majesty will become acquainted with it. I wonder if she will honour me with a knighthood ha ha.

Abberline says, he was never amazed,
I did my work with such honour.
For his decree
370 he had to agree,
I deserve at least an honour
so all for a whim,

I can now rise Sir Jim – I cannot think of another word to accompany Jim. I like my words to rhyme damn it. It is late, mine is waiting, I will enjoy this evening. I will be gentle and not give anything away.

I miss Edwin. I have received but one letter from him since his arrival in the whores country. The bitch is vexing me more as each day passes. If I could I would have it over and done with. I visited my mother and fathers grave. I long to be reunited with them. I believe they know the torture the whore is putting me through. I enjoy the thrill of thinking of all I have done. But there has been, but once, regret for my deeds. I dispelled my remorse instantly. The whore still believes I have no knowledge of her whoring master. I have considered killing him, but if I was to do so I would surely be caught. I have no desire for that, curse him and the whore their time will come.

To my astonishment I cannot believe I have not been caught. My heart felt as if it had left my body. Within my fright I imagined my heart bounding along the street with I in desperation following it. I would have dearly loved to have cut the head of the damned horse off and stuff it as far as it would go down the whores throat. I had no time to rip the bitch wide, I curse my bad luck. I believe the thrill of being caught thrilled me more than cutting the whore herself. As I write I find it impossible to believe he did not see me, in my estimation I was less than a few feet from him. The fool panicked, it is what saved me. My satisfaction was far from complete, damn the bastard, I cursed him and cursed him, but I was clever, they could not out do me. No one ever will. Within the quarter of the hour I found another dirty bitch willing to sell her wares. The whore like all the rest was only too willing. The thrill she gave me was unlike the others, I cut deep deep deep. Her nose annoyed me so I cut it off, had a go at her eyes, left my mark, could not get the bitches head off. I believe now it is impossible to do so. The whore never screamed. I took all I could away with me. I am saving it for a rainy day ha ha.
371 Perhaps I will send Abberline and Warren a sample or two, it goes down well with an after dinner port. I wonder how long it will keep? Perhaps next time I will keep some of the red stuff and send it courtesy of yours truly. I wonder if they enjoyed my funny Jewish joke? Curse my bad luck had no time to write a funny little rhyme. Before my next will send Central another to remember me by. My God life is sweet. Will give them something to know it is me.

Red – head
horse,
cryed
smelt breath

~~A rose matched the red~~
~~I did cut the head~~

~~damn it I cried, hence forth I did hide,~~
~~The horse went and shied~~

With a rose to match the red
I tried to cut off the head
Damn it I cried,
The horse went and shied
But I could still smell her sweet scented breath

I

Sir Jim,
tin match box empty
~~cigarette case~~
~~make haste~~
~~my shiny knife~~
~~the whores knife~~
first whore no good

One whore no good,
decided Sir Jim strike another.
I showed no fright and indeed no light,
damn it, the tin box was empty

II

tea and sugar 372
~~away, pay, did say~~
me, plea, be
~~tea and sugar paid my fee~~
Sweet sugar and tea, could have paid my small
fee ha ha
~~then I did flee~~
Showed my glee
A kidney for supper

Sweet sugar and tea,
could have paid my small fee.
But instead I did flee
and by way showed my glee
By eating cold kidney for supper

III

bastard
Abberline
bonnett
hides all
clue
clever
will tell you more

~~Mr Abberline is a funny little man~~

Oh Mr Abberline, he is a clever little man

he keeps back all that he can.
~~But I know better~~
For do I know better, indeed I do
did I not leave him a very good clue
Nothing is mentioned, of this I know sure
ask clever Abberline, ~~he does know more~~

Oh Mr Abberline, he is a clever little man
he keeps back all that he can.
For do I not know better, Indeed I do
did I not leave him a very good clue.
Nothing is mentioned, of this I am sure,
ask clever Abberline, could tell you more

IV

Sir Jim trip over
fear
have it near
redeem it near
case
poste haste

373 He believes I will trip over
but I have no fear
~~I cannot redeem it here~~
For I could not possibly redeem it here
of this certain fact, I could send him poste haste
if he requests that be the case.

Am I not a clever fellow

That should give the fools a laugh, it has done so for me, wonder if they have enjoyed the name I have given? I said it would be on the lips of all, and indeed it is. Believe I will send another. Include my funny little rhyme. That will convince them that it is the truth I tell. Tonight I will celebrate by wining and dining George. I am in a good mood, believe I will allow the whore the pleasure of her whore master, will remark an evening in the city will do her good, will suggest a concert. I have no doubt the carriage will take the bitch straight to him. ~~I will go~~—— I will go to sleep thinking about all they are doing. I cannot wait for the thrill.

With a rose to match the red
I tried to cut off the head.
Damn it I cried,
the horse went and shied
hence forth I did hide,
but I could still smell
her sweet scented breath

One whore no good, decided Sir Jim strike another.
I showed no fright, and indeed no light.
Damn it, the tin box was empty

Sweet sugar and tea
could have paid my small fee
But instead I did flee and by way showed my glee
by eating cold kidney for supper

Oh, Mr Abberline he is a clever little man,
he keeps back all that he can.
For do I not know better, Indeed I do,
did I not leave him a very good clue
Nothing is mentioned of this I know sure,
ask clever Abberline, could tell you more

He believes I will trip over, 374
but I have no fear.
For I could not possibly
redeem it here.
Of this certain fact I could send them poste haste
If he requested that be the case

It has been far too long since my last, I have been unwell. The whole of my body has pained. Hopper did not believe me. One day I will take revenge on him. The whore has informed the bumbling buffoon. I am in the habit of taking strong medicine. I was furious when the bitch told me. So furious I hit her ha. The whore begged me not to do so again. It was a pleasure, a great deal of pleasure. If it was not for my work, I would have cut the bitch up there and then. But I am clever. Although the gentle man has turned, I did not show my hand true. I apologised, a one off instance, I said, which I regretted and I assured the whore it would never happen again. The stupid bitch believed me.

I have received several letters from Michael. In all he enquires about my health and asked in one if my sleepwalking has resumed. Poor Michael he is so easily fooled. I have informed him it has not. My hands still remain cold. I shall be dining tonight. I hope kidneys are on the menu, ha ha. Will put me in the mood for another little escapade. Will visit the city of whores soon, very soon. I wonder if I could do three?

If it were not for Michael insisting that we take dinner I would have tried my hand that very night. I cursed my brother as I have never cursed him before. I cursed my own stupidity, had I not informed Michael that I no longer sleepwalked I was forced to stop myself from indulging in my pleasure by taking the largest dose I have ever done. The pain that night has burnt into my mind. I vaguly recall putting a handkerchief in my mouth to stop my cries. I believe I vomited several times. The pain was intolerable, as I think I shudder. No more.

I am convinced God placed me here to kill all whores, for he must have done so, am I still not here. Nothing will stop me now. The more I take the stronger I become.

Michael was under the impression that once I had finished my business I was to return to Liverpool that very day. And indeed I did one day later ha ha. I fear not, for the fact will not come to his attention as he addresses all letters to me. 375

I have read about my latest, my God the thoughts, the very best. I left nothing of the bitch, nothing. I placed it all over the room, time was on my hands, like the other whore I cut off the bitches nose, all of it this time. I left nothing of her face to remember her by. She reminded me of the whore. So young unlike I. I thought it a joke when I cut her breasts off, kissed them for a while. The taste of blood was sweet, the pleasure was overwhelming, will have to do it again, it thrilled me so. Left them on the table with some of the other stuff. Thought they belonged there. They wanted a slaughterman so I stripped what I could, laughed while I was doing so. Like the other bitches she riped like a ripe peach. One of these days I will take the head away with me. I will boil it and serve it up for my supper. The key and burnt clothes puzzle them ha ha..

key	rip
flee	initial
hat	
handkerchief	whore master
whim	look to the whore
Mother	light
father	fire

~~With the key I did flee~~
I had the key,
and with it I did flee
~~the clothes I burnt~~
~~along with the hat~~
The hat I did burn
for light I did yearn.
~~For the sake of the whoring mother~~
And I thought of the whoring mother

I had the key,
And with it I did flee
The hat I did burn
for light I did yearn
And I thought of the
whoring mother

I
376 A handkerchief red,
led to the bed
and I thought of the whoring mother

II
~~For Sir Jim with his whim~~
A whores whim,
Caused Sir Jim
to cut deeper, deeper and deeper.
~~away with it I did go~~
~~back to the whoring mother~~
All did go
As I did so
back to the whoring mother

A whores whim,

caused Sir Jim
to cut deeper deeper and deeper.
All did go,
As I did so
back to the whoring mother.

III
~~Her initial there~~
An initial here and a initial there
would tell of the whoring mother

I had a key,
and with it I did flee.
The hat I did burn,
for light I did yearn.
And I thought of the whoring mother
A handkerchief red,
led to the bed
And I thought of the whoring mother.

A whores whim
caused Sir Jim,
to cut deeper, deeper and deeper
All did go,
As I did so,
back to the whoring mother.
An initial here and an initial there 377
will tell of the whoring mother.

I left it there for the fools but they will never find it. I was too clever. Left it in front for all eyes to see. Shall I write and tell them? That amuses me. I wonder if next time I can carve my funny little rhyme on the whores flesh? I believe I will give it a try. It amuses me if nothing else. Life is sweet, very sweet. Regret I did not take any of it away with me it is supper time, I could do with a kidney or two ha ha.

I cannot live without my medicine. I am afraid to go to sleep for fear of my nightmares reoccuring. I see thousands of people chasing me, with Abberline in front dangling a rope. I will not be topped of that fact I am certain. It has been far too long since my last, I still desire revenge on the whore and the whore master but less than the desire to repeat my last performance. The thoughts still thrill me so. I am tired and I fear the city of whores has become too dangerous for I to return. Christmas is approaching and Thomas has invited me to visit him. I know him well. I have decided to accept his offer, although I know the motive behind it will strictly be business. Thomas thinks of nothing else except money unlike me, ha ha.

My first was in Manchester so why not my next? If I was to do the same as the last, that would throw the fools into a panick, especially that fool Abberline. The children constantly ask what I shall be buying them for Christmas they shy away when I tell them a shiny knife not unlike Jack the Rippers in order that I cut their tongues for peace and quiet. I do believe I am completely mad. I have never harmed the children in the years since they have been born. But now I take great

delight in scaring them so. May God forgive me. I have lost my battle and shall go on until I am caught. Perhaps I should top myself and save the hangman a job. At this moment I have no feeling in my body, none at all. I keep assuring myself I have
378 done no wrong. It is the whore who has done so, not I. Will peace of mind ever come? I have visited Hopper too often this month. I will have to stop, for I fear he may begin to suspect. I talk to him like no other.

~~Sir Jim shall,~~
Am I insane?
Cane, gain
~~Sir Jim with his fancy cane~~
~~Will soon strike again~~

~~One whore in heaven,~~
~~two whores side by side,~~
~~three whores all have died~~
~~four~~

~~Sir Jim he cuts them first~~
damn it

~~Abberline says he is now amazed,~~
~~Sir Jim has not struck another~~
~~He waits patiently~~
~~to see hastily~~

~~Christmas save the whores mole bonnett~~
~~damn the bitches damn Michael~~
~~Give Sir Jim his due~~
~~He detests all the Jews~~
~~For he has no favourite men~~
~~As he runs away to his den.~~

~~He likes to write with his pen~~

~~Give Sir Jim his dues~~
~~He detests all the Jews~~
~~and indeed was it not in t e~~

379 ~~I kissed them,~~
~~I kissed them~~
~~They tasted so sweet~~
~~I thought of leaving them by the whores feet~~
~~but the table it was bear~~
~~so I went and left them there~~

damn it damn it damn it

so help me God my next will be far the worst, my head aches, but I will go on damn Michael for being so clever the art of verse is far from simple. I curse him so. Abberline Abberline, I shall destroy that fool yet, So help me God. Banish him from my thoughts, he will not catch Sir Jim yet

Abberline Abberline Abberline Abberline
The devil take the bastard

I am cold curse the bastard Lowry for making me rip. I keep seeing blood pouring from the bitches. The nightmares are hideous. I cannot stop myself from wanting to eat more. God help me, damn you. No no-one will stop me. God be damned. Think think think write tell all prove to them you are who you say you are make them believe it is the truth I tell. Damn him for creating them, damn him damn him damn him. I want to boil boil boil. See if there eyes pop. I need more thrills, cannot live without my thrills. I will go on, I will go on, nothing will stop me nothing. Cut Sir Jim cut. Cut deep deep deep.

~~Sir Jim will cut them all~~
Oh costly intercourse
of death

Banish the thoughts banish them banish them ha ha ha,
look towards the sensible brother
Chickens running round with their heads cut off

ha ha ha ha ha ha ha ha ha
Am I not a clever fellow
out foxed them all, they will never know

~~Sir Jim will cut them all~~ 380
~~Sir Jim he does so walk tall~~

~~Sir Jim makes his call~~
~~he cuts them all,~~
~~with his knife in his bag~~

will have to take up lodgings on my return. Middlesex Street that was a joke. The fools, several times they could have caught me if they had looked good and proper. My God am I not clever? Indeed I am. My head spins will somehow have to find the strength for my journey home. The devil take this city, it is too cold for me. Tomorrow I will make Lowry suffer. The thought will thrill me on my journey home.

I cannot bring myself to look back, all I have written scares me so. George visited me today. I believe he knows what I am going through, although he says nothing. I can see it in his eyes. Poor George, he is such a good friend. Michael is well, he writes a merry tune. In my heart I cannot blame him for doing so. I regret I shall not see him this Christmas.

Encountered an old friend on the Exchange floor. I felt regret for was he not Jewish. I had forgotten how many Jewish friends I have. My revenge is on whores not Jews. I do believe I am truly sorry for the scare I have thrown amongst them. I believe that is the reason I am unable to write my funny little rhymes. I thank God I have had the courage to stop sending them. I am convinced they will be my undoing.

I am tired, very tired. I yearn for peace, but I know in my heart I will go on. I will be in Manchester within a few days. I believe I will feel a great deal better when I have repeated on my last performance. I wonder if I can improve on my fiendish deeds. Will wait and see, no doubt I will think of something. The day is drawing to a close, Lowry was in fine spirits. I am pleased. I regret, as with my Jewish friends I have shown my wrath. This coming Christmas I will make amends.

---

381 The bitch, the whore is not satisfied with one whore master, she now has eyes on another. I could not cut like my last, visions of her flooded back as I struck. I tried to quosh all thoughts of love. I left her for dead, that I know. It did not amuse me. There was thrill. I have showered my fury on the bitch. I struck and struck. I do not know how I stopped. I have left her penniless, I have no regrets. The whore will suffer unlike she has ever suffered. May God have mercy on her for I shall not, so help me.

Thomas was in fine health. The children enjoyed Christmas. I did not. My mood is no longer black, although my head aches. I shall never become accustomed to the pain. I curse winter. I yearn for my favourite month, to see flowers in full bloom would please me so. Warmth is what I need, I shiver so. Curse this weather and the whoring bitch. My heart has been soft. All whores will feel the edge of Sir Jims shining knife. I regret I did not give myself that name, curse it, I prefer it much much more than the one I have given.

Sir Jim with his shining knife,
cuts through the night,
and by God,
does he not show his might ha ha

It shall not be long before I strike again. I am taking more than ever. The bitch can take two, Sir Jim shall take four, a double double event ha ha. If I was in the city of whores I would do my fiendish deeds this very moment. By God I would.

I curse myself for the fool I have been, I shall have no more regrets, damn them all. Beware Mr Abberline I will return with a vengeance. Once more I will be the talk of England. What pleasure my thoughts do give me. I wonder if the whore will take the bastard? The bitch is welcome to him. I shall think about their deeds, what pleasure. Tonight I shall reward myself, I will visit mine, but I will not be gentle. I will show my whore what I am capable of. Sir Jim needs to wet his appetite, all
382 whore be damned. A friend has turned, so be it, Sir Jim will turn once more. When I have finished my fiendish deeds, the devil himself will praise me. But he will have a long wait before I shake hands with him. I have works to do a great deal of works ha ha. kidney for supper.

I am tired of keeping up this pretence of respectability. I am finding it increasingly difficult to do so. I believe I am a lucky fellow. Have I not found a new source for my medicine. I relish the thoughts that it will bring me. I enjoy thinking of the whores waiting for my nice shining knife. Tonight I write to Michael. Inform him I shall be visiting the city of whores soon, very soon. I cannot wait. The whore may take as many whore masters as she wishes. I no longer worry. I have my thoughts and pleasure of deeds to come, and oh what deeds I shall commit. Much, much finer than my last. Life is indeed sweet, very very sweet.

Dear Mr. Abberline

I am a lucky man
Next time I will do all that I can
~~ram, can, fan, damn~~
~~cut and thrust~~
with a little cut here,
and a little cut there
I will go laughing
away to my lair

Dear Mr. Abberline,
I am a lucky man
Next time I will do
all that I can.
With a little cut here
and a little cut there
I will go laughing
away to my lair

Damn it damn it damn it the bastard almost caught me, curse him to hell, I will cut 383
him up next time, so help me. A few minutes and I would have done, bastard. I will seek him out, teach him a lesson. No one will stop me. Curse his black soul. I curse myself for striking too soon, I should have waited until it was truly quiet so help me I will take all next time and eat it. Will leave nothing not even the head. I will boil it and eat it with freshly picked carrots. I shall think about Abberline as I am doing so, that will give me a laugh ha ha the whore will suffer tonight for the deed she has done.

The bitch has written all,
tonight she will fall.

So help me God I will cut the bitch up and serve her up to the children. How dare the whore write to Michael. the damn bitch had no right to inform him of my medicine. If I have my funny little way the whore will be served up this very night. I stood my ground and informed Michael it was a damn lie.

The bitch visits the city of whores soon, I have decided I will wait until the time is ripe then I will strike with all my might. I shall buy the whore something for her visit. Will give the bitch the impression I consider it her duty to visit her aunt. She can nurse the sick bitch and see her whoring master ha ha.

Ha, what a joke, let the bitch believe I have no knowledge of her whoring affairs. When she returns the whore will pay. I relish the thoughts of striking the bitch once more. Am I not a clever fellow. I pride myself no one knows how clever I am. I do believe if George was to read this, he would say I am the cleverest man alive. I yearn to tell him how clever I have been, but I shall not, my campaign is far from over yet. Sir Jim will give nothing away, nothing. How can they stop me now this Sir Jim may live for ever. I feel strong, very strong, strong enough to strike in this
damn cold city, believe I will. Why not, nobody does suspect the gentle man born. 384
Will see how I will feel on my journey home, if the whim takes me then so be it. Will have to be careful not to get too much of the red stuff on me. Perhaps I will just cut the once, fool the fools, oh what a joke, more chickens running around with their heads cut off, ha ha I feel clever.

Sir Jimay
live
forever
ha ha ha ha ha

This clever Sir Jim,
he loves his whims
tonight he will call
and take away all. ha ha ha ha

---

385 Am I not a clever fellow, the bitch gave me the greatest pleasure of all. Did not the whore see her whore master in front of all, true the race was the fastest I have seen, but the thrill of seeing the whore with the bastard thrilled me more so than knowing his Royal Highness was but a few feet away from yours truly ha ha what a laugh, if the greedy bastard would have known he was less than a few feet away from the name all England was talking about he would have died there and then. Regret I could not tell the foolish fool. To hell with sovereignity, to hell with all whores, to hell with the bitch who rules.

~~Victoria the bitch~~
~~Queen fool Sir Jack knows all~~
~~The queen she knows all~~

Victoria, Victoria
The queen of them all
When it comes to Sir Jack
She knows nothing at all

I
~~She knows one day~~
who knows,
perhaps one day
I will give her a call

II
~~Shining knife~~
~~my life~~
~~honour my knife~~
Show her my knife
and she will honour me for life

III
~~Come Sir Jim she will say~~
Arise Sir Jack she will say,
and now you can go,
as you may ha ha ha
ha ha ha ha

386 Victoria, Victoria
the queen of them all
when it comes to Sir Jack
she knows nothing at all

who knows,
Perhaps one day,
I will give her a call

Show her my knife
and she will honour me for life

Arise Sir Jack she will say
and now you can go
as you may

Jim, Jack Jack Jim ha ha ha

I was clever. George would be proud of me, told the bitch in my position I could not afford a scandal. I struck her several times an eye for an eye, ha ha too many interfering servants, damn the bitches. Hopper will soon feel the edge of my shining knife, damn the meddling bufoon, damn all. Once more the bitch is in debt, my God I will cut her. Oh how I will cut her. I will visit the city of whores I will pay her dues and I shall take mine, by God I will. I will rip rip rip May seek the bastard out who stopped my funny little games and rip him to. I said he would pay. I will make sure he damn will. I feel a numbness in my body, the whores will pay for that. I wonder if Edwin is well? I long for him to return. I have decided that next time I will take the whores eyes out and send them to that fool Abberline.

bastard
bastard

take the eyes, 386
take the head,
leave them all for dead

It does not amuse me. Curse that bastard Abberline, curse him to hell I will not dangle from any rope of his. I have thought often about the whore and her whoring master. The thoughts still thrill me. Perhaps one day the bitch will allow me to participate. Why not? All have taken her. Have I no right to the whore. I wish to do so.

The bitch
the bitch
the bitch

Fuller believes there is very little the matter with me. Strange, the thoughts he placed into my mind. I could not strike, I believe I am mad, completely mad. I try to fight my thoughts I walk the streets until dawn. I could not find it in my heart to strike, visions of my dear Bunny overwhelm me. I still love her, but how I hate her. She has destroyed all and yet my heart aches for her, oh how it aches. I do not know which pain is the worse my body or my mind.

My God I am tired, I do not know if I can go on. Bunny and the children are all that matter. No regrets, no regrets. I shall not allow such thoughts to enter my head. Tonight I will take my shinning knife and be rid of it. Throw it deep within the river. I shall return to Battlecrease with the knowledge that I can no longer continue my campaign. 'Tis love that spurned me so, 'tis love that shall put an end to it.

388 I am afraid to look back on all I have written. Perhaps it would be wiser to destroy this, but in my heart I cannot bring myself to do so. I have tried once before, but like the coward I am, I could not. Perhaps in my tormented mind I wish for someone to read this and understand that the man I have become was not the man I was born.

My dear brother Edwin has returned. I wish I could tell him all. No more funny little rhymes. Tonight I write of love.

> tis love that spurned me so,
> tis love that does destroy
> tis love that I yearn for
> tis love that she spurned
> tis love that will finish me
> tis love that I regret

May God help me. I pray each night he will take me, the disappointment when I awake is difficult to describe I no longer take the dreaded stuff for fear I will harm my dear Bunny, worse still the children.

I do not have the courage to take my life. I pray each night I will find the strength to do so, but the courage alludes me. I pray constantly all will forgive. I deeply regret striking her, I have found it in my heart to forgive her for her lovers.

I believe I will tell her all, ask her to forgive me as I have forgiven her. I pray to God she will understand what she has done to me. Tonight I will pray for the women I have slaughtered. May God forgive me for the deeds I commited on Kelly, no heart no heart.

---

389 The pain is unbearable. My dear Bunny knows all. I do not know if she has the strength to kill me. I pray to God she finds it. It would be simple, she knows of my medicine, and for an extra dose or two it would be all over. No one will know I have seen to that. George knows of my habit and I trust soon it will come to the attention of Michael. In truth I believe he is aware of the fact. Michael will know how to act he is the most sensible amongst us all I do not believe I will see this June, my favourite of all months. Have begged Bunny to act soon. I curse myself for the coward I am. I have redressed the balance of my previous will. Bunny and the children are well cared for and I trust Michael and Thomas will carry out my wishes.

Soon, I trust I shall be laid beside my dear mother and father. I shall seek their forgiveness when we are reunited. God I pray will allow me at least that privilege, although I know only too well I do not deserve it. My thoughts will remain in tact, for a reminder to all how love does destroy. I place this now in a place were it shall be found. I pray whoever should read this will find it in their heart to forgive me. Remind all, whoever you may be, that I was once a gentle man. May the good lord have mercy on my soul, and forgive me for all I have done.

I give my name that all know of me, so history do tell, what love can do to a gentle man born.

Yours truly
Jack the Ripper
Dated this third day of May 1889

Postscript

By David Canter,
Professor of Psychology,
Centre for Investigative Psychology,
University of Liverpool

In 1927 a little known Russian psychologist gave her name to a fascinating phenomenon: the Zeigarnick effect. Bluma Zeigarnick carried out some psychological experiments on human memory and found that those tasks that were stopped before completion were remembered more readily and in more detail than those that were brought to a natural end. Over the subsequent seventy years her discovery has been applied to many areas of human experience. The power of wanting to complete a puzzle or solve a conundrum remains a gnawing motivator across many domains. Without a sense of closure, as it is often called, people still feel the stress of the original challenge.

The Zeigarnick effect is the best explanation I have come upon for why the murders of Jack the Ripper, and the search for the identity of their perpetrator, still holds people in its grip well over a century after the last victim was laid to rest. There have, sadly, been many more vicious and more numerous serial murders since then, but none seems to hold the public interest in the same way. Bookshops devote whole shelves of books to this one set of crimes. Online bookstores list around 200 books currently available on the topic.

The power of the psychological drive to scratch this scab has many significant consequences but one is the constant search for new ways of getting at it – as if the itch were between the shoulder blades, and any corner or device will be used to get access to it and gain a few minutes' respite. We ask others to help reach it and, before anyone realises what is happening, a whole family becomes involved. To change the metaphor, the desire to finish off the crossword puzzle involves the whole train carriage full of people.

Once presented, even casually, with a problem to be solved, especially one that others have had no success with, many of us are drawn into the puzzle. The identity of Jack the Ripper is just such a puzzle and solving it has become an obsession for a small army of historians, researchers, novelists and journalists.

Looking down from my ivory tower, with all the superciliousness I could muster, I felt content to leave others to squabble over this historical conundrum. Then, I made the mistake of all naïve drug users, and agreed just to take a look, not to get involved or to commit myself in any way, not even to inhale. I agreed to take a look, that is, at the curious document that had surfaced, proclaimed as Jack the Ripper's Diary. What had raised my interest and lowered my defences was that the Diary identified this London killer as a Liverpool cotton merchant. I have a long-standing interest in fraud, how it is perpetrated and the characteristics of the suckers. This was so self-evidently fraudulent that I thought it was worth looking at to see how, yet again, sensible people had been conned.

At the time, I lived quite near the Liverpool house in which the purported Whitechapel murderer had resided. Indeed on my drive into the University of Liverpool each morning, I passed Riversdale Road. It is a sleepy cul-de-sac that stretches from the elegant, tree-bedecked boulevard of Aigburth Drive down to the wide, grey River Mersey. The only sign of any note at the entrance to the road is one warning motorists that it does not give them access to the pleasant park that is a respite for courting couples, and the promenade that is a haven for joggers and anglers, now that the Mersey has been cleaned.

Riversdale Road is thus an unlikely setting for the erstwhile residence of probably the most notorious serial killer of all time, Jack the Ripper. It is still a select area of Liverpool. In the 1880s it was even grander, not at all the underbelly of the city in which we might expect a serial killer to hang out. Particularly not the likely residence for a murderer who was awarded his sobriquet because of the violent way he mutilated his victims.

The magical mystery tour that takes visitors to Liverpool around the mundane, youthful haunts of John Lennon, Paul McCartney and other Liverpool celebrities does not even pass the end of Riversdale Road. No. 7 (now number 8) where James Maybrick lived, attracts no stream of casual visitors, even though the area of London in which the killings took place over 100 years ago brings in as many as half a million visitors a year.

Clearly, for most people, it seems highly unlikely that a Victorian businessman, who lived in such pleasant and affluent surroundings, committed so many sickening killings 220 miles away.

My assumption that the Diary was a hoax was further fuelled when I found out the remarkable way in which opposing camps so quickly formed, advocating or denigrating claims to the authenticity of the 'Ripper Diaries'. Instead of the steady drip of systematic research that such an important historical document would demand, with a consensus slowly emerging after careful consideration of all options, there has been a feast of claim and counter-claim, fed by opinions from every bizarre sort of 'expert' that could be got hold of.

Indeed, before I met Shirley Harrison and was approached by Paul Feldman to comment on the Diary, not only was it impossible to get any clear or detailed information about its provenance, or the tests that had been carried out on it, it was not feasible to enter into any sensible dialogue about the claims and counter-claims, so vociferous were the advocates. Since those early harangues, comments on the Ripper Diary from astrologers, graphologists and a small army of psychics, none of which has ever withstood careful, systematic, scientific validation, have masked the growing body of scholarly and objective information, which Shirley Harrison and her publishers have garnered about this most curious of documents. It was when I eventually became aware that serious-minded people were attempting, with very limited resources, to carry out careful studies, that I began to think it should be looked at closely.

It was tough trying to cut through the nonsense that was being purveyed by anyone who could see an opportunity of riding their hobbyhorse through the newly available territory. By their nature clairvoyants, and all other suppliers of paranormal interpretations, express their opinions with great confidence. They offer up a proliferation of views that the unwary and gullible can pick amongst until they find something they can clasp as a gem that supports their beliefs. These apparently glittering crystals of insight make the cautious, specific opinions of scientists look pale by comparison. The steady build-up of rather dour, technical information politely asks for consideration amongst their yapping claims and the counter-claims of professional cynics.

Out of this unproductive exchange of polemic a clan of the converted emerges, holding aloft the fake baubles and icons of their faith. Thus, when I have tried to find the evidence for and against the genuineness of the Ripper Diary, I am regaled with wondrous accounts of psychics flown in from foreign lands and astrologers poring over Mr and Mrs Maybrick's birth charts. I have seen TV presenters sniffing the Victorian album in which the Diary is written as if it were a bottle of wine that would reveal its origins in a distinctive bouquet. I have witnessed a psychic swinging a pendulum over the document intoning, 'Was this written in 1888… 1889… 1890?' whilst apparently well-informed, intelligent people watch without even a smile to cloud their gullibility. This is all such arrant twaddle that I have been tempted, more than once, to dismiss the Diary as one more component of the myth of Jack the Ripper, and see it as another millennial, new-age flowering, half fiction, half fantasy.

Then, a pause at the traffic lights by Riversdale Road, whilst listening to the banter of Billy and Wally on local radio, makes me wonder how such a strange concoction of a Scouse Ripper who kept a diary could ever have been invented. What sort of a person, or team even, could have come up with such an unlikely notion? Psychological Offender Profiles of Jack the Ripper are ten-a-penny, but what would be the profile of the hoaxer who perpetrated such an inventive scam?

The first point to come to mind is that the author of the Diary, be he hoaxer or fraudster, was a remarkably subtle man. (Most crime and the majority of frauds are committed by men, although fraud does attract more women, but even they – contrary to feminist aspirations – are often secondary to their male partners.) When I first read the Diary I was struck by how unstructured the writing was. It is not really a diary in the usual sense at all, but more of a journal of thoughts and feelings, or even at times a notebook recording sketches of half-hearted doggerel. There are no clear or regular dates, it meanders from thoughts to accounts of events to plans for action. In the same section that describes the most horrific post-mortem mutilation there is the search for a rhyme scheme. The record of the crimes and reactions to relatives and acquaintances are all mixed together.

This is inventive psychological writing of the highest order. If most people sat down to write a convincing diary about another's life I am sure they would want to place the publicly known events of that life clearly for the reader to see. Indeed, the fraudulent diarist would have to take the public events as a starting point and build the diary around them. But our fraudster is much more cunning than that. The Diary deals with the feelings of the writer. A record of his experiences dominates it. The things noted in the Diary are those that would be of interest to the author. It does not focus on what others have seen him do.

Many serial killers write autobiographies and some keep a journal. These typically capture the self-centred, narcissistic focus that drives these people to such disgusting excesses of depravity. There are examples that immediately occur to me. Fred West's memoir is full of trivial detail of daily life dotted with casual reference to outrageous sexual exploitation of his children, larded with gooey declarations of love. Pee-Wee Gaskins describes with glee how he killed babies by sexually assaulting them, implying in a mock sermonising tone that his pleasure in this was enough justification. Charles Manson keeps a manic, self-centred diatribe going throughout his extensive correspondence. Sadly, there are many more examples in the archives. They are all leagues away from the ponderous seriousness of those who write about Jack the Ripper. Indeed, few novelists could capture the all-embracing egocentricity with its mix of gloating irony that this Diary has.

There is another, rather more objective test that psychologists have fashioned to help determine the authenticity of an account. It has been graced with the rather grand title of 'Criteria Based Content Analysis', but what it amounts to is a list of aspects of an account. These aspects are taken to reveal the density of experience on which the account draws and the sort of detail that would be more likely to come from genuine experience than fabrication. Of course, creative writers, as they work, unconsciously tick off the criteria for making invention seem genuine, but less effective imaginations do miss a few tricks. The point most often missed is the almost irrelevant detail, or casual aside, that embeds the narrative within a particular context, especially when that detail does not really move the story line forward and may actually undermine its obvious purpose.

The author of the Diary is a particular master of the casual aside, the irrelevant detail that implies a person whose mind is not entirely on the events he is describing, who seems to be writing to sort out his own feelings not just to tell a story. He may be bragging about having fooled the police, yet there is still the need to record how cold his hands felt. Amidst the gruesome writing about removing body parts is the domestic aside of wondering 'how long it will keep'. This is the sort of specific comment that, because it apparently derives directly from the immediate concerns whilst writing, brings the reader back to thinking about the person writing, not just his deeds. It is therefore a powerful literary device if used effectively, but easily turns into self-parody.

The author of the Diary has a particularly clever way of keeping these irrelevancies coherent with the character he is creating. We are given a man who thinks nothing of murdering and mutilating others but is nonetheless psychologically vulnerable. He is desperately concerned with his own state of health and a determination to get rid of intrusive thoughts about his children that might distract him from his campaign. After the most violent outburst he notes that 'the children enjoyed Christmas'. By these asides a surprisingly insecure protagonist is created. No implacable Bruce Willis, or steely, emotionless Clint Eastwood is he, but a man who misses his brother, who is astonished that he has not been caught, dependent on his 'medicine', but who eventually becomes obsessed with his own actions and their consequences.

So, our literary profile of the perpetrator of this fraudulent Diary, if such it be, is already revealing some distinct characteristics. Here is a subtle writer who is determined to envelop us in Maybrick's thoughts and feelings, even if that introduces ambiguities into the details of his actions. But he is also remarkably crafty in the way he develops his fiction. If you had not been told this was the actual writing of a notorious serial killer the opening pages would not have made you any the wiser. There are oblique references that indicate more that the author is engaged in nefarious activities that cannot be specified too precisely for fear of discovery. There are emotional words that raise more questions than they answer. Especially the curious term 'whore master' that shows an anger with someone who, although execrated as a 'whore', is still of great emotional significance to the writer.

The opening paragraphs lead us further into an intriguing world of subterfuge and emotional tension with just the necessary sexual undertones to raise our interests without giving too much of the plot away. We are hooked by the time it is clear that the writer has a 'campaign', as he calls it, although we are not told explicitly what that 'campaign' is. Only once our interest has been raised does this skilled storyteller begin to feed in connections to a world we might recognise.

The reader is led on by hints of the danger of actually writing things down, 'it is unwise to continue writing'. But we are given the strangely ambiguous phrase 'to down a whore'. This is almost a hunting term as in 'the dogs downed a fox'. Its true significance is indicated by the suggestion that the act of recording it is dangerous. That ambiguous caution continues throughout the Diary, but after the visit to Manchester and the apparent strangulation of a 'whore' the accounts get ever more explicit and caution is eventually put aside to enjoy the delight of recording the experiences.

He measures his pace very well, slowly involving us in ever more gruesome details, capturing a mood of increased anger mixed with pain and delight. What starts as an unclear reference to a 'campaign' gets more explicit with a reference to the purchase of a knife. Then all is made terribly clear when the difficulty of cutting off the head is mentioned. As if that is not enough the Diary moves into angry despair: 'I want to boil boil boil', an almost incoherent tirade against himself and the God that made him. Lucid moments of self-doubt intervene and a growing refrain that perhaps he should give himself up or commit suicide, but the ending is much more effectively resolved than that. The author actually asks the reader for forgiveness.

The whole document emerges as a justification of his actions. Others and the external forces of 'love', not evil within himself, brought them on. Only someone who has carefully explored how serial killers see the world could be so perceptive as to notice that in the end they always seek to justify their actions by some means or other. Typically these justifications place the blame outside their own nature.

Most novelists struggle for years to gain the ability to look at the world as if through the eyes of another. Then they usually fail and are only able to give us one of their own perspectives. The Diary writer, though, brilliantly captures the mixture of adolescent delight in fooling others and getting away with crimes he finds exciting. He also has the unselfconscious thrill of seeing his deeds written about. This fraudster really enables us to get into the mind of a 'Ripper' character and see the turmoil of emotions and the tumult of thought that keep him going.

This is masterly psychological thriller writing, deftly indicating why the Diary is being written, at the same time as drawing us into the anger and confusions of the author. These moods are seasoned with the game of writing poems, a use of frivolity and dark humour to highlight the deadly seriousness of the drama that Shakespeare could have been proud of. Constant anger or polemic would have been tedious and unconvincing, but the mixture of emotional expression and banality keep the reader mesmerised as by the slight twitches of a snake.

There are just enough hints at facts to allow us to tie the experiences into known events. These historical cards are not over-played. It has taken Shirley Harrison and her advisers a considerable amount of time and effort to unravel all the references to actual events. A more conventional fraudster would have made sure that the critical events were clearly present. There are even hints at events that have no place in the Ripper canon, most especially the early murder in Manchester, mentioned twice in the Diary. Did an author who was so meticulous in all his other details make a mistake here? Or is this a devilish nuance to hint at things that only Maybrick would know, but which no-one else could ever verify? This murder is, notably, a strangulation that would never have been linking to the 'rippings' that were used to link the Whitechapel murders.

What of the character the fraudster has created? What sort of person is James Maybrick revealed to be in the Diary? He is certainly the centre of his own world. The Diary is written for his own pleasure but also in the arrogant belief that his views are inevitably of public significance. He has enormous mood swings from the heights of delight to the depths of despair. He is an inveterate gambler who gets real enjoyment from taking risks. But his arrogance is based on profound doubts about his own self-worth, especially in comparison to his brother. This does seem to be what gives him such preening satisfaction in duping others, his pleasure on showing them to be 'fools'.

Yet for all these explosive emotions and wild mood swings he is able to present himself as mild mannered and is aware enough to recognise that duplicity and gloat over it. He is not uncontrollably impulsive, but plans ahead, enjoying the planning and reminiscence of past acts as much as the acts themselves. This is a man others would recognise as intelligent, but not easy to know because he would hide so much of what he feels. There are some well-established British authors who would fit this picture. What has any of them to gain from remaining anonymous all this time?

A subtle novelist capable of giving the feeling of what it is like to be inside the Ripper's skull, but who also knows how to tread softly and pull back from revealing all too readily, is clearly a master of his art. But the fraudster/novelist had to do more than be convincing by carefully ambiguous statements. He had to have a thorough knowledge of Jack the Ripper and his activities. There are, of course, far too many books about the Victorian killings, so a study of these might have provided the basis for the prank. But, as I found when I tried to put some thoughts together for my own book *Mapping Murder*, the plethora of material on the Whitechapel murders is actually the problem. There are huge disagreements about most details including who Jack actually killed.

The fraudster/novelist would have to have been very heavily immersed in the Ripper literature for some time. He would also have to have had a very good understanding of Victorian England and police investigations in order to distill from all the writings those facts that the experts would agree on. Such a person would be known to the experts and could indeed be recognised as one of them. However, having had to plough through many Ripper books I have to say there are not many, if any, that reveal the writing skills apparent in the invention of the Diary.

Our profile of the fraudster, then, has narrowed down the field to gifted writers who are also Ripper experts. But there is one more clear indication of the character of the fraudster/novelist/expert. This is the very clever focus on a Liverpudlian.

Jack the Ripper is a London character par excellence. If he is not one of the professionals or aristocracy that crowd our image of Victorian London, then we can almost see him as a sort of Dick van Dyke classic cockney. Liverpool can claim to be the birthplace of many of the metropolitan developments of the last century, from medical officers of health to recalcitrant strikers, but Liverpool is not usually thought of as an especially violent city or one from which the modern serial killer would have originated. It is a stroke little short of genius to spot the trial of Florence Maybrick for murdering her husband, and determine to work the fiction backwards from that point to invent her alleged victim as Jack the Ripper.

It may be my own origins in Liverpool that bias my opinion, but surely only people from Liverpool are convinced enough of the fecundity of their city and its central position in the known universe to believe that Jack the Ripper could have been a Scouser? But as the quietness of Riversdale Road demonstrates, that is certainly not an idea that has caught the imagination of present day citizens. So whichever of their number invented the Diary she or he was certainly swimming against the Merseyside tide. The author of the Diary was not picking up one of the popular myths of Liverpool and cloaking it with invention.

This Liverpool fraudster/novelist/expert was also, of course, very knowledgeable about the Maybricks and their doings. Florie's trial was of great note in Britain and her native America so, once again, tireless research would have provided the depth of insight to be able to scatter references to major and minor figures in James Maybrick's life. A variety of names would be available from the trial, but once again the author does not over-use them. For example, the outburst against a subordinate in the railing against Lowry is a delightful touch and further evidence of the control and skill of the novelist. I must confess that if I were to invent such an interesting walk-on character as Lowry, I would have wanted to develop his involvement and use him as more than a cipher.

The knowledge of inks and paper, of Victorian vocabulary and handwriting styles and the other objective aspects of the Diary that Shirley Harrison has painstakingly examined, were of course available to the fraudster in much the same way as they were available to her. Readers of crime fact and fiction books will be aware of the forensic sciences that can be drawn upon. Our fraudster is no Liverpool scally, no slouch throwing a few possibilities together. He has devoted considerable time and effort to getting the Diary just right. He would not make the mistake of getting the forensic science obviously wrong.

Our profile of the author of the Diary then has him (or just possibly her) based in Liverpool with a very good knowledge of life and times of the Maybrick family. He also has excellent knowledge of Victorian England and the Jack the Ripper murders and their investigation. In addition, he can very plausibly capture and express the mixture of thoughts and feelings that the Whitechapel murderer might have had. Furthermore, he is likely to be a careful scholar who enjoys taking risks. Those who know him very well will recognise the turmoil of emotions deeply hidden by a placid façade. He has access to, and knows how to use effectively, Victorian writing implements and writing styles. But above all he does not display these consummate creative and scholarly skills by writing a gripping novel or screen play, but produces a personal, meandering document that is so unlike a Diary that it finds a publisher almost accidentally.

This is a person so fascinated by Jack the Ripper that he has devoted a large portion of his life to trying to be him. A person who gets such delight in recreating the feelings that Jack the Ripper might have had and such excitement by the stir that the Diary might cause, that this shy genius has still not stepped forward to claim his rightful glory. His story would be a certainty for Hollywood treatment.

These musings, then, give us two broad possibilities for the authorship of the Diary. One is that it was written by a shy, but emotionally disturbed genius, who combined the novelist's art with an intelligent understanding of serial killers, the agreed facts of Jack the Ripper and James Maybrick. The other possibility is a rather different person. He knew how Jack the Ripper felt and had knowledge and experience of his killings. He also was totally familiar with the world of James Maybrick. He fits the personality profile revealed in the Diary exactly and had ready access to all the necessary writing materials. He also had a plausible reason for writing the Diary. He desperately wanted others to know the secret festering within him. He lived at No. 7 Riversdale Road in the late 1880s.

The question that arises from this challenging conclusion is, has James Maybrick got a convincing alibi? Does it make sense to think of a

London serial killer living in Liverpool. I cannot think of any known serial killer who did not have some sort of base near to his crimes. Indeed, I have been struggling with the geographical patterns of serial killers and rapists whilst writing *Mapping Murder* and have yet to find one who did not have some location not too far from his crimes, even if it were a moving base such as with the recent Washington Snipers. The striking discovery on reading the Diary is that the Diarist is almost aware of that and tells us that he has rented rooms within the Whitechapel area. He goes further and tells us they are in Middlesex Street. From careful analysis of the distribution of the crime locations, applying principles used in many police investigations, often referred to as 'geographical profiling', Middlesex Street turns out to be a plausible location for the Ripper to have his base.

Watch and beware. That is what is does to you. The nagging puzzle sucks you in. These ruminations on the characteristics of the author of the Diary show how seductive the document is. The search for closure on this case is a part of our popular culture. Anything that hints at helping us solve it grabs our attention. So much energy and resource has been put into describing, debating and attempting to resolve this mystery that a great fistful of habitual reactions are in place.

I am therefore not surprised that other mock diaries and other serial killings have been found that seem to be a coincidence too far. As we turn our attention from Victorian London, and look ever more closely at James Maybrick, all sorts of accidental co-occurrences will be seen in a new light. The Austin murders happened when Maybrick was in that part of the world. Will we discover linked murders in Manchester? What about a network of arsenic addicts using a cotton cover?

If we dismiss the Diary as bogus, then we can return to all the lovely conspiracy theories that drag in minor royals and famous painters. Like the now passé Rubik's cube, hours of pleasure can be gained from turning the puzzle round and round even though we are no nearer solving it. Bluma Zeigarnik will smile down on us, aware that the itch to solve it will keep the interest alive.

If we take the rather more courageous stance of regarding the Diary as genuine, a whole new raft of unsolved puzzles float to the surface. What did the torn out earlier pages of the Diary contain? What drove James Maybrick to wreak his jealousy in such a bizarrely vicious way? Why did his wife, who lived into the middle of the twentieth century, long after the revelation would have had any material significance, never even hint at the possibility that the husband she had been convicted of murdering was Jack the Ripper? How could a document of this significance have been missed when 7 Riversdale Road was searched by the police, scoured by family and servants and eventually all sold at public auction?

Conspiracy and cock-up will continue to be purveyed as we struggle to resolve the puzzle. The only thing that is certain is that the question of who exactly was Jack the Ripper will not go away.

David Canter
Ruthun, 2003

A more extensive study of The Diary is to be found in David Canter's book *Mapping Murder: The Secrets of Geographical Profiling*, Virgin Books 2003.